PRAYER PASSPORT

TO CRUSH

OPPRESSION

DR. D. K. OLUKOYA

PRAYER PASSPORT TO CRUSH OPPRESSION
© 2006 by DR. D. K. OLUKOYA
ISBN 978-0615920733
1st Printing - August 2006

A Publication of
Mountain of Fire and Miracles Ministries
Press House
13, Olasimbo Street, off Olumo Road,
(By Unilag 2nd Gate), Onike, Iwaya,
P. O. Box 2990, Sabo, Yaba, Lagos, Nigeria.
website: www.mountain-of-fire.com
email: mfmhqworldwide@mountainoffire.org

All Scripture quotation is from the King James Version
Cover illustration: Sister Shade Olukoya

DEDICATION

This book, **Prayer Passport To Crush Oppression**, is dedicated to late Apostle Joseph Ayodele Babalola, a minister of God, who understood the power of prayer. He was a man mightily used by God to ignite the fire of the first Christian revival in this country, in the nineteen thirties.

Brother J. A. and his team of aggressive prayer warriors entered forbidden forests, silenced demons that demanded worship and paralysed deeply-rooted, anti-gospel activities. Sometimes, beginning from the highest places, they openly disgraced satanic agents, emptied hospitals by the healing power of the Lord Jesus Christ, rendered witchdoctors jobless, and they started the first indigenous Holy-Ghost filled church in Nigeria. So far - and we stand to be corrected - none has equalled, let alone surpassed this humble brother in the field of aggressive evangelism in this country.

TABLE OF CONTENTS

TABLE OF CONTENTS CONTD.

TABLE OF CONTENTS CONTD.

TABLE OF CONTENTS CONTD.

TABLE OF CONTENTS CONTD.

Prayer is a gift to you and a privilege. The gift is offered to all and all may become the wielders of the great power of prayer. However, the fact remains that the power of prayer is least exercised by the average believer. You will do well to learn the art of warfare prayer. The present temperature of the prayer of many Christians needs to rise if they expect serious breakthroughs.

The prayer points in this book are targeted at certain needs so that as you pray, you will not be beating the air.

This is how to use this book

1. Locate your area of need by looking at the table of contents.

2. Select appropriate scriptures promising you what you desire. Meditate on them and let them sink into your spirit.

3. Go about the prayers in any of the following ways as you are led by the Holy Spirit:

   a. Three days vigil, i.e. praying from 10:00 P.M. to 5:00 A.M. three-consecutive nights.

   b. Three days fast (breaking daily), i.e. praying at intervals and breaking the fast at 6.00 P.M. or 9:00 P.M. daily.

   c. Seven days vigil, i.e. praying from 10:00 P.M. to 5:00 A.M. seven consecutive nights.

   d. Seven days fast (breaking daily), i.e. praying at intervals and breaking the fast at 6:00 P.M. or 9:00.P.M. daily.

   e. Three or more days of dry fast, i.e. praying and fasting three or more days without any food or drink.

4. Pray aggressively.

NOTE

> Spend part of the vigil or fast praying in the Spirit - Praying in the Spirit is an ability to pray in tongues as given utterance by the Holy Spirit. To pray in the Spirit, you must have been baptised in the Holy Ghost (not water baptism) - 1 Cor. 14:15.

You will be victorious in Jesus' name.

THE ANALYSIS OF OPPRESSION

What does it mean to be oppressed?

1. To be oppressed means to be put under subjection by a force stronger than you are.

2. It means to be tortured by certain forces that are beyond your control.

Oppression is not only experienced physically, it could be psychological, financial, marital, educational and most importantly spiritual. For a person to be under oppression physically, the oppression must have been planted spiritually. Nothing can come into manifestation unless it has been accomplished in the spirit.

Oppression is a state of captivity in which you rely on your enemy for survival. It is the foundation for difficulties, frustrations, hardships and unbearable sufferings. For an individual to be oppressed, he must have fulfilled certain criteria consciously or unconsciously. An oppressed fellow might be completely unaware of his state until trouble starts.

> **Psalm 42:9:** I will say unto God my rock, Why hast thou forgotten me? why go I mourning because of the oppression of the enemy?

These questions form the basis of what I am writing about. I want you to attempt to answer them sincerely, as you read on.

No matter what form, shape or manner it takes, oppression is always from the camp of the enemy.

> **Isaiah 54:14:** In righteousness shalt thou be established: thou shalt be far from oppression; for thou shalt not fear: and from terror; for it shall not come near thee.

As Christians and children of the Most High God, oppression is meant to be far from us. This is God's plan and purpose for our lives. However, it is not automatic that it works in our lives. It depends on the individual.

> **Eccl. 7:7:** Surely oppression maketh a wise man mad; and a gift destroyeth the heart.

From this verse, one can deduce that a man can only lay claim to wisdom when he is not oppressed. When oppression comes upon a man, he becomes another creature. He cannot regulate or control his affairs anymore because a power stronger than him is now in place. He really needs the mercy of God.

> **Acts of the Apostles 10:38:** How God anointed Jesus of Nazareth with the Holy Ghost and with power: who went about doing good, and healing all that were oppressed of the devil.

In this verse, we are introduced to the power that can break the backbone of oppression. It is the Holy Ghost and the power of God. We can also notice that when a fellow has been under the power of oppression, he needs healing.

Many of us look and feel quite happy with ourselves. We are not quarreling with anybody or at war with any force. But when oppression sets in, our countenance changes and a kind of force takes control of our lives. As a result, many of us cannot explain the mystery we find ourselves in. When oppression comes upon a person, it introduces an evil load upon him. And because of the heavy load that has been introduced, the person who used to be good becomes bad all of a sudden.

What does it mean to oppress?

To oppress means to weigh down. It also means to sit upon a person. To oppress means to cruelly exercise power over a person.

It could also mean to cause a person to be depressed. "Surely," the Bible says, "oppression maketh a wise man mad."

To be oppressed means to be under a very hard yoke and a heavy burden. Jesus Christ says, "Come unto me all you whose yokes are hard and your burdens are heavy and I will give you rest. For my yoke is easy and my burden is light."

Jesus recognized the implication of a yoke or burden in our lives. Like God the Father, Jesus gives each and everyone free will to choose whom to serve. But you must realize that we shall all reap what we sow in this world.

One of our brothers, who found a lady he wanted to marry, claimed he loved her with the whole of his heart and that she was God's choice for him. Things began to happen quickly over the marriage.

Oppression makes the yoke hard and the load heavy

Each time he wanted to sleep, he would dream that the lady dressed like a man. He got confused and told her not to come to his house anymore. The next morning, the first person to come to him was the lady. She told him that he had entered into her and she had entered into him, so his glory was now in her hands. He sent her away, but when he got to the office that morning, he saw a letter waiting for him. He was ordered to submit his car and his house to his employers, and to tender a letter of resignation immediately.

He went home to console himself, but on getting there, he noticed that thieves had come and stolen everything in the house, including the refridgerator. He ran back to the lady and said that he had made a slip of tongue. She forgave him and in less than a week, those who sacked him came back, apologized and reinstated him. This fellow died of oppression three years ago. The yoke he chose was too hard for him.

Oppression makes the yoke hard and the load heavy. The bible says Christ's yoke is easy and His burden is light. What does it still mean to be oppressed? It is for a wicked spirit to sit on someone's shoulder, consistently harassing the person. It is sad but true that over 90 per cent of church-goers or so-called Christians suffer from one form of oppression or the other. You may deceive yourself by saying it is a lie but I know what I am talking about. Even in places where they shout and pray against the devil, if you are not free from doing his will, you are in deeper oppression compared to the unbelievers. The devil will deceive the unbeliever into committing sin for which he will get his reward, but the devil will torture you for praying against him and still doing his will.

Oppression is a terrible thing. It is a form of slavery.

Oppression is usually the first point of attack of the enemy. Most cases reported in the hospitals, either early or late, are usually cases of oppression.

15 KINDS OF OPPRESSION

There are 15 different kinds of oppression. I want you to read them carefully so you can realise their consequences and appreciate the need for you to be free from their captivity.

1. BODILY OPPRESSION

You just find out that something is not right with your body. You do not feel the way you should feel. There is something oppressing your body.

One of the greatest deliverance cases I have ever seen in my life was the one of a fellow who used to be very bright. All of a sudden, he became very dull. When the number of students in the class was 30, his position was the last and when they became 36, he took the 36th position. The teachers were confused. Nobody knew that there could be a padlock in the head of a person. As they laid hands on him on the deliverance ground, he coughed out a padlock. Right from that day, he moved again from 36th position to the 1st position.

"Every padlock of witchcraft locking my virtue, die, in the name of Jesus."

> 2. **PHYSICAL OPPRESSION**
> 3. **MENTAL OPPRESSION**
> 4. **SPIRITUAL OPPRESSION**

Many people are under these categories of oppression. The devil has limited the anointing upon their lives and they are now confused about what is happening to them.

> 5. **MARITAL OPPRESSION**

Many marriages are of convenience. Many couples are suffering day and night. I went to visit a couple and the hair of the madam was wet with water. She greeted me well, smiling at me, instead of telling me the truth that her husband had just put her head into a water closet and flushed it, and that he was still there, getting ready to beat her up. This is a case of marital oppression.

Now let me say that it is not only the man that oppresses the woman. Women now know how to oppress fellow women, and how to oppress and deal ruthlessly with men. I have seen a man trying to go out and the woman said if he stepped out of the door, hunger would kill him. He quickly went back because it was only the woman that was working.

Oppression has been programmed by the devil into an institution like marriage whose founder and chief proprietor is God Himself. This is very sad.

6. FINANCIAL OPPRESSION
7. CAREER OPPRESSION

Those who know about the university system of promotion know that before one can move from one level to the other, one is asked to publish papers that would meet international standards and be reckoned with around the world. Some lecturers write as if they want to die, yet their works are not recognized. This man spent days and nights writing but they were not seen as materials. This is a situation where effort is not used to measure achievement.

8. DREAM OPPRESSION

Instead of people or Christians to fulfil the scripture that "The young shall dream dreams and the old shall see visions," every night is another battle ground of war with forces that are stronger than they are. Some situations have got so serious that those concerned attempt not to sleep at night so as to avoid being fed or battered in the dream. Some see dead relatives, others experience terrible nightmares.

9. VERBAL OPPRESSION

Verbal oppression is a case where the tongue becomes a snare to the whole body. Although a small member of the body, the tongue can set the whole world ablaze. As lifeless as it may seem, the tongue is tougher and stronger than a gun or a sword. It is a weapon, which when not controlled, could cause mass destruction. With it we bless, with it we curse; with it we give life, with it we take life.

10. EMOTIONAL OPPRESSION

Is a state when you notice that most of the time, for inconsequential and unnecessary issues, you just feel sad and downcast. You can't explain why or what happened. You just know that something keeps telling you that all is not well.

11. WITCHCRAFT OPPRESSION

Has become as common as bread and butter. In those days, witches were ashamed and used to hide their identity and association. But today, they have become as important as the United Nations, as some people have become dependent on them for their existence and survival. This may sound strange but it has continuea to wax stronger and stronger as many Christians have given room to modernism and liberty to enjoy the pleasures or ordinances of the world.

12. INHERITED OPPRESSION

Inherited oppression is transferred from parents to children. The bible says that curses which are issued on some people are carried onto their third and fourth generations. You may not have offended anyone; you may not have done anything wrong but for the mere fact that you belong to a certain lineage or kindred, certain forces have been put in place before you were born to oppress you, except you are delivered by the mercy of God.

13. FORCED OPPRESSION

Those who experience forced oppression, like those who are oppressed unconsciously can do nothing about it. They fight by the means they know, yet they remain oppressed. Many of such people are Christians. For them to be saved, they need to pray specific and targeted prayers that will locate the unprotected forehead of their oppressors.

14. UNCONSCIOUS OPPRESSION
15. CONSCIOUS OPPRESSION

When oppression goes beyond tolerance, madness results. That is why the bible says, "Surely oppression maketh a wise man mad." Oppression is a destroyer and has a maddening power. Oppression has an imprisonment power. It has a dominating and demoting power. It has a burdening and yoke power. It is not the normal function of oppression to kill a person. It will just keep the person unsettled, uncomfortable and depressed. It can be likened to a parasite.

They say that a good parasite does not kill the host. But a bad parasite, like cancer, will kill its host and have nothing to eat again. Like a tapeworm that stays inside the tummy, it waits for you to eat and digest your food. It only begins to operate when the individual is trying to absorb the nutrients into the body. Oppression is a terrible satanic spirit. It sometimes comes upon a person and the person would say he feels like a breeze coming upon him. It can be compared to when you're trying to sleep and suddenly feel like a deep freezer is plugged to your bed, and the cold runs through your body and then goes away.

The spirit of oppression has done an unquantifiable amount of havoc to men and women. Oppression is the center forward player in the enemy's football team. If it gets in, other more terrible spirits would move in. There is no amount of work you will do that will prevent some people from getting into conscious oppression with their eyes wide open. Some of the victims don't just know what to do. The devil has so bamboozled them that they believe there is no way out.

Oppression is a masquerading spirit that comes in different forms

Oppression is a demon assigned by the devil to trap and to cage. Once it is dispatched against you, you must fight it to a standstill with all your strength and heart. It causes heavy and antagonistic feeling in the body, soul and spirit. Like a virus in a computer system, it will prepare a person for a total and permanent shut-down.

Oppression can originate in early childhood

Oppression is a masquerading spirit that comes in different forms. It can enter into the life of an individual through all kinds of avenues. Anytime you no longer know whether to follow God or the devil, you are being oppressed. If you are always at the cross-roads in your spiritual life, not knowing if you should hold on to Jesus or go back to the world, you're being oppressed.

Oppression is particularly stubborn. When you find a particular sin holding a person captive, then it is oppression. When you see someone who, in spite of praying hard, his instrument of sin is in his pocket, he is under oppression.

In 1994 after a message on 'Brokenness,' a minister of God from another church came to see me. Immediately he entered my office he broke down, cried and said I should help him. He was a pastor who kept cigarettes in his pocket. Even after the sermon on brokenness, he still kept his cigars. He was under oppression.

Oppression can originate in early childhood. Many spoilt their kids by oppressing them at a very young age. So, oppression can become a major factor in shaping a child's life.

Oppression presses you down when you are struggling to succeed.

Oppression is when you are going from one disappointment to the other. It is a mind destroyer. It has no respect for persons or races. Oppression is when your sleep is being disturbed or when you over-sleep.

Oppression is when you have an abnormal appetite; when you eat too much or eat too little.

Oppression is when a person is so upset with life that he refuses to go out or he wants to end it all.

Oppression is when you refuse to forgive yourself.

Oppression brings a spirit of worthlessness with it. All forms of addictions are oppressions. It starts from small things like tobacco, snuff, drinks and cigarettes.

Oppression can cause fear in the mind of a person.

Oppression can remove a person from those that will help him so that the enemy can have unmolested control over him. It is when satan becomes an authoritative figure in a person's life. It is when problems are packaged neatly for the future. This means that many people are just bombs walking around and getting ready to explode.

Oppression is spiritual weight. It is known for its ability to make a person stray from his divine destination. It is progressive insanity.

Unfortunately, at times, relevant prayers are not employed to make amend to what oppression has destroyed.

If you notice that you are being tormented by wicked oppressive spirits, then you are under oppression. Is the enemy attacking every area of your life? You should know you are suffering from multiple oppression. Do you notice that you are spiritually stagnant? Do you notice uncomfortable financial embarrassment? Do you discover that your helpers are running away? Is your marriage a cat and mouse marriage?

Do you notice that all those evil family patterns are happening to you one after the other? Are all other members of your family doing very well, but you seem to be the only one not doing well? If yes, then you must know that there is oppression on ground.

How Do We Break The Backbone of Oppression

SALVATION You must give your life to Jesus so that through the baptism and anointing of the Holy Spirit, shackles of oppression can be destroyed completely. God first loved us and gave His only begotten Son to die for us. We need not remain under any form of oppression.

THROUGH THE WORD OF GOD The Bible says the word of God is like a hammer that breaks rocks into pieces. When we renew our minds with the word of God, bondage must be broken, no matter how old they are; no matter who put them there or where they came from. I expect anyone who wants to be immune to oppression to know, at least, 52 memory verses.

GENUINE BAPTISM OF THE HOLY SPIRIT

At one of the Prayer Rain meetings, I shared a testimony about a woman with a very terrible problem. She had the result of two scans in her hand. Scan one said she was six months pregnant, while scan two said her womb was completely empty. For this, she went for a crusade and went to the section for the fruit of the womb but was directed to join the section for Holy Ghost baptism. She got baptized in the Holy Ghost, got into labour and was delivered of a large snail. When you receive the genuine baptism of the Holy Ghost, there is no way the wonder-working power of God will not come upon you and something will definitely happen.

THROUGH REPENTANCE

When we repent of our sins, the Lord promises us forgiveness and deliverance. Repentance removes the ladder and the legal ground of the enemy. Many of us need to repent of the wrong use of our eyes, ears, mouths, hearts and most especially, our tongues. The activities are known to you, but once the tongue issues forth a statement, it goes into the wind to your listener and can never return to you. You can plead to be forgiven but you can never get back your words.

CAST OUT THE DEMON ON OPPRESSION By the powers in the name and the blood of Jesus, you can cast out the demon of oppression. Our bodies are the sacred temples of God and a spirit or a false personality is not supposed to dwell therein.

VIOLENT FAITH By this I mean the kind of faith exercised by Bartimaeus. He called on the Most High God: "Jesus, thou Son of David, have mercy on me." He was told to keep quiet, but the more he was silenced, the more he screamed. His voice was not the loudest but his faith was the strongest. He held our Lord Jesus at one spot and made Him to return and attend to him. The day you have violent faith, you will experience what to some others is "Impossible." For with our God, all things are possible.

BY WARFARE PRAYERS There are many methods of deliverance but the best remains the power of prayer. Prayer has prevailed over fire, water and the earth. Joshua prayed in the bible and stopped the movement of the sun. Prayer has prevailed over angels. It has cast out the devil and broken down his kingdom.

Prayer has power over good angels to bring them from heaven.

Prayer has healed the sick and raised the dead. In the case of Daniel, prayer has stopped the mouth of lions. It has subdued evil powers and put then to flight.

Prayer has opened prison gates and completely blindfolded the enemy. There is no artillery of hell fire that can stand against prayer. It is like an engine that makes the enemy tremble. The power of prayer remains undefeatable. The power of prayer is beyond human comprehension.

PRAYER POINTS

1. Holy Ghost fire, come upon my life, in the name of Jesus.

2. Thou power of spiritual dowries, die, in the name of Jesus.

3. Every counterfeit spiritual honeymoon, scatter, in the name of Jesus.

4. (Lay your hands on your stomach) Every sexual serpent and scorpion, die, in the name of Jesus.

5. Inherited oppression in my life, die, in the name of Jesus.

6. Environmental darkness in my area, scatter, in the name of Jesus.

7. Dream robbers, die, in the name of Jesus.

8. I fire back every arrow of oppression, in the name of Jesus.

POWER TO SUPPRESS THE SUPPRESSOR

Luke 24:49: And, behold, I send the promise of my Father upon you: but tarry ye in the city of Jerusalem, until ye be endued with power from on high.

One of the greatest weaknesses of modern-day Christianity is powerlessness. The enemy is aware of this and he is using it to terrorize and oppress us. Do you know that when a greater power comes across a smaller power, the smaller power bows? Do you believe that if you have the power to operate at a certain level of authority, the devil and his agents will be subject to you?

You must understand the fact that like every other organization or institution, there is a hierarchy in the school of power. There is the topmost level which is God Almighty, followed by His Son, Jesus Christ, who is followed closely by the Holy Spirit.

This is a trinity which simultaneously operates at a level or magnitude of power that is incomprehensible to human knowledge. Just like when Jesus asked Peter, "Who do you think I am," and Peter responded: "Jesus, the Son of the Most High God, the Messiah." Jesus said that this was not revealed to Peter by man but by God.

The only power that can suppress the suppressor is the Power from On High

So, for you to have a clear understanding of the principle of power, you have to move closer to God. The closer you are to God, the more you can experience and exercise His divine authority. The farthest person from the power of God is the devil. God is at one extreme and so is the devil at the other extreme.

The devil will try to prevent you from receiving power from God by enticing you with the cares of this world. Whatever he gives you now is only a facade or a mirage. After a while, it disappears and you are in trouble. You have to decide to follow Jesus. Key in to His power so you can experience Him as the "I am that I am."

The fellow who operates in the heavenlies is stronger than the fellow who operates down here or underneath the earth. The fellow on earth can experience the power from on high if he chooses to serve God, or he can decide to be deceived by the power from below which is determined to lure mankind from God in order to kill man's eternity.

The only power that can suppress the suppressor is the power from on high. When Jesus was crucified, the state of His disciples was sorrowful. Peter went back to fishing. Thomas, "The I am a scientist. I am an honest and logical doubter," said he saw Jesus dying and was there when Jesus said he would come back. However, "Until I see Him and I put my finger into the holes in His hands, I won't believe He lives."

The disciples of Jesus were like the sheep, whose shepherd had been killed and they had to scatter. They behaved as if they had never known the Messiah.

> ## Once the power of God comes into your life, you are a winner

The Messiah, who raised the dead in their presence was also the Healer, who cast out a legion of demons from the man at the grave-side. They saw all these, yet they were in a sorry state after His death. Why were they in this sorry state? It was because something was missing in their lives.

The reason something or someone is threatening you in your dream, or someone issued a curse upon you and it is working is that there is no power in you. Anytime a greater power comes against a lesser power, the lesser power must bow as a matter of necessity.

When I was in secondary school, a man was brought to our school and we had to contribute 10 kobo each to watch him. This amount was very big money then. They told us that he was a "Superman." When he undressed, one of his hands with its muscles was almost more than my size then. I was really surprised. The man said he wanted to display his power. So he tied a string to a Volkswagen Beetle car and held it in his teeth and began to pull it and the car was moving.

Later, 50 boys held one end of the rope and he started pulling it at the other end as if all the boys were just as light as pieces of paper. He could do this because he had power in him which could not be understood.

A lady took her fiancé home to introduce to her daddy. The father ran inside the room and brought out a cutlass. He was surprised that the girl wanted to marry. He asked her how she managed to break the yoke he put upon her. He then chased the young man away. If not for the mercy of God, that lady would never have married in her life.

Anytime a greater power comes against a lesser power, the lesser power must bow as a matter of necessity

A lion came upon Samson but something happened to him that the lion did not understand. The Bible says, "And the Spirit of the Lord came upon him." Immediately the Spirit of the Lord came upon Samson, he tore the lion into pieces."

Beloved, if you read your Bible carefully, you will realize that Samson was not a muscular or very huge person. He was just like an ordinary man, but when the Sprit of God came upon him, he became unstoppable.

Once the power of God comes into your life, you are a winner. When that power enters into your life, your yoke will break, those things that have been boasting that they are strong and have been suppressing you will flee.

Are you ready to receive the power from on high? When it comes upon you, your yoke will break and you can suppress your suppressors. When the power from on high rests upon you, you will torture and harass the devil to the uttermost. The devil and his demons will fear you like fire fears water.

In a city where the Mountain of Fire and Miracles Ministries is now located, there was a tree that the people of that community had been worshiping for 70 years. Anytime they wanted to worship this tree, practically the whole town would be summoned to be there. Fortunately and unfortunately, the Mountain of Fire and Miracles Ministries is situated at the back of this tree. So, after every service, the pastor in charge of that branch told the congregation to pray one prayer point free of charge for the community: "Let the fire of God consume every evil tree, in the name of Tesus."

Are you ready to receive the Power from On High?

One day, they noticed smoke coming out right from the root of the tree. Later it became a great fire. The chief priest was called and they started pouring water on the tree, but the more they poured water, the more the fire burnt. Rain fell, but the fire did not quench and the tree fell and was destroyed. I pray that every evil tree growing in any life today shall be roasted, in the name of Jesus.

The Bible says that on the day of Pentecost, the apostles were of one accord. All of a sudden as they sat together, there was a noise like a mighty wind, and it filled the whole place. And there was a burning tongue of fire on the head of each of them. They were 120. That fire will fall on your head, in the name of Jesus. Then their lives changed.

One man of God has said that the sign of Christianity is not the cross but the tongue of fire. When that power comes upon you, you will feel the existence of the Almighty in you. When you walk into a demonic environment, the demons will walk out immediately.

O that you will have the power that the apostles had burning in them. You will not have to pray against evil forces, problems or frustration because the grand-father of any evil spirit that would want to torment your life has not been born. You would be completely immune to the devices of the devil.

Your life would become too hot for the enemy to handle or for the enemy to live in. Oh that the power from on high will enter into our bones like it entered into the life of Elisha! Even when Elisha was dead, the fire was still inside his bones and it was enough to raise the dead. If the bone of a dead man had fire in it to raise the dead, is that the kind of person that witches would want to attack? It is possible for us to receive this same power from on high to suppress the suppressors to the uttermost.

It is not good that someone will be speaking in tongues and will still be having dreams of spirit husbands or spirit wives, poverty and frustration, and every single day becomes a day of lamentation for him.

Many of us say that we have received the baptism of the Holy Spirit. Then why are you still afraid of witches and wizards? It is because you have not received it. When you receive it, you will become as bold as a lion.

Our present-day Christians wear materials and ornaments that are dedicated to demons without knowing it. Some of us have houseboys and maids that are serpents, and we don't know. Others are being surrounded by unfriendly friends and they don't know.

It is like that sister who attended our Prophetic Prayer Meeting. That was the first time in her life that she did three days dry fast. And God opened her eyes at the meeting. She went to look for her prayer partner and found her eating rice. But God opened her eyes and she saw that the stew on the rice was not stew but blood. She was offered some of the rice which she declined to eat and took her leave.

We need to wake up and become very serious. I know of a man of God who went to a crusade after beating his wife at home. He was asked to pray with someone. He laid his hands on the fellow's head and began to pray violently. After a while, he realized that his hands were bleeding. When he opened his eyes, he saw two horns on the fellow's head. These horns had pierced his palms. It took him about a year to use those hands actively again. Perhaps you still waste your time dancing every Sunday, when witchcraft powers are pursuing you, or you are on the side of witches who are the cause and are in charge of your problems. You really need deliverance from the suppressors.

Each and every one of us needs to have a divine encounter with the Holy Ghost. After such an encounter, your life can never be the same again. You ought to know that as a Christian, you are a champion in your school, your work place and where you live. You should not be a spiritual coward. You must note that until that power from on high comes upon you, you will continue to be suppressed by the enemy. I believe God that if you can pray like a mad person, He will deliver you.

In this world, before you can achieve anything to make your life move forward, you have to run a little bit mad. Somebody might want a first class degree from the university and he reads seven hours a day. That's a kind of madness. To achieve the unbelievable, you need to do the unusual, the unimaginable. Jesus said, "you shall receive power from on high." So you must try to possess this power to set yourself free. Why should the bible say that we are seated at the right hand of Jesus in heavenly places and powers of the earth are troubling our lives? It is because we lack power.

To suppress means to put under oppression, to be tortured by the devil beyond human comprehension. In these last days, the devil has put many Christians under his false authority. He has limited many lives and destinies by force or by deceit. He has built a stronghold with which he has captured and caged many people.

The devil has suppressed many to the point of madness. Many Christians today have lost faith in the absolute power of God because they have been suppressed for too long. The devil prevents people from expressing themselves and their emotions in prayers. He uses deceit to prevent people from growing spiritually, financially and materially. He cuts short development which he believes is dangerous for his hold upon his captives. You need to understand this, so that very soon, when it is time for you to pray, you should pray like a wounded lion. You should liberate yourself from the seemingly inescapable captivity of the enemy.

PRAYER POINTS

1. Thou power from on high, come upon my life, in Jesus' name.

2. Let the power of God locate me by fire, in Jesus' name.

3. You the oppressor and suppressor of my life, die, in the name of Jesus.

4. Every pillar of suppression in my life, collapse, in the name of Jesus.

5. Every evil pattern of suppression in my life, break, in the name of Jesus.

6. Every stubborn oppressor working against my marriage, die, in the name of Jesus.

7. Every ancestral suppressor, die, in the name of Jesus.

8. You the serpent of suppression, die, in the name of Jesus.

OPPRESSION MAKETH A MAN MAD

What is Oppression?

To oppress means to rule or treat in a continually cruel or harsh way. It could also mean to make somebody feel unnecessarily anxious, uncomfortable or unhappy.

Oppression is not just the physical act of torture or depriving people of their fundamental human rights. In the school of prayer, oppression is one of the greatest weapons of the enemy with which he totally confuses many Christians. The devil or Lucifer has been an oppressor since he was cast down from heaven. He had a pretty good idea of what heaven looks like, so if he can't go back there and continue to enjoy the wonders of being in the presence of the Almighty God, then why should he allow ordinary men (i.e. humans) to go there?

Oppression is a form of physical, psychological, financial, mental, academic, marital and spiritual disorganization in which the victim or the oppressed does not and cannot comprehend the vices or manner of oppression used by the devil to deprive them of their privileges of being members of a chosen generation.

Oppression is a tool of the enemy. It must die in every area of your life, in the name of Jesus.

> Eccl. 7:7: Surely oppression maketh a wise man mad; and a gift destroyeth the heart.

When you take a close look at that verse and meditate on it, you can interpret it like this- Wise people are troubled by the ways and deeds of the wicked.

Oppression can be so heavy at times. It can be so terrible that it can disgrace the wisest man's knowledge. The storms of life have a maddening power; they can make a fellow senseless. One of the most pathetic scenes I have ever seen in my life was the one I saw at Idi-Araba, around the Lagos University Teaching Hospital. We took a boy there at night from the Lagos University campus. A trailer tyre ran over his leg. I decided to take a stroll to the gate and through the corner of my eye, I saw a naked woman carrying a pot. From the look of her hair, I saw that she was not mad. She looked well-educated and sophisticated. In those days, I was more of a trouble maker than I am now, so I ran over to meet her and I asked her why she was carrying that pot. I told her that there was a better solution to her problem than to make such a sacrifice. She broke down and cried her eyes out.

She told me she came from the United States with her husband. She had three children and was an orphan. She accompanied her husband back to Nigeria and on arrival, her in-laws took her things and threw her out. They also took the children from her. She had no one to run to and no place to turn until she was taken to a herbalist who told her to make the sacrifice, that it would bring her solution. She told me she was a banker and had a master's degree. Here was a woman, schooled to the level of a master's degree, carrying a pot of sacrifice on her head, stark naked at night. Oppression had made her mad.

"Any power carrying sacrifices against me, die, in the name of Jesus."

The enemy raises a storm against you, when he sees your name in the plan of God. If he looks at the plan and sees that you are not serious, that you are not even listed among the elect, he would leave you alone. But immediately he sees your destiny being connected to the will of God, he would raise a storm against you. Many of us are not happy with our situations, at the same time, we are not mad against them yet.

Many people are losing their minds because of oppression. You should be able to know that the maddening power of the storm is more than able to make a man insane. Once we prayed with a man who wanted money at all cost. Fortunately for him, he got the money. Despite all the money, he developed cancer of the liver and was told to put his house in order and prepare to die. Eventually he found a person who told him that to be free from the sickness, he should sleep with his youngest daughter. He agreed and did. We had to conduct deliverance for him and his 19-year-old daughter. This incident is just to show you how extreme these maddening powers could be.

A sister wanted a husband desperately, and she met someone who took an egg and rubbed it all over her body three times and gave it to her to swallow. Not only did she not get a husband after that, she found herself in a bondage. She always felt the urge to have sexual affairs with the fellow who rubbed the egg over her body. I am sure you should, by now, have a clear picture of what I am trying to explain to you.

Oppression is a tool
of the enemy.

The truth is this, madness can only listen to a higher madness. The bible says, "For this cause was the Son of God made manifest that he might destroy the works of the devil." The devil himself is a destroyer, for we know it is written that he came solely to kill, to steal and to destroy while our Lord and Saviour, Jesus Christ, came that we might be saved that we might have life and have it abundantly.

The desire of the devil is to see humanity beg him, crave for him, wish he were God Almighty, and for many people to follow him to hell on the Day of Judgment. The path to destruction is wide and sadly, many find it. The path that leads to life and a peaceful eternity is narrow, and very few find it. Jesus is here to deliver and redeem, to the uttermost, as many as are willing to let Him into their lives as their Lord and personal Saviour.

A king looked at Paul and said: "What kind of person is this, thou hast destroyed thyself Too much learning has made you mad." Violence will only yield to the control of higher violence. The maddening power of oppression, which has been made manifest in very many lives today, can only be silenced by a higher power. When a strongman keepeth his palace, the Bible says, his goods are in peace. But when a stronger man comes upon him, he will take away his strength and plunder his goods. Only a higher voice can silence the voice of oppression.

> **Oppression by the enemy can raise unprofitable conflict against you.**

After one of the anointing services we had some years ago, a brother, who used to hear the cry of a cat at night beside his window, anointed that window. He went to sleep but was suddenly awakened by the cry of the cat. He got up, took his bible and his anointing oil and went outside. The cat was glued to the window and began to talk:

"Please, I did not come on my own, I was sent here." He summoned courage, killed the cat and burnt it.

The devil thought he was mad enough to torture this fellow by programming a cat to his window. But when he met a higher level of madness, his power was subdued. Evil cats being sent against you shall die, in the name of Jesus.

What I am trying to explain to you is that any power that tries to make the wise foolish is not a power to joke or toy with at all. If you think you can dine with the devil with a long spoon, he will climb on your spoon and get at you. Jesus spoke to the storms that felt that they were mad.

Although these storms tormented His disciples and they thought they would die, when a higher madness stood up and spoke just three words, "Peace, be still," the demonstration of the little power of the devil fell like a pack of cards. When Jesus got into the temple, He drove out all those who had turned His Father's house into a place of buying and selling.

The devil had infiltrated into the house of God and turned it into what, today, you would call a business center, a place for profit and loss and a playground for dubious people. Jesus went in and it was not recorded in the Bible that He was accompanied by any disciple. So it is safe to assume that He solely drove out those bargainers of destiny in the house of His father. There is a great possibility that even the local authorities could not have successfully driven them out, but one with a madness higher than theirs had come into the place and they bowed.

Oppression can
remove your alertness

Oppression by the enemy can raise unprofitable conflict against you. I have seen people who say, "I don't know what is wrong but I don't just like that man or woman."

Oppression can frighten us. It can even make you, a believer, to become half-hearted in your faith.

Oppression can make you think of giving up. You will suddenly feel that 'Enough is enough,' "I don't want to be oppressed by the devil anymore. I want to be free from all those hardships and frustrations," you may say. Then the devil sends in the spirit of suicide as a solution to your problem. It takes the grace of God to oppress your oppressors.

Oppression can remove your alertness.

Oppression can make you to sometimes forget Jesus who is your captain. A fellow can be so oppressed by the devil that he begins to wonder if there is God at all. The problem before you becomes very big because the devil puts magnifying glasses on you when the spirit of fear comes in. Then you will begin to doubt if Jesus really is a Saviour.

Oppression can make you lose your focus

Oppression can make you lose your focus. If you are not ready for the enemy to destroy your life physically and spiritually, then you need to quicken yourself to the fact that if you fail to fight now that you still can, you may not fight again but live or die to regret it. In one way or the other, all men have some madness in them. Many are mad for money. At least, I saw a man who was mad for money and was asked to swallow a live serpent and he did. Love, which many have ignorantly turned to lust today, is a form of madness. Love is known for its ability to intoxicate. If you think alcohol can make a man lose his senses, then wait till you find a fellow who is deeply, truly and whole-heartedly in love. All the endless list of desires of humanity like ambitions, passions, cares, regrets, lust, addictions – are all quiet madness. They have the capacity to grow, spread and consume people.

One of the popular madness is the desire to be noticed. Some of us derive pleasure from being noticed. Many are usually seriously disappointed if they go through a lot to prepare, suffer, stay awake all night, dress to kill and they are not noticed at the end of the day. The fellows who are noticed for good are mostly those who have the divine favour of God upon their lives.

All men have madness in them, but what varies is its degree or magnitude. Some are outright mad, like those in the psychiatric hospitals. Others require situations to quicken up their madness and there is a group whose madness grows unconsciously. They cannot control or stop themselves, once it's fully blown.

Fortunately and unknown to many, you can channel this madness to the right direction. You can decide to channel your madness against the oppressor. The energy you waste in backbiting, talking to unprofitable and unfriendly friends, fighting or having evil discussion should be gathered and directed against the oppressor. You need to ride on the wings of your madness so that you can oppress your oppressors.

I shared this somewhere before, about somewhere I lived for a long time called Akure. One day, the whole of the town went into uproar. A brother used to do morning cry in front of a shrine everyday at about 5 a.m.

One day, all the people in the shrine came out, called him and told him that they did not have any problem with him but that they wanted him to stop passing through that way. He refused and said that the Holy Ghost did not ask him to stop going through that path. The next day when he got there, about 21 of them came out naked and began to issue incantation against him. He started speaking in tongues. When they noticed that the incantations had no effect on him, they resorted to a physical assault of his person.

Another brother saw him and ran to the church where a service was going on and soon, members of the church arrived there and the shrine was bombarded with all kinds of tongues.

Eventually, the town crier arrived and said that the king needed to see the quarrelling parties immediately. This incident caused a serious uproar because those who served the idols and offered sacrifices in the shrine wanted to see their gods in action. Those who had surrendered their lives to Jesus also wanted to see His much talked about awesome power in physical manifestation. The king later decided that the Christians should follow their Jesus while the shrine worshippers should call on their own gods.

He stressed that the land belongs to everybody and anyone could take whatever road he or she chooses. The beauty of the incident was that many of those who came out naked gave their lives to Jesus because they could not understand why their incantations did not work.

"Every incantation of darkness against my destiny, die, in the name of Jesus."

WHO ARE THE OPPRESSORS?

There are very many of them. The way things are going on in our country now, we need a lot of prayer if our people don't want to become an example of the proverbial saying that "A knife was put in the center of what bound us together and things have fallen apart."

Many lives in our country today are under oppression and they need God before it is too late. National oppression is as a result of individual oppression. If there is individual deliverance, there will be national deliverance. The oppressors include:

PROBLEM EXPANDERS

These powers climb on top of problems already on ground and begin to expand them. Somebody might already be in trouble with household wickedness and the devil, wanting to destroy him, propels him to annoy a genuine man of God who now issues a curse upon his head. For example, Gehazi was already battling with covetousness and the problem expanders came upon him and added leprosy to it. I pray that any power enlarging any problem in your life shall die, in the name of Jesus.

STAR HUNTERS

Every man has a star and if the enemy can hunt down your star, you are in trouble. You will undergo constant oppression. An occultic man came to church to give his testimony. He had already surrendered his life to Jesus. He arrived at the pulpit but instead of talking, he broke down at the altar and started crying. He was asked what was wrong. When he got control of himself, he told the congregation to stand up and help him pray some prayers.

He said on his way to the crusade, he saw a boy with tattered dress sitting under a bridge. He said he recognized the boy, that on the day the boy was named, he was there and there were four stars on the boy's head and he took them all away. Now, he felt very bad because he was the one that destroyed the life of that boy. He asked the congregation to pray that the stars be returned to the boy and there would be a divine rearrangement in his life.

"Thou star of my life, reject the prison of darkness, in the name of Jesus."

DESTINY KILLERS

When a person's destiny is killed, he will suffer from oppression. When your life is not going in the right direction, the enemy has the right to oppress you.

EVIL SPIES

These come to spy and monitor your progress. I was at the church one afternoon when somebody brought a dozen chairs for the anointing service. This fellow was very happy. He said before he came to Mountain of Fire, he wore one shirt and a pair of trousers for six months. But now, we could see the way he was dressing expensively. He said he had some evil people in his house who kept reporting to the devil that he was making progress in his endeavours and everything had been going back to zero point. I pray that every power monitoring your progress shall be blinded, in the name of Jesus.

HEAD MANIPULATOR

Consider the case of a well-groomed marriage which suddenly became a living hell. The husband became a dog and the wife a cat. They used to agree before, but now they have agreed to disagree. A student might be the best in school but all of a sudden, he moves to the tail of the class where he battles to become the last runner- up.

MONEY SWALLOWERS

They wait for you to invest, they watch the interest grow and when it is time for you to reap your harvest, they move in and swallow everything. They are the types of forces that feed on their hosts from time to time. They are not permanent parasites but they come when the harvest is near. I pray that all money swallowers shall vomit all they have eaten, in the name of Jesus.

PROGRESS ARRESTERS

The victim moves slowly for a while, then all of a sudden, he is arrested and he becomes confused.

SATANIC MINISTERS

In this our generation more than in any other, satanic ministers are more rampant. They are the group that say, "Thus saith the Lord," when the Lord does not say anything. They are the ones Jesus warned about when he said, "In the last days, many shall come in my name performing miracles and deceiving many." They will end up in hell. Do you know that no matter how powerful your church is, you will still find someone who will take you to the house of a herbalist if you want to go there?

POVERTY ACTIVATORS

These powers activate poverty out of apparent wealth and affluence. They make a man lose his divine favour before they plunder his goods. Most of the time, they are programmed against a person over a period and the fellow whom they are draining does not realise he is being drained until it is too late. He then begins to run helter-skelter, looking for a solution. They are very wicked powers and are no respecters of persons. They move in over a period of time, operate and move out suddenly.

COFFIN SPIRITS

These spirits come in through fear. They first of all withdraw your peace and you become restive. The growing fear becomes a voice which continues to implant the spirit of death. At every point, even when it is a common headache, the person sees death approaching. Some cases are so bad that the victims see the coffins coming to them. I pray that every coffin spirit in your life shall die, in the name of Jesus.

VAGABOND ANOINTING

The victim becomes a wanderer, roaming all over the place without a focus, aim or objective. Just like the wind blows and we don't know where it is coming from or where it's going, so does a person with vagabond anointing wander. It's a pity that many who are possessed by this spirit are not even aware. It destroys destinies and puts the people in bondage.

SPIRITS OF DEATH AND HELL

These spirits are bent on killing people and sending them to hell fire. That's why Jesus died and went to hell and it is written in Revelation 1:8:, I am Alpha and Omega, the beginning and the ending, saith the Lord, which is, and which was, and which is to come, the Almighty.

Jesus went to hell, fought with the devil and collected the keys of death and hades, and so He is in charge. All you need to do is get connected to the One who holds the keys and you will become free. You shall not die but live to declare the works of God, in the name of Jesus.

RAIN OF AFFLICTION

This force torments people. Some victims have big files in the hospitals. But it is written that, as children of the Most High, by the stripes of Jesus we are healed. So we have no reason to be afraid of the devil. I pray that every rain of affliction will backfire, in the name of Jesus.

STRANGE MONEY

Once you get this kind of money and it touches your own money, your money disappears in a mysterious way. You won't know what happened to your money. You must be very careful about those from whom you collect money. Plead the blood of Jesus on any balance of money you receive and pay your tithes regularly and faithfully. Your tithe is one tenth of your income, but wise people pay more.

WITCHCRAFT HANDWRITING

Some people sleep and when they wake up there are scratches all over their bodies. The devil gives such evil marks to people so he can manipulate their lives. They are signatures of the devil over his own properties.

SATANIC ARROWS AND BULLETS

These are fired at people from different directions. They are carriers of problems, diseases and troubles. When the bible talks about the arrows that fly by day and the fiery darts of the enemy, it is referring to satanic arrows and bullets. The blood of Jesus which speaks better things than the blood of Abel will keep you from the reach of these devices of the devil.

DESERT SPIRITS

These spirits cause whatever you do or you are involved in to become desolate like a dry land. The life of the victim becomes an arid region where nothing seems to work right. The dews of heaven and the rains of heaven are completely prevented from falling on such a life by desert spirits.

EVIL MARK

This is a mark of dis-favour and oppression. Anywhere the victim goes, he does not find favour or mercy. Everyone else would be allowed to go, but that fellow with the evil mark will be detained. When it is the person's turn for something, the thing goes upside down. Try as nothing can be done.

CONTENDERS WITH ANGELS OF BLESSINGS

These are the kind of contenders that stopped the angel sent to Daniel for 21 days . He prayed and God answered, but the prince of Persia refused to let the angel go until angel Gabriel came from heaven to help the angel. These contenders hold people's blessings and prevent them from achieving their goals.

BUSINESS BEWITCHMENT

It possesses the goods before they enter the market. People would search through the whole town looking for these goods but once they reach the market, no one would be interested because this oppressing spirit has possessed it.

MARRIAGE KILLERS

A research showed that 25 per cent of the women in psychiatric hospitals are there because of marital stress. Marriage is an institution created by God. Two people (a male and a female) are to come together to live as one to the glory of God and for the purpose of procreation. Like he challenges other institutions of God, the devil has also attacked marriages, right from the time of Adam and Eve up till today.

CHILDREN KILLERS

These prevent children from, even, entering the wombs of their mothers. When the children enter, they try to snuff life out of them before they are born.

SATANIC PRAYERS

There are churches of satan all over the places. These days, people pray these prayers to the devil to strengthen him to fight against Christians, but our God is more than able to deal with him.

TERRITORIAL DEMOTION

It is impossible to prosper in certain areas. Even if you had so much before you moved into such places, the forces of demotion will not allow you to prosper there. They suffocate all forms of progress.

POCKET WITH HOLES

There are pockets that have holes. No matter how hard you try to safeguard what belongs to you, it keeps disappearing or slipping out of your hands.

**DESTRUCTIVE INCANTATIONS
DEMON IDOLS
DREAM MANIPULATORS**

These enter into people's dreams and make them experience practical nightmares that are horror. They never dream of heaven or prosperity, but of torture and masquerades that continue to oppress them. Some people's cases are so serious that they are even afraid to sleep.

UNFRIENDLY FRIENDS

This is terrible because those whom you call your close friends are the ones that go behind you to carefully plan your downfall. Some appear to be caring and loving, but are more wicked than the devil himself.

HOUSEHOLD WICKEDNESS

The Bible says that the enemies of a man are the members of his household and those he loves are the ones he should fear the most. It happened to Samson when Delilah got his secret and traded him to the Philistines. It also happened to Joseph when his brothers sold him to the Ishmeelites who took him to Egypt.

The forces of oppression are doing a lot of havoc. The Bible says, "Surely oppression maketh a wise man mad."

WHAT TO DO

Decide that you will take your circumstances into your hands – you cannot be delivered until you decide wholeheartedly to fight and say, 'Enough is enough.' Take that decision right now in your mind.

You must exhibit holy violence, a higher madness to deliver your destiny from the hands of the oppressors.

Pray barricading prayers so that the oppressors will not be able to disgrace you.

Somebody said that for any success you want to achieve in life, to win a race, pass an exam excellently or to rise in your career, you definitely need a little bit of madness.

PRAYER POINTS

1. Every power that wants to swallow my destiny, what are you waiting for? Die, in the name of Jesus.

2. Every agenda of oppression for my life, I bury you today, in the name of Jesus.

3. Every oppressor of the night, what are you waiting for? Die, in the name of Jesus.

4. By reason of the anointing, every yoke in my life, break, in the name of Jesus.

5. Anointing that breaks the yoke, break my yoke, in the name of Jesus.

6. Yoke-breaking power of the Holy Ghost, fall upon my life, in the name of Jesus.

IMMUNITY AGAINST OPPRESSORS

Daniel 2: 22: He revealeth the deep and secret things: he knoweth what is in the darkness, and the light dwelleth with him.

There is only one person who qualifies for the above description and that is the Almighty God. He can reveal what is deep and secret; He knows what is in the darkness and the light dwells with Him. He is the only Person who can see into the two worlds very well.

In this message, we would be considering some of the secrets of freedom from the hands of the oppressors, particularly in our environment. Anything that is affecting your body, soul, spirit, life or business in a negative way is an oppressor. When you earnestly want to grow up spiritually but something seems to be dragging you back, that thing is an oppressor. Anything that is ruling a person's life in a hard or cruel way is an oppressor.

CERTAIN THINGS YOU OUGHT TO KNOW ABOUT THE POWERS OF THE OPPRESSORS

☞ *Their main purpose is to keep men from serving the true God*

If witches, wizards and demons do not succeed in that, they will ensure that a person who has started with God does not make much progress.

☞ *They need a door to enter into any life*

They just cannot enter anywhere and begin to operate. No, a door is required for them to get in. Many people open these doors for them by themselves. Others get the doors open by their parents.

☞ *The oppressors vary in power*

A man of God prayed hard to God for somebody to be delivered from a particular thing. While he was praying, he saw a vision that the person was being guarded by some soldiers and lions. Each time he tried to move near, the lions roared and tried to jump at him and he ran away. This continued until the vision cleared.

The problem of that person remained and the man of God cried unto the Lord saying, "Why is the lion preventing me from setting this person free?" The Lord said, "You need to obtain sufficient power because the power oppressing this person is higher than you think." So, he went into fasting and prayer. It was then he could conquer the lions and the person was set free. Sometimes, certain things go easily when you order them once to do so in the name of Jesus. But some would not go at a single command.

☞ Oppressors like unhappy people

They like them because a sad spirit creates a gateway for demons to enter into a person's life and oppress him. So, anybody suffering from depression would continually have a traffic of evil spirits in his life.

Most of the time, human beings invite them in through many things they do.

For example, when a small girl is raped at a very young age, a big door is opened in the world of the spirits to something that may happen to her later. Immorality is an open door. Sacrificing things to idols or eating food anyhow, anywhere; maybe because you do not have enough food in the house or because the food is attractive, is opening doors through which these spirits enter. If you eat beans cooked on Fridays for twins, you are opening doors to the oppressors.

A person who is guilty concerning a matter and is cursing himself that he is not guilty is opening a door to the oppressors. When a young person of about 14 or 15 peeps through the keyhole of a door to see what a man and a woman are doing inside the room, he is opening a door through which oppressors can enter. When they have entered, the person could struggle all his life and may not be able to find the cause of his problems.

The Bible says that it is wrong to pray with the name of angels. There is nothing like Six and Seven Books of Moses anywhere. Moses never wrote any six or seven Books. If a person begins to read such books, he gets into trouble and the Lord would look at him twice before he gets deliverance.

I want you to look back a little bit into your life to identify where you went wrong so that you can retrace your steps.

A certain mother brought her son to me and said that he was reading the Sixth and Seventh Books of Moses because he wanted a

Carrying of sacrifices to the cross-roads is also an invitation to oppressors

visa. She asked me to appeal to him to stop reading the books before he got into trouble. But before I talked to the boy, he had read a little bit of it and that was enough for the devil to operate in his life.

Somebody whose father was a chief hunter learnt and memorized demonic incantations. When he became born again, he forgot about them and did not even pray to God to wipe them off from his brain. Now that he is excited when he sees masquerades, he should know that there is an open door in his life. His father put his leg on something which must be taken out.

When a young girl of 15 sees men coming to sleep with her in the dream, it is quite possible that she has been committing fornication in real life, and through the act, a ladder has been created for oppressors. Such a girl needs to repent.

Carrying of sacrifices to the cross-roads is also an invitation to oppressors. Those, who visit false prophets, obey their instructions and use their materials are also opening doors for the oppressors to come in. Whether those instructions are simple or complicated, they are invitations to tormentors or oppressors.

Borrowing clothes from people to wear is a dangerous thing to do in this environment. If the person you borrowed from is possessed, you too would be possessed and a transfer would be carried out through the clothes. Since the anointing power of God can be transferred through handkerchiefs and it will heal the sick, evil spirits too can move through people's clothes.

Mothers who seek the fruit of the womb through charms are not only endangering their lives, the children would also get their share of the trouble. All those who invite the oppressors cannot blame the devil or God because they issued the invitations themselves.

Many people have been spiritually contaminated and have to be purged. There are different types of ink. Some, you can easily clean off with water and some you cannot. In the spirit world, spiritual marks are like that. There are some you can easily remove by praying for half an hour while others cannot be easily removed like that.

Sometime ago, as I was praying with somebody, a spirit spoke to me from the person's mouth: "Leave me alone. This girl has been dedicated to me from birth, so leave us alone. After all, does she tell you that she wants to be free?" A door had been opened and the enemy had rushed in and there was trouble.

When somebody is suffering from spiritual contamination, his problems would be multiplied. God did not create drug addicts. He did not create mad people. He did not create ulcer patients or broken homes. These things have been happening since the world became contaminated. Many people have been spiritually contaminated, some from birth. Even some people who call themselves Christians still need deliverance in one area of their lives or the other. Hot temper opens the doors for the oppressors, even in the life of a Christian. A Christian, who is hot-tempered, needs to repent so that he can be delivered.

Many people come from idolatrous homes and some bear idol names. All these open doors. Some people are fond of praying and at the same time consulting herbalists, while some are stylishly worshipping nature. Looking at the stars and believing that the horoscope is dictating your life is opening doors to evil powers. You have life and they do not have life, so they cannot control or dictate your life in anyway.

Our lives are in the hands of God, not in the hands of stars. A star may fall down and crash but God can never fall down. We may not know about tomorrow but we know the Person who owns tomorrow in His hands. Let this be settled in our spirits.

People dedicate their children to idols, thereby starting problems for them early in life. Sometimes at naming ceremonies, people eat dead rats and from there, trouble begins. You must withdraw yourself from all these things today through prayer.

Many times while evil spirits keep to themselves, people go to look for their trouble. Distributing cakes and things like that to people have no biblical backing at all. Collecting names of a child from false prophets creates an evil door. Such names must be changed because they will not do him any good since their spiritual source is evil.

Many people are doing what you call astral travel. They read books that help them to take their bodies from this physical world to the river or somewhere else. The devil allows them to do all that, but contaminates their spirits before they come back to their bodies, and when they come back, they will start behaving funny.

Some people worship angels. This is wrong. The bible says that we would judge the angels. John was addressing an angel and when the angel spoke to him, he prostrated. But the angel said, "No, no, no, don't worship me. Just worship God."

Incense burning is a serious invitation to demons. All the special perfumes and special use of Psalms are invitations to the oppressors.

A woman came to one of our meetings about three years ago and said that her husband was not loving her enough. One white garment priest told her to bring the picture of her wedding and she took it to him. He tied some strings around the picture and did something to it saying, "As from now, when you say, 'go,' the man would go and when you say, 'run,' he would run to you.' She found that the thing was working and was excited.

However, her husband made a roundabout turn and it became so serious that the woman rushed back to the white garment man and told him that the charm was no longer working. Then the man started making passes at her and she knew that there was trouble. So she came to our meeting and the Lord revealed that she did something that she hid in her room. She was asked to bring the picture. It was after we destroyed that picture and prayed very well that the man began to follow her to church.

All these things are traps that people put their legs into. You must seriously examine everything you put on your body. Find out where they came from. Be sure that you get them from a source that you can explain or a source that is not cloudy. These things may be open gateways for the oppressors.

A lot of black people are worried by ancestral spirits which have caused them one trouble or the other. Some people kiss the dead and from there, the demons that are yet to go out of the dead person get into them. It is like a trap set by the devil and when people get into it, they start struggling to get out.

At times, the devil operates like the fly. When the fly lays eggs in a particular place, the eggs may be difficult to see. The same stands for the eggs of evil spirits. They may be difficult to see but when they start becoming maggots and develop further, then we will see that there is trouble.

If you know that you are being oppressed, it is not good to leave the oppressors alone. Give them no peace. Take action and do not allow them to work unmolested in your life.

But you must first clean the temple of your life. Once you clean the temple of your life, God will fill it for you because He will not live in a dirty environment, just as you would not find houseflies living in a very clean environment.

HOW TO BE IMMUNE AGAINST THE OPPRESSORS

LIVE A HOLY LIFE

I have said that things do not just happen; maybe a gate or a door has been opened. A holy life annoys the devil. A Christian with a pure heart, mind and body is surrounded by fire which burns brightly all the time. Your naked eyes may not be able to see it, but satan and his agents can see it, and they avoid people with such fire because they know that when they are attacked, they react violently.

Unfortunately, today, sin and immorality have removed holiness from many people's lives and many Christians have been unequally yoked with unbelievers. When they mix so much with unbelievers, they make themselves vulnerable to all the attacking forces. When we begin to say foul things with our mouths and begin to do bad things, we are giving the oppressors a foothold. But when we clean our temples and fill them with good spirits, we are immune.

But the fact is that a lazy Christian can never be holy because holiness requires reading the bible, it requires disciplining our bodies; it requires our praying very well, and it requires our praying in the Holy Ghost which is vaccine number one.

So if we want to be free from oppressors, we must go back to holy life which the devil cannot pollute or touch. We must examine our lives very well and see to it that there is nothing there which can invite him in: no envy, no malice, no quarrelsome spirit, no spirit of anger. All these things must go to render the devil powerless.

Sometime ago, a man took his friend's case to a herbalist. The herbalist asked him, "Have you quarrelled?" He said, "No, we have never quarrelled." The herbalist said, "Go and quarrel with him then come back." The man did not succeed because his friend was somebody who would not talk when you look for his trouble. He would smile at you and go away. Such people are difficult to attack. When you attack them, the evil will come back to you.

WALK IN THE SPIRIT

Galatians 5:16-17 says, "This I say then, Walk in the Spirit, and ye shall not fulfil the lust of the flesh. For the flesh lusteth against the Spirit, and the Spirit against the flesh: and these are contrary the one to the other: so that ye cannot do the things that ye would."

When you give your life to the Holy Ghost and you are genuinely baptized in Him, one of His symbols is fire. It makes the environment too hot for the devil. It brings every thought to captivity. When you begin to walk in the Spirit, your life will be filled with Him. You would pray in tongues in the morning, pray in tongues in the afternoon and at night, and even before you take your actions, you would ask the Holy Spirit. When somebody talks to you, before you react, you would say, "Holy Spirit, what should I say to this person." But when the flesh is in control, we open the gate for the enemy.

BE HUMBLE

When you set humility against the devil, he will flee. The bible says that the humble man occupies a high place. He takes the place of the fallen angels. Isaiah 57:15 says, "For thus saith the high and lofty One that inhabiteth eternity, whose name is Holy; I dwell in the high and holy place, with him also that is of a contrite and humble spirit, to revive the spirit of the humble, and to revive the heart of the contrite ones." So, the Lord would actually bless those who are humble and He hates the proud because pride is a character of the devil. The devil committed only one sin before he was cast out of heaven. He wanted to exalt himself above God.

So, demons would be far away from any person who is humble, but to an angry or proud person, they will always be close. What we are saying is that, you must totally submit yourself to God. That is the easiest way to force satan out of his stronghold. You must totally submit your body to God. The devil recognises that once you are living a life of submission to God, he cannot touch you. Every area of your life must be brought under the power of God.

> **1 Peter 5: 6-9:** Humble yourselves therefore under the mighty hand of God, that he may exalt you in due time: Casting all your care upon him; for he careth for you. Be sober, be vigilant; because your adversary the devil, as a roaring lion, walketh about, seeking whom he may devour: Whom resist stedfast in the faith, knowing that the same afflictions are accomplished in your brethren that are in the world.
>
> **James 4:7:** Submit yourselves therefore to God. Resist the devil, and he will flee from you.

It is when you submit yourself to God that you can resist the devil. The reason all the parts of the body are functioning well is that they are under a particular authority. So, submit yourself to God in every area of your life and let us see how the oppressor can come in.

READ THE WORD OF GOD AND MEDITATE UPON IT DAILY

The word of God is the mirror of the Spirit. All our faults are exposed in the mirror and the word is able to transform our lives.

KEEP THE RIGHT COMPANY

1Corinthians 15:33: Be not deceived: evil communications corrupt good manners.

We are supposed to be separated from the world and keep away from possible sources of contamination.

An unbeliever should not be a believer's closest friend. In fact, the bible asks us to keep away from certain groups of people. If God delivers you from drinking of alcohol, you must not go back and fellowship with those who drink it because you are now a different person.

MAKE SURE YOU GO TO THE RIGHT CHURCH

It is important for you to go to a Bible-believing church, a church where you can grow. You must not stay in a church where your spiritual life is dying out and you are not doing anything to improve on it. If you stay there because you were born there, you may end up in trouble. Look for a bible-believing church which believes in the totality of the word of God; which believes in the power of the Holy Ghost and which believes in the gifts of the Holy Spirit, not where there is corruption and people are doing things contrary to the word of God. Look for a bible-believing church where the power of God is present.

PUT ON THE WHOLE ARMOUR OF GOD

Ephesians 6:12: For we wrestle not against flesh and blood, but against principalities, against powers, against the rulers of the darkness of this world, against spiritual wickedness in high places.

Verses 13-18: Wherefore take unto you the whole armour of God, that ye may be able to withstand in the evil day, and having done all, to stand. Stand therefore, having your loins girt about with truth, and having on the breastplate of righteousness. And your feet shod with the preparation of the gospel of peace. Above all, taking the shield of faith, wherewith ye shall be able to quench all the fiery darts of the wicked. And take the helmet of salvation, and the sword of the Spirit, which is the word of God: Praying always with all prayer and supplication in the Spirit, and watching thereunto with all perseverance and supplication for all saints.

All these things are the armour of God.

Deuteronomy 7:26: Neither shalt thou bring an abomination into thine house, lest thou be a curse thing like it: but thou shalt utterly detest it, and thou shalt utterly abhor it, for it is a cursed thing.

You must remove all demonic materials from your house so that you don't have a ladder through which oppressors can come in. Re-examine all the pictures that you have, examine all those things that are put in your house as decorations. Deeply look at them again from your spirit. Removing abominable things from your house would help to set you free from the oppressors. The devil uses them to set traps and deceive people to step into bondage from which they will be struggling to get out. The people I feel sorry for most are those who enter into these traps unconsciously.

One day, a girl who could not walk was carried to our church. What happened to her? Her classmate belonged to a mermaid group which told its members to bring one person each within a specified period. The girl tried but could not get anybody to join voluntarily.

So she went and wrote down the name of this girl. And from that night the immobile girl would find herself swimming at the Bar-beach without knowing what was happening to her. It was later she discovered that her friend wrote down her name in the group and the important thing for her was to get out.

Please pray the following prayer points very well. Do not allow your mind to wander. Forget about past failures. Trust God today. Stand against monitoring spirits with great anger and violence because the kingdom of God suffers violence and the violent takes it by force.

PRAYER POINTS

1. Every spirit monitoring any area of my life, I bind you, in Jesus' name.

2. I withdraw my leg and my life from any monitoring spirit, in Jesus' name.

3. Holy Spirit, incubate me with your fire, in Jesus' name.

4. You foul spirits, tormenting and harassing my life, loose your hold, in Jesus' name.

PRAYERS POINTS TO CRUSH OPPRESSION

PRAYERS TO RECEIVE FRESH FIRE

☞ When you need personal revival.

☞ When you need fresh fire for fighting the battles of life.

☞ When you need the power of the Holy Ghost to enable you to fulfil your destiny in life.

Fire is one thing which the enemy cannot withstand. When you receive fresh fire, you become untouchable. When the totality of your life is set on fire, you will emerge a winner in the battles of life. The fire of the Holy Ghost is one major weapon which we need for victory in life. God has promised to slay His

For by fire and by his sword will the LORD plead with all flesh: and the slain of the LORD shall be many. Isa 66:16.

Fire is one of the weapons which God has freely given to you to enable you to go through life successfully. Whenever the fire of your life goes down, you will be enveloped with fear. But the moment your fire level increases, it will be victory all the way. The shortest route to your testimonies is to pray fresh fire upon your life. God dwells in the midst of fire. When God envelops your life with fresh fire, His mighty presence will also envelope your life. You need to pray the prayer points that follow aggressively if you want to experience the fire of God afresh. Pray the prayer points aggressively and the God who answereth by fire shall manifest Himself in your life.

> **Galatians 3:13-14:** Christ hath redeemed us from the curse of the law, being made a curse for us: for it is written, Cursed is every one that hangeth on a tree: That the blessing of Abraham might come on the Gentiles through Jesus Christ; that we might receive the promise of the Spirit through faith.
>
> **2 Tim. 4:18:** And the Lord shall deliver me from every evil work, and will preserve me unto his heavenly kingdom: to whom be glory for ever and ever. Amen.
>
> **Col. 1:13:** Who hath delivered us from the power of darkness, and hath translated us into the kingdom of his dear Son:
>
> **Col. 2:15:** And having spoiled principalities and powers, he made a shew of them openly, triumphing over them in it.

And call ye on the name of your gods, and I will call on the name of the LORD: and the God that answereth by fire, let him be God. And all the people answered and said, It is well spoken. 1 Kings 18:24.

Confessions:

Aggressive Praise worship

1. Thank God for His mighty power to save to the uttermost and for the power to deliver from any

form of bondage.

2. Confess your sins and those of your ancestors, especially those sins linked to evil powers and idolatry.

3. I cover myself with the blood of Jesus.

4. I release myself from any inherited bondage and limitation, in the name of Jesus.

5. O Lord, send Your axe of fire to the foundation of my life, and destroy every evil plantation therein.

6. Blood of Jesus, flush out from my system, every inherited satanic deposit, in the name of Jesus.

7. Any rod of the wicked, rising up against my family line, be rendered impotent for my sake, in the name of Jesus.

8. I cancel the consequences of any evil local name attached to my person, in the name of Jesus.

9. You evil foundational plantations, come out of my life with all your roots, in the name of Jesus.

10. I break and loose myself from every form of demonic bewitchment, in the name of Jesus.

11. I release myself from every evil domination and control, in the name of Jesus.

19. Every gate, opened to the enemy by my foundation, be closed forever with the blood of Jesus.

20. Lord Jesus, walk back into every second of my life and deliver me where I need deliverance; heal me where I need healing and transform me where I need transformation.

21. Thou power in the blood of Jesus, separate me from the sins of my ancestors.

12. I release myself from the grip of any problem transferred into my life from the womb, in the name of Jesus.

13. Blood of Jesus and the fire of the Holy Ghost, cleanse every organ in my body, in the name of Jesus.

14. I break and loose myself from every inherited evil covenant, in the name of Jesus.

15. I break and loose myself from every inherited evil curse, in the name of Jesus.

16. I vomit every evil consumption, that I have been fed with as a child, in the name of Jesus.

17. I command all foundational strongmen attached to my life to be paralysed, in the name of Jesus.

18. O Lord, let the blood of Jesus, be transfused into my blood vessel.

22. Blood of Jesus, remove any unprogressive label from every aspect of my life.

23. O Lord, create in me a clean heart by Your power.

30. O Lord, establish me as a holy person unto You.

31. O Lord, restore my spiritual eyes and ears.

32. O Lord, let the anointing to excel in my spiritual and physical life fall on me.

33. O Lord, produce in me the power of self-control and gentleness.

34. Holy Ghost, breathe on me now, in the name of Jesus.

35. Holy Ghost fire, ignite me to the glory of God.

36. O Lord, let every rebellion flee from my heart.

24. O Lord, let the anointing of the Holy Spirit break every yoke of backwardness in my life.

25. O Lord, renew a right spirit within me.

26. O Lord, teach me to die to self.

27. Thou brush of the Lord, scrub out every dirtiness in my spiritual pipe, in the name of Jesus.

28. O Lord, ignite my calling with Your fire.

29. O Lord, anoint me to pray without ceasing.

37. I command every spiritual contamination in my life to receive

38. Every rusted spiritual pipe in my life, receive wholeness, in the name of Jesus.

39. I command every power, eating up my spiritual pipe to be roasted, in the name of Jesus.

40. I renounce any evil dedication placed upon my life, in the name of Jesus.

41. I break every evil edict and ordination, in Jesus' name.

42. O Lord, cleanse all the soiled parts of my life.

43. O Lord, deliver me from every foundational Pharaoh.

44. O Lord, heal every wounded part of my life.

45. O Lord, bend every evil rigidity of my life.

46. O Lord, re-align every satanic straying in my life.

47. O Lord, let the fire of the Holy Spirit warm every satanic freeze in my life.

48. O Lord, give me a life that kills death.

49. O Lord, kindle in me the fire of charity.

50. O Lord, glue me together where I am opposed to myself.

51. O Lord, enrich me with Your gifts.

52. O Lord, quicken me and increase my desire for the things of heaven.

cleansing by the blood of Jesus.

53. By Your rulership, O Lord, let the lust of the flesh in my life die.

54. Lord Jesus, increase daily in my life.

55. Lord Jesus, maintain Your gifts in my life.

56. O Lord, refine and purge my life, by Your fire.

57. Holy Spirit, inflame my heart with your fire, in the name of Jesus.

58. Holy Ghost fire, begin to burn away every power of the bond woman in me, in the name of Jesus.

59. O Lord, make me ready to go wherever You send me.

60. Lord Jesus, never let me shut You out.

61. Lord Jesus, work freely in me and through me.

62. Thank God for answers to your prayers.

PRAYERS TO KILL GOLIATH IN YOUR DESTINY

A lot of people have problems in the area of fulfilling their destinies today. These problems can be traced to the presence of a stubborn Goliath in their lives. Goliath is a symbol of the wicked one. The terrifying presence of a local goliath in your life will invite confusion and chaos into your destiny. The threats of Goliath, as well as his wicked acts, will make the fulfilment of your destiny impossible.

CONFESSION: Luke 10:19: Behold, I give unto you power to tread on serpents and scorpions, and over all the power of the enemy: and nothing shall by any means hurt you.

Praise Worship

1. Praise the Lord for the power in His name, at which every knee must bow.

2. Thank God, for providing deliverance from any form of bondage.

3. I cover myself with the blood of Jesus.

4. Confess any sin that can hinder answers to your prayers, and ask God to forgive you.

5. Stand against any power already organised against this prayer.

6. I destroy the power of every satanic arrest in my life, in Jesus' name.

7. All satanic-arresting agents, release me, in the mighty name of our Lord Jesus Christ.

8. Everything that is representing me in the demonic world against my career, be destroyed by the fire of God, in the name of Jesus.

9. Spirit of the living God, quicken the whole of my being, in the name of Jesus.

10. O God, smash me and renew my strength, in the name of Jesus.

11. Holy Spirit, open my eyes to see beyond the visible to the invisible, in the name of Jesus.

14. Holy Spirit, teach me to pray through problems instead of praying about them, in the name of Jesus.

15. O Lord, deliver me from the lies I tell myself.

16. Every evil spiritual padlock and evil chain hindering my success, be roasted, in the name of Jesus.

17. I rebuke every spirit of spiritual deafness and blindness in my life, in the name of Jesus.

18. O Lord, empower me to resist satan so that he would flee from me.

19. I choose to believe the report of the Lord and none other, in the name of Jesus.

20. O Lord, anoint my eyes and my ears that they may see and hear wondrous things from heaven.

12. O Lord, ignite my career with Your fire.

13. O Lord, liberate my spirit to follow the leading of the Holy Spirit.

21. O Lord, anoint me to pray without ceasing.

22. In the name of Jesus, I capture and destroy every power behind any career failure.

23. Holy Spirit, rain your fire

on me now, in the name of Jesus.

24. Holy Spirit, uncover my darkest secrets, in the name of Jesus.

25. You spirit of confusion, loose your hold over my life, in Jesus' name.

26. In the power of the Holy Spirit, I defy satan's power upon my career, in the name of Jesus.

27. You water of life, flush out every unwanted stranger in my life, in the name of Jesus.

28. You the enemies of my career, be paralysed, in Jesus' name.

29. O Lord, begin to wash away from my life, all that does not reflect You.

30. Holy Spirit fire, ignite me for the glory of God, in Jesus' name.

31. Oh Lord, let the anointing of the Holy Spirit break every yoke of backwardness in my life.

32. I frustrate every demonic arrest of my spirit-man, in Jesus' name.

33. Blood of Jesus, remove any unprogressive label from every aspect of my life, in Jesus' name.

34. Anti-breakthrough decrees, be revoked, in Jesus' name.

35. Holy Ghost fire, destroy every satanic garment in my life, in the name of Jesus.

36. Oh Lord, give unto me the key to good success, so that anywhere I go, the doors of good success will be opened unto me.

37. Every wicked house, constructed against me and my career, be demolished, in the name of Jesus.

38. Oh Lord, establish me a holy person unto You, in Jesus' name.

39. Oh Lord, let the anointing to excel in my career fall on me, in the name of Jesus.

40. I shall not serve my enemies. My enemies shall bow down to me, in the name of Jesus.

41. I bind every desert and poverty spirit in my life, in Jesus' name.

42. I reject the anointing of non-achievement in my career, in Jesus' name.

43. I pull down all the strongholds erected against my progress, in the name of Jesus.

44. I recall all my blessings thrown into the river, forest and satanic bank, in the name of Jesus.

45. I cut down all the roots of problems in my life, in Jesus' name.

46. Satanic scorpions, be rendered stingless in every area of my life, in the name of Jesus.

47. Demonic serpents, be rendered venom-less in every area of my life, in the name of Jesus.

48. I declare with my mouth, that nothing shall be impossible with me, in the name of Jesus.

49. You the camp of the enemy, be put in disarray, in Jesus' name.

51. All my Herods, receive spiritual decay, in the name of Jesus.

52. Oh Lord, in my career, let Your favour and that of man encompass me this year, in the name Jesus.

53. I reject any demonic limitation on my progress, in Jesus' name.

54. All evil handwritings against me, be paralysed, in Jesus' name.

55. I reject the spirit of the tail, I choose the spirit of the head, in the name of Jesus.

56. All those circulating my name for evil, be disgraced, in the name of Jesus.

57. All evil friends, make the mistakes that would expose you, in Jesus' name.

58. You the strongmen from both sides of my family, attacking my career, destroy yourselves, in Jesus' name.

59. I refuse to wear the garment of tribulation and sorrow, in the name of Jesus.

60. Every rebellion, flee from my heart, in the name of Jesus.

61. O Lord, let the spirit that flees from sin incubate my life.

62. I claim all my rights now, in the name of Jesus.

63. Holy Ghost, grant me a glimpse of Your glory now, in Jesus' name.

64. Holy Ghost, quicken me, in the name of Jesus.

65. I release myself from any inherited bondage, affecting my career, in Jesus' name.

66. O Lord, send Your axe of fire to the foundation of my life and destroy every evil plantation attacking the success of my career.

67. Blood of Jesus, flush out from my system, every inherited satanic deposit, in Jesus' name.

68. I command all foundational strongmen attached to my life to be paralysed, in the name of Jesus.

69. Any rod of the wicked, rising up against my career, be rendered impotent for my sake, in the name of Jesus.

70. I cancel the consequences of any evil local name attached to my person, in the name of Jesus.

71. I release myself from every evil domination and control, in the name of Jesus.

72. Every evil imagination, against my career, wither from the source, in the name of Jesus.

73. O Lord, let the destructive plan of the enemies aimed at my career blow up in their faces, in the name of Jesus.

74. O Lord, let my point of ridicule be converted to a source of miracle, in Jesus' name.

75. All powers sponsoring evil decisions against me, be disgraced, in the name of Jesus.

76. You the stubborn strongman, delegated against me and my career, fall down to the ground and become impotent, in the

80. Every spirit of Herod, be disgraced, in Jesus' name.

81. Every spirit of Goliath, receive the stones of fire, in Jesus' name.

82. Every spirit of Pharaoh, fall into your Red Sea and perish, in Jesus' name.

83. All satanic manipulations, aimed at changing my destiny, be frustrated, in the name of Jesus.

84. All unprofitable broadcasters of my goodness, be silenced, in Jesus' name.

85. All evil monitoring eyes, fashioned against me and my career, become blind, in the name of Jesus.

86. All demonic reverse gears, installed to hinder the progress of my career, roast, in Jesus' name.

name of Jesus.

77. You the stronghold of every spirit of Korah, Dathan and Abiram militating against me, be smashed to pieces, in the name of Jesus.

78. Every spirit of Balaam, hired to curse me, fall after the order of Balaam, in the name of Jesus.

79. Every spirit of Sanballat and Tobiah, planning evil against me, receive the stones of fire, in the name of Jesus.

87. Any evil sleep, undertaken to harm me and my career, be converted to the sleep of death, in Jesus' name.

88. All weapons and devices of oppressors and tormentors, be rendered impotent, in Jesus' name.

89. Fire of God, destroy the power operating any spiritual vehicle working against me and my career, in Jesus' name.

90. All evil advice given against my favour, crash and disintegrate, in the name of Jesus.

91. Every spirit of Egypt, fall after the order of Pharaoh, in Jesus' name.

92. You the wind, the sun and the moon, run contrary to every demonic presence in my environment, militating against my career, in the name of Jesus.

93. I prophesy, that all those laughing me to scorn, shall witness my testimony, in the name of Jesus.

94. Every wicked pot, cooking my affairs, roast, in Jesus' name.

95. Every witchcraft pot, working against me, I bring the judgment of God against you, in Jesus' name.

96. Begin to thank God for answering your prayers.

MY HAMAN AND BALAAM SHALL DIE

A prayer programme to be done:

☞ **When you are surrounded by enemies.**

☞ **For those who are experiencing deep opposition.**

☞ **For those who are facing recurrent battles.**

☞ **For those under the attack of very hostile powers.**

Haman and Balaam stand out in the Scriptures as enemies of God's people. One major characteristic of these two enemies is that they carried out their activities in broad daylight. You need this prayer programme when you face attacks from the enemies who fight you openly.

Haman and Balaam represent principal agents from the kingdom of darkness. When the spirit of Haman is at work, enemies will try to destroy you completely.

And he thought scorn to lay hands on Mordecai alone; for they had showed him the people of Mordecai: wherefore Haman sought to destroy all the Jews that were throughout the whole kingdom of Ahasuerus, even the people of Mordecai. Est 3:6.

You need the prayer points in this section to get rid of your Haman.

Balaam, on the other hand, fought against God's people with the power of curses and bewitchment.

This kind of power uses the weapon of demonic manipulation and tries to curse the people whom God has blessed

And God said unto Balaam, Thou shalt not go with them; thou shalt not curse the people: for they are blessed. Num 22:12.

When you pray the prayers in this section aggressively, those who have been hired to curse you will fail woefully and will declare that no one can curse you since your God has blessed you. When you are praying this prayer, you may receive certain reports along the way. Keep on praying until your Haman and Balaam are dead.

CONFESSION: Numbers 23:8: How shall I curse, whom God hath not cursed? or how shall I defy, whom the Lord hath not defied?

Praise Worship

1. I prophesy that my place of birth will not become my caldron, in Jesus' name.

2. I prophesy that this city where I live will not be my caldron, in Jesus' name.

3. Every pot of darkness, programmed against my life, be destroyed by fire, in Jesus' name.

4. Every witchcraft pot, using remote control against my health, break into pieces, in Jesus' name.

5. Every power, calling my name into any caldron, fall down and die, in Jesus' name.

6. Every caldron, making noise against me and monitoring my life, disintegrate, in Jesus' name

7. Every power, cooking my progress in an evil pot, receive the fire of judgment, in the name of Jesus.

8. Every satanic programme, emanating from the caldron of darkness, be reversed, in the name of Jesus.

9. Any evil fire, boiling any satanic programme in my life, be quenched, in the name of Jesus.

10. I prophesy that the counsel of the wicked against my life in this city shall not stand and I command it to perish, in Jesus' name.

11. Every counsel of God for my life, begin to prosper, in the name of Jesus.
12. Every power, cooking my flesh and my health in any evil caldron, receive the fire of God, in the name of Jesus.
13. Every evil bird of satanic programme, emanating from any cauldron of darkness, fall down and die, in Jesus' name.
14. Every pot, cooking my affairs, the Lord rebukes you, in Jesus' name.
15. I remove, the spell of any witchcraft pot over my neck, in the name of Jesus.
16. I break every witchcraft pot over my life, in Jesus' name.
17. O Lord, let every evil pot hunt its owners.

18. Every evil caldron or pot, be judged from heaven, in Jesus' name.

19. I prophesy that no evil caldron will cook up my life, in the name of Jesus.

20. Every council of witchcraft, working against me, you will not prosper, in the name of Jesus.

21. Every agreement with satan over my life, I cancel you now, in Jesus' name.

22. Every astral projection against me, I frustrate you, in Jesus' name.

23. I disentangle myself and my family from every witchcraft cage and pot, in the name of Jesus.

24. Every enemy that will not let go easily, I bring the judgment of death against you, in Jesus' name.

25. I prophesy that this year, my blessings will not sink, in the name of Jesus.

26. O Lord, let the spirit of salvation fall upon my family, in the name of Jesus.

27. Every grip of the evil consequences, of the ancestral worship of my forefathers' gods over my life and ministry, break by fire, in Jesus' name.

28. Every covenant with water spirits, desert spirits, witchcraft spirits, spirits in evil sacred trees, spirits inside / under sacred rocks / hills, family gods, evil family guardian spirits, family / village serpentine spirits, masquerade spirits, inherited spirit husbands / wives, break by the blood of Jesus.

29. Every unconscious evil soul-tie and covenant with the spirits of my dead grandfather, grandmother, occultic uncles, aunties, custodian of family gods/oracles/shrines, break by the blood of Jesus.

30. Every decision, vow or promise made by my forefathers contrary to my divine destiny, loose your hold by fire, in the name of Jesus.

31. Every legal ground, that ancestral/guardian spirits have in my life, be destroyed by the blood of Jesus.

32. Any ancestral bloodshed of animals or human beings affecting me, loose your hold by the blood of Jesus.

33. Every generational curse of God, resulting from the sin of idolatry of my forefathers, loose your hold, in Jesus' name.

34. Any curse, placed on my ancestral line by anybody cheated, maltreated or at the point of death, break now, in Jesus' name.

35. Every ancestral evil altar, prospering against me, be dashed against the Rock of Ages, in the name of Jesus.

36. Every garment of ancestral infirmity, disease, sickness, untimely death, poverty, disfavour, dishonour, shame and failure at the edge of miracles, passed down to my generation, roast by fire, in the name of Jesus.

37. Every ancestral placenta manipulation of my life, be reversed, in Jesus' name.

38. Every evil ancestral river, flowing down to my generation, dry up, in the name of Jesus.

39. Every evil ancestral life pattern, designed for me through vows, promises and covenants, be reversed, in Jesus' name.

40. Every evil ancestral habit and weakness of moral failures, manifesting in my life, loose your grip and release me now, in Jesus' name.

41. Every hold of any sacrifice ever offered in my family or on my behalf, I break your power in my life, in the name of Jesus.

42. Any power, from my family background, seeking to make a shipwreck of my life and ministry, be destroyed by the fire of God, in the name of Jesus.

43. Every rage and rampage of ancestral and family spirits, resulting from my being born again, be quenched by the liquid fire of God, in Jesus' name.

44. Any ancestral power, frustrating any area of my life, in order to discourage me from following Christ, receive multiple destruction, in the name of Jesus.

45. Every ancestral chain of slavery, binding my people from prospering in life, break in my life by the hammer of God, in the name of Jesus.

46. I prophesy that I will reach the height nobody has attained in my generation, in Jesus' name.

47. I recover every good thing, stolen by ancestral evil spirits from my forefathers, my immediate family and myself, in the name of Jesus.

48. Every ancestral embargo, be lifted; good things, begin to break forth in my life and in my family, in Jesus' name.

49. I release myself from any inherited bondage, in Jesus' name.

50. O Lord, send Your axe of fire to the foundation of my life and destroy every evil plantation therein.

51. Blood of Jesus, flush out from my system, every inherited satanic deposit, in Jesus' name.

52. I release myself from the grip of any problem, transferred into my life from the womb, in Jesus' name.

53. I break free from every inherited evil covenant, in Jesus' name.

54. I break loose from every inherited evil curse, in Jesus' name.

55. I vomit every evil food or drink, that I have been fed with as a child, in Jesus' name.

56. All foundational strongmen, attached to my life, be paralysed, in Jesus' name.

57. Any rod of the wicked, rising up against my family line, be rendered impotent for my sake, in the name of Jesus.

58. I cancel all the consequences of any evil local name, attached to my person, in the name of Jesus.

59. You evil foundational plantations, come out of my life with all your roots, in the name of Jesus.

60. I break loose from every form of demonic bewitchment, in Jesus' name.

61. I release myself from every evil domination and control, in Jesus' name.

62. Every gate, opened to the enemy by my foundation, be closed forever with the blood of Jesus.

63. Lord Jesus, walk back into every second of my life and deliver me where I need deliverance; heal me where I need healing and transform me where I need transformation.

64. Every evil imagination against me, wither from the source, in the name of Jesus.

65. I prophesy that all those laughing me to scorn shall witness my testimony, in Jesus' name.

66. All the destructive plans of the enemies, aimed at me, blow up in their faces, in Jesus' name.

67. O Lord, let my object of ridicule be converted to a source of miracle, in Jesus' name.

68. All powers, sponsoring evil decisions against me, be disgraced, in Jesus' name.

69. O Lord, let the stubborn strongman, assigned against me, fall down to the ground and become impotent, in the name of Jesus.

70. O Lord, let the stronghold of every spirit of Korah, Dathan and Abiram militating against me be smashed to pieces.

71. Every spirit of Balaam, hired to curse me, fall after the order of Balaam, in the name of Jesus.

72. Every spirit of Sanballat and Tobiah, planning evil against me, receive the stones of fire, in the name of Jesus.

73. Every spirit of Egypt, fall after the order of Pharaoh, in Jesus' name.

74. Every spirit of Herod, be disgraced, in Jesus' name.

75. Every spirit of Goliath, receive the stones of fire, in Jesus' name.

76. Every spirit of Pharaoh, fall into the Red Sea of your own making and perish, in the name of Jesus.

77. All satanic manipulations, aimed at changing my destiny, be frustrated, in Jesus' name.

78. All unprofitable broadcasters of my goodness, be silenced, in the name of Jesus.

79. All leaking bags and pockets, be sealed up, in Jesus' name.

80. All evil monitoring eyes, fashioned against me, be blind, in Jesus' name.

81. Every evil effect of any strange touch, be removed from my life, in the name of Jesus.

82. All demonic reverse gears, installed to hinder my progress, roast, in Jesus' name.

83. Any evil sleep, undertaken to harm me, be converted to death sleep, in Jesus' name.

84. All weapons and devices of the oppressors and tormentors, be rendered impotent, in Jesus' name.

85. Thou fire of God, destroy every power operating any spiritual vehicle working against me, in Jesus' name.

86. All evil advice given against my favour, crash and disintegrate, in Jesus' name.

87. O Lord, let the wind, the sun and the moon, run contrary to every demonic presence in my environment.

88. O you devourers, vanish from my labour, in Jesus' name.

89. Every tree, planted by fear in my life, dry up from the roots, in the name of Jesus.

90. I cancel all the enchantments, curses and spells that are against me, in the name of Jesus.

91. All iron-like curses, break, in the name of Jesus.

92. Divine tongues of fire, roast any evil tongue that is against me, in Jesus' name.

93. O Lord, I thank You very much for everything You have done for me through these prayer points.

BEWITCHMENT MUST DIE

☞ For those suffering witchcraft attacks.
☞ For those who have experienced demonic manipulations.
☞ For victims of household witchcraft.

God is a man of war. He will always rise up in the full strength of His military power to deal death blows on bewitchment.

There are agents of witchcraft in the nooks and crannies of every community. One of the major preoccupations of these witchcraft agents is to bewitch men, women and children. They infiltrate into the lives of their victims and manipulate, intimidate, oppress, subdue and attack them. Hence, many people find themselves in all forms of demonic actions as a result of bewitchment.

Additionally, marriages experience bewitchment, business ventures are bewitched; houses and business premises are also bewitched. You need to take up the prayer points below to pass the judgment of death on every form of bewitchment. When bewitchment is eliminated, the glory of God will envelop you and whatever belongs to you

CONFESSION: Numbers 23:23: "Surely *there is* no enchantment against Jacob, neither *is there* any divination against Israel: according to this time it shall be said of Jacob and of Israel, What hath God wrought!"

Aggressive praise worship

1. Every problem in my life, that originated from witchcraft, receive divine instant solution, in the name of Jesus.

2. All the damages done to my life by witchcraft, be repaired, in the name of Jesus.

3. Every blessing, confiscated by witchcraft spirits, be released, in Jesus' name.

4. Every witchcraft power, assigned against my life and marriage, receive ... (pick from the under listed), in the name of Jesus.

- the thunder and lightning of God.

- hail and fire mixed with the Blood of the Lamb.

- unbearable heat   - concentrated acid-destroying flood

- destruction   - raging fire- continuous plagues

- failures   - confusion

5. I loose myself from any power of witchcraft, in Jesus' name.

6. Every power of witchcraft, gathered against my prosperity, fall down and die, in the name of Jesus.

7. Every witchcraft pot, working against me, I bring the judgment of God upon you, in the name of Jesus.

8. Every witchcraft pot, using remote control against my health, break into pieces, in Jesus' name.

9. Witchcraft opposition, receive the rain of affliction, in the name of Jesus.

10. You the spirit of witchcraft attack and familiar spirits fashioned against me, die, in the name of Jesus.

11. I retrieve my integrity from the hands of household witchcraft, in the name of Jesus.

12. I break the power of the occult, witchcraft and familiar spirits, over my life, in the name of Jesus.

13. In the name of Jesus, I break loose from all evil curses, chains, spells, jinxes, bewitchments, witchcraft or sorcery which may have been put upon me.

14. Thou thunder of God, locate and dismantle the throne of witchcraft in my household, in Jesus' name.

15. Every seat of witchcraft in my household, roast with the fire of God, in the name of Jesus.

16. Every altar of witchcraft in my household, roast, in the name of Jesus.

17. Thou thunder of God, scatter the foundation of witchcraft in my household beyond redemption, in the name of Jesus.

18. Every stronghold of refuge of my household witches, be destroyed,

in the name of Jesus.

19. Every hiding place and secret place of witchcraft in my family, be exposed by fire, in the name of Jesus.

20. Every local and international witchcraft network of my household witches, be shattered to pieces, in the name of Jesus.

21. Every communication system of my household witches, be frustrated, in the name of Jesus.

22. Thou terrible fire of God, consume the means of transportation of my household witchcraft, in Jesus' name.

23. Every agent, ministering at the altar of witchcraft in my household, fall down and die, in the name of Jesus.

24. Thunder and fire of God, locate the storehouses and strongrooms of any household witchcraft, harbouring my blessings and pull them down, in the name of Jesus.

25. Any witchcraft curse, working against me, be revoked by the blood of Jesus.

26. Every decision, vow and covenant of household witchcraft, affecting me, be nullified by the blood of Jesus.

27. I destroy with the fire of God, every weapon of witchcraft used against me, in Jesus' name.

28. Any material taken from my body and now placed on a witchcraft altar, roast by the fire of God, in Jesus' name.

29. I reverse every witchcraft burial, fashioned against me,

in the name of Jesus.

30. Every trap, set for me by witches, begin to catch your owners, in Jesus' name.

31. Every witchcraft padlock, fashioned against any area of my life, roast, in Jesus' name.

32. O Lord, let the wisdom of my household witches be converted to foolishness, in Jesus' name.

33. O Lord, let the wickedness of my household enemies overtake them, in the name of Jesus.

34. I deliver my soul from every witchcraft bewitchment, in the name of Jesus.

35. Any witchcraft bird, flying for my sake, fall down, die and roast to ashes, in Jesus' name.

36. Any of my blessings, that had been traded with by household witches, be returned to me, in the name of Jesus.

37. Any of my blessings and testimonies, swallowed by witches, be converted to hot coals of fire of God and be vomited, in Jesus' name.

38. I break loose from every bondage of witchcraft covenants, in Jesus' name.

39. Any witchcraft coven, where any of my blessings is hidden, roast by the fire of God, in the name of Jesus.

40. (Lay your right hand on your head) Every witchcraft spirit plantation, pollution, deposit and material in my body, melt by the fire of God and be flushed out by the blood of Jesus.

41. Every evil, ever done to me through witchcraft attack, be reversed, in Jesus' name.

42. Every witchcraft hand, planting evil seeds in my life through dream attacks, wither and burn to ashes, in the name of Jesus.

43. Every witchcraft obstacle and hindrance, put on the road to my desired miracle and success, be removed by the east wind of God, in the name of Jesus.

44. Every witchcraft chant, spell and projection directed at me, I bind you and turn you against your owner, in the name of Jesus.

45. I frustrate every plot, device, scheme and projection of witchcraft, designed to affect any area of my life, in the name of Jesus.

46. Any witch, projecting herself into the body of any animal, in order to harm me, be trapped in the body of such an animal forever, in the name of Jesus.

47. Any drop of my blood, sucked by any witch, be vomited now, in the name of Jesus.

48. Any part of me, shared out among household / village witches, I recover you, in the name of Jesus.

49. Any organ of my body, that has been exchanged for another through witchcraft operations, be replaced now, in Jesus' name.

50. I recover any of my virtues / blessings shared out among village / household witches, in the name of Jesus.

51. I reverse the evil effect of any witchcraft summon of my spirit, in the name of Jesus.

52. I loose my hands and feet from any witchcraft bewitchment and bondage, in the name of Jesus.

53. Blood of Jesus, wash away from my life, every witchcraft identification mark on me or on any of my property, in Jesus' name.

54. I forbid any re-union of household and village witches against my life, in Jesus' name.

55. O Lord, let the entire body system of my household witches begin to run contrary, until they have confessed all their wickedness, in the name of Jesus.

56. O Lord, let your mercies be withdrawn from them, in the name of Jesus.

57. O Lord, let them begin to grope in the daytime as in the thickness of a dark night, in the name of Jesus.

58. O Lord, let everything that has ever worked for them begin to work against them, in the name of Jesus.

59. O Lord, let them not have a garment to cover their shame, in the name of Jesus.

60. Thank God for answers to your prayers.

KILLING THE WITCHCRAFT IN YOUR DESTINY

You need to bar any form of witchcraft interference in the affairs of your destiny because you are meant to shine like stars. God has given you a colourful destiny and it is His divine plan that you fulfil it. But whenever witchcraft succeeds in eating the root of your destiny, you will find it difficult to experience the manifestation of God's plan for your life and destiny.

The Bible says, "Thou shall not suffer a witch to live." This shows that any witchcraft toying with your destiny must receive the sentence of death.

With this prayer, you will succeed in killing the witchcraft in your destiny. Once witchcraft is dead, you will be able to fulfil your destiny in life.

Confession: Matthew 15:13: "But he answered and said, every plant, which my heavenly Father hath not planted, shall be rooted up."

PRAYER POINTS

1. O Lord, let as many witches and the entire body system of my household witches that are stubbornly unrepentant be smitten by the sun in the day and by the moon in the night.

2. O Lord, let each step they take lead them to greater destruction, in the name of Jesus.

3. But as for me, O Lord, let me dwell in the hollow of Your hand, in the name of Jesus.

4. O Lord, let the goodness and mercies of God now overwhelm me, in the name of Jesus.

5. Any witchcraft fashioned under any water against my life, receive immediate judgment of fire, in the name of Jesus.

6. Every witchcraft power, that has introduced spirit husband/wife or child into my dreams, roast by fire, in Jesus' name.

7. Every agent of witchcraft power, posing as my husband, wife or child in my dreams, roast by fire, in Jesus' name.

8. Every agent of witchcraft power, physically attached to my marriage, be frustrated, fall down and perish now, in the name of Jesus.

9. Every agent of witchcraft power, assigned to attack my finances through dreams, fall down and perish, in Jesus'

. name.

10. Thunderbolts of God, locate and destroy every witchcraft coven where deliberations and decisions are being fashioned against me, in the name of Jesus.

11. Any water spirit from my village or in the place of my birth, practising witchcraft against me and my family, be amputated by the Word of God, in the name of Jesus.

12. Any power of witchcraft, holding any of my blessings in bondage, receive the fire of God and release it, in the name of Jesus.

13. I loose my mind and soul from the bondage of marine witches, in the name of Jesus.

14. Any witchcraft chain binding my hands and feet from prospering, break and shatter to pieces, in the name of Jesus.

15. Every arrow, shot into my life from under any water through witchcraft, come out of me a   n   d go back to your sender, in the name of Jesus.

16. Any evil material, transferred into my body through contact with .any witchcraft agent, roast by fire, in the name of Jesus.

17. Any evil done against me so far through witchcraft oppression and manipulation, be reversed by the blood of Jesus.

18. I bind every witchcraft controlling and mind-blinding spirit, in the name of Jesus.

19. I cast out every witchcraft arrow affecting my senses (sight, smell, taste, hearing), in the name of Jesus.

20. I command every witchcraft arrow to depart from my

   - spinal cord - spleen

   - navel   - heart

   - throat - eyes

   - top of the head.

21. Blood of Jesus, purge me of every witchcraft contaminating material, in the name of Jesus.

22. I destroy the hand of any witch-doctor working against me, in the name of Jesus.

23. Every witchcraft spirit, attempting to build a wall against my destiny, fall down and die, in the name of Jesus.

24. I send the rain of affliction upon every witchcraft power working against me, in the name of Jesus.

25. O sun, moon, stars, earth, water and other elements of creation, vomit every enchantment that is against me, in Jesus' name.

26. Every power, using the heavenlies against me, fall down and be disgraced, in the name of Jesus.

27. O Lord, let the stars of heaven begin to fight for me, in the name of Jesus.

28. O God, arise and scatter every conspiracy against me in the heavenlies, in the name of Jesus.

29. I break with the blood of Jesus, all evil soul ties affecting my life, in the name of Jesus.

30. Spirit of the living God, come upon my life and place a shield of protection around me, in the name of Jesus.

31. Every chain of inherited witchcraft in my family, break, in the name of Jesus.

32. Every ladder, used by witchcraft against me, roast, in the name of Jesus.

33. Any door that I have opened to witchcraft in any area of my life, be closed for ever by the blood of Jesus.

34. I revoke every witchcraft verdict on my marital life, in the name of Jesus.

35. I send confusion into the camp of household witchcraft, in the name of Jesus.

36. Stubborn witchcraft, release me, in the name of Jesus.

37. Every witchcraft power, working against my destiny, fall down and die, in the name of Jesus.

38. Every incantation, ritual and witchcraft power against my destiny, fall down and die, in Jesus' name.

39. I break the power of the occult, witchcraft and familiar spirits over my life in the name of Jesus.

40. Witchcraft opposition, receive the rain of affliction, in the name

of Jesus.

41. I cancel every witchcraft verdict against my life, in the name of Jesus.

42. Every arrow of witchcraft in my life, come out with all your roots, in the name of Jesus! (Lay your hands on your stomach and pray aggressively.)

43. Every witchcraft pot, using remote control against my health, break into pieces, in the name of Jesus.

44. I rebuke the spell of any witchcraft pot over my neck, in the name of Jesus.

45. I break every witchcraft pot over my life, in Jesus' name.

46. Every council of witchcraft, working against me will not prosper, in the name of Jesus.

47. I disentangle myself and my family from every witchcraft cage and pot, in the name of Jesus.

48. I retrieve my integrity from the hands of household witchcraft, in the name of Jesus.

49. Every witchcraft hand, planting evil seeds in my life through dream attacks, wither and burn to ashes, in the name of Jesus.

50. O Lord, let all friendly witchcraft powers be exposed and disgraced, in the name of Jesus.

51. O Lord, plant Your warring angels around me, to dismantle and destroy evil stronghold of internal witchcraft.

52. I exercise my authority over stubborn witchcraft and I pull down

its structures, in the name of Jesus.

53. Every placenta witchcraft, targeted at my destiny, what are you waiting for? die, in the name of Jesus.

54. Placenta witchcraft, manipulating my destiny, die, in the name of Jesus.

55. Every blessing, that I have lost through placenta witchcraft, I re-possess you, in Jesus' name.

56. Every witchcraft coven and marine banks, release my placenta, in Jesus' name.

57. Every cage of family witchcraft, release my divine partner, in Jesus' name.

58. Oh Lord, let my dreams and visions reject every witchcraft projection, in the name of Jesus.

PRAYERS TO BREAK THE BACKBONE OF POVERTY

Poverty is not just the absence of prosperity; it is an attack from the kingdom of darkness. There is a spiritual entity responsible for afflicting people with poverty. When you come across people who work like elephants and eat like ants, you have come across people who are attacked by the spirit of poverty.

Wealth or prosperity is not mainly achieved by working hard or labouring from dawn to dusk. If you want to experience prosperity in life, first and foremost, you must deal with the spirit of poverty. The principality behind the spirit of poverty must be stripped of his power and rendered impotent.

You need to use the prayer points below as a potent weapon for breaking the backbone of poverty. Once the backbone of

poverty is broken, every trace of poverty will be removed from your life.	

Confession: Obad. 1:17; Deut. 8:18

Aggressive Praise Worship

1. I release myself from every ancestral demonic pollution, in Jesus' name.

2. I release myself from every inherited demonic pollution, in Jesus' name.

3. I release myself from every demonic pollution emanating from my past involvement in any demonic religion, in Jesus' name.

4. I break loose from every idol and related association, in Jesus' name.

5. I release myself from every dream pollution, in Jesus' name.

6. Satanic attacks against my life in the dreams, be converted to victory, in Jesus' name.

7. O Lord, let all rivers, trees, forests, evil companions, evil pursuers, pictures of dead relatives, snakes, spirit husbands, spirit wives and masquerades, manipulated against me in the dream, be completely destroyed by the power in the blood of the Lord Jesus.

8. Every evil plantation in my life, come out with all your roots, in the name of Jesus! (Lay your hands on your stomach and keep repeating the emphasised area.)

9. I withdraw my wealth from

the hand of the bondwoman and her children, in Jesus' name.

10. By the power of the living God, I will not squander my divine opportunities, in Jesus' name.

11. I dismantle any power working against my efficiency, in Jesus' name.

12. I refuse to lock the door of blessings against myself, in Jesus' name.

13. I refuse to be a wandering star, in the name of Jesus.

14. I refuse to appear and disappear suddenly, in Jesus' name.

---

15. O Lord, let the riches of the Gentiles be transferred to me, in the name of Jesus.

16. Angels of God, pursue every enemy of my prosperity to destruction, in Jesus' name.

17. O Lord, let the sword of the Goliath of poverty turn against it, in the name of Jesus.

18. Holy Father, let wealth change hands in my life, in Jesus' name.

19. O Lord, make a hole in the roof for my prosperity.

20. My Father, let the yoke of poverty upon my life be dashed to pieces, in the name of Jesus.

21. Father Lord, let every satanic siren, scaring away my helpers be silenced, in the name of Jesus.

22. O Lord, let every masquerading power, swallowing my prosperity be destroyed, in Jesus' name.

23. Every coffin, constructed against my prosperity,

swallow your owner, in Jesus' name.

24. My God, let the ways of the evil angels of poverty commissioned against me become dark and slippery, in the name of Jesus.

25. Lord Jesus, hold my purse.

26. Every demonic scarcity, be dissolved by fire, in Jesus' name.

27. Thou Awesome God, bring the day of evil upon every enemy of my prosperity and destroy him with double destruction.

CONFESSIONS FOR PROSPERITY

There is a strong link between the physical and spiritual realm. When you take control of a situation in the spiritual, you will surely experience mastery over the same situation in the physical. You can confess and command prosperity to come into manifestation in your life. Prophetic confession is a powerful weapon in the school of spiritual warfare.

When you desire prosperity and wealth, you must keep making the confessions below until prosperity becomes a glorious possibility in your life. The power of the spoken word is a tool which poverty cannot resist. Make use of these confessions of prosperity today; you will climb the ladder of prosperity with ease

Jesus is Lord of this earth. The earth with all its

fullness belongs to God. As a joint heir with Jesus, I claim the wealth of this earth, for it belongs to Jesus. I claim all that Jesus' death made available for me to receive. In Jesus' name, I command you devil to loose the wealth of this earth! Take your hands off now! I command every hindering force to stop! In Jesus' name, I bind you and render you ineffective against me! In Jesus' name, I command wealth to come to me now! Jesus is Lord of my life. Jesus is Lord of my finances. Jesus is Lord!

I delight myself in the word of the Lord, therefore, I am blessed. Wealth and riches shall be in my house and my righteousness endureth forever. (Psalm 112:1-3.)

I remember the Lord my God, for it is He that giveth me power to get wealth. (Deut. 8:18.)

With me are riches and honour, enduring wealth and prosperity. (Prov. 8:18.)

I am crowned with wealth. (Prov. 14:24.)

I know the grace of my Lord Jesus Christ, that, though He was rich, yet for my sake He became poor, that through His poverty I might be rich. (2 Corn. 8:9.)

I shout for joy: Let the Lord be magnified, which hath pleasure in my. (Psalm 35:27.)

The Lord is my shepherd. (Psalm 23:1.)

The Lord prepares a table before me in the presence of my enemies, He anoints my head with oil, my cup runneth over. (Psalm 23:5.)

The blessing of the Lord makes

me rich and He adds no trouble to it. (Prov. 10:22.)

I receive wealth from the Lord and the good health to enjoy it. (Eccl. 5:19.)

I am blessed because I trust in the Lord. I reverence the Lord, therefore there is no want in my life. The young lions do lack and suffer hunger: But I shall not want any good thing. (Psalm 34:8-10.)

I have given and it shall be given unto me, good measure, pressed down, shaken together and running over, shall men give into my bosom. For with the same measure that I mete withal it shall be measured to me again. (Luke 6:38.)

God is able to make all grace abound toward me, that I, always having all sufficiency in all things, may have an abundance for every good work. (2 Corn. 9:8.)

I am prospering in every way. My body keeps well, even as my soul keeps well and prosper. (3John 2.)

Whatsoever I ask the Father in the name of His Son Jesus, He will give it to me. (John 16:23.)

Abraham's blessings are mine. (Gal. 3:14.)

What things soever I desire, when I pray, I believe that I have received them and I shall have them. (Mark 11:24.)

I delight myself in the Lord, and He gives me the desires of my heart. (Psalm 37:4.)

I seek first the kingdom of God, therefore everything I need shall be added unto me. (Lk. 12:31.)

The wealth of the sinner is laid up for me. (Prov. 13:22.)

My inheritance shall be forever. I shall not be ashamed in the evil time: and in the days of famine I shall be satisfied. (Psalm 37:18-19.)

Every burden shall be taken away from off my shoulder, and every yoke from off my neck, and the yoke shall be destroyed because of the anointing. (Isa. 10:27.)

I am like a tree that's planted by the rivers of water. Everything I do shall prosper. (Psalm 1:3.)

I will not faint, for in due time and at the appointed season I shall reap, if I faint not. (Gal. 6:9.)

My God supplies all of my need according to His riches in glory by Christ Jesus. (Phil. 4:19.)

MY CALLING SHALL NOT BE WASTED

DELIVERANCE PRAYERS FOR MINISTERS

To be called into the ministry is a great privilege. But it is one thing to be called and another to fulfil one's calling. Many people have had their calling wasted by wasters of callings. The war against wasters of callings should be fought with the totality of your strength. Many who were called started on a very good note but ended badly. Every Christian worker or member of the gospel ministry should make it a point of duty to carry out this prayer programme on regular basis. Some gospel workers and ministers never bargained for the attacks they have suffered in the course of fulfilling their calling.

It is the responsibility of those who are called into the ministry to wage prayer war against all wasters of callings. You must use the prayer points below to safeguard your calling. These prayer points will chase away every power trying to waste your calling.

Confession: Psalms 1 & 2

Praise Worship

1. Thank the Lord for the privilege of working in His vineyard.

2. Since many are called but few are chosen, thank the Lord for choosing you.

3. Bring quality repentance before the Lord.

4. I shall not be a misfired arrow in the hands of my Maker, in Jesus' name.

5. Any foundational power, working against my calling, be destroyed, in the name of Jesus.

6. Every yoke, working against spiritual growth in my life, break, in the name of Jesus.

7. By the power of God, the enemy will not make me a bad example, in the name of Jesus.

8. Every destructive habit, designed to waste my calling, die, in the name of Jesus.

9. Power to finish well, come upon my destiny, in the name of Jesus.

10. Every area of incomplete deliverance in my life, receive complete deliverance by fire, in the name of Jesus.

11. Every spiritual cataract, clear away from my vision, in the name of Jesus.

12. Every spirit of slumber, I bury you today, in the name of Jesus.

13. You the eagle of my calling, mount up by the power in the blood of Jesus.

14. Every anti-ministry arrow, fired into my life, backfire, in Jesus' name.

15. Holy Ghost fire, destroy all works of darkness in my life, in Jesus' name.

16. Every door, opened to the enemy of my calling, be closed, in Jesus' name.

17. My Father and my God, let the waters of life flow into every dead area of my spiritual life, in the name of Jesus.

18. Every weapon, fashioned against my high calling, be destroyed, in the name of Jesus.

19. Any foundational serpent and scorpion, programmed into my life to destroy my calling in the future, die, in Jesus' name.

20. O God of Elijah, arise and give unto me my mantle of fire, in the name of Jesus.

21. Anything planted within me, that has not manifested now but will manifest in the future to make me backslide, dry up, in Jesus' name.

22. Every witchcraft power, drinking the blood of my spiritual life, die, in the name of Jesus.

23. Glory of God, overshadow me, in the name of Jesus.

24. Strength of God, empower me, in the name of Jesus.

25. Every internal bondage, magnetizing external bondage, break, in the name of Jesus.

26. O glory of my calling, arise and shine, in the name of Jesus.

27. By the power of God, I will not mortgage my calling on the lap of Delilah and Jezebel, in the name of Jesus.

28. I refuse to retire, I must re-fire, in the name of Jesus.

29. Every enemy of my divine commendation of 'well done,' at the end of my race, die, in the name of Jesus.

30. I decree that my Samson will not be shaven, in the name of Jesus.

31. I receive power to meet the needs of this present generation, in the name of Jesus.

32. All the rough places in my life, targeted at my spiritual breakthroughs, be smoothened by the blood of Jesus.

33. O Lord, let Your glory overshadow my destiny, in Jesus' name.

34. I refuse to tarry in the valley of powerlessness, in the name of Jesus.

35. I rise above my roots by the power in the blood of Jesus.

YOKE BREAKING PRAYERS

Every demonic yoke can be broken through the power of the Almighty. To deal with the yoke of the enemy, you have to use the weapon of aggressive prayer. If a particular yoke has remained entrenched in your life for 20 years, the amount of prayer efforts which you must apply must be equally strong.

The satanic yoke must be broken such that the manifestations are non-existent. The prayer points below are specially vomited by the Holy Ghost to do some specific things in your life. Make use of them and the yoke of the enemy will be completely broken.

CONFESSION: Psalm 2

Praise Worship

1. Praise the Lord for the power in His name at which every knee must bow.

2. Thank God for making the provision for deliverance from any form

of bondage.

3. I cover myself with the blood of Jesus.

4. Confess any sin that can hinder answers to your prayers and ask God to forgive you.

5. Stand against any power already organised against this prayer programme.

6. O Lord, anoint my eyes and ears, that they may see and hear wondrous things from heaven.

7. Holy Spirit, uncover my darkest secrets, in the name of Jesus.

8. O Lord, let the anointing of the Holy Spirit break every yoke of backwardness in my life.

9. Blood of Jesus, remove any unprogressive label from every aspect of my life, in the name of Jesus.

10. O Lord, establish me a holy person unto You, in the name of Jesus.

11. O Lord, let the anointing to excel in my career fall on me, in the name of Jesus.

12. By the power of God, I shall not serve my enemies; my enemies shall bow down to me, in the name of Jesus.

13. I pull down all the strongholds erected against my progress, in the name of Jesus.

14. Every generational curse of God on my forefathers, resulting from the sins of idolatry, loose your hold, in Jesus' name.

15. I release myself, from any inherited bondage, in Jesus' name.

16. All you powers, that are sucking the peace of my destiny, be bound, in the name of Jesus.

17. O Lord, ordain a terrifying noise unto the camp of the enemy of my destiny, in the name of Jesus.

18. Father Lord, put your seal on every miracle You have performed in this church, in the name of Jesus.

19. I reject every evil arrangement concerning this church and I receive the arrangement of God, in Jesus' name.

20. All the evil forces opposing this church, begin to rise up against one another, in the name of Jesus.

21. Angels of God, hinder and stop all the works of darkness in this church, in the name of Jesus.

22. I stand against every form of tragedy in the lives of the congregation, in the name of Jesus.

23. I cast down every evil imagination against the ministers, in the name of Jesus.

24. Any power, working against the vision of God for my destiny, scatter by fire, in the name of Jesus.

25. My destiny, arise by fire and possess your possessions, in Jesus' name.

26. Every arrangement by sorcerers and witches in the heavenlies, fashioned against my life, scatter, in the name of Jesus.

27. I take a divine insurance for my family and I, against all forms of accidents, in the name of Jesus.

28. I raise the whirlwind of the Lord to blow away every stubborn pursuer, in the name of Jesus.

29. Every negative anointing, targeted at me, dry up, in the name of Jesus.

30. You spirit of confusion, loose your hold over my life, in Jesus' name

31. I cut down all the roots of problems in my life, in Jesus' name.

32. I recall all my blessings thrown into the water, forest and satanic bank, in the name of Jesus.

33. O Lord, let the camp of my enemies be put in disarray, in Jesus' name.

PRAYERS TO RECEIVE SPIRITUAL STRENGTH

The devil takes delight in weakening the strength of the saints. If he succeeds in weakening his victim, he will succeed in executing his wicked programmes. As long as you are spiritually strong, the devil will not be able to execute his agenda in your life. You need this prayer programme to renew your strength in the presence of God. You need this programme to mount up with wings as eagles.

You should make use of the prayer points until your spiritual batteries are charged. You can turn your closet into an arena where you receive power.

This prayer programme is your personal antidote to failure in the day of battle.

BIBLE STUDY: Nehemiah 8:10; Isa. 40:29-31; 2 Sam. 22:33-36

Praise Worship

Confession: In the name of Jesus Christ, I am a beloved child of God. I believe in God. I believe in Jesus Christ and I believe in the blessed Holy Spirit, which is dwelling inside me. I believe in the unshakable and eternal power in the word of God. I believe that life and death are in the power of my tongue. I believe that as I make this confession unto life with the power in my tongue, according to the words which the Lord has put in my mouth this day, I shall prosper therewith.

It is written that Jesus Christ offered His blood as a drink and His flesh as bread, that whosoever drinks and eats them shall not die forever. Now, with strong faith in my heart, I hold in my hand, a cup containing the blood of the Lamb of God and I drink it that I may have eternal life.

I receive unto myself, the virtues, strength, power, might and anointing in the blood.

And I say, let the blood quicken all that is dead within me. Let all sucked, sapped and paralysed spiritual milk and strength of my life resurrect by the blood.

Let the blood re-energize, revitalize, reactivate and revive all dead potentials and spiritual gifts within me.

Let the blood flush out of me, all inherited or self-acquired evil deposits in my system.

Let it purify my blood system. Let it make old things pass away in my life and transform everything to become new.

Let the power in the blood clean my spiritual vision and wash my spiritual pipe, that I may be receiving from the Lord unhindered.

I eat the flesh of Jesus with the heart of faith; for it is written, "His flesh is bread indeed." I eat it now, so that I can also eat with Him in His glory.

I eat the flesh of Jesus to receive new spiritual strength and vigour. I receive new spiritual strength and vigour: to put all the works of the flesh under subjection; to paralyse the desires of my flesh; to buffet my flesh; to paralyse the power of my flesh and make it obedient to the laws of the Lord.

As I eat and drink the flesh and blood of my Lord Jesus Christ, I renew my covenant with Him and I receive the life therein for it is written, "Life is in the blood." Thus, I possess the life and the Spirit of Christ in me, Amen.

Jeremiah found the words of God and ate them, and they became the joy of his heart. I have found the words of God and now, I throw them in my mouth like vitamin pills and chew, and digest them. Let them produce within me, the power to rejoice in the Holy Ghost, the power to be steadfast in following God, the power to walk circumspectly, the power of holy living and the power of unashamed faithfulness in all circumstances.

The word of God is spirit and life. It entered Ezekiel and he was put back on his feet.

Let the word of God raise every downtrodden area of my life. Let the word, like fire, purify me like the refiner's fire. Let the word recreate in me everything stolen or destroyed by the enemy. Let the word build me up and give me inheritance among all sanctified brethren.

Let the joy of the Lord strengthen me. Let His right hand of righteousness uphold me. Let His countenance brighten up my life. Let the horn of His salvation lift me up, out of the valley of death and let his life giving anointing oil fall on me like the Dew of Hermon, and fill my life till I want no more.

Lord, make me drunk with the blood of Jesus and I shall be full of life eternally.

Father Lord, as it is written, that I should be strong in the Lord and in the power of His might, as you will be my might and my strength all the days of my life according to Your word, gird me with Your strength and let me not fall into the pit of my enemies, and I will praise You all the days of my life.

With my heart, I believe the word of God; with my mouth, I have confessed unto salvation and justification. O Lord, let it be performed unto me, as I have prayed, in the one and only Jesus Christ's mighty name, Amen.

1. Thank God for the strength with which He has been upholding you all these years.

2. Cover yourself with the blood of Jesus.

3. I hold the blood of Jesus, as a shield against any power that is already poised to resist me, in the name of Jesus.

4. By the blood of Jesus, I stand against every device of distractions, in the name of Jesus.

5. I stand upon the word of God and I declare myself unmoveable, in the name of Jesus.

6. Father Lord, inject me with Your spiritual vitamins that will make me spiritually

healthy, in the name of Jesus.

7. Father Lord, inject me with spiritual vitamins that will boost my appetite to eat Your word, in the name of Jesus.

8. Father Lord, infuse my blood with spiritual vitamins that will produce hunger and thirst for prayers in me, in the name of Jesus.

9. Lord God, inject me with spiritual vitamins that will clear my vision and strengthen its clarity, in the name of Jesus.

10. Lord God, inject me with spiritual vitamins that will sustain me in the evil days, in the name of Jesus.

11. Lord God, inject me with divine immunity that will always kill spiritual germs and evil deposits in me, in the name of Jesus.

12. Lord God, inject me with spiritual energy that will make me tireless with You, in the name of Jesus.

13. Lord God, feed me with the food of the champions, in the name of Jesus.

14. Lord God, boost my energy to run the race that is set before me, in the name of Jesus.

15. I receive the comforting anointing and power in the Holy Ghost, in the name of Jesus.

16. I receive the unsearchable wisdom of the Holy Ghost, in the name of Jesus.

17. I take the shield of faith to quench every fiery dart of the enemy, in the name of Jesus.

18. I run into the name of the Lord, which is a strong tower, and I am safe, in the name of Jesus.

19. Father Lord, always make me drink from Your everlasting well of joy, in the name of Jesus.

20. Begin to bless the Lord for all answered prayers.

I AM FOR BLESSING AND NOT FOR CURSES

The world is filled with satanic agents who place curses on people with impunity. Curses are placed upon people from several quarters. At the end of the day, the curses manifest in the lives of many people. However, curses can be turned into blessings through the prayer points in this section. You can deal with generational curses, as well as self-inflicted curses, by making use of the prayer points below.

Additionally, you can use them to command blessings to come upon you. Make use of the prayer points until you completely get rid of curses and your life becomes a symbol of the blessings of God.

Praise Worship

Confessions

Jesus Christ has purchased my freedom from the curse of the law and all its condemnation, by offering Himself as a curse for me. I can no longer labour under the burden of the law for I have become a saint, a lively stone, a built-up spiritual stone and a holy priesthood to offer up spiritual sacrifices acceptable to God by Christ. I am a chosen generation, a royal priesthood, a peculiar person that shows forth the praises of Him, who has called me out of darkness into His marvellous light.

The name of Jesus Christ is given unto me to exercise authority in three different worlds: the earth, seas and beneath the earth. For theBible says, "God has highly exalted Him and has freely bestowed upon him the name that is above every name." So, when I pronounce that name, it becomes a strong tower for me; it makes everything against my prayers in the heavenlies to bow. Also, those in the earth and seas beneath the earth surrender to the authority of that name.

In Jesus' name, I take authority over the heavenlies, the earth, the seas, the earth beneath and the things in them. I destroy, with the sword of the Spirit, every dark person that is poised to stand against my prayer or to reinforce against me.

Jesus Christ is my personal Lord He is my Saviour., my Redeemer and Deliverer. His blood has done so much for me and it is the reason for my living today. The blood saves me from the wrath of God, inspired by the consequences of my sins. Through the blood, I have received forgiveness of my sins; through the blood, God becomes merciful to my unrighteousness and He no longer remember my past. Now, I am justified by the blood of Jesus Christ, for faith in the blood of Jesus delivers me from every accusation that the devil makes against me.

It is written that if Jesus Christ sets me free, I am free indeed. I confess and receive freedom from every ancestral curse of untimely death, ancestral curse of marital destruction or frustration, poverty or financial handicap, infirmities and failure at the edge of breakthroughs.

By the blood of Jesus, there is no condemnation for me. I am in Christ Jesus, for I walk not after the flesh, but after the Spirit and the law of the Spirit of life in Christ Jesus has made me free from the law of sin and death. I confess that every ancestral dedication of children to idols, god's sacred waters and trees in my family lineage is broken in my life. For, I shall not suffer for the sins of my forefathers; everyone shall bear his own iniquity. By the blood of Jesus, every unconscious covenant with familiar spirits in my family shall break and release me.

By the power in the blood of Jesus, I decree that every curse of sexual immorality over my life, as a result of incest, lesbianism, homosexuality, bestiality, fornication, adultery, oral sex, abortion, sexual sins of my father, sexual iniquities of my mother should break now, in the name of Jesus. For Jesus was bruised for my transgressions.

Every curse, affecting my dwelling place, positions, land and properties, as a result of any past ritual or sacrifice performed on them shall break by the power in the blood of Jesus.

It is written that life and death are in the power of the tongue and by the words of our mouth, we shall be condemned or justified. Every curse placed on my life and property through witchcraft, spells, jinx, enchantments and incantations shall break by the blood of Jesus. Every curse that I have personally attracted to my life through my actions, promises, vows, oaths and negative confessions shall break by the blood of Jesus. The Scripture says, "Whatsoever I bind here on earth shall be bound in heaven." I bind the activities of these curses and loose myself from their grip.

The Bible says, "Where I sold myself without money, the Lord will buy me back." Every curse resulting from my consultations with evil spirits, herbalists, oracles, mediums and palmists, I break you with the blood of Jesus and I command you to loose your grip over my life.

Every curse activated through my personal sins, be removed by the blood of Jesus. I confess that I am now in the service of God. My body is the temple of God, as it is written, God will dwell in me and walk in me. He shall be my God and I shall be His. I command all the demons operating these curses to come out of my life and property. Let their activities come to an end and the blessings of God begin to replace their curses.

In the place of the curse that ever affects me, I confess these scriptures: And I have peace through the blood of His cross, by Him to reconcile all things unto Himself. I confess that everything that pertains to me is reconciled to Christ.

The Lord will give me strength. He will bless me and my household with peace. The Lord God will bless me as He promised me, I shall lend unto many nations, I shall not borrow. I shall reign over many nations. The Lord shall open unto me His good treasure. The heaven shall give rain unto my land in its season and bless all the works of my hand. The Lord shall cause my enemies, who rise up against me, to be defeated before my face. They shall come out against me in one way and shall be defeated before me in seven ways. The Lord will establish me a holy person to Himself as He has spoken.

I shall be the head and not tail. Blessed shall be my land, my storehouse, my business place, my dwelling place and the works of my hand. The Lord shall not allow destruction and peril to come upon me all the days of my life. I seal my confession with the precious blood of the Lamb of God.

PRAYERS TO DEAL WITH EVIL SOUL TIES

An evil soul-tie represents a spiritual link with individuals or groups of people. An evil soul-tie can be acquired by association. Friends can be involved in evil soul-ties. Parents and children can be united through soul-ties. It is also possible to experience an evil soul-tie through past involvement with a religious group.

An individual or group of people can have influence over your life to the detriment of your destiny. Ungodly and immoral relationships have also led to evil soul-ties. It is therefore difficult to break a relationship when it is entrenched in an evil soul-tie. If you want to be free from any form of undue influence from anyone, living or dead, you must make use of the following prayer points. You must separate yourself from every evil soul-tie, if you want to experience total freedom.

Confession: Gal. 3:13-14

Praise Worship

1. Praise the Lord for the power in His name at which every knee must bow.

2. Every ancestral covenant, affecting my life, break and loose your hold, in the name of Jesus.

3. Every inherited family covenant, affecting my life, break and loose your hold, in the name of Jesus.

4. Every inherited covenant, affecting my life, break and release me, in the name of Jesus.

5. Any evil covenants, prospering in my family, break by the blood of Jesus.

6. Every soul tie and covenant between me and ancestral spirits, break and release me, in the name of Jesus.

7. Every soul-tie and covenant with any dead relation, break now and release me, in the name of Jesus.

8. Every soul tie and covenant with family gods, shrines and spirits, break now and release me, in the name of Jesus.

9. Every soul tie and covenant between me and my parents, break and release me, in the name of Jesus.

10. Every soul tie between me and my grandparents, break and release me, in the name of Jesus.

11. Every soul tie and covenant between me and my former boyfriends or girlfriends, break and loose your hold, in the name of Jesus.

12. Every soul tie covenant between me and any spirit husband or wife, break and loose your hold, in the name of Jesus.

13. Every soul tie covenant between me and any demonic minister, break and loose your hold, in the name of Jesus.

14. Every soul tie and covenant between me and my former house, office or school, break and loose your hold, in the name of Jesus.

15. Every soul tie and covenant between me and water spirits, break and loose your hold, in the name of Jesus.

16. Every soul tie and covenant between me and serpentine spirits, break and loose your hold, in the name of Jesus.

17. I break any covenant, empowering my household enemy; loose your hold, in the name of Jesus.

18. Every soul tie and covenant between me and any occultic relation, break and loose your hold, in the name of Jesus.

19. Every soul tie covenant between me and any dead relation, break and loose your hold, in the name of Jesus.

20. Any evil covenant, strengthening the foundation of any bondage, break, in the name of Jesus.

21. Every soul tie covenant between me and familiar spirits, break and loose your hold, in the name of Jesus.

22. Every soul tie covenant between me and spiritual night caterers, break and loose your hold, in the name of Jesus.

23. Every soul tie covenant between me and any territorial spirit, break and loose your hold, in the name of Jesus.

24. Every soul tie and covenant between me and any demonic church I have ever attended, break and loose your hold, in the name of Jesus.

25. Every soul tie and covenant between me and any herbalist, break and loose your hold, in the name of Jesus.

26. Every soul tie and covenant between me and marine kingdom, break and loose your hold, in the name of Jesus.

27. Every soul tie and covenant between me and witchcraft spirits, break and loose your hold, in the name of Jesus.

28. Every soul tie and covenant between me and the spirit of barrenness, break and loose your hold, in the name of Jesus.

29. Every soul tie and covenant between me and the spirit of poverty, break and loose your hold, in the name of Jesus.

30. Every soul tie and covenant between me and the spirit of infirmity and sickness, break and loose your hold, in the name of Jesus.

31. Every soul tie and covenant between me and the spirit of insanity, break and loose your hold, in the name of Jesus.

32. Every soul tie and covenant between me and the spirit of backwardness and demotion, break and loose your hold, in the name of Jesus.

33. Every soul-tie and covenant between me and the spirit of failure, break and loose your hold, in the name of Jesus.

DESTROYING THE DESTROYER

The best strategy for any battle is the offensive rather than the defensive.

Offensive warfare enables you to determine the result of a battle. Most people in life are at the receiving end of spiritual attacks, but effective students in the school of spiritual warfare have learnt to attack the attacker and destroy the destroyer. You should not wait for the enemy to attack you.

Rather, you should confront satanic agents and destroy their weapons of war before they raise a finger against you. Don't wait for agents of destruction to convert your life to an experimental guinea pig. Rise up, take up your weapons of war and destroy the destroyer before he charges at you.

The prayer points below are God's weapons for killing the destroyers assigned against your destiny. Remember, don't spare the destroyer. Let the power of the destroyer be consumed by fire!

Confessions: Luke 10:19; Matt.18:18-19; 1 John 3:8; James 4:7; Ps. 27:2; Job 8:22; Jer. 30:23; Isa. 54:17; Matt. 15:13; 3:1; 2 Cor. 10:1-5.

Praise Worship

Praise the Lord for the power in His name at which every knee must bow.

1. In this prayer session, Lord, empower me to prevail, in Jesus' name.
2. I anoint every prayer point I shall pray with the fire of God, in the name of Jesus.
3. I receive divine power to destroy every destroying power in my life, in the name of Jesus.
4. Every instrument of destruction, fashioned against me from birth, roast by fire, in the name of Jesus.
5. Every agent of the destroyer, assigned against my life to specifically destroy me, fall down and die, in the name of Jesus.
6. O Lord, let the stronghold of the destroyer be destroyed by the thunder of God, in the name of Jesus.
7. Every demonic wall, constructed around me by the destroyer, receive the thunderbolt of God and be destroyed, in Jesus' name.
8. Every route and channel of the destroyer in my life, become dark and slippery, in the name of Jesus.

9. Every property of the destroyer, deposited into my life, roast by fire, in the name of Jesus.

10. Every activity of the destroyer, manifesting in the form of frustration in my life, be destroyed, in the name of Jesus.

11. Every spirit of frustration, assigned against my life by the destroyer, fall down and die, in the name of Jesus.

12. I refuse to be frustrated out of the programme of God for my life, in the name of Jesus.

13. Every source of frustration, made available for me, receive the fire of God and dry up, in the name of Jesus.

14. I recover, every good miracle and testimony snatched out of my hand by the spirit of frustration, in the name of Jesus.

15. Every activity of the destroyer, manifesting in the form of discouragement in my life, be paralysed, in the name of Jesus.

16. Every good blessing, opportunity and chance that I have ever missed as a result of discouragement, I recover you, in the name of Jesus.

17. Every activity of the destroyer, manifesting in the form of time- wasting, be paralysed, in the name of Jesus.

18. Every demon of time-wasting in my life, loose your hold, fall down and die, in the name of Jesus.

19. Every evil power, fashioned to waste my divine chances and opportunities, loose your hold, fall down and die, in Jesus' name.

20. Any agent of the destroyer, assigned to waste my goods, loose your hold, fall down and die.

21. Any agent of the destroyer, assigned to waste my life, loose your hold, fall down and die, in the name of Jesus.

22. I recover, all my wasted years, in the name of Jesus.

23. I recover, all my wasted chances and opportunities, in the name of Jesus.

24. I recover, all my wasted goods, in the name of Jesus.

25. Any power of the destroyer, destroying good things in my life at the edge of manifestation, fall down and die, in the name of Jesus.

26. Any power of the destroyer, cutting off good visions and dreams at the edge of manifestation, fall down and die, in Jesus' name.

27. Any power, assigned by the destroyer to be killing good things at birth in my household, fall down and die, in the name of Jesus.

28. Any power, assigned by the destroyer to be cutting short my joy, loose your hold, fall down and die, in Jesus' name.

29. Every good thing, that has been amputated in my life, receive new life and begin to germinate and prosper, in the name of Jesus.

30. Any power of the destroyer, assigned to be swallowing my goodness like the grave, roast by fire, in Jesus' name.

31. Any spirit of death, harbouring my blessings and potentials, receive the fire of God and vomit them unto me now, in the name of Jesus.

32. Any power of the grave, that had swallowed my blessings and potentials, receive the fire of God and vomit them unto me now, in the name of Jesus.

33. Any power in any water that has ever swallowed my blessings, receive the fire of God and vomit them unto me now.

34. Any spiritual animal, that has ever swallowed my blessings, melt by fire.

35. Any satanic strongman, keeping my blessings as his goods, fall down and die; I recover my goods now.

36. Any evil swallower, assigned by the destroyer against my life, vomit my blessings, fall down and die.

37. Any power of the destroyer, assigned to destroy my body organs, fall down and die.

38. Any power of the destroyer, drinking my blood and eating my flesh, fall down and die.

39. Any power of the destroyer, assigned to pollute my body, fall down and die.

40. You strongman of body destruction, loose your hold over my body, fall down and die.

41. I wash every polluted organ in my body with the blood of Jesus.

42. Any organ of my body, that has been eaten up spiritually, receive the blood of Jesus and be made whole.

43. Any power of the destroyer, specifically assigned to destroy my relationship with my God, fall down and die.

44. Any power of the destroyer, attacking my spiritual life, fall down and die.

45. Any power of the destroyer, fighting against my spiritual well being, fall down and die.

46. Any damage, done so far to my spiritual relationship with God, be repaired.

47. All spiritual gifts, blessings, virtues and benefits that have been paralysed, damaged or amputated, I recover them now, in the name of Jesus.

48. Begin to thank God for the victory.

DEFEATING DEFEAT

Confession: Psalm 142:7

Praise Worship

1. Praise the Lord for the power in His name at which every knee must bow.

2. I issue a divine curse on every satanic agent and satanic instrument set against my life, in the name of Jesus.

3. Terror of the living God, scatter every evil altar constructed against me, in the name of Jesus.

4. Every power, trying to bury me alive, fall down and die, in Jesus' name.

5. Every programme after my life, by household wickedness, fall down and die, in Jesus' name.

6. Every power, circulating my name for evil, fall down and die, in the name of Jesus.

7. Every decision, taken against my life by witchcraft spirits, fall down and die, in the name of Jesus.

8. Every internal coffin, roast by fire, in Jesus' name.

9. Every satanic animal in my dream, fall down and die, in Jesus' name.

10. You owners of the load of sickness, carry your load now, in Jesus' name.

11. I refuse satanic substitution for my life, in the name of Jesus.

MOVE ME FORWARD BY FIRE

This prayer programme is specially designed for those who want to experience spiritual progress in every department of their lives. There are times progress seems impossible, as the enemy must have drawn a line saying, you will not exceed this point. At such times, you need a prayer programme that will enable you move forward by fire. You must cry unto God and ask Him to move you forward through the instrumentality of the fire of the Holy Ghost

Since nothing can hinder fire, the fire of God will enable you to move beyond every barrier, jump over every hurdle and exceed every demonic limit. You must command the stumbling blocks of darkness to be dismantled. These prayer points will enable you to move forward, even when all odds are against your making progress in life.

Confession: Eph. 4:8-10

Praise Worship

1. All my blessings imprisoned by the grave, come forth, in the name of Jesus.

2. I release my blessings from the hands of my dead relatives, in the name of Jesus.

3. I withdraw my blessings from the hands of all dead enemies, in the name of Jesus.

4. I disgrace every witchcraft burial, in the name of Jesus.

5. Just as the grave could not detain Jesus, no power will detain my miracles, in the name of Jesus.

6. That which hinders me from greatness, give way now, in Jesus' name.

7. Whatsoever has been done against me, using the ground, be neutralized, in the name of Jesus.

8. Every unfriendly friend, be exposed, in the name of Jesus.

9. Anything representing my image in the spirit world, I withdraw you, in the name of Jesus.

10. All the camps of my enemies, receive confusion, in the name of Jesus.

11. O Lord, empower my life with Your authority over every demonic force, in Jesus' name.

12. O Lord, let all the impossible begin to become possible for me in every department of my life, in Jesus' name.

13. O Lord, take me from where I am to where You want me to be.

14. O Lord, make a way for me where there is no way.

15. O Lord, grant me the power to be fulfilled, successful and prosperous in life, in the name of Jesus.

16. O Lord, break me in every department of my life, in the name of Jesus.

17. O Lord, make me to break through into dumbfounding miracles in all areas of my life, in the name of Jesus.

18. O Lord, make me to break loose from every obstacle on my way to progress in life, in the name of Jesus.

19. O Lord, establish me in the truth, godliness and faithfulness.

20. O Lord, add flavour to my work, in the name of Jesus.

21. O Lord, add increase to my work, in the name of Jesus.

22. O Lord, add profitability to my work, in the name of Jesus.

23. O Lord, promote and preserve my life, in the name of Jesus.

24. I reject the plans and agenda of the enemies for my life, in the name of Jesus.

25. I reject the assignments and weapons of the enemy against my life, in the name of Jesus.

26. Every weapon and evil designs against me, fail totally, in Jesus' name

27. I reject premature death, in the name of Jesus.

28. I reject nightmares and sudden destruction, in the name of Jesus.

29. I reject dryness in my walk with God, in the name of Jesus.

30. I reject financial debt,

in the name of Jesus.

31. I reject lack and famine in my life, in Jesus' name.

32. I reject physical and spiritual accidents in my going in and coming out, in Jesus' name..

33. I reject sickness in my spirit, soul and body, in the name of Jesus.

34. I stand against every work of evil in my life, in the name of Jesus.

35. I overcome powerlessness, confusion and every attack of the enemy, in the name of Jesus.

36. I command spiritual divorce between me and every power of darkness, in Jesus' name.

37. Every poison and arrow of the enemy, be neutralized, in Jesus' name.

38. I break every yoke of unfruitfulness in my life, in the name of Jesus.

39. I cancel the plans and the mark of the enemy upon my life, in the name of Jesus.

40. Lord Jesus, break all harmful genetic ties in my life, in Jesus' name.

41. Begin to thank God for answered prayers.

POWER AGAINST MISCARRIAGE 1

This prayer programme is specially designed by the Holy Ghost for those who are looking up to God for the fruit of the womb. It is also meant specially for those who are pregnant and want to cancel evil threats of miscarriage.

Those who have had repeated miscarriages and are struggling with threatening abortion can destroy the enemy's plan through these powerful prayer points. Whether the reasons behind the miscarriage are physical or spiritual, you can issue a divine decree saying; "It shall not come to pass." You can carry your pregnancy full time and experience safe delivery. These prayer points have been used by God to make many people joyful mothers. Your case shall not be an exception, in the mighty name of Jesus.

Confession: Exodus 23:26; Eccl. 3:14

Praise Worship

1. O Lord, make way for me where there is no way, in Jesus' name.

2. Any of my clothes that the enemy has set aside to afflict my conception, roast, in Jesus' name.

3. Any decoration in my apartment that is bewitched, O Lord, reveal it to me.

4. Any garment that the enemy is using to destroy my pregnancy, roast.

5. Every demonic instrument of operation set aside to abort my pregnancy, break into pieces, in the name of Jesus.

6. Every demonic doctor /nurse delegated by satan to destroy my pregnancy, inject yourself to death, in the name of Jesus.

7. Every evil remote controlled gadget being used to manipulate my pregnancy, roast by fire, in the name of Jesus.

8. I render every weapon fashioned against my pregnancy impotent, in the name of Jesus.

9. I close down every satanic broadcasting station fashioned against my pregnancy, in the name of Jesus.

10. I refuse to harbour any pregnancy killer, in any department of my life, in the name of Jesus.

11. I bind every spirit of error assigned against my pregnancy, in the name of Jesus.

12. I bind the spirit of almost there. You will not operate in my life, in the name of Jesus.

13. I break every grip and hold of witchcraft over my pregnancy, in the name of Jesus.

14. I paralyse every opposition to my pregnancy, in the name of Jesus.

15. Any member of my family reporting my pregnancy to the evil ones, receive the slap of the angel of God, in the name of Jesus.

16. Every territorial demon working against my marriage, receive the thunder fire of God, in the name of Jesus.

17. I nullify every satanic threat against my pregnancy, in Jesus' name.

18. Every power/spirit visiting me at night or in the dream in order to terminate my pregnancy, fall down and die, in the name of Jesus.

19. I nullify every evil influence of satanic visitation upon my pregnancy, in the name of Jesus.

20. O Lord, let the plug of my womb receive the power of the Holy Spirit to carry my pregnancy to the point of delivery, in the name of Jesus.

21. I reject every manifestation of fever during my pregnancy, in the name of Jesus.

22. I reject every satanic stress during my pregnancy, in the name of Jesus.

23. Thank God for answers to your prayers.

POWER AGAINST MISCARRIAGE 2

MEDITATION POINTS

☞ Marriage to unseen spouse.

☞ Seeing yourself carrying children or someone collected your child in the dream.

☞ Abortion in time past.

☞ Appearances of evil objects, e.g., palm oil, red pepper, goat, dog, cow, etc. This speaks of evil dedication in time past. It can hinder your ability to conceive and deliver safely.

☞ The spirit of error or mistake.

☞ Mismanagement of the pregnancy by quack doctors.

☞ Medical pollution; deliverance must be sought.

CONFESSIONS: Genesis 1:28: And God blessed them, and God said unto them, Be fruitful, and multiply, and replenish the earth, and subdue it: and have dominion over the fish of the sea, and over the fowl of the air, and over every living thing that moveth upon the earth.

Exodus 23:26: There shall nothing cast their young, nor be barren, in thy land: the number of thy days I will fulfil.

1 Samuel 2:4-6: The bows of the mighty men are broken, and they that stumbled are girded with strength. They that were full have hired out themselves for bread; and they that were hungry ceased: so that the barren hath born seven; and she that hath many children is waxed feeble. The Lord killeth, and maketh alive: he bringeth down to the grave, and bringeth up.

Psalm 119:89: For ever, O Lord, thy word is settled in heaven.

Eccles. 3:1: To every thing there is a season, and a time to every purpose under the heaven:

Eccles. 3:14: I know that, whatsoever God doeth, it shall be for ever: nothing can be put to it, nor any thing taken from it: and God doeth it, that men should fear before him.

Hosea 9:13-14: Ephraim, as I saw Tyrus, is planted in a pleasant place: but Ephraim shall bring forth his children to the murderer. Give them, O Lord: what wilt thou give? give them a miscarrying womb and dry breasts.

Rev. 12:14-16: And to the woman were given two wings of a great eagle, that she might fly into the wilderness, into her

place, where she is nourished away of the flood. And the
for a time, and times, and half earth helped the woman, and the
a time, from the face of the earth opened her mouth, and
serpent. And the serpent cast swallowed up the flood which the
out of his mouth water as a dragon cast out of his mouth.
flood after the woman, that he
might cause her to be carried

Aggressive Praise Worship

1. I confess and repent of the sin of bloodshed, committed in my days of ignorance, in the name of Jesus.

2. Lord Jesus, wash away the sins and consequences of my past.

3. Lord Jesus, let the sword depart from my marriage, in Jesus' name.

4. O Lord, make ways for me where there is no way, in Jesus' name.

5. I break any covenant between me and any evil husband or wife, in the name of Jesus.

6. Any of my clothes, that the enemy has set aside to afflict my conception, roast, in Jesus' name.

7. Every bow of the mighty, contending with my fruitfulness, break, break, break, in the name of Jesus.

8. Any decoration in my apartment that is bewitched, O Lord, reveal it to me.

9. I destroy every evil stone or goat, destroying my children in pregnancy, in the name of Jesus.

10. Any garment, that the enemy is using to destroy my pregnancy, roast.

11. You the strong east wind of the Lord, blow against the Red Sea in my womb now, in the name of Jesus.

12. Every demonic instrument of operation, set aside to abort my pregnancy, break to pieces, in the name of Jesus.

13. O Lord, fight against the destroyer, working against my increase and fruitfulness, in the name of Jesus.

14. Every demonic doctor /nurse, delegated by satan to destroy my pregnancy, inject yourself to death, in Jesus' name.

15. Blood of Jesus, wash me and show me mercy, in the name of Jesus.

16. Every evil remote control gadget being used to manipulate my pregnancy, roast by fire, in Jesus' name.

17. Thou Man of war, save me out of the hand of wicked midwives, in the name of Jesus.

18. I render every weapon fashioned against my pregnancy impotent, in the name of Jesus.

19. Oh Lord, overthrow every Egyptian, working against me in the midst of the sea, in the name of Jesus.

20. I close down every satanic broadcasting station, fashioned against my pregnancy, in the name of Jesus.

21. I prophesy that I will see the great work of the Lord, as I deliver my children safely, in the name of Jesus.

22. I refuse to harbour any pregnancy-killer in any department of my life, in the name of Jesus.

23. Every horse and its rider in my womb, family or office, be thrown into the sea of forgetfulness, in the name of Jesus.

24. I bind every spirit of error, assigned to my pregnancy, in Jesus' name.

25. O Lord, send Your light before me to drive miscarriages away from my womb and life, in the name of Jesus.

26. I bind the spirit of almost there; You will not operate in my life, in the name of Jesus.

27. I cast out every power casting out my children, in Jesus' name

28. I break every grip and hold of witchcraft over my pregnancy, in the name of Jesus.

29. From today, I shall not cast away my young, in the name of Jesus.

30. I paralyse every opposition to my pregnancy, in Jesus' name.

31. I will fulfil the numbers of the days of this pregnancy, in Jesus' name.

32. Any member of my family, reporting my pregnancy to the evil ones, receive the slap of the angels of God, in Jesus' name.

33. I shall not cast out my pregnancy before delivery, in Jesus' name.

34. Every territorial demon, working against my marriage, receive the thunder fire of God, in the name of Jesus.

35. Every spirit of stillbirth and threatened abortion, be consumed by fire, in the name of Jesus.

36. I nullify every satanic threat against my pregnancy, in Jesus' name.

37. I shall not bring forth to murderers, in the name of Jesus.

38. Every power/spirit, visiting me at night or in the dream in order to terminate my pregnancy, fall down and die, in Jesus' name.

39. Every power of murderers, shatter, in the name of Jesus.

40. I nullify every evil influence of satanic visitation upon my pregnancy, in Jesus' name.

41. O Lord, deliver me from the womb that miscarries, in the name of Jesus.

42. O Lord, let the plug of my womb receive the power of the Holy Spirit to carry my pregnancy to the point of delivery, in Jesus' name.

43. O Lord, let every violence of miscarriages stop permanently, in Jesus' name.

44. I reject every manifestation of fever during my pregnancy, in Jesus' name.

45. Every evil power, appearing through a dog, a man or a woman, be destroyed by fire, in the name of Jesus.

46. I reject every satanic stress during my pregnancy, in the name of Jesus.

47. You evil children, causing abortion, die, in the name of Jesus. I am loosed from your oppression, in Jesus' name.

48. I decree death to spirit husband or spirit wife, killing my children, in Jesus' name.

49. O earth, help me to conquer the power of miscarriages, in the name of Jesus.

50. O Lord, give me wings of a great eagle to escape from miscarriages, in Jesu' name.

51. O Lord, give me a man-child, in the name of Jesus.

52. I declare that I am fruitful and I will bring forth in peace, in the name of Jesus.

53. I overcome miscarriages by the power of the Lord, in Jesus' name.

54. My Father, cover me with Your shield and put me under Your banner, in the name of Jesus.

55. Every power, that has swallowed my children, vomit them now, in Jesus' name.

56. Every foundation of miscarriages, receive the judgment of God, in the name of Jesus.

57. You fibroid, drop off my womb, in the name of Jesus.

58. Every low sperm count, be converted to full sperm count, in the name of Jesus.

59. I decree that throughout the period of my pregnancy, I shall not be stressed. I receive angelic ministration, in the name of Jesus.

60. You my body, become strong to labour, in Jesus' name.

61. O Lord, send Your heavenly nurse to minister to me throughout the period of this pregnancy, in Jesus' name.

62. I prophesy that I shall bring forth a normal child to the glory of God, in Jesus' names.

63. O Lord, deliver me from the spirit of error, in Jesus' name.

64. I judge the hold of mismanagement through wrong medical advice or wrong medication, in Jesus' name.

65. My cervix, close up, let there be no contraction or dilation before the nine months period, in the name of Jesus.

66. I receive power from above to bring forth, in Jesus' name.

67. I break the horn of the wicked, exercising evil against me, in the name of Jesus.

68. Holy Spirit, envelope and overshadow me throughout the period of this pregnancy, in the name of Jesus.

69. I will neither labour in vain nor bring forth for trouble, in the name of Jesus.

70. As I build, I will inhabit; and as I plant, I shall eat, in the name of Jesus.

71. I and the children that God has given me are for signs and wonders, in the name of Jesus.

72. Thank God for answers to your prayers.

POWER AGAINST MISCARRIAGE
3

Marital Jericho stands for every shade of demonic hindrance to marital fulfilment. This is the prayer to pray when the enemy has set up a strong wall between your dreams of marital bliss and its fulfilment.

However, the prayer is intercessory in nature. It is best undertaken by those concerned about marital problems in the lives of their family members, neighbours or acquaintances. Even if victims of marital Jericho are thousands of miles away, this prayer programme will pull down the evil walls and there will be restoration, harmony and peace. You can use the prayer points when you come across hopeless situations in the marriage or the homes of your beloved ones.

MEDITATION POINTS

☞ Marriage to unseen spouse.

☞ Seeing yourself carrying children or someone collected your child in the dream.

☞ Abortion in time past.

☞ Appearances of evil objects, e.g., palm oil, red pepper, a goat, a dog, a cow, etc. These speak of evil dedication in time past and can hinder your ability to conceive and deliver safely.

☞ The spirit of error or mistake.

☞ Mismanagement of the pregnancy by quack doctors.

☞ Medical pollution; deliverance must be sought.

CONFESSIONS: *Genesis 1:28: And God blessed them, and God said unto them, Be fruitful, and multiply, and replenish the earth, and subdue it: and have dominion over the fish of the sea, and over the fowl of the air, and over every living thing that moveth upon the earth.*

Exodus 23:26: There shall nothing cast their young, nor be barren, in thy land: the number of thy days I will fulfil.

1 Samuel 2:4-6: The bows of the mighty men are

broken, and they that stumbled are girded with strength. They that were full have hired out themselves for bread; and they that were hungry ceased: so that the barren hath born seven; and she that hath many children is waxed feeble. The Lord killeth, and maketh alive: he bringeth down to the grave, and bringeth up.

Psalm 119:89: For ever, O Lord, thy word is settled in heaven.

Eccles. 3:1: To every thing there is a season, and a time to every purpose under the heaven:

Eccles. 3:14: I know that, whatsoever God doeth, it shall be for ever: nothing can be put to it, nor any thing taken from it: and God doeth it, that men should fear before him.

Hosea 9:13-14: Ephraim, as I saw Tyrus, is planted in a pleasant place: but Ephraim shall bring forth his children to the murderer. Give them, O Lord: what wilt thou give? give them a miscarrying womb and dry breasts.

Rev. 12:14-16: And to the woman were given two wings of a great eagle, that she might fly into the wilderness, into her place, where she is nourished for a time, and times, and half a time, from the face of the serpent. And the serpent cast out of his mouth water as a flood after *the woman, that he might cause her to be carried away of the flood. And the earth helped the woman, and the earth opened her mouth, and swallowed up the flood which the dragon cast out of his mouth.*

Aggressive Praise Worship

1. I confess and repent of the sin of bloodshed, committed in my days of ignorance, in the name of Jesus.

2. O Lord, make way for me where there is no way, in Jesus' name.

3. Lord Jesus, wash away my sins and their consequences.

4. I break any covenant between me and any evil husband or wife, in the name of Jesus.

5. Lord Jesus, let the sword depart from my marriage, in the name of Jesus.

6. Any of my clothes that the enemy has set aside to afflict my conception, roast, in Jesus' name.

7. Every bow of the mighty, contending with my fruitfulness, break, break, break, in the name of Jesus.

8. Any garment that the enemy is using to destroy my pregnancy, roast.

9. Any decoration in my apartment that is bewitched, O Lord, reveal it to me.

10. You the strong east wind of the Lord, blow against the Red Sea in my womb now, in Jesus' name.

11. I destroy every evil stone or goat destroying my children in pregnancy, in Jesus' name.

12. Every demonic instrument of operation, set aside to abort my pregnancy, break to pieces, in the name of Jesus.

13. O Lord, fight against the destroyer, working against my increase and fruitfulness, in the name of Jesus.

14. Every demonic doctor/nurse, delegated by satan to destroy my pregnancy, inject yourself to death, in Jesus' name.

15. Blood of Jesus, wash me and show me mercy, in the name of Jesus.

16. Every evil remote control gadget being used to manipulate my pregnancy, roast by fire, in Jesus' name.

17. Thou Man of war, save me from the hands of wicked midwives, in the name of Jesus.

18. I render every weapon fashioned against my pregnancy impotent, in the name of Jesus.

19. O Lord, overthrow every Egyptian, working against me in the midst of the sea, in the name of Jesus.

20. I close down every satanic broadcasting station, fashioned against my pregnancy, in the name of Jesus.

21. I decree that I will see the great work of the Lord, as I deliver my children safely, in the name of Jesus.

22. I refuse to harbour any pregnancy killer in any department of my life, in the name of Jesus.

23. Every horse and its rider in my womb, family or office, be thrown into the sea of forgetfulness, in the name of Jesus.

24. I bind every spirit of error, assigned against my pregnancy, in the name of Jesus.

25. O Lord, send Your light before me to drive miscarriage from my womb and life, in the name of Jesus.

26. I bind the spirit of almost there. You will not operate in my life, in the name of Jesus.

27. I cast out every power, casting out my children, in Jesus' name.

28. I break every grip and hold of witchcraft over my pregnancy, in the name of Jesus.

29. From today, I shall not cast away my young, in Jesus' name.

30. I paralyse every opposition to my pregnancy, in Jesus' name.

31. I will fulfil the number of days of this pregnancy, in the name of Jesus.

32. Any member of my family, reporting my pregnancy to the evil ones, receive the angelic slap of angels of God, in Jesus' name.

33. I shall not cast out my pregnancy before delivery, in the name of Jesus.

34. Every territorial demon, working against my marriage, receive the thunder fire of God, in the name of Jesus.

35. Every spirit of stillbirth and threatened abortion, be consumed by fire, in the name of Jesus.

36. I nullify every satanic threat against my pregnancy, in the name of Jesus.

37. I shall not bring forth to murderers, in Jesus' name.

38. Every power/spirit, visiting me at night or in the dream in order to terminate my pregnancy, fall down and die, in the name of Jesus.

39. Every power of murderers, shatter, in the name of Jesus.

40. I nullify every evil influence of satanic visitation upon my pregnancy, in Jesus' name.

41. O Lord, deliver me from the womb that miscarries, in the name of Jesus.

42. O Lord, let the plug of my womb receive the power of the Holy Spirit to carry my pregnancy to the point of delivery, in Jesus' name.

43. Every violence of miscarriage, stop permanently, in the name of Jesus.

44. I reject every manifestation of fever during my pregnancy, in Jesus' name.

45. Every evil power, appearing through a dog, a man or a woman, be destroyed by fire, in the name of Jesus.

46. I reject every satanic stress during my pregnancy, in the name of Jesus.

47. You evil children, causing abortion, die, in the name of Jesus. I am loosed from your oppression, in Jesus' name.

48. I decree death of every spirit husband or spirit wife, killing my children, in Jesus' name.

49. O earth, help me to conquer the power of miscarriages, in the name of Jesus.

50. O Lord, give me wings of a great eagle to escape from miscarriage, in Jesus' name.

51. O Lord, give me a male-child, in the name of Jesus.

52. I declare that I am fruitful and I will bring forth in peace, in the name of Jesus.

53. I overcome miscarriage by the power of the Lord, in the name of Jesus.

54. My Father, cover me with Your shield and put me under Your banner, in Jesus' name.

55. Every power, that has swallowed my children, vomit them now, in Jesus' name.

56. Every foundation of miscarriage, receive the judgment of God, in Jesus' name

57. I command fibroid, drop off my womb, in Jesus' name.

58. Every low sperm count, be converted to full sperm count, in the name of Jesus.

59. I decree that throughout the period of the pregnancy, I shall not be stressed. I

receive angelic ministration, in the name of Jesus.

60. My body, become strong to labour, in the name of Jesus.

61. O Lord, send Your heavenly nurse to minister to me throughout the period of this pregnancy, in Jesus' name.

62. I shall bring forth a normal child to the glory of God, in the name of Jesus.

63. O Lord, deliver me from the spirit of error, in Jesus' name.

64. I judge the hold of mismanagement through wrong medical advice or wrong medication, in Jesus' name.

65. My Cervix, be closed up, let there be no contraction or dilation before the nine months period, in the name of Jesus.

66. I receive power from on high to bring forth, in Jesus' name.

67. I break the horn of the wicked exercising evil against me, in the name of Jesus.

68. Holy Spirit, envelop me and overshadow me throughout the period of this pregnancy, in the name of Jesus.

69. I will neither labour in vain nor bring forth for trouble, in the name of Jesus.

70. As I build, I will inhabit and as I plant, I shall eat, in the name of Jesus.

71. I and the children that God has given me are for signs and wonders, in the name of Jesus.

72. Thank God, for the answers to your prayers.

POWER AGAINST SPIRITUAL BURIAL

Living on earth as if one is dead is a terrible thing to experience. There are multitudes that, though alive, but are living as if they are dead. The powers of darkness muster every effort to subject people to ugly spiritual burial through some form of deadly spiritual operations, powers of darkness bury people's destinies and virtues. Immediately the burial is concluded, a victim loses every virtue.

Those who are subjected to spiritual burial live frustrated lives. They go through life aimlessly and achieve nothing at the end of the day. To be buried spiritually is to be robbed of your potentials. Those who are buried generally have an evil aura around them. Such people need to go through deliverance.

You need the prayer points below to experience the resurrection power of our Lord Jesus Christ. You will use them as weapons for exhuming your buried virtues.

Confession: Rev. 12:11

Praise Worship

1. O Lord, I reject every financial burial, in Jesus' name.

2. Every spiritual anchor of financial failure attached to my life, receive the axe of fire, in the name of Jesus.

3. Every strange money in my possession, be flushed out by the blood of Jesus.

4. O Lord, cleanse my hands from every sort of failure and financial collapse, in Jesus' name.

5. My name, business and handiwork will not record anything for the spirit of financial collapse, in Jesus' name.

6. O Lord, rescue my finances from every satanic well, in Jesus' name.

7. O Lord, let all the powers oppressing my finances sit on the seat they constructed for me, in the name of Jesus.

8. Every tree of heaviness, procrastination and discouragement, operating in any area of my life, be cut down by the axe of fire, in Jesus' name.

9. O Lord, give me the key to any goodness you have kept in Your bank for me, in the name of Jesus.

10. Every stronghold of loss, be dashed to pieces, in the name of Jesus.

11. Every stronghold of debt, fashioned against my finances, be dashed to pieces, in the name of Jesus.

12. Every satanic traffic warden, directing profit away from my career, business and handiwork, receive the hailstones of fire, in Jesus' name.

13. Whatever the enemies say would be impossible with my hands, you hands, hear the word of the Lord, begin to perform the impossible, in the name of Jesus.

14. Anointing to prosper, fall upon my hands, in the name of Jesus.

15. I release my hands from every satanic bondage affecting my finances, in the name of Jesus.

16. You spirit of confusion and satanic inspiration of overdraft, loose your hold upon my life and business, in the name of Jesus.

17. Every anchor of financial collapse affecting my finances, be uprooted by the axe of fire, in the name of Jesus.

18. By the arrows of fire, I challenge all the agencies of financial collapse, fashioned against my finances, in the name of Jesus.

19. Every demon, strongman and associated spirit of financial collapse, receive the hailstones of fire, and be roasted beyond remedy, in Jesus' name.

20. O Lord, prosper me beyond my wildest imaginations, in Jesus' name.

21. O Lord, I reject every leaking hole in the pocket of my life, in the name of Jesus.

22. O Lord. I shall not labour in vain or bring forth trouble, in Jesus' name.

23. O Lord, I decree a hedge of fire around my finances, in Jesus' name.

DEMOTION MUST DIE

It is God's plan that His children should be above only. Therefore, whatever looks like a valley experience is contrary to His plan for His beloved children.

However, there are powers whose major pre-occupation is to programme demotion into the lives of people. They are the reason people fall from grace to grass. Such people are victims of the spirit of demotion. The spirit of demotion will make a man to fall from great heights and remain in the lowest dungeon.

There are people who were once princes, riding on horses but later they began to trek. This prayer programme can make those who are victims of satanic demotion to rise again and become prominent men and women. They will prevent you from being demoted in any area of your life. The God that answereth by fire will relocate you. You will mount up with wings and get to the top once again.

Give this prayer programme all the seriousness it deserves.

Confession: Nahum 1:7

Praise Worship

1. Let the serpent of impossibility be dissolved by the fire of the God of Elijah, in the name of Jesus.

2. Every magic mirror, conjuring my face, break, in the name of Jesus.

3. Dream animals, release my destiny, in the name of Jesus.

4. I bury every hunter of my star today, in the name of Jesus.

5. Every Goliath of poverty, die, in the name of Jesus.

6. O God, arise and throw stones at the head of my enemies, in the name of Jesus.

7. Every river of trouble, flowing in my family, dry up, in the name of Jesus.

8. Every organised enemy, be disorganised, in the name of Jesus.

9. O God of signs and wonders, manifest Your power, in the name of Jesus.

10. The Pharaoh of my destiny, die, in the name of Jesus.

11. Any bewitched organ in my body, receive deliverance, in the name of Jesus.

12. Fire of God, shatter blindness and darkness in my life, in the name of Jesus.

13. My body, refuse to co-operate with any arrow of darkness, in the name of Jesus.

14. Every witchcraft broom, sweeping away my blessings, die, in the name of Jesus.

15. Every yoke manufacturer, die with your yoke, in the name of Jesus.

16. Every satanic investment in my life, be wasted, in the name of Jesus.

17. O Lord, let my life experience divine acceleration, in the name of Jesus.

18. Satanic agenda for my life, vanish, in the name of Jesus.

19. Every satanic pregnancy in my life, die, in the name of Jesus.

20. Thou swallower of my breakthroughs, die, in the name of Jesus.

21. Every unconscious evil association, release me and scatter, in the name of Jesus.

22. Every arrow of oppression, fly away, in the name of Jesus.

23. I call forth my Lazarus from the grave of witchcraft, in the name of Jesus.

24. Every power that swallows divine opportunities, die, in the name of Jesus.

25. Every enemy, that has refused to let me go, receive double destruction, in the name of Jesus.

26. Every evil candle and incense, working against me, backfire, in the name of Jesus.

27. Every arrow of rituals and sacrifices, backfire, in the name of Jesus.

28. If my enemy is saying that I can only prosper over his dead body, so be it, because it is now time for me to prosper.

29. I enter into my prophetic destiny, in the name of Jesus.

30. I speak to the belly of the waters, release my breakthroughs, in the name of Jesus.

31. You Pharaoh in my home town, I bury you in the Red Sea, in the name of Jesus.

32. I take the wheels off the chariot of my enemies, in the name of Jesus.

33. I cut off the ministry of Judas Iscariot from my finances, in the name of Jesus.

34. O Lord, breathe Your glory upon me.

35. O God, arise and abort the pregnancy of the devil that is against my life, in the name of Jesus.

36. O Lord, let every resurrection of affliction die, in the name of Jesus.

37. Every power, sponsoring repeated problems, die, in the name of Jesus.

I CLAIM DIVINE FAVOUR

It is God's desire to favour His children. When divine favour is unleashed by God upon your life, He will bless you beyond your wildest dreams and people will stumble upon themselves to bestow favour upon you, simply because you have found favour with God.

Much as divine favour has been provided, you need to pray fervently in order to experience it.

God has given lots of promises to His children in the area of divine favour. These promises must be claimed through prayer. You need to set time apart for the prayer points in this section and you must continue praying them vigorously until favour begins to locate you from the North, South, East and West. Don't live a life that is characterized by lack of favour. Claim divine favour today and your story will change. Doors that were closed will be thrown wide open.

Confession: Matthew 7:1-10

Praise Worship

1. I receive the goodness of the Lord, in the land of the living, in the name of Jesus.

2. Everything done against me to spoil my joy this year, be destroyed, in the name of Jesus.

3. O Lord, as Abraham received favour from you, let me also receive Your favour so that I can excel, in the name of Jesus.

4. Lord Jesus, deal bountifully with me this year, in the name of Jesus.

5. It does not matter, whether I deserve it or not, I receive unquantifiable favour from the Lord, in the name of Jesus.

6. Every blessing God has earmarked for me this year will not pass me by, in the name of Jesus.

7. My blessing will not be transferred to my neighbour, in the name of Jesus.

8. Father Lord, disgrace every power, that is out to steal Your programme for my life, in the name of Jesus.

9. Every step I take this year shall lead to outstanding success, in the name of Jesus.

10. I shall prevail with man and with God, in the name of Jesus.

11. Spend quality time to bless the name of the Lord.

I SHALL NOT BACKSLIDE

The devil may not prevent a man from giving his life to Christ but he will put up a wicked plan towards making him to backslide. Backsliding is not just a physical problem, it is a spiritual one. When people backslide, it is often programmed from the kingdom of darkness. Once the powers of darkness have concluded their evil plans, those who are on the pilgrimage to heaven will mysteriously become flabby, grow lukewarm and become cold. To continue to live the christian life and remain on fire for the Lord, you need a good knowledge of spiritual warfare.

To escape the snare of backsliding, you need to fight spiritually. This prayer programme will prove invaluable when you begin to notice traces of lukewarmness or marks of backsliding.

These aggressive prayer points are antidotes to backsliding. They will help	quicken the restoration of backsliders and enhance the stability of the fervent.

Confession: Col. 1:20-21

Praise Worship

1. I refuse to give the accuser of the brethren any legal ground in my life.
2. Holy Spirit, help me not to depart from the faith.
3. Holy Spirit, help me not to give heed to seducing spirits.
4. Holy Spirit, let no work of darkness thrive in my life.
5. Every power, assigned by the host of darkness to draw me away from eternal life will not prosper in my life, in Jesus' name.
6. By the power of God, no lying spirit will have his way in my life, in Jesus' name.
7. I reject the activities of the spirit of hypocrisy, in Jesus' name.
8. Every power, specifically assigned to distract me, be bound, in Jesus' name.
9. Any spirit of the world, beckoning to me, be bound, in Jesus' name.
10. Any part of me, thirsting for friendship with the world, receive divine deliverance, in Jesus' name.
11. Every spirit, polluting the gifts of God in my life, be bound, in Jesus' name.
12. Any power, manipulating my decision-making, be bound in Jesus' name.
13. Every invitation to rebellion, roast, in Jesus' name.

14. Holy Spirit, hold back my steps from falling, in Jesus' name.

15. Holy Spirit, renew a steadfast spirit within me, in Jesus' name.

16. Deliver me, O Lord, from the grip of spiritual weakness and negligence, in Jesus' name.

17. Father Lord, do not allow me to run away from Your presence, in Jesus' name.

18. O God, create in me a clean and pure heart, in the mighty name of Jesus.

19. O God, plant and establish my feet upon the Rock of Ages, in the name of Jesus.

20. O God, strengthen me where I am weak, in the name of Jesus.

21. O God, open my ears to the instructions and warnings of the Holy Ghost, in the name of Jesus.

22. O Lord, do not allow my heart to be seared with a hot iron, in Jesus' name.

23. O Lord, wash my conscience, with the cleansing power of Your word.

24. O Lord, remove completely from me, every lust drawing me away from You, in the name of Jesus.

25. Father Lord, uphold me with Your right hand of righteousness, in Jesus' name.

26. Thank God for all answered prayers.

POWER AGAINST THE SPIRIT OF THE SNAIL

The spirit of the snail is one of the most wicked weapons used by the devil. Satan's intention is to make people hoist the flag of their lives at half mast. It is the spirit of slow motion. It makes the victims go back and forth sluggishly, while their counterparts are breaking new grounds and achieving great feats.

The spirit of the snail manifests itself in various ways. Students who are under the attack of this ugly spirit keep writing the same examination without achieving any success.

When victims undertake a journey that should last for two weeks, they spend two years. The spirit of the snail is the spirit of non-achievement. It makes men sluggish in their endeavours. Lots of people become too slow and have no tangible achievement to show for their efforts. They eventually give up in the race of life.

The ultimate aim of the devil is to make the runners

in the race of life trail behind through an embarrassingly slow movement. These prayer points will destroy the manifestations of the spirit of the snail and make you experience accelerated progress.

Confession: Luke 10:19

Praise Worship

1. Every power, prolonging my journey to breakthroughs, fall down and die, in Jesus' name.

2. Every problem, that I brought into my life through my association with the spirit of the snail, die now, in Jesus' name.

3. I cancel the activities and powers of the snail spirit in my life, in the name of Jesus.

4. I break the covenants and curses of the snail spirit over my life, in the name of Jesus.

5. Every effect of the spirit of the snail over my life, be nullified by the blood of Jesus.

6. Every spirit of sluggishness and backwardness in my life, receive the fire of God now and be destroyed, in the name of Jesus.

7. Every spirit, preventing good things in my life, be destroyed, in the name of Jesus.

8. O Lord, I reject left-over blessings.

9. By the grace of God, I will not

feed from waste bins, in the name of Jesus.

10. I refuse to have boneless blessings, in the name of Jesus.

11. Every spirit of irritation in my life, be washed off by the blood of Jesus.

12. I reject the spirit of fear, anxiety and discouragement, in the name of Jesus.

13. Every evil instruction, prophecy or prediction, issued against my life with snail shell, be cancelled by the blood of Jesus.

14. I reject the spirit of the tail; I claim the spirit of the head, in the name of Jesus.

15. I receive angelic transportation to where God wants me to be now, in the name of Jesus.

16. Every evil deposit in my life as a result of eating snail, be washed away by the blood of Jesus.

17. O Lord, catapult me into greatness as You did for Daniel in the land of Babylon.

18. I reject slippery blessings, in the name of Jesus.

19. I reject the spirit of over-sensitivity, in the name of Jesus.

20. Holy Father, let all my enemies and their strongholds be shattered to pieces by the thunder of God, in the name of Jesus.

21. I deliver myself from the grip of my enemies, in the name of Jesus.

DEALING WITH THE SPIRIT OF THE DOG

The spirit of the dog is the spirit of spiritual pollution. The devil will attack the victims in two major ways. The first way is the spirit- husband and spirit- wife. Many people experience dirty or wet dreams and keep seeing a particular spirit- husband or spirit- wife on regular basis.

Another method is through the projection of the spirit of immorality into the lives of unsuspecting victims.

When this spirit has fully injected its poison into the lives of its victims, they will go about manifesting every form of immoral behaviour. Often times the victims are not able to control their· sexual appetite since they have inherited terrible propensity towards licentious lifestyle. Some victims have been initiated into the cult of the dog. They go from one place to another, exhibiting all forms of lewdness.

To experience freedom from the power of the dog, you need to pray against this stubborn spirit. Use these prayer points as your battle weapons against every kingdom of darkness targeted at looting your life and destiny.

Confession: Eph. 4:8-10

Praise Worship

1. I break loose from every spirit of the dog, in the name of Jesus.

2. I release myself from every spirit of pollution, emanating from past sins of fornication and sexual immorality, in Jesus' name

3. I release myself from every ancestral pollution, in Jesus' name.

4. I release myself from every dream pollution, in Jesus' name.

5. I command every plantation of sexual immorality in my life, come out with all your roots, in Jesus' name.

6. Every demon in dog, working against my life, be paralysed and get out of my life, in Jesus' name.

7. Every demon in dog assigned to my life, be bound, in Jesus' name.

8. Father Lord, let the power of the dog oppressing my life receive the fire of God and roast, in the name of Jesus.

9. Every inherited demon in dog, receive the arrows of fire, in the name of Jesus.

10. Every force of the power of the dog, come against

yourselves, in the mighty name of Jesus.

11. Father Lord, let every demonic stronghold, built into my life by the spirit of the dog be pulled down, in the name of Jesus.

12. Every power of the dog that has possessed my life, shatter to pieces, in Jesus' name.

13. My soul, be delivered from the forces of the dog, in Jesus' name.

14. Lord God of Elijah, arise with a strong hand against every spirit husband/wife and power of the dog, in the name of Jesus.

15. I break the hold of any evil power over my life, in the name of Jesus.

16. I nullify every effect of the bite of the dog upon my life, in the name of Jesus.

17. Every evil stranger and satanic deposit in my life, be paralysed and get out of my life, in the name of Jesus.

18. Holy Ghost fire, purge my life completely, in Jesus' name.

19. I claim my complete deliverance from the spirit of fornication and sexual immorality, in the name of Jesus.

20. My eyes, be delivered from lust, in the name of Jesus.

21. As from today, my eyes, be controlled by the Holy Spirit, in Jesus' name.

22. Holy Ghost fire, fall upon my eyes and burn to ashes every evil force and satanic power, controlling my eyes, in Jesus' name.

23. I move from bondage to liberty in every area of my life, in Jesus' name.

DEALING WITH ANTI-PROMOTION WITCHCRAFT

There are times when getting promoted from one level to another becomes mysteriously impossible. When the power of witchcraft is behind the inability to attain promotion, you need to use the weapon of spiritual warfare. There is a department in the realm of witchcraft charged with making promotion impossible. But we all need promotion in life.

When we are promoted, God is glorified. You must therefore deal with anti-promotion witchcraft. Remember the Bible has declared that there is no enchantment against God's children.

Confession: Psalm 119:15

Praise Worship

1. I revoke every satanic decree issued against my promotion, in the name of Jesus.

2. O God, let terrors like a flood pursue, overtake and consume

enemies of my breakthroughs, in the name of Jesus.

3. Finger of God, unseat my household strongman, in the name of Jesus.

4. Every evil bird, flying about for my sake, be trapped, in Jesus' name.

5. Every agent of disgrace, backwardness and shame, release me, in the name of Jesus.

6. I overthrow every evil throne, installed against my life, in Jesus' name

7. Every agent of disorder in my life, scatter unto desolation, in the name of Jesus.

8. Every power, fueling my problems, fall down and die, in Jesus' name.

9. I release myself from any curse working in my family, in Jesus' name.

10. Every spiritual vulture, delegated against me, eat your own flesh, in the name of Jesus.

11. I receive the shoes of iron, and I trample upon serpents and scorpions, in the name of Jesus.

12. Every root of cleverly concealed problem, be uprooted, in Jesus' name.

13. I disgrace every evil wisdom working against my breakthroughs, in the name of Jesus.

14. In the power of the Holy Spirit, I crush all my enemies, in Jesus' name.

15. In the power of the Holy Spirit, I put every evil under my feet, in the name of Jesus.

16. O Lord, let me be extraordinary.

17. Holy Spirit, deposit Your wonders in my life, in the name of Jesus.

18. Lord Jesus, break my infirmity into pieces and destroy my disease.

19. Lord Jesus, destroy satanic foundations and build me upon Your word.

20. Lord Jesus, set me ablaze with Your Spirit.

21. Divine earthquake, shake down the foundation of every satanic prison, in the name of Jesus.

22. I let loose confusion, shame and reproach into the camp of the enemy, in the name of Jesus.

23. I bind every evil spirit, withstanding good testimonies in my life, in the name of Jesus.

24. Every satanic river of backwardness, dry up, in the name of Jesus.

25. I destroy every evil dedication, made by my parents for my sake, in the name of Jesus.

26. O Lord, let all prayer failures cease in my life, in the name of Jesus.

27. Holy Ghost, fulfil Your purpose in me now, in the name of Jesus.

28. I refuse to be controlled by environmental situations or satanic revival, in the name of Jesus.

29. By thunder and by fire, I will receive all that the Lord has purposed for me, in this programme, in the name of Jesus.

30. O Lord, create within me, a hunger and thirst for purity and holiness.

31. Holy Spirit, promote divine possibility in my life, in the name of Jesus.

32. Holy Spirit, liberate my spirit, that I may scorn the works of the flesh, in the name of Jesus.

33. I take the thoughts of accusation against me captive, in Jesus' name.

34. Everything working contrary to the obedience of Christ in my life, wither away, in the name of Jesus.

35. Holy Spirit, transform my weakness to strength, in the name of Jesus.

36. Holy Spirit, unmask any portion of me that has not surrendered to you, in the name of Jesus.

37. Holy Spirit, begin to expose all the hidden sins, in the name of Jesus.

NEUTRALIZING SATANIC VERDICTS

Just as there are divine verdicts, there are also satanic verdicts. The good news is that divine verdicts overrule any satanic verdict and also that evil verdicts can be changed.

This prayer programme is to deal with situations when evil decisions have been taken against you or you are a victim of evil conspiracy.

Confession: Isa. 54:16-17

Praise Worship

1. No evil vow, decision or prophecy shall come to pass in my life, in the name of Jesus.

2. My life, you will not be used by the devil, in the name of Jesus.

3. Father Lord, anoint my life to do powerful things in your kingdom.

4. Father Lord, let every curse

of impossibility against me backfire sender, in the name of Jesus.

5. Father Lord, let every agent of impossibility, fashioned against me, receive permanent failure, in the name of Jesus.

6. I refuse to be diverted from the path of blessings, in the name of Jesus.

7. Every hole in my hand, be sealed by the blood of Jesus.

8. Holy Spirit, help me to discover myself, in Jesus' name.

9. My life, refuse every bewitchment, in Jesus' name.

10. Every evil door that I have used my hand to open for the enemy to come into my life, close by the blood of Jesus.

11. Every evil power, drinking the milk of my life, vomit it, in the name of Jesus.

12. Light of God, shine upon my life, in the name of Jesus (spend 30 minutes on this).

13. Holy Ghost fire, burn away every satanic deposit in my life, in the name of Jesus.

14. Father Lord, give me knowledge, wisdom and understanding, in Jesus' name.

15. I receive the power to become great in life, in Jesus' name.

16. Father Lord, baptize me with Your divine favour, in Jesus' name.

17. O Lord, impress my matter into the hearts of those who will help me, in the name of Jesus.

18. In the name of Jesus, spirit of error, you will not prosper in my life.

19. Father Lord, let it be known that You are God in every situation of my life.

20. I cancel the manifestation of every satanic dream, in the name of Jesus.

21. Father Lord, anoint my prayers with Your fire, in the name of Jesus.

22. O Lord, let me touch heaven today and let heaven touch me, in the name of Jesus.

23. Anything in my life that will hinder my prayer, blood of Jesus, flush it out.

24. I receive the power to mount up with wings like an eagle, in the mighty name of Jesus.

25. My Father, let the power of resurrection of our Lord Jesus Christ resurrect every dead potential and virtue in my life, in the name of Jesus.

26. I release myself from every satanic prison, in Jesus' name.

27. I paralyse every evil power working against my career, in the name of Jesus.

28. Every contrary power in my family, loose your peace until you repent and leave me alone, in Jesus' name.

29. Every satanic camp, reinforcing against me, scatter, in the name of Jesus.

30. I reject every spirit of the crossroads, in the name of Jesus.

31. Any evil kingdom, reigning in my life, be utterly destroyed, in the name of Jesus.

32. By the power of God, no evil gathering shall hold in my environment, in the name of Jesus.

33. Every demon, reigning in my life, bow, in the name of Jesus.

34. Every satanic attempt to downgrade my potentials, be frustrated, in the name of Jesus.

35. Every evil prophecy against my life, be rendered impotent, in the name of Jesus.

36. Father Lord, expose all my hidden enemies to me, in the name of Jesus.

37. All those who want me out of the way because I am disturbing them, be paralysed, in the name of Jesus.

38. Every evil finger, pointing at my progress, dry up, in the name of Jesus.

39. I pronounce the curse and destruction of God upon every evil plantation in my life and I command them to wither away, in the name of Jesus.

40. I cast down every vain imagination against my success, in Jesus' name.

41. I seal all my prayers with the blood of Jesus.

POWER AGAINST ROCK SPIRITS

Students of spiritual warfare know that certain powers in the kingdom of darkness either make their abode in the rock or draw their powers from there. The rock spirits are stubborn spirits. They are responsible for ruling nations, communities and families.

The spirits of the rock are spirits that generally have records for perpetrating evil for a very long time. Many ancient rocks habour spirits that are as old as the history of the communities where they are located.

Prayers against rock spirits are not ordinary prayers. The virtues and blessings of so many people are stored in some evil vaults in the rock. You must pray against every rock affecting your destiny and recover your stolen virtues.

Confession: Numbers 20:8; Psalm 91; Matthew 24:1-2

Praise Worship

Confess these words (3 times) with faith in your heart: Oh Lord, my

God, I thank you for loving me. I know you have good things in stock for me. Lord Jesus, I thank You for Your steadfast love and faithfulness to me and my family. My Father and my God, as I open my mouth to pray these warfare prayers, Oh Lord, answer me by fire, in the name of Jesus.

1. I receive power to overcome every spirit of the rock, in Jesus' name.

2. You spirit of the rock, release my destiny by fire, in Jesus' name.

3. You power of the rock, release my blessings by the blood of Jesus.

4. All my blessings, deposited inside the rock, receive fire and locate me now, in the name of Jesus.

5. You power of the rock, assigned to afflict me, die, in Jesus' name.

6. Every rock spirit of poverty, break and release my money by fire, in the name of Jesus.

7. Anything programmed against me inside the rock, break into pieces, in the name of Jesus.

8. Rock of Ages, fight against every rock of failure in my life, in the name of Jesus.

9. Every evil load in my life, come out by fire, in the name of Jesus.

10. Anything planted in my life by the enemy, die, in Jesus' name.

11. You evil stone in my body, come out by fire, in the name of Jesus.

12. Every stone of problem in my life, die, in the name of Jesus.

13. Oh Lord, purge me with your fire, in the name of Jesus.

14. Every evil material in my body, die by fire, in the name of Jesus.

15. Every evil monitoring power inside the rock, assigned against my life, break by fire, in the name of Jesus.

16. Begin to thank the Lord for answered prayers.

BEELZEBUB MUST DIE

Beelzebub is the evil spirit which operates in the kingdom of flies. The fly kingdom forms an integral part of the demonic kingdom. Flies generally dominate any environment that is dominated by dirts.

Flies are carriers of evil demonic messages in the dark kingdom. Since evil spirits can materialize and dematerialize, they operate as flies to inflict spiritual epidemic on their victims. Those who are under the attack of these categories of evil spirits experience contamination of their destinies. Once they are invaded by a swam of evil flies in the spiritual realm, their problems will be legion in their physical lives. You must fight against the spirit of Beelzebub and destroy it in the physical realm.

The prayer programme is meant for men and women.

Confession: Psalm 23

Praise Worship

1. I receive power to fight against every power of the air, in Jesus' name.

2. You flying evil spirit, receive fire and die, in the name of Jesus.

3. Every power, flying in the air against me, fall down and die, in the name of Jesus.

4. Oh Lord, deliver me today from the evil power of the air, in Jesus' name.

5. Every instrument of the night flying against me in the dream, die, in the name of Jesus.

6. You wind, refuse to co-operate with my enemy, in Jesus' name.

7. Every storm, raging against me at night, be silent, in Jesus' name.

8. Every arrow, fired against me by witchcraft, backfire, in Jesus' name.

9. Every instrument of witchcraft, working against my life, die, in the name of Jesus.

10. Arrows of the night, I am not your victim, go back to your sender, in the name of Jesus.

11. Any whirlwind, evoked against me, encircle your sender for destruction, in the name of Jesus.

12. Any power, speaking into the air against my life, die, in Jesus' name

13. Father Lord, protect my life with your fire, in the name of Jesus.

resistant to prayers.

Confession: Gal. 3:13

Praise Worship

1. Father Lord, let the foothold and the seat of the enemy in my life be destroyed completely, in the name of Jesus.

2. Blood of Jesus, erase all the legal ground that the enemy has against my life, in the name of Jesus.

3. I close all the doors opened to the enemies in my life with the blood of Jesus.

4. Every concrete barrier, constructed by the enemy to stop the germination of the seed of my life, break down completely, in the name of Jesus.

5. Every foundation, constructed by the enemy in my life, be destroyed completely, in the name of Jesus.

6. All the words contrary to God's words spoken against me, fall down to the ground and bear no fruit, in the name of Jesus.

7. I bind the strongman in my life, and I clear my goods from his possession.

8. You strongman of body destruction, be bound, in Jesus' name.

9. You strongman of mind destruction, be bound, in Jesus' name.

10. You strongman of financial destruction, be bound, in Jesus' name.

11. Every battle, waged against me by the kingdom of darkness, receive defeat, in the mighty name of Jesus.

12. Distributors of spiritual poison, swallow your poison, in Jesus' name.

13. All the forces of Egypt in my life, rise up against yourselves in the name of Jesus.

14. Father Lord, let the joy of the enemy over my life be turned to sorrow.

15. You demonic armies, stationed against my life, receive the judgment of leprosy, in the name of Jesus.

16. Every evil power source, in my place of birth, be destroyed completely, in the name of Jesus.

17. Every access to my life by the enemy, be closed, in the name of Jesus.

18. Every problem, that came into my life by personal invitation, depart, in the name of Jesus.

19. Any problem, that has come into my life through my parents, depart, in the name of Jesus.

20. Any problem, that has come into my life, as a result of attacks by satanic agents, depart, in the name of Jesus.

21. All my trapped blessings, be released, in the name of Jesus.

22. Bondage repairers, be bound, in the name of Jesus.

23. Every locked-up blessings, be uncaged, in the name of Jesus.

24. Every evil agreement, fashioned against me, be dissolved, in the name of Jesus.

25. I disallow the strengthening of any problem, in the name of Jesus.

26. All evil thrones, fashioned/set up against me, be destroyed completely, in the name of Jesus.

27. You God of promotion, promote me beyond my wildest dreams, in Jesus' name.

28. I fire back sevenfold, every arrow of witchcraft, in Jesus' name.

29. Every satanic agent in my family, who refuses to repent, I destroy your power, in the name of Jesus.

30. Shadow of death, flee away from me; heavenly light, shine on me, in the name of Jesus.

31. I rebuke all the spirits that are against the soundness of my mind, in the name of Jesus.

32. I possess the mind of Christ.

ALONE WITH GOD

There is a time in life when your life needs thorough spiritual sanitation and total elimination of whatever has the tendency of corrupting your virtues and making your life lose its value.

To make your life and destiny attain the highest level, you need to set time apart to be alone with God. Such prayer retreats will enable you to get the best out of life and make your destiny attain the highest height. Much time needs to be spent, much prayer efforts need to be put in and aggression must be added to your prayers as you painstakingly undertake the prayer points below.

This prayer programme will turn your life around and make you to mount up with wings as eagles.

Praise Worship

Prayer points

1. I oppose every opposition, I pursue every pursuer, I oppress every

oppressor, in the name of Jesus.

2. Every yoke manufacturer, arise, carry your yoke and die, in Jesus' name.

3. I release myself from every ancestral demonic pollution, in Jesus' name.

4. I release myself from every demonic pollution, emanating from my parents' religion, in the name of Jesus.

5. I release myself from demonic pollution, emanating from my past involvement in any demonic religion, in the name of Jesus.

6. I break loose from every idol and related association, in Jesus' name.

7. I release myself, from every dream pollution, in the name of Jesus.

8. Every satanic attack, against my life in my dreams, be converted to victory, in the name of Jesus.

9. All rivers, trees, forests, evil companions, evil pursuers, pictures of dead relatives, snakes, spirit husbands, spirit wives and masquerades manipulated against me in the dream, be completely destroyed by the power in the blood of the Lord Jesus.

10. Every evil plantation in my life, **come out with all your roots, in the name of Jesus!** (*Lay your hands on your stomach and keep repeating the emphasised area.*)

11. Evil strangers in my body, come all the way out of your hiding places, in the name of Jesus.

12. I disconnect any conscious or unconscious link with demonic

caterers, in the name of Jesus.

13. O Lord, let all avenues to eat or drink spiritual poisons be closed, in the name of Jesus.

14. I cough out and vomit any food eaten from the table of the devil, in the name of Jesus. (*Cough them out and vomit them in faith. Prime the expulsion.*)

15. All negative materials circulating in my blood stream, come out and catch fire, in the name of Jesus.

16. I drink the blood of Jesus. (*Physically swallow and drink it in faith. Keep doing this for some time.*)

17. (*Lay one hand on your head and the other on your stomach or navel and begin to pray like this*): Holy Ghost fire, burn from the top of my head to the sole of my feet. *Begin to mention every organ of your body; your kidney, liver, intestines, blood, etc. You must not rush at this level, because the fire will actually come and you may start feeling the heat.*

18. I cut myself off from every spirit of ... (*mention the name of your place of birth*), in the name of Jesus.

19. I uproot, (pick from the underlisted) from the foundation of my life, in the name of Jesus.

- poison of darkness   - ancestral initiation

-negative programming   - poverty   - triangular trap

- bewitchment power   - idol deposit   - sexual pollution

- witchcraft hatred

- spirit of polygamy   - cultural bondage   - dream harassment

- family disgrace   - ancestral curses   - mind fragmentation

- animal spirit   - water domination   - Pharisees' anointing

- vagabond bondage   - non-achievement   - Goliath problem

- spirit of death and hell   - witchcraft cage

- blood pollution   - spirit of defilement

- seed of powerlessness

- anointing of the snail   - nakedness

- failure at the edge of miracle- spiritual blindness

- spiritual deafness   - poor finishing   - curses and spells

- familiar spirits   - evil patterns   - marine covenants

- evil padlock   - demonic dog bite   - spirit of the dead

- vagabond lifestyle   - untimely death   - marital instability

- arrow of frustration   - sicknesses and diseases

- parental curses   - violent death   - abnormal behaviour

- uncontrollable anger   - mental blackout   - strange voices

20. I cut myself off from every tribal spirit and curse, in Jesus' name.

21. I cut myself off from every territorial spirit and curse, in Jesus' name.

22. Holy Ghost fire, purge my life.

23. I claim my complete deliverance from the spirit of . . . (*mention those things you do not desire in your life*), in Jesus' name.

24. I break the hold of any evil power over my life, in the name of Jesus.

TERRITORIAL DELIVERANCE

Territorial deliverance can be classified among the categories of advanced deliverance and spiritual warfare. Its purpose is to stem the tide of evil and set the captives of a particular territory free. Since every territory or geographical location is under the jurisdiction or satanic agents, the power of God cannot flow freely in such areas and the people of God there cannot enjoy completely the benefits God has provided for them. Territorial deliverance will unleash upon you the power to excel and the ability to succeed where others fail. You can also make use of these prayer points if you want to get away with spiritual warfare in the area of deliverance.

You can rise up as a soldier of Christ, challenge the powers that be in your territory, disgrace them, and uphold the banner of the gospel of the Lord Jesus Christ.

With these prayer points, you will surely overcome

territorial powers.

Praise Worship

Confessions:

Hosea 10:2: Their heart is divided; now shall they be found faulty: he shall break down their altars, he shall spoil their images.

Deut. 7:5: But thus shall ye deal with them; ye shall destroy their altars, and break down their images, and cut down their groves, and burn their graven images with fire.

Deut. 12:2-3: Ye shall utterly destroy all the places, wherein the nations which ye shall possess served their gods, upon the high mountains, and upon the hills, and under every green tree: And ye shall overthrow their altars, and break their pillars, and burn their groves with fire; and ye shall hew down the graven images of their gods, and destroy the names of them out of that place.

PRAYER POINTS

1. As I go into this level of warfare, I receive a cover of the blood of Jesus. I stay in the strong tower which is the name of the Lord.

2. I receive God's unction and power upon my tongue, in the name of Jesus.

3. I forbid any satanic backlash or retaliation against me and my family, in the name of Jesus.

4. In this battle, I shall fight and win I shall be the victor and not the victim, in the name of Jesus.

5. I put on the helmet of salvation, the belt of truth, the breastplate of righteousness; I wear the shoe of the gospel and I take the shield of faith, as I go into this territorial intercession and warfare, in the name of Jesus.

6. I bind and rebuke the princes and powers in charge of this (mention the name of the city), in the name of Jesus.

7. I command the fire of God on all the idols, traditions, sacrifices and rituals on this land, in the name of Jesus.

8. I break all the agreements made between the people of this city and satan, in the name of Jesus.

9. I dedicate and claim this city for God, in the name of Jesus.

10. O Lord, let the presence, dominion, authority and blessings of God be experienced in this city, in the name of Jesus.

11. I destroy and decree total removal of arsons, strikes, juvenile delinquencies, lawlessness, nakedness, pornography, immoralities, homosexuality and drug addiction from this city, in the name of Jesus.

12. I prophesy against all the satanic altars, in high places in this city to be consumed by the fire of God and their ashes blown away by the East wind, in the name of Jesus.

13. Every satanic altar, around this vicinity, become desolate; and all covenants being serviced by these altars, be revoked and break, in the name of Jesus.

14. Most Holy God, let the sword and the hand of the Lord be against the priests and priestesses ministering at all these satanic altars and high places and let their places be found no more, in the name of Jesus.

15. I silence every evil directive from all satanic altars and high places of this city, in the name of Jesus.

16. My Father, let all curses brought about by ritual sacrifices and satanic tokens be revoked, in the name of Jesus.

17. I paralyse the evil powers of idolatrous priests of this city, in the name of Jesus.

18. I command the stars, the sun, the moon and the wind to begin to fight against the diviners and astrologers, who have been using these elements against the move of God in this city, in the name of Jesus.

19. Judgment of God, come upon the ancient and scornful men, who rule over this city by sorcery, satanic manipulation and witchcraft, in Jesus' name.

20. I deprogramme whatever the enemy has programmed into the lives of the people of this city, in the name of Jesus.

21. By the blood of Jesus, I destroy every blood covenant made upon any satanic altar, that has brought untold hardships upon the people of this city, in the name of Jesus.

22. I frustrate the tokens of liars and make mad all diviners, enchanters and sorcerers, who are operating against this city at any altar, in the name of Jesus.

23. I desecrate every satanic altar in this city with the blood of Jesus and cancel all their associated covenants, in Jesus' name.

24. Every marine altar in this city, catch fire, in the name of Jesus.

25. All territorial altars in this city, catch fire, in the name of Jesus.

26. All astral altars, in this city, catch fire, in the name of Jesus.

27. Every marine spirit, operating in this neighbourhood, be paralysed and suffocated, in the name of Jesus.

28. I break every limitation brought on this city by the influence of satanic altars, in the name of Jesus.

29. Every devoted land and evil forest, in this city, be demolished, in the name of Jesus.

30. By the power in the name of our Lord Jesus Christ, I command the citadel of the wicked forces to shift base from this city, in the name of Jesus.

31. I prophesy and decree that the peace, glory, love and mercy of God, be established in this city, in the name of Jesus.

32. O Lord, let Your fear, righteousness, godliness, knowledge and wisdom be established in this city, in the name of Jesus.

33. Father Lord, let there be repentance of the heart and hunger for God in this city, in the name of Jesus.

34. I decree, that the gospel of the kingdom of God shall no longer be restricted by any satanic altar or high places in this city, in the name of Jesus.

35. In the name of the Lord Jesus Christ, I declare a new day of divine visitation and deliverance for this city and its neighbourhood.

36. I prophesy that an altar to Jehovah God, will be raised in every household of this city, in the name of Jesus.

37. Henceforth, I declare that Jesus Christ is Lord over this city, in the name of Jesus.

TURN-AROUND BREAKTHROUGHS

There are breakthroughs and there are breakthroughs. There is no limit to the height which you can attain by making use of certain explosive prayer points.

A number of people have experienced breakthroughs that have remained unforgettable in their experiences. It is possible to go through life in circles around the frontiers of breakthroughs. But it is far more possible to go beyond that point and exceed all known frontiers in the area of breakthroughs. Breakthroughs are not meant for lazy men and women. To experience a turn-around breakthrough, you must pray with the totality of your energy or strength. Those who have experienced turn-around breakthroughs have discovered that there is a wall of difference between such breakthroughs and emptiness. No amount of prayer efforts can be too much to be invested in the kind of breakthroughs that will permanently change your history.

These prayer points have been specially packaged to enable you experience great changes in every department of your life.

Praise Worship

Confessions: Isaiah 32:15-20 : Until the spirit be poured upon us from on high, and the wilderness be a fruitful field, and the fruitful field be counted for a forest. Then judgment shall dwell in the wilderness, and righteousness remain in the fruitful field. And the work of righteousness shall be peace; and the effect of righteousness quietness and assurance for ever. And my people shall dwell in a peaceable habitation, and in sure dwellings, and in quiet resting places; When it shall hail, coming down on the forest; and the city shall be low in a low place. Blessed are ye that sow beside all waters, that send forth thither the feet of the ox and the ass.

Rev. 2:12 : And to the angel of the church in Pergamos write; These things saith he which hath the sharp sword with two edges.

Rev. 3:9: Behold, I will make them of the synagogue of Satan, which say they are Jews, and are not, but do lie; behold, I will make them to come and worship before thy feet, and to know that I have loved thee.

| 1. Holy Spirit, multiply Your grace upon my life, in Jesus' name. | 2. Anointing of revelation, fall upon my spirit man, in the name of Jesus. |

3. Anointing of wisdom, fall upon my inner man, in Jesus' name.

4. Holy Ghost fire, open the eyes of my spirit, in Jesus' name.

5. Oh Lord, let all the angels assigned to assist me in my ministry receive fire, in the name of Jesus.

6. Any power, that has arrested my angels, be arrested and release my angels, in the name of Jesus.

7. Oh mighty hand of God, fall upon me for ministry and protection, in Jesus' name.

8. Oh Lord, let me and my descendants dwell under the shadow of the Almighty, all the days of our lives, in Jesus' name.

9. Oh Lord, keep me, my ministry, my family and my descendants after me in Your pavilion, in the name of Jesus - for in Your pavilion, evil arrows cannot locate us.

10. Evil arrows, that came into my life by night, jump up and come out of my life by night, in Jesus' name.

11. Oh Lord God of Elijah, arise in Your power and let all my enemies fall before me, in the name of Jesus.

12. Oh Lord, whenever my enemies plan any attack against me, in the future, let their counsel turn into foolishness, in Jesus' name.

13. Oh Lord, whenever my enemies take evil decisions against me, let Your truth deliver me according to Thy Word, in the name of Jesus. (Pray for those who are victims of false accusations and slanders by brethren in the house

of God).

14. Oh Lord, Man of War, destroy the teeth of all those that the devil will use against me in Your sanctuary, in Jesus' name.

15. Oh Lord, break me and mould me for Your glory, in the name of Jesus.

16. Every synagogue of satan, erected against me, fall down before me now, for I am the beloved of the Lord, in the name of Jesus.

17. Anything in me, that will allow the arrow of the enemy to prosper, be removed now, in the name of Jesus.

18. Every demonic alteration of my destiny, loose your hold upon my life and come out of my foundation, in Jesus' name.

19. All powers, behind demonic alteration of my destiny, die, in the name of Jesus.

20. Any power, behind demonic alteration of my handwriting and virtues, die, in the name of Jesus.

21. Demonic marriage, loose your hold over my life, and be purged out of my foundation, in the name of Jesus.

22. Every strange child, assigned to me in the dream, roast by fire, in the name of Jesus.

23. Fire of God, pursue all strange children and women, assigned to me in the dream, in the name of Jesus.

24. Every evil effect of laying on of hands, loose your hold over my life and be purged out of my foundation, in Jesus' name.

25. Evil idols from my father's house, fight against idols from my mother's house and destroy yourselves, in Jesus' name.

26. Every idol,in my city of birth, holding down my destiny, roast by fire, in Jesus' name.

27. Every demonic authority, attacking my life, as a result of my past relationship with strange sexual partners, roast by fire, in Jesus' name.

28. Every demon, activated against me, go back to your owner, in the name of Jesus.

29. All demons and principalities assigned against me, be decommissioned, in the name of Jesus.

30. Every evil voice, rising up against my glory, be silenced, in the name of Jesus.

31. Holy Spirit of God, do something new in my life today, in the name of Jesus.

32. Oh Lord, make me an instrument of revival in Your hand.

33. I shake off powers of demotion in my life, in the name of Jesus.

34. Thou serpent of demotion, release my glory, in the name of Jesus.

35. Oh heaven, arise and release me from captivity, in the name of Jesus.

UPROOTING EVIL PLANTATIONS

Satan's major pre-occupation is to pollute the foundation of men and women, thereby subjecting them to wicked spiritual attacks. He carries out this evil assignment by programming evil plantations in the lives of people. Such plantations generally have roots that are strongly entrenched. To uproot them you will need several sessions of aggressive prayers. You need to give time and attention to these life-transforming prayer points. All evil plantations must be uprooted. Every problem that has been planted in your life and destiny by the enemy must be totally uprooted. These prayer points can be likened to laying the axe of fire to every tree which the enemy has planted. Do not spare any evil plantation.

Praise Worship

1. What the enemy has programmed into my life to destroy me, Oh Lord, remove it by fire, in the name of Jesus.

2. Oh Lord my God, remove whatever the enemy has planted in my life, in the name of Jesus.

3. Every good thing that the enemy has destroyed in my life, Oh Lord my God, restore it unto me today, in Jesus' name.

4. My spiritual antenna, be connected to the kingdom of God, in the name of Jesus.

5. Every pollution in my spiritual life, be purged with holy fire, in the name of Jesus.

6. Holy Spirit, visit the dark room of my life and destiny and expose every unwanted material, in the name of Jesus.

7. Every evil spirit in my foundation, release me by fire and die, in the name of Jesus.

8. Every short and long term project of the enemy in my life, be aborted, in the name of Jesus.

9. All organs of my body, I charge you, don't be used to destroy me, in the name of Jesus.

10. You organs of my body, become fire, in the name of Jesus.

11. Spirit of excellence, take control of my life, in the name of Jesus.

12. O Lord, let the gift of revelation promote my ministry, in the name of Jesus.

13. Holy Spirit, lay Your hands upon me, in the name of Jesus.

14. O Lord, let the power of resurrection activate holiness and purity in me, in the name of Jesus.

15. Oh Lord, let every marriage conducted for me in the dream be destroyed, in the name of Jesus.

16. Evil marriage, that is destroying my holiness and purity, die, in the name of Jesus.

17. Evil marriage, that is destroying my ministry and calling, die, in the name of Jesus.

18. Every power, that has turned my life upside-down, roast by fire, in the name of Jesus.

19. Oh Lord my God, re-arrange my destiny according to Your plan, in the name of Jesus.

20. Oh Lord my God, crush every power that says I will not fulfil my destiny, in the name of Jesus.

ARRESTING DARK CLOUD OVER YOUR DESTINY

Whenever a dark cloud hangs over your destiny, you will have problems with destiny fulfilment. The dark cloud is an attempt by the enemy to create an artificial barrier between you and the destination earmarked for you by God. To have a dark cloud hang over your destiny can be likened to driving on a highway that is over-shadowed by palpable darkness. A driver on such a highway will hit the ditch sooner or later. The devil generally targets colourful and glorious destinies. His ultimate intention is to create so much darkness that the one who is undertaking the journey to destiny fulfilment will lose his bearing and miss the target. The only way to forestall what the enemy wants to achieve is to put your battle in high gear and arrest the dark cloud.

The prayer points in this section will enable you to speak against the dark cloud and force it to disappear by fire. Do not spare any dark cloud sponsored by the enemy to divert destiny.

Praise Worship

Scripture Reading: Matthew 12:37: For by thy words thou shalt be justified, and by thy words thou shalt be condemned.

1. I thank You Lord for Your angels, You have released to bless me during this prayer session, in Jesus' name.

2. Lord, I pray for the forgiveness of all our sins (personal and collective), in the name of Jesus.

3. Holy Spirit, cleanse me of all sins so that the Lord can hear me, in the name of Jesus.

4. Blood of Jesus, saturate this environment now, in the name of Jesus.

5. Any demon that is assigned to attack me, what are you waiting for? Be arrested, in the name of Jesus.

6. Any satanic border or boundary attacking me, be pulled down, in the name of Jesus.

7. I register my life in the ministry of glory, in the name of Jesus.

8. O Lord, let my buried glory be exhumed, in the name of Jesus.

9. Any power, assigned to bury me alive, be arrested by fire, in the name of Jesus.

10. Any power, sitting upon my glory, be unseated by fire, in the name of Jesus.

11. Every satanic prophecy, against my destiny, backfire, in the name of Jesus.

12. Weapons of destruction against me, backfire, in the name of Jesus.

13. Every weapon of darkness, attacking my glory, ministry and marital fulfilment, backfire, in the name of Jesus.

14. Every evil cloud upon my life, disappear by fire, in the name of Jesus.

15. Every evil cloud, bringing confusion, frustration, disappointment, stagnancy and non-achievement upon my life, disappear by fire, in the name of Jesus.

16. Oh Lord my God, deliver me from every satanic prison, in the name of Jesus.

17. Every local wickedness, walking upon my destiny, release me by fire, in the name of Jesus.

18. Every spiritual lion, roaring against me, be silenced, in the name of Jesus.

19. Every spiritual serpent, arresting my glory, receive fire, in the name of Jesus.

20. Every spiritual coffin, prepared for me and my household, be arrested by fire, in the name of Jesus.

21. Every evil mark upon my life, be blotted out by the blood of Jesus, in the name of Jesus.

22. Every satanic label upon my life, be removed by fire, in the name of Jesus.

23. Every demonic king, opposing me, be dethroned, in the name of Jesus.

24. Every satanic crown upon my life, be removed by fire, in the name of Jesus.

25. Oh Lord my God, let every word that I have spoken against my life be reversed, in the name of Jesus.

26. My God is the God of the living, therefore He will answer me, in the name of Jesus.

27. Every prince of this world, opposing me, die, in the name of Jesus.

28. Every prince of this world, reigning in my life, I cast you out, in the name of Jesus.

29. Any strange power or personality, living with me in my house, receive fire, in the name of Jesus.

30. Every man/woman, raising evil altar above or around me, roast by fire, in the name of Jesus.

31. Every demonic authority in my environment, opposing me, be arrested by the Holy Ghost, in the name of Jesus.

32. I receive deliverance from evil powers and demonic authorities controlling this land, in the name of Jesus.

33. Any part of my body or organ, that has been stolen, be returned by fire, in the name of Jesus.

34. I proclaim that the shout of Alleluia, will not cease in my life, in the name of Jesus.

WHEN THE ENEMY WILL NOT LET GO

In every generation, there is a stubborn Pharaoh who will not let Israel go. Satan is not soft. He is stubborn to the core.

He will not release his victims with ease. The only language he understands is violence. There is a type of prayer to pray when the enemy is hell bent on denying you your freedom. Such a drastic situation requires some drastic prayer points.

These prayer points will enable you to send confusion into the camp of demonic agents. You will send the task master parking and disgrace Pharaoh and all his horsemen. The enemy that will not let you go will also not call you to a conference table to negotiate your release. This prayer programme will lead to the re-enactment of the burial of Pharaoh and his agents.

Praise Worship

Scripture Reading: Exodus 6:10-11: And the Lord spake unto Moses, saying, go in, speak unto Pharaoh king of Egypt, that he let the children of Israel go out of his land.

Exodus 7:1-4: And the Lord said unto Moses, see, I have made thee a god to Pharaoh: and Aaron thy brother shall be thy prophet. Thou shalt speak all that I command thee: and Aaron thy brother shall speak unto Pharaoh, that he send the children of Israel out of his land. And I will harden Pharaoh's heart, and multiply my signs and my wonders in the land of Egypt. But Pharaoh shall not hearken unto you, that I may lay my hand upon Egypt, and bring forth mine armies, and my people the children of Israel, out of the land of Egypt by great judgments.

Psalm 71:7: I am as a wonder unto many; but thou art my strong refuge.

Exodus 8:28: And Pharaoh said, I will let you go, that ye may sacrifice to the Lord your God in the wilderness; only ye shall not go very far away: intreat for me.

Exodus 10:8: And Moses and Aaron were brought again unto Pharaoh: and he said unto them, Go, serve the Lord your God: but who are they that shall go?

1. Thou power of God, penetrate my spirit, soul and body, in the name of Jesus.

2. Association of

demons, gathered against my progress, roast by the thunder fire of God, in the name of Jesus.

3. Blood of Jesus, redeem me, in the name of Jesus.

4. Every satanic decision, taken against my progress, be nullified, in the name of Jesus.

5. Every evil deposit, in my spirit, soul and body, be flushed out by the blood of Jesus, in the name of Jesus.

6. Oh Lord my God, promote me in the spiritual and in the physical, in the name of Jesus.

7. Every stranger, in my body, ministry, life and calling, jump out, in Jesus' name.

8. Any satanic arrow, fired at me, go back, locate and destroy your sender, in the name of Jesus.

9. Holy Ghost, arise and destroy the habitation and works of the wicked in my life (home, finances, ministry), in the name of Jesus.

10. Every serpentine spirit, spitting on my breakthrough, roast, in the name of Jesus.

11. Every enemy of the perfect will of God for my life, die, in the name of Jesus.

12. Thou anointing of joy and peace, replace heaviness and sorrow in my life, in Jesus' name.

13. O Lord, let abundance replace lack and insufficiency in my life, in Jesus' name.

14. Every Pharaoh in my life, destroy yourself, in the name of Jesus.

15. Garment of Pharaoh that is upon my life, be removed by fire, in Jesus' name.

16. Thou power of impossibility in my

destiny, die, in the name of Jesus.

17. Every task master, assigned against me, somersault and die, in the name of Jesus.

18. I refuse to continue eating from the crumbs of the task master's table, in the name of Jesus.

19. Any man or woman, who wouldn't let me prosper, Oh Lord, declare his/her obituary, in the name of Jesus.

20. Oh Lord, give me a new inner man if I have been altered, in Jesus' name.

21. Oh Lord,

activate Your high calling in my life, in the name of Jesus.

22. Oh Lord, anoint me to recover the wasted years in every area of my life, in Jesus' name

23. Oh Lord, if I have fallen behind in any area of my life, empower me to recover all lost opportunities and wasted years, in the name of Jesus.

24. Any power that says I will not go forward, be arrested, in the name of Jesus.

25. Any power that

wants to keep me in want in the midst of plenty, die, in Jesus' name.

26. Any power that wants to draw me away from the presence of the Lord to destroy me, die, in the name of Jesus.

27. I prophesy that I will get to my promised inheritance, in the name of Jesus.

28. Any power that wants me to fulfil my destiny partially, die, in the name of Jesus.

29. Oh Lord, anoint

me with power, to destroy all foundational covenants, in the name of Jesus.

30. Oh Lord, use my substance for the furtherance of the gospel, in the name of Jesus.

31. Oh Lord, arise and bless my inheritance, in the name of Jesus.

32. All my stolen virtues, be returned to me, in the name of Jesus.

33. O Lord, let my release bring revival, in the name of Jesus.

34. Oh Lord, reveal all unprofitable ways in me, by Your Holy Spirit, in the name of Jesus.

35. Today, you my spirit man will not bewitch me, in the name of Jesus.

36. Power in the blood of Jesus, redeem my destiny, in the name of Jesus.

37. Every satanic weapon, formed against my destiny, backfire, in the name of Jesus.

38. Arrows of deliverance, locate my destiny, in the name of Jesus.

39. Every spiritual cobweb on my destiny, burn, in the name of Jesus.

40. Every serpent in my foundation, swallowing my destiny, die, in the name of Jesus.

41. Every red candle, burning against my destiny, roast, in the name of Jesus.

42. Song: God of deliverance, send down fire. (Sing for 15 minutes clapping your hands).

43. Every lid the enemy has put on my destiny, jump up, in the name of Jesus.

44. Every serpent in my blood, die, in the name of Jesus.

45. Every serpent, caging my destiny, die, in Jesus' name.

46. Every power of darkness, that is following me about, die, in the name of Jesus.

POWER TO BE CONNECTED WITH GREAT MEN IN HIGH PLACES

These prayer points are specially designed for those who want to be connected. Those who matter in the society can be used of the Lord to advance you in life. Not every one of us is naturally connected to the high and the mighty, but God can catapult you to great heights through the prayer programme in this section. These prayer points will be used by God to supernaturally connect you to high places. Connection is spiritual in nature. If you take these prayer points aggressively, you will begin to experience wonderful connections with men and women of substance from the North, South, East and West. You can say these prayer points on daily basis. Through them you can be connected to the noble, locally and internationally.

Great men who would fulfil God's agenda for your life will come looking for you as you faithfully pray these prayer points. Take them very seriously as one major contact can change your life positively.

Praise Worship

Scripture Reading: Deut. 28:13: And the Lord shall make thee the head, and not the tail; and thou shalt be above only, and thou shalt not be beneath; if that thou hearken unto the commandments of the Lord thy God, which I command thee this day, to observe and to do them:

1. Holy Spirit, do the work of deliverance in my life today, in the name of Jesus.

2. Every evil spirit, assigned against me, disappear by fire, in the name of Jesus.

3. Blood of Jesus, remove every curse in my life, in the name of Jesus.

4. Holy Spirit, connect me with great men of this world, in the name of Jesus.

5. Fire of God, explode in my life, in the name of Jesus.

6. Every sickness in my life, die, in the name of Jesus.

7. Anointing for prosperity, fall upon me now, in the name of Jesus.

8. Anointing for revival, explode in my life and ministry, in the name of Jesus.

9. Every demonic authority in this vicinity, be crippled and silenced, in the name of Jesus.

10. O Lord, let the heaven open upon me now, in the name of Jesus.

11. Every power, working against my prosperity, fall down and die, in the name of Jesus.

12. Every power, that wants to deny me of my destiny, roast, in the name of Jesus.

13. It is written concerning me, that I will divide the spoil of the land with the great and mighty and it shall be so, in the name of Jesus.

14. I prophesy that I will take my position among the rulers of this world, in the name of Jesus.

15. Holy Spirit, You are my Passport, I have come to the treasured city, but it is walled against me; Lord, wave to me to come in, in the name of Jesus.

16. Every power, that wouldn't allow me to reach my potential, roast, in the name of Jesus.

17. Power of redemption, locate me, in the name of Jesus.

18. Oh Lord my God, connect me with my glory, in the name of Jesus.

19. Holy Spirit, arrest any power that wants to deny me of my glory, in the name of Jesus.

20. Oh heaven, fight for me against powers sitting on my glory, in the name of Jesus.

21. Any satanic agent, using evil horn to torment my life, be tormented, in the name of Jesus.

22. O Lord, let the horn of the wicked be cut off, in the name of Jesus.

23. Every satanic horn, speaking against my greatness, be silenced, in the name of Jesus.

24. Every demon, in charge of satanic horn, be arrested, in Jesus' name.

25. Every spiritual embargo, placed upon my destiny, be consumed by fire, in the name of Jesus.

26. Every evil conspiracy, against my life, roast by fire, in Jesus' name.

27. Every power, that says that I will not make it in life, scatter by fire, in the name of Jesus.

28. Every satanic conspiracy, against my glory, scatter unto desolation, in the name of Jesus.

29. Every power, increasing itself against me, be pulled down by fire, in the name of Jesus.

30. All those who are gathered against my glory, be put to shame, in the name of Jesus.

31. Holy Spirit, arise in Your majesty, and touch every area of my life, in the name of Jesus.

32. Anointing for glory, enter my life, in the name of Jesus.

33. Spirit of impossibility, jump out of my life, in the name of Jesus.

34. Anointing for prosperity, overshadow my life, in the name of Jesus.

35. Evil wounds and injuries in my spirit and body, be healed, in the name of Jesus.

36. Every evil fly hovering over my spirit and body, die, in Jesus' name.

37. Fire of God, heal all my spiritual injuries, in the name of Jesus.

38. Balm of Gilead, heal all my spiritual injuries, in the name of Jesus.

39. Blood of Jesus and fire of God, heal my spiritual injuries, in the name of Jesus.

40. Anything that has been stolen from me, I repossess you back, in the name of Jesus.

41. My soul, come out of the valley of darkness and failure, in Jesus' name.

42. My destiny, come out of the valley of darkness and oppression, in the name of Jesus.

43. My glory, come out of the valley of defeat and stagnancy, in the name of Jesus.

44. Oh Lord, cause every demonic security around my life to be consumed by fire, in the name of Jesus.

45. As from today, I begin to walk in the anointing of glory, in Jesus' name.

46. Oh Lord, let Your glory and fire fall upon me, in the name of Jesus.

47. Oh Lord, let Your anointing of wisdom and understanding fall upon me, in the name of Jesus.

48. Every clock, set against my destiny to move anti-clock wise, be reversed and move clock- wise, in the name of Jesus.

49. I refuse to have the clock of my life move anti-clock wise, in the name of Jesus.

50. My destiny, receive the anointing to move forward, in Jesus' name.

MY LIFE IS NOT FOR SALE

God takes delight in drawing a line of demarcation between strangers and His beloved sons and daughters.

While the people of the world go through life, confused and disenchanted, children of God simply follow the glorious highway mapped out for them. You can choose to move from the valley to the mountain top and live a life that is unique in every sense by making use of the prayer points below. You do not need to go through life as if life was not worth living. Do not allow the

These prayer points afford you the opportunity to declare that your life is not for sale and that no matter what happens, you will fulfil your divine destiny.

Praise Worship

Scripture Reading: Psalm 36:9-11: For with thee is the fountain of life: in thy light shall we see light. O continue thy lovingkindness unto them that know thee; and thy righteousness to the upright in heart. Let not the foot of pride come against me, and let not the hand of the wicked remove me.

1. Evil cord of wickedness, sin or iniquity, blocking my communication with heaven, be cut off, in the name of Jesus.

2. Every power, spirit or personality, listening to my prayers in order to report them to the demonic world, Father, tear them, in Jesus' name.

3. Every authority of darkness, upon which wealth and blessings are based, crumble suddenly in one day, in the name of Jesus.

4. Father, expose and destroy the workers of iniquity, in Jesus' name.

5. Father, in the name of Jesus, let the mystery and secret of my fulfilment be revealed.

6. My Father, let the heaven open, let the anointing speak, let my hidden blessings be revealed and released, in Jesus' name.

7. Forgive me, Oh Lord, where I have judged others out of ignorance and pride, in the name of Jesus.

8. Oh Lord, remove the penalty of judgment upon my life and calling, in the name of Jesus.

9. O Lord, let the heavens fight for me today, in Jesus' name.

10. Increase me, Oh Lord, so that Your name may be glorified, in the name of Jesus.

11. Any power diverting the will of God from my life, somersault and die, in Jesus' name.

12. Oh Lord, arise and let every poison in my life be arrested, in Jesus' name.

13. I write the obituary of all contrary powers attacking my glory and calling, in Jesus' name.

14. Holy Spirit, activate the will of God in my life and calling, in Jesus' name.

15. I decree the will of my enemies against me to backfire, in Jesus' name.

16. Every plot of the enemy, against me, be reversed, in Jesus' name.

17. Every confidence of my enemies, dash to pieces, in Jesus' name.

18. Every spiritual manipulation against my glory and calling shall be a failure, in Jesus' name.

19. All those who live to destroy my personality, Oh Lord, destroy their personalities, in Jesus' name.

20. Oh Lord, vindicate my position in this city (company, country, nation, etc.), in Jesus' name.

21. Oh Lord, reveal to me what You have called me to be in life (in this city, country, company), in Jesus' name.

22. Every strange god, assigned to attack my destiny, personality, glory or calling, attack your sender, in Jesus' name.

23. Ark of God, pursue every dragon assigned against me, in Jesus' name.

24. Hosts of heaven, pursue those who are raging against me, in Jesus' name.

25. Ark of God, come into my house today to locate and fight the power of the opposition against me, in the name of Jesus.

26. Ark of God, wherever I had been accepted in the past and they are now refusing me, arise and fight for me, in Jesus' name.

27. Lion of Judah, devour every opposition, raging against me now, in Jesus' name.

28. Wherever they have rejected me, let my spirit man be accepted now, in Jesus' name.

29. I resist and refuse the sale of my glory and calling, for a pair of shoes or for silver, in the name of Jesus.

30. Wine of condemnation, drunk against me, become poison to my enemies, in Jesus' name.

31. Oh Lord, let the mighty among my enemies flee away from me naked, in Jesus' name.

32. Every power of darkness, that has arrested my ministry and calling, release me now, in the name of Jesus.

33. I prophesy that I am coming out of captivity, in Jesus' name.

34. Holy Ghost, arise and promote me, in the name of Jesus.

35. Every association of demons, cooperating with workers of iniquity from my father's house, be shattered unto desolation, in Jesus' name.

36. Vehicle of my destiny, be repaired and put back on the road, in the name of Jesus.

37. Holy Ghost, arise and send me divine help, in the name of Jesus.

38. Oh Lord my God, pour blessings upon me now from Your reservoir of blessings and power, in Jesus's name.

39. Holy Ghost, arise and activate my ministry and calling, in Jesus' name.

40. All roadblocks and impediments to the fulfilment of my life and calling, be removed, in Jesus' name.

41. Thou yoke of frustration, failure and unfulfilment over my life, be destroyed by fire, in the name of Jesus.

42. Thou siege of the wicked over my life, be lifted by the hand of God, in Jesus' name.

LET GOD ARISE

There are times in the ministry of prayer, when the battle becomes very intense, and God begins to demonstrate His full strength as a man of war. Such a battle is described below.

"For every battle of the warrior is with confused noise, and garments rolled in blood; but this shall be with burning and fuel of fire." Isa 9:5

During sessions of intensive spiritual warfare, you can invoke the divine presence saying: "Let God arise and all his enemies scattered." God will surely arise at that moment and the battle becomes His. I have stated time and again that any power that tries to challenge a true child of God is set for instant burial.

When you are involved in a battle with an array of evil forces, you simply need to shout with holy anger saying: "Let God Arise!" When you pray like that, you are throwing a challenge to the Almighty and asking Him to grant you more strength in the fullness of His power.

These prayer points would always grant you victory in all your battles.

Praise Worship

Scripture Reading: Psalm 107:23-24; 42:7; 36:8; 1 Peter 3:19; Ps 142:7; Amos 2:6; Job 20:15; Ps 97:3; 118:8-10

1. Holy Ghost, arise and destroy every evil habitation in me, in Jesus' name.

2. Every satanic incantation, pronounced against me, be rendered null and void, in Jesus' name.

3. It is illegal for powers of darkness to show up where children of the living God are gathered. Therefore, I destroy all demons and association of demons in this area right now, in the mighty name of our Lord Jesus.

4. Every satanic gathering, against this gathering, scatter, in Jesus' name.

5. Every association of demons against this gathering, scatter by lightning, in Jesus' name.

6. Holy Ghost, arise in Your power and wage war against my adversaries, in Jesus' name.

7. All you crocodiles, I command you to vomit everything you have swallowed up in my life, in the name of Jesus.

8. Oh Lord, show me where the enemy has kept or buried my blessings, in the name of Jesus.

9. Holy Ghost, arise and chase away every evil dog pursuing me, in Jesus' name.

20. All flesh and demons, be silenced before God now. Speak, Oh Lord, Your servant heareth, in the name of Jesus.

Pause for 5 to 15 minutes or more to hear from God.

21. I connect to the anointing of the Ancient of Days, in Jesus' name.

22. I connect to the anointing of glory and honour, in Jesus' name.

23. I connect to the anointing of fire, in Jesus' name.

24. I connect to the anointing of multiplication, in Jesus' name.

STUBBORN PROBLEMS MUST DIE

There are certain problems that can be classified as extremely stubborn: problems that border on violent attacks from the kingdom of darkness; that are meant to terminate lives; problems meant to put people into perpetual bondage; enchantment from the kingdom of darkness and that are targeted against your destiny. Such problems must be dealt with decisively.

When a problem has proved stubborn and has remained entrenched in your life for a long time, you need to settle down and address it or face it squarely. Dealing with such a problem can be likened to uprooting a tree with firm roots. Cutting off a branch cannot give you lasting results. You need to lay the axe of prayer to the root of every wicked tree.

Many who go about with stubborn problems have not really addressed them with seriousness. You must use the weapon of aggressive prayers to address every stubborn tenant bent on making your life their permanent place of residence.

Pray until the powers behind stubborn problems bow and take their leave. The battle against them must be fought and won.

Praise Worship

Confession: Psalm 2:1-12: Why do the heathen rage, and the people imagine a vain thing? The kings of the earth set themselves, and the rulers take counsel together, against the Lord, and against his anointed, saying, Let us break their bands asunder, and cast away their cords from us. He that sitteth in the heavens shall laugh: the Lord shall have them in derision. Then shall he speak unto them in his wrath, and vex them in his sore displeasure. Yet have I set my king upon my holy hill of Zion. I will declare the decree: the Lord hath said unto me, Thou art my Son; this day have I begotten thee. Ask of me, and I shall give thee the heathen for thine inheritance, and the uttermost parts of the earth for thy possession. Thou shalt break them with a rod of iron; thou shalt dash them in pieces like a potter's vessel. Be wise now therefore, O ye kings: be instructed, ye judges of the earth. Serve the Lord with fear, and rejoice with trembling. Kiss the Son, lest he be angry, and ye perish from the way, when his wrath is kindled but a little. Blessed are all they that put their trust in him.

PRAYER POINTS

1.O wind of God, sweep away every power of the ungodly, rising against my destiny, in the name of Jesus.

2.O Lord, let the rage of the wicked against me be rendered impotent, in the name of Jesus.

3.Father Lord, let the imagination of the wicked against me be neutralized, in the name of Jesus.

4.Every counsel of evil kings against me, scatter, in the name of Jesus.

5.O God, arise and speak in great wrath against the enemy of my breakthroughs, in the name of Jesus.

6.Every chain of the wicked, that is arresting my progress, break, in the name of Jesus.

7.Every cord of darkness, militating against my breakthroughs, die, in the name of Jesus.

8.I decree that I will not be afraid of ten thousand people, that have set themselves against me, in the name of Jesus.

9.O God, smite my enemies on the cheekbones, in Jesus' name.

10.My Father, break the teeth of the ungodly, in Jesus' name.

11.O God, visit with destruction every power, lying against me, in the name of Jesus.

12.Father Lord, let my enemies fall by their own counsel, in the

name of Jesus.
13.My Father, cast out my enemies in the multitude of their transgressions, in the name of Jesus.
14.Every organised worker of iniquity, depart from me, in the name of Jesus.
15.O Lord, let all my enemies be ashamed and sore vexed, in Jesus' name.
16.O Lord, let sudden shame be the lot of all my oppressors, in Jesus' name
17.Every power, planning to tear my soul like a lion, be dismantled, in the name of Jesus.
18.My Father, let the wickedness of the wicked come to an end, O Lord, in the name of Jesus.
19.O God, prepare the instruments of death against my enemies, in the name of Jesus.
20.O God, ordain Your arrows against my persecutors, in the name of Jesus.
21.Every pit, dug by the enemy, become a grave for him, in the name of Jesus.
22.I render null and void, the effect of any interaction with satanic agents, moving around as men, in the name of Jesus.

23. I pull down the stronghold of evil strangers in every area of my life, in the name of Jesus.

24. Any negative transaction, currently affecting my life negatively, be cancelled, in the name of Jesus.

25. All the dark works, done against me in secret, be exposed and be nullified, in the name of Jesus.

26. I loose myself from any dark spirit, in the name of Jesus.

27. O Lord, let all incantations against me be cancelled, in the name of Jesus.

28. I command all oppressors to retreat and flee in defeat, in the name of Jesus.

29. I bind every strongman, having my goods in his possessions, in the name of Jesus.

30. I break, the curse of automatic failure, working upon my life, in the name of Jesus.

31. The anointing to prosper, fall mightily upon me now, in the name of Jesus.

GLORY REVIVAL

God has an agenda of greatness for you. But the problem with many people today is that those whose destinies are meant to be colourful are languishing in the dustbin and require aggressive prayers to effect resurrection of their destinies that are dead. When a particular destiny is dead, its glory becomes shame. Good prospects are rubbished and brilliant stars are hidden in darkness.

It requires serious prayer battle for lost glory to be found. You must pray fervently if the glory which God destined you to experience and enjoy must be revived.

When your glory is revived, those who once disregarded you will begin to reckon with you.

Revival of glory is an important prayer programme which must be undertaken by those who are serious about becoming who God wants them to be.

Praise Worship

Confession: Psalm 27:6: And now shall mine head be lifted up above mine enemies round about me: therefore will I offer in his tabernacle sacrifices of joy; I will sing, yea, I will sing praises unto the Lord.

Deut 28:13: And the LORD shall make thee the head, and not the tail; and thou shalt be above only, and thou shalt not be beneath; if that thou hearken unto the commandments of the LORD thy God, which I command thee this day, to observe and to do them.

Prov. 21:1: The king's heart is in the hand of the LORD, as the rivers of water: he turneth it whithersoever he will.

Prayer Points

1. Thou King of glory, arise, visit me and turn around my captivity, in the name of Jesus.
2. I shall not regret, I will become great, in the name of Jesus.
3. Every habitation of humiliation and demotion, fashioned against me, be battered, shattered and swallowed up by the power of God.
4. O Lord, station and establish me in Your favour.
5. God of restoration, restore my glory, in the name of Jesus.
6. As darkness gives up before light, O Lord, let all my problems give up before me, in the name of Jesus.
7. Thou power of God, destroy every trouble in my life, in the name of Jesus.

8. O God, arise and attack every lack in my life, in the name of Jesus.

9. Power of liberty and dignity, manifest in my life, in the name of Jesus.

10. Every chapter of sorrow and slavery in my life, be closed forever, in the name of Jesus.

11. Thou power of God, usher me out of the balcony of disgrace by fire, in the name of Jesus.

12. Every obstacle in my life, give way to miracles, in the name of Jesus.

13. Every frustration in my life, become a bridge to my miracles, in the name of Jesus.

14. Every enemy, exploring devastating strategies against my progress in life, be disgraced, in the name of Jesus.

15. Every residential permit for me to stay in the valley of defeat, be revoked, in the name of Jesus.

16. I decree that bitter life shall not be my portion. A better life shall be my testimony, in the name of Jesus.

17. Every habitation of cruelty, fashioned against my destiny, become desolate, in the name of Jesus.

18. My Father, let all my trials become gateways to my promotions, in the name of Jesus.

19. Anger of God, write the obituary of all my oppressors, in Jesus' name.

20. Almighty God, let your presence begin a glorious story in my life.

21. Every strange god, attacking my destiny, scatter and die, in the name of Jesus.

22. Every horn of satan, fighting against my destiny, scatter, in the name of Jesus.

23. Every altar, speaking hardship into my life, die, in Jesus' name.

24. Every inherited battle in my life, die, in Jesus' name.

25. All my blessings that have been buried with dead relatives, come alive now and locate me, in Jesus' name.

26. All my blessings that are presently not in this country, arise now and locate me, in the name of Jesus.

27. Every stronghold of my father's house, be dismantled, in Jesus' name.

28. Father, let all my proposals find favour in the sight of . . . in the name of Jesus. (Insert name).

29. O Lord, let me find favour, compassion and loving-kindness with . . . concerning this matter. (Insert name).

30. All demonic obstacles, that have been established in the heart of . . . against this matter, be destroyed, in Jesus' name. (Insert name).

31.	O Lord, show . . . dreams, visions and restlessness that would advance my cause. (Insert name).
32.	I command my money being caged by the enemy to be completely released, in the name of Jesus.
33.	O Lord, give me supernatural breakthroughs in all my present proposals.
34.	I bind and put to flight, all the spirits of fear, anxiety and discouragement, in the name of Jesus.
35.	O Lord, let divine wisdom fall upon all who are supporting me in these matters.
36.	I break the backbone of any spirit of conspiracy and treachery, in the name of Jesus.
37.	O Lord, hammer my matter into the mind of those who will assist me, so that they do not suffer, from demonic loss of memory.
38.	I paralyse the handiwork of household enemies and envious agents in this matter, in the name of Jesus.
39.	You devil, take your legs away from the top of my finances, in the mighty name of Jesus.
40.	Fire of the Holy Spirit, purge my life from any evil mark put upon me, in the name of Jesus.
41.	Thank the Lord for answered prayers.

COMMAND THE MORNING 1

The mystery of spiritual warfare can only be understood by those who have decided to venture into certain areas which other people hardly explore. Those who belong to the dark kingdom have invented a particular strategy for carrying out their wicked antics. They rise up in the early hours of the morning and programme into the day. By so doing, they succeed in having negative impact on the lives of their victims. Soldiers of spiritual warfare have learnt to turn the tide against their enemies by employing a more powerful weapon.

To command the morning is to take charge of the day. It is to exercise dominion and to order the elements of nature, as well as the agents of the enemy, to bow to the wish of the Almighty. By so doing, evil plans are captured.

The sentence of the enemy is rendered null and void. Those who have leant to command the morning experience first class victory. This is undoubtedly the greatest success tablet. Use it on daily basis and you will be more than a conqueror.

Start by singing songs of praises and thanksgiving to God for giving you another new day.

Confessions: Psalm 5:1-3; Psalm 2:1-12; Psalm 121:1-8; Psalm 91:1-16; Psalm 16:1-11.

1. I take authority over this day, in the name of Jesus.

2. I draw upon heavenly resources today, in the name of Jesus.

3. I confess that this is the day the Lord has made, I will rejoice and be glad in it, in the name of Jesus.

4. I decree that all the elements of this day will cooperate with me, in Jesus' name.

5. I decree that these elemental forces will refuse to cooperate with my enemies this day, in Jesus' name.

6. I speak unto you the sun, the moon and the stars, you will not smite me and my family this day, in Jesus' name.

7. I pull down every negative energy, planning to operate against my life this day, in Jesus' name.

8. I dismantle any power that is chanting incantations to capture this day, in the name of Jesus.

9. I render null and void, such incantations and satanic prayers over me and my family, in the name of Jesus.

10. I retrieve this day from their hands, in the name of Jesus.

11. Every battle in the heavenlies, be won by angels conveying my blessings today, in Jesus' name.

12. My Father, let everything You have not planted in the heavenlies be uprooted, in Jesus' name.

13. O Lord, let the wicked be shaken out of my heavens, in the name of Jesus

14. O sun, as you are coming out today, uproot every wickedness targeted at my life, in the name of Jesus.

15. I programme blessings into the sun for my life, in the name of Jesus.

16. O sun, I have risen before you, cancel every evil programme projected into you against me by wicked powers, in the name of Jesus.

17. You this day, you will not destroy my prosperity, in the name of Jesus.

18. O sun, moon and stars, carry your afflictions back to the sender and release them against him, in Jesus' name.

19. O God, arise and uproot everything You have not planted in the heavenlies that is working against me, in Jesus' name.

20. O Lord, let the wicked be shaken out of the ends of the earth, in the name of Jesus.

21. O sun, as you come forth, uproot all the wickedness that has come against my life, in the name of Jesus.

22. I programme blessings into the sun, the moon and the stars for my life today, in the name of Jesus.

23. O sun, cancel every daily evil programme drawn up against me, in the name of Jesus.

24. O sun, torment every enemy of the kingdom of God in my life, in the name of Jesus.

25. O sun, throw away those who spend the night pulling me down, in the name of Jesus.

26. O elements, you shall not hurt me, in Jesus' name.

27. O heavenlies, you shall not steal from my life today, in the name of Jesus.

28. I establish the power of God over the heavenlies, in the name of Jesus.

29. O sun, moon and stars, fight against the stronghold of witchcraft targeted at me today, in Jesus' name.

30. O heavenlies, torment every unrepentant enemy to submission, in Jesus' name.

31. O heavens, fight against the stronghold of witchcraft, in the name of Jesus.

32. Every wicked altar in the heavenlies, I pull you down, in the name of Jesus.

33. Every caldron in the stars, the moon and the sun, break, in the name of Jesus.

34. Every evil pattern in the heavenlies, break, in the name of Jesus.

35. O God, arise and destroy every astral altar, in Jesus' name.

36. I destroy every satanic connection between the heavenlies and my place of birth, in Jesus' name.

37. Every spiritual wickedness in the heavenlies that will reinforce against me and my destiny today, be disgraced by the blood of Jesus.

38. Thus saith the Lord: "Let no principality, power, ruler of darkness, spiritual wickedness in the heavenlies and local wickedness, trouble me, for I bear in my body, the marks of the Lamb of God," in the name of Jesus.

39. Every dark power, hidden in the heavenlies against me, I pull you down, in the name of Jesus.

40. Any evil power, floating or hanging in the heavenlies against me, I bring you down, in the name of Jesus.

COMMAND THE MORNING 2

The mystery of spiritual warfare can only be understood by those who have decided to venture into certain areas which other people hardly explore. Those who belong to the dark kingdom have invented a particular strategy for carrying out their wicked antics. They rise up in the early hours of the morning and program into the day. By so doing, they succeed in having negative impact on the lives of their victims. Soldiers of spiritual warfare have learnt to turn the tide against their enemies by employing a more powerful weapon.

To command the morning is to take charge of the day. It is to exercise dominion and to order the elements of nature, as well as the agents of the enemy, to bow to the wish of the Almighty. By so doing, evil plans are captured.

The sentence of the enemy is rendered null and void. Those who have learnt to command the morning experience first class victory. This is undoubtedly the greatest *success tablet. Use it on daily basis and you will be more than a conqueror.*

Start by singing songs of praises and thanksgiving to God, for giving you another new day.

Confessions: Psalm 5:1-3; Psalm 2:1-12; Psalm 121:1-8; Psalm 91:1-16; Psalm 16:1-11.

1. I take authority over this day, in the name of Jesus.
2. I draw upon heavenly resources today, in the name of Jesus.
3. I confess that this is the day the Lord has made; I will rejoice and be glad in it, in the name of Jesus.
4. I decree that all the elements of this day will cooperate with me, in Jesus' name.
5. I decree that these elemental forces will refuse to cooperate with my enemies this day, in Jesus' name.
6. I speak unto you the sun, the moon and the stars: you will not smite me and my family this day, in Jesus' name.
7. I pull down every negative energy, planning to operate against my life this day, in Jesus' name.
8. I dismantle any power that is chanting incantations to capture this day, in the name of Jesus.
9. I render such incantations and satanic prayers over me and my family null and void, in the name of Jesus.

10. I retrieve this day from their hands, in the name of Jesus.

11. Spirit of favour, counsel, might and power, come upon me, in Jesus' name.

12. I shall excel this day and nothing shall defile me, in the name of Jesus.

13. I shall possess the gates of my enemies, in the name of Jesus.

14. The Lord shall anoint me with the oil of gladness above others, in the name of Jesus.

15. The fire of the enemy shall not burn me, in the name of Jesus.

16. My ears shall hear good news; I shall not hear the voice of the enemy, in the name of Jesus.

17. My future is secured in Christ, in the name of Jesus.

18. God has created me to do certain definite services. He has committed into my hands some assignments which He has not committed to anybody else. He has not created me for nothing. I shall do good. I shall do His work. I shall be an agent of peace. I will trust Him in whatever I do and wherever I am. I can never be thrown away or downgraded, in the name of Jesus.

19. There will be no poverty of body, soul and spirit in my life, in the name of Jesus.

20. The anointing of God upon my life gives me favour in the eyes of God and men, all the days of my life, in Jesus' name.

21. I shall not labour in vain, in the name of Jesus.

22. I shall walk in victory and liberty of the spirit everyday, in the name of Jesus.

23. I receive the mouth and the wisdom, which my adversaries are not able to resist, in Jesus' name.

24. Every battle in the heavenlies, be won in favour of the angels conveying my blessings today, in Jesus' name.

25. My Father, everything which You have not planted in the heavenlies, let it be uprooted, in Jesus' name.

26. O Lord, let the wicked be shaken out of my heavens, in the name of Jesus

27. O sun, as you are coming out today, uproot every wickedness targeted at my life, in the name of Jesus.

28. I programme blessings into the sun for my life, in the name of Jesus.

29. O sun, I have risen before you, cancel every evil programme, projected into you against my life by wicked powers, in the name of Jesus.

30. You this day, you will not destroy my prosperity, in the name of Jesus.

31. O sun, moon and stars, carry your afflictions back to the sender and release them against him, in Jesus' name.

32. O God, arise and uproot everything You have not planted in the heavenlies, that is working against me, in Jesus' name.

33. Oh Lord, let the wicked be shaken out from the ends of the earth, in the name of Jesus.

34. O sun, as you come forth, uproot all the wickedness that has come against my life, in the name of Jesus.

35. I programme blessings into the sun, the moon and the stars for my life today, in the name of Jesus.

36. O sun, cancel daily evil programme, drawn up against me, in the name of Jesus.

37. O sun, torment every enemy of the kingdom of God in my life, in the name of Jesus.

38. Those who spend the night pulling me down, o sun, throw them away, in the name of Jesus.

39. O elements, you shall not hurt me, in Jesus' name.

40. O heavenlies, you shall not steal from my life today, in the name of Jesus.

41. I establish, the power of God over the heavenlies, in the name of Jesus.

42. O sun, moon and stars, fight against the stronghold of witchcraft, targeted at me today, in Jesus' name.

43. O heavenlies, torment every unrepentant enemy to submission, in Jesus' name.

44. O heavens, fight against the stronghold of witchcraft, in Jesus' name.

45. Every wicked altar in the heavenlies, I throw you down, in Jesus' name.

46. Every cauldron in the stars, the moon and the sun, break, in Jesus' name.

47. Every evil pattern in the heavenlies, break, in the name of Jesus.

48. O God, arise and destroy every astral altar, in Jesus' name.

49. I destroy every satanic connection between the heavenlies and my place of birth, in Jesus' name.

50. Every spiritual wickedness in the heavenlies, that will reinforce against me and my destiny today, be disgraced by the blood of Jesus.

51. Thus saith the Lord: "Let no principality, power, ruler of darkness, spiritual wickedness in the heavenlies and local wickedness trouble me, for I bear in my body the marks of the Lamb of God," in Jesus' name.

52. Every dark power, hidden in the heavenlies against me, I pull you down, in the name of Jesus.

53. Any evil power, floating or hanging in the heavenlies against me, I bring you down, in the name of Jesus.

OVERTHROWING THE WALL OF JERICHO 1

There are times in life when the barrier between you and your breakthroughs appears as the impregnable walls of Jericho.

Jericho is a symbol of barrier put up by the devil. It is the plan of the devil to make you view your miracles afar off, but incapacitates you by surrounding your miracles with the walls of Jericho. Jericho walls represent the totality of the might of the enemy. When he wants to do his worst, he erects the walls of Jericho. It is one way of challenging the power of God.

In the Old Testament, the walls of Jericho amounted to a statement of defiance by the enemy. The walls of Jericho were so strong and fortified that the enemies of the children of Israel could go on boasting.

According to ancient history, the walls of Jericho were so massive that a vehicle could ply on them. The walls were so huge that penetrating Jericho was impossible. The picture painted by Jericho walls is that of a strong barricade. When the enemy succeeds in erecting wicked walls around you, he begins to boast, feeling that he has done everything necessary to hinder or prevent you from receiving and enjoying your breakthroughs.

The walls of Jericho cannot allow you to fulfil your destiny in life. As long as they stand, your dreams may remain shattered, your hopes may remain dashed and your prospects may remain a far cry from what you want to experience.

Allow God to intervene in your situation today. Enough is enough. Do not tolerate satanic walls in your life. Let the bulldozer of the Holy Ghost crush all Jericho walls.

Ask God to turn your tragedies to triumph, your tears to testimonies, sorrow to joy, problems to promotions and inadequacies to uncommon strength. The same God who made Jericho walls to fall down will arise in your life and the existence of Jericho walls will become a thing of the past.

God is set to do something unique in your life and when He arises as a man of war, no Jericho wall will remain intact. Remember the following Scripture:

And the God of peace shall bruise Satan under your feet shortly. The grace of our Lord Jesus Christ be with you.
Amen. Rom 16:20

Start by singing songs of praises and thanksgiving to God for giving you another new day.

Confessions: Jer. 20:11

1. Lord, I pray that . . . will not find peace until he returns in repentance to his/her Creator.

2. I command the ways of all unfriendly friends confusing . . . to become dark and slippery, in the name of Jesus.

3. Angels of God, arise and block the path of . . . with thorns after the order of Balaam until . . . runs back to the Saviour, in the name of Jesus.

4. O Lord, let all strange lovers begin to avoid . . . as from today, in the name of Jesus.

5. Lord, ordain terrifying noises against all evil collaborators confusing . . .

6. O Lord, build a wall of hindrance around . . . so that he will be unable to carry out any ungodly activity.

7. O Lord, let all the good things that . . . is enjoying that is hardening his heart to the truth be withdrawn, in Jesus' name.

8. Let . . . become sick and restless on tasting any alcohol or using any addictive substance, in the name of Jesus.

9. I break every curse of the vagabond upon the life of . . ., in the mighty name of Jesus.

10. Angels of the living God, begin to pursue all strange lovers caging . . ., in Jesus' name.

11. O Lord, walk back to the foundation of my marriage and carry out the necessary surgical operation.

12. I bind every strongman, militating against my home, in Jesus' name.

13. Every gadget of marriage destruction in my home, be frustrated, in Jesus' name.

14. Every evil anti-marriage link with our parents, break, in Jesus' name

15. Every evil effect of external interference in our marriage, be completely neutralized, in the name of Jesus.

16. I paralyse every architect of conflict and hostility in my home, in the name of Jesus.

17. Every evil power, trying to re-draw my marriage map, be put to shame, in Jesus' name.

18. All extra-marital relationships with other "partners," collapse and die, in the name of Jesus.

19. I paralyse the activities of the following spirits (*listed hereunder*) and I command them to loose their hold upon... in the name of Jesus.

- Criticism   - Unreasonableness
- Accusation   - Argument
- Intimidation - Rejecting truth
- Pride   - Self-importance
- Self-centredness
- Self-exaltation - Selfishness
- Stubbornness - Superiority
- Intolerance - Cruelty
- Retaliation - Impatience
- Bitterness   - Anger
- Hatred   - Fighting
- Contention   - Violence
- Rebellion   - Deception
- Restlessness - Withdrawal

- Confusion
- Family molestation
- Lust of the eyes
- Lust of the flesh
- Dishonesty   - Disrespect
- Personality disorder
- Cursing   - Lying
- Inherited curses
- Occult practices

20. All powers, encamping against my goodness and breakthroughs, become confused and scatter, in the name of Jesus.

21. All powers of my adversaries, be rendered impotent , in the name of Jesus.

22. Every evil tongue, uttering curses and other evil things against my life, be completely silenced, in the name of Jesus.

23. I command every evil stronghold and power, housing my rights and goodness to be violently overthrown, in the name of Jesus.

24. I pursue, overtake and recover my properties from the hands of spiritual robbers, in the name of Jesus.

25. Every counsel, plan, desire, expectation, imagination, device and activity of the oppressors against my life, be rendered null and void, in the name of Jesus.

26. I terminate every contract and cancel every evil promissory note, kept in satanic files for my sake, in the name of Jesus.

27. I release myself from the powers and activities of the wasters, in the name of Jesus.

28. I refuse to be tossed around by any evil remote control device fashioned to delay my miracle, in Jesus' name.

29. All the citadels of summons to my spirit, receive the fire of God and burn to ashes, in the name of Jesus.

30. Holy Spirit, teach me to avoid unfriendly foods, and unprofitable discussions, in the name of Jesus.

31. All my goodness, presently in the prison of the enemy, begin to pursue me and overtake me from today, in Jesus' name.

32. All strange fires, prepared against my life, be quenched, in the name of Jesus.

33. Every tongue, issuing destruction against me, be condemned, in Jesus' name.

34. All the troublers of my Israel, be disbanded and be confused, in Jesus' name.

35. Blood of Jesus, wipe off all unprofitable marks in any department of my life, in the name of Jesus.

36. All strange hands that have touched my blood, catch fire, in the name of Jesus.

37. You the spirit that prevents blessings, be bound, in the name of Jesus.

38. I receive victory over the host of wickedness surrounding me, in the name of Jesus.

39. I stand against dream defeats and their effects, in the name of Jesus.

40. Every spirit, attacking me in the form of animals, receive the fire of God, in Jesus' name.

41. I stand against the operations of the spirit of death in my life, in the name of Jesus.

42. Every counsel of the devil against me, be destroyed and be frustrated, in Jesus' name.

43. I bind the spirit of doubt, unbelief, fear and tradition, in the name of Jesus.

44. Father, destroy every stronghold of the powers of darkness in my family, in the name of Jesus.

45. Every problem, affecting my brain, be neutralized, in the name of Jesus.

46. Every effect of ritual killings by my ancestors upon my life, be neutralized, in Jesus' name.

47. All terminal, genetic and ancestral sicknesses, be healed, in the name of Jesus.

48. O Lord, give me the power to pursue and overtake the enemy, and to recover my stolen property, in the name of Jesus.

49. O God, let Your fire destroy every foundational problem in my life, in Jesus' name.

50. Every link, label and stamp of the oppressors, be destroyed, by the blood of Jesus.

51. Every evil spiritual pregnancy in my life, be aborted, in the name of Jesus.

52. Every dirty hand, be removed from the affairs of my life, in the name of Jesus.

53. Every effect of evil access to my blood, be reversed now, in the name of Jesus.

54. Everything done against me, under the devil's anointing, be neutralized now, in Jesus' name.

55. All evil vessels, dispatched to do me harm, crash, in the name of Jesus.

56. Satanic banks, release my property in your hand, in Jesus' name.

57. I remove my name from the book of untimely death, in the name of Jesus.

58. I remove my name from the book of tragedy, in Jesus' name.

59. All evil umbrellas, preventing heavenly showers from falling upon me, roast, in Jesus' name.

60. All evil associations, summoned for my sake, scatter, in Jesus' name.

61. Every problem, connected to polygamy in my life, be nullified, in Jesus' name.

62. Every satanic reinforcement against me, scatter, in the name of Jesus.

63. I cancel all evil vows, affecting me negatively, in Jesus' name.

64. I destroy the clock and the time-table of the enemy for my life, in the name of Jesus.

65. O Lord, reschedule my enemies to useless and harmless assignments, in Jesus' name.

66. Every evil device against me, fail, in Jesus' name.

67. Healing power of the Holy Spirit, overshadow me, in the name of Jesus.

68. I bind every spirit, working against answers to my prayers, in Jesus' name.

69. I disarm any power, that has made a covenant with the ground, water and wind against me, in Jesus' name.

70. O Lord, make my life invisible to demonic observers.

71. I bind all evil remote control spirits, in the name of Jesus.

72. I withdraw all the bullets and ammunition made available to the enemy, in Jesus' name.

73. I revoke any conscious or unconscious covenant with the spirit of death, in Jesus' name.

74. In the name of Jesus, I call on the heavenly surgeon to perform surgical operations where necessary in my life.

75. I refuse to be spiritually amputated, in Jesus' name.

76. I refuse to wage war against myself, in the name of Jesus.

77. O Lord, wake me up from any form of spiritual sleep.

78. All evil seeds, planted by fear into my life, be uprooted, in Jesus' name.

79. Father of our Lord Jesus Christ, let Your kingdom be established in every area of my life, in the name of Jesus.

80. I cancel all former negotiations with the devil, in Jesus' name.

81. All my buried goodness and prosperity, receive divine resurrection, in Jesus' name.

82. I refuse to turn back at the edge of victory, in the name of Jesus.

83. Father, pour out shame on all the powers struggling to put me to shame, in Jesus' name.

84. All drinkers of blood and eaters of flesh, turn against yourselves, in Jesus' name.

85. Spiritual problems, attached to the months of: January, February, March, April, May, June, July, August, September, October, November and December, be nullified, in Jesus' name

86. O Lord, deliver me from coldness of the heart and weakness of will.

87. O Lord, let my life shine forth the light of goodness and love.

88. O Lord, let my will be lost in Your will.

OVERTHROWING THE WALL OF JERICHO 2

There are times in life when the barrier between you and your breakthroughs appears as stubborn as the impregnable walls of Jericho.

Jericho is a symbol of barrier put up by the devil. It is the plan of the devil to make you view your miracles afar off, but incapacitates you by surrounding them with the walls of Jericho. Jericho walls represent the totality of the might of the enemy. When the devil wants to do his worst, he erects the walls of Jericho. It is one way of challenging the power of God.

In the Old Testament, the walls of Jericho amounted to a statement of defiance by the enemy. The walls of Jericho were so strong and fortified, that the enemies of the children of Israel could go on boasting.

According to ancient history, the walls of Jericho were so massive that a vehicle could ply on them. The walls were so huge that penetrating Jericho was impossible. The picture painted by Jericho walls is that of a strong barricade. When the enemy succeeds in erecting wicked walls, he begins to boast, feeling that he has done everything necessary to hinder or prevent you from receiving and enjoying your breakthroughs.

The walls of Jericho cannot allow you to fulfil your destiny in life. As long as Jericho walls stand, your dreams may remain shattered, your hopes may remain dashed, your prospects may remain a far cry from what you want to experience.

Allow God to intervene in your situation today. Enough is enough. Do not tolerate satanic walls in your life; let the bulldozer of the Holy Ghost crush all Jericho walls.

Ask God to turn your tragedies to triumph, your tears to testimonies, sorrow to joy, problems to promotions and your inadequacies to uncommon strength. The same God who made Jericho walls to fall down will arise in your life and the existence of Jericho walls will become a thing of the past.

God is set to do something unique in your life and when He arises as a man of war, no Jericho wall will remain intact. Remember:

And the God of peace shall bruise Satan under your feet shortly. The grace of our Lord Jesus Christ be with you. Amen.

Rom 16:20

Confessions: Jer. 20:11 Ezek. 33:11

1. Lord, I pray that . . . will not find peace until he returns in repentance to his/her Creator.

2. I command the ways of all unfriendly friends confusing . . . to become dark and slippery, in the name of Jesus.

3. Angels of God, arise and block the path of . . . with thorns after the order of Balaam until . . . runs back to the Saviour, in Jesus' name.

4. O Lord, let all strange lovers begin to avoid . . . as from today, in the name of Jesus.

5. Lord, ordain terrifying noises against all evil collaborators confusing . . .

6. O Lord, build a wall of hindrance around . . . so that he will be unable to carry out any ungodly activity.

7. O Lord, let all the good things that . . . is enjoying that is hardening his heart to the truth be withdrawn, in Jesus' name.

8. Let . . . become sick and restless on tasting any alcohol or using any addictive substance, in the name of Jesus.

9. I break every curse of the vagabond upon the life of . . ., in the mighty name of Jesus.

10. Angels of the living God, begin to pursue all strange lovers caging . . . in the name of Jesus.

11. O Lord, walk back to the foundation of my marriage and carry out the necessary surgical operation.

12. I bind every strongman, militating against my home, in the name of Jesus.

13. Every gadget of marriage destruction in my home, be frustrated, in the name of Jesus.

14. Let every evil anti-marriage link with our parents break into pieces, in the name of Jesus.

15. Every evil effect of external interferences in our marriage, be completely neutralized, in the name of Jesus.

16. I paralyse every architect of conflict and hostility in my home, in the name of Jesus.

17. Every evil power, trying to re- draw my marriage map, be put to shame, in the name of Jesus.

18. All extra-marital relationships with other "partners," collapse and die, in the name of Jesus.

19. I paralyse the activities of the following spirits (*listed hereunder*) and I command them to loose their hold upon . . ., in the name of Jesus.

- Criticism	- Unreasonableness	- Accusation
- Argument	- Intimidation	- Rejecting truth
- Pride	- Self-importance	- Self-centredness
- Self-exaltation	- Selfishness	- Stubbornness
- Superiority	- Intolerance	- Cruelty

- Retaliation   - Impatience   - Bitterness

- Anger   - Hatred   - Fighting

- Contention   - Violence   - Rebellion

- Deception   - Restlessness   - Withdrawal

- Confusion   - Family molestation - Lust of the eyes

- Lust of the flesh-Dishonesty   - Disrespect

- Personality disorders   - Cursing

- Lying   - Inherited curses - Occult practices

20. Father, in the name of Jesus, give unto .   . ., the spirits of wisdom and revelation in the knowledge of You.

21. Every stronghold of the enemy, barricading the mind of .   . ., from receiving the Lord, be pulled down, in the name of Jesus.

22. All hindrances, coming between the heart of .   . . and the gospel, melt away by the fire of the Holy Spirit.

23. In Jesus' name, I bind the strongman, attached to the life of .   ., keeping him from receiving Jesus Christ as his Lord and Saviour.

24. Lord, build a hedge of thorns around .   . ., so that he turns to You.

25. In the name of Jesus, I break the curse placed on .   . ., binding him from receiving the Lord.

26. You spirit of death and hell, release .   . ., in the name of Jesus.

27. Every desire of the enemy on the soul of . . ., refuse to prosper, in the name of Jesus.

28. I bind every spirit of mind blindness, in the life of . . ., die, in the name of Jesus.

29. Spirit of bondage, lukewarmness and perdition, release . . ., in the name of Jesus.

30. I bind the strongman, shielding . . ., from receiving the gospel, in the name of Jesus.

31. Father, let spiritual blindness be erased from the life of . . ., in the name of Jesus.

32. I come against the powers of darkness, blinding and holding . . ., back from receiving the gospel, in Jesus' name.

33. You spirit of the power of the air, loose your hold on . . . so that he will be free to accept Jesus as his/her Lord and Saviour, in the name of Jesus.

34. I tear down and smash every stronghold of deception, keeping . . ., in the enemy's camp, in Jesus' name.

35. O Lord, let . . . come out from the kingdom of darkness, into the kingdom of light, in the name of Jesus.

36. Lord, let Your plan and purpose for the life of . . . prevail.

37. Let every evil imagination against me wither from the source, in the name of Jesus.

38. I decree that those laughing me to scorn shall witness my testimony, in the name of Jesus.

39. Father, let my point of ridicul, be converted to a source of miracle, in the name of Jesus.

40. All powers, sponsoring evil decisions against me, be disgraced, in the name of Jesus.

41. You stronghold of the spirit of Korah, Dathan and Abiram, militating against me, shatter into pieces , in the name of Jesus.

42. Every spirit of Balaam, hired to curse me, fall after the order of Balaam, in the name of Jesus.

43. Every spirit of Sanballat and Tobiah, planning evil against me, receive the stones of fire, in Jesus' name.

44. Every spirit of Egypt, fall after the order of Pharaoh, in the name of Jesus.

45. Every spirit of Herod, be disgraced, in the name of Jesus.

46. Every spirit of Goliath, receive the stones of fire, in the name of Jesus.

47. Every spirit of Pharaoh, fall into your Red Sea and perish, in the name of Jesus.

48. All satanic manipulations, aimed at changing my destiny, be frustrated, in the name of Jesus.

49. All unprofitable broadcasters of my goodness, be silenced, in the name of Jesus.

50. All leaking bags and pockets, be sealed up, in Jesus' name.

51. All evil monitoring eyes, fashioned against me, receive blindness, in the name of Jesus.

52. All demonic reverse gears, installed to hinder my progress, roast, in the name of Jesus.

53. All evil advice given against my favour, crash and disintegrate, in the name of Jesus.

54. You devourers, vanish from my labour, in the name of Jesus.

55. I loose myself from every satanic bondage, in the name of Jesus.

56. I cancel the power of all curses upon my head, in Jesus' name.

57. Every spiritual contamination in my life, receive cleansing by the blood of Jesus.

58. You brush of the Lord, scrub out every dirt in my spiritual pipe, in the name of Jesus.

59. Every rusted spiritual pipe in my life, receive wholeness, in the name of Jesus.

60. Every power, eating up my spiritual pipe, roast, in the name of Jesus.

61. Every blockage in my spiritual pipe, be removed, in the name of Jesus.

62. Every hole in my spiritual pipe, be closed, in the name of Jesus.

63. O Lord, ignite my calling with Your fire.

64. I receive heavenly flushing in my spiritual pipe, in Jesus' name.

65. Every evil spiritual padlock and evil chain, hindering my spiritual growth, roast, in the name of Jesus.

66. I rebuke every spirit of deafness and blindness in my life, in the name of Jesus.

67. I bind the strongman that is behind my spiritual blindness and deafness; and, I paralyse his operations in my life, in the name of Jesus.

68. I anoint my eyes and my ears with the blood of Jesus.

69. O Lord, restore my spiritual eyes and ears, in the name of Jesus.

70. O Lord, anoint my eyes and my ears, that they may see and hear wondrous things from heaven.

71. I send the fire of God to my eyes and ears to melt away satanic deposits, in the name of Jesus.

72. In the name of Jesus, I capture every power behind my spiritual blindness and deafness.

73. My spiritual sight and eardrum, receive healing, in Jesus' name.

74. I decree that I will not loose my calling, in the name of Jesus.

75. You the enemies of the gospel in my life, be paralysed, in the name of Jesus.

76. I reject every spiritual pollution, in the name of Jesus.

77. O Lord, put the gift that will elevate my calling into my hand, in

the name of Jesus.

78. O Lord, let the anointing of the Holy Spirit break every yoke of backwardness in my life, in Jesus' name.

79. I reject the spirit of the tail, I choose the spirit of the head, in the name of Jesus.

80. I reject any demonic limitation to my progress, in Jesus' name.

81. Lord, give unto me the key to good success, so that anywhere I go, the doors of good success will open unto me.

82. O Lord, let the anointing to excel in my spiritual and physical life fall on me, in the name of Jesus.

83. I reject the anointing of non-achievement in my handiwork, in Jesus' name.

84. All those circulating my name for evil, be disgraced, in the name of Jesus.

85. All evil friends, make mistakes that would expose you, in the name of Jesus.

86. I refuse to wear the garment of tribulation and sorrow, in the name of Jesus.

87. O Lord, let the spirit that flees from sin incubate my life.

88. O Lord, produce in me the power of self-control and gentleness.

89. By the blood of Jesus, I loose . . . from the bondage that the powers of darkness are putting on him / her.

90. By the blood of Jesus, I cancel and render null and void, all commands issued by the powers of darkness, in . . .'s life.

91. I bind the god of this age and I declare that he can no longer bind . . . in darkness, in the name of Jesus.

92. Father Lord, let Your power draw . . . out of every trap, in the name of Jesus.

93. O Lord, let the powers of darkness that seek after . . ., be confounded and be put to shame, in the name of Jesus.

94. Father Lord, grant . . . open eyes and ears, understanding heart and grace, to be converted and healed, in the name of Jesus.

95. Lord, bring all of . . .'s thoughts captive to the obedience of Christ.

96. O Lord, Let the hedge of thorns be built around . . . and let it repel all the workers of darkness in his / her life, in Jesus' name.

97. O Lord, grant . . . conviction of sin with godly sorrow to repentance.

98. Thank God for answers to your prayer.

BAPTISM OF FIRE 1

One of the greatest weapons for crushing oppression is to be baptized with the fire of the Holy Ghost.

Generally, oppression will thrive where there is no fire. The devil and his agents will perpetrate all kinds of wicked acts when they find the atmosphere comfortable. You cannot say no to oppression until you have fire in your life. When you become baptized in the fire of the Holy Ghost, your life will become too hot for the enemy to handle. If you have noticed symbols of oppression, intimidation, manipulation and wickedness, it is an indication of the fact that your fire has been extinguished. Rather than box shadows, you need to go back to the presence of God and receive fresh fire. The baptism of fire is a symbol of the overflowing presence of the Holy Spirit in your life.

The moment you are endued with fire from on high, you will become master over circumstances and forces of darkness. This prayer programme will restore your lost

glory and make you to declare that there is something in your life that can repel the enemy.

Praise Worship

Scriptures: John 12:24; 2Cor. 6; 1Cor. 9:16; Deut. 28:13; Rom. 8:35-39

1. Thank God for the privilege of your calling.

2. Thank the Lord for the power of the Holy Spirit.

3. Make confession of sins and repent.

4. Father, let the Holy Spirit fill me afresh.

5. Father, let every unbroken area in my life be broken, in the name of Jesus.

6. Father, incubate me with the fire of the Holy Spirit, in Jesus' name.

7. Every anti-power bondage in my life, break, in Jesus' name.

8. O Lord, let all strangers flee from my spirit and let the Holy Spirit take control, in the name of Jesus.

9. O Lord, catapult my spiritual life to the mountaintop.

10. Father, let heavens open and let the glory of God fall upon me, in the name of Jesus.

11. Father, let signs and wonders be my lot, in the name of Jesus.

12. Every joy of the oppressors upon my life, be turned into sorrow, in the name of Jesus.

13. All multiple strongmen, operating against me, be paralyzed, in the name of Jesus.

14. O Lord, open my eyes and ears to receive wondrous things from You.

15. O Lord, grant me victory over temptations and satanic devices.

16. O Lord, ignite my spiritual life so that I will stop fishing in unprofitable waters.

17. O Lord, release Your tongue of fire upon my life and burn away all spiritual filthiness present within me.

18. Father, make me to hunger and thirst for righteousness, in the name of Jesus.

19. Lord, help me to be ready to do your work without expecting any recognition from others.

20. O Lord, give me victory, over emphasizing the weaknesses and sins of other people, while ignoring my own.

21. O Lord, give me depth and root in my faith.

22. O Lord, heal every area of backsliding in my spiritual life.

23. Lord, help me to be willing to serve others, rather than wanting to exercise authority.

24. O Lord, open my understanding concerning the scriptures.

25. O Lord, help me to live each day, recognizing that the day will come when You will judge secret lives and innermost thoughts.

26. O Lord, let me be willing to be the clay in Your hands, ready to be moulded as You desire.

27. O Lord, wake me up from any form of spiritual sleep and help me to put on the armour of light.

28. O Lord, give me victory over all carnality and help me to be at the centre of Your will.

29. I stand against anything in my life that will cause others to stumble, in the name of Jesus.

30. O Lord, help me to put away childish things and put on maturity.

31. O Lord, empower me to stand firm against all the schemes and techniques of the devil.

32. O Lord, give me a big appetite for the pure milk and solid food in Your word.

32. O Lord, empower me to stay away from anything or anybody, who might take God's place in my heart.

33. O Lord, I thank You for the testimonies that will follow.

33. I declare that I am called of God; no evil power shall cut me down, in the name of Jesus.

34. O Lord, give me the power to be faithful to my calling, in the name of Jesus.

35. I receive the anointing to remain steady, committed and consistent in my ministerial life, in Jesus' name.

36. I declare that I shall not be lured into politics, church rivalry or rebellion, in the name of Jesus.

37. O Lord, give me the wisdom to respect my teachers and seniors who have trained me, in the name of Jesus.

38. O Lord, give me the heart of a servant, so that I can experience Your blessings everyday, in the name of Jesus.

39. I receive power

to rise with wings as eagles, in the name of Jesus.

40. I decree that the enemy will not waste my calling, in the name of Jesus.

41. By the power of the living God, the devil will not swallow my ministerial destiny, in Jesus' name.

42. Power for effective development in my calling, come upon me now, in the name of Jesus.

43. I declare war against spiritual ignorance, in the name of Jesus.

44. I bind and cast out every unteachable spirit, in the name of Jesus.

45. I receive the anointing for success in my ministry, in the name of Jesus.

46. I shall not be an enemy of integrity, in Jesus' name.

47. I shall not steal God's money, in the name of Jesus.

48. I shall not disgrace the call of God upon my life, in Jesus' name

49. I shall walk in holiness everyday, in Jesus' name.

50. I bind the spirit of sexual immorality, in Jesus' name

51. I receive the culture of loyalty in my ministry, in the name of Jesus.

52. I shall not become an old king that is resistant to advice, in the name of Jesus.

53. I shall not live a wasteful and extravagant life, in the name of Jesus.

54. I shall not serve my wonderful Saviour for

filthy financial gain, in the name of Jesus.

55. I prevent every spirit of quarrel and opposition from my wife/husband, in the name of Jesus.

56. M y wife/husband, shall not scatter my church members, in the name of Jesus.

57. Every Judas in my ministry, fall into your own trap, in the name of Jesus.

58. My ministry will not destroy my marriage, in the name of Jesus.

59. My marriage will not destroy my ministry, in the name of Jesus.

60. My children will not become misfired arrows in my ministry, in the name of Jesus.

61. I claim progress and excellence for my ministry, in the name of Jesus.

62. My church shall experience prosperity, in the name of Jesus.

63. O Lord, let my ministry reach the unreached, in the name of Jesus.

64. A multitude of people will go to heaven because of my ministry, in the name of Jesus.

65. I kill every attack on my ministry. I shall prevail, in the name of Jesus.

66. I shall not bite the fingers that fed me, in Jesus' name.

67. I shall not engage in rebellion, in the name of Jesus.

68. Every power of my father's house, working against my calling, die, in the name of Jesus.

69. Anointing for excellence, fall

upon me, in the name of Jesus.

70. O Lord, break me and re-mould me, in Jesus' name.

71. I will not surrender to the enemy, in the name of Jesus.

72. I shall not die before my time, in the name of Jesus.

73. I shall not covet the prosperity of Naaman, in the name of Jesus.

74. Let God arise and let every enemy of my calling scatter, in Jesus' name.

75. I receive fresh fire and fresh anointing, in the name of Jesus.

BAPTISM OF FIRE 2

The fire of the Holy Ghost is the antidote for rescuing a perpetual candidate of satanic attack. This programme is for those who have laboured under negative anointing at one time or the other. When you are baptized by the fire of the Holy Ghost, its presence will consume and expel every form of negative anointing in your life.

Baptism by fire will exert a sanitizing influence upon your life. One simple way of carrying out thorough internal environmental sanitation is to seek baptism by fire if you have never experienced it. If you have sensed in any way that your fire level is low, you need a refreshing experience of fresh baptism in the Holy Ghost. You need to seek God's face for baptism by fire. This prayer programme will thoroughly eliminate every stranger hibernating in your life.

Scriptures for meditation: 2 Chro. 6; 7:1-6.

Confession: Jer. 20:9.

Prayer points

1. Thank God for the purifying power of the fire of the Holy Ghost.

2. I cover myself with the blood of the Lord Jesus.

3. Father, let Your fire that burns every deposit of the enemy fall upon me, in the name of Jesus.

4. Holy Ghost fire, incubate me, in the name of the Lord Jesus Christ.

5. I reject any evil stamp or seal, placed upon me by ancestral spirits, in the name of Jesus.

6. I release myself from every negative anointing, in the name of Jesus.

7. Every door of spiritual leakage, close, in the name of Jesus.

8. I challenge every organ of my body with the fire of the Holy Spirit (methodically lay your right hand on various parts of your body beginning from the head), in the name of Jesus.

9. Every human spirit, attacking my spirit, release me, in the name of Jesus.

10. I reject every spirit of the tail, in the name of Jesus.

11. Sing the song: "Holy Ghost, fire, fire fall on me."

12. All evil marks on my body, be burnt off by the fire of the Holy Spirit, in the name of Jesus.

13. The anointing of the Holy Ghost, fall upon me and break every negative yoke, in the name of Jesus.

14. Every garment of hindrance and dirtiness, be dissolved by the fire of the Holy Ghost, in the name of Jesus.

15. All my chained blessings, be released, in the name of Jesus.

16. All spiritual cages, inhibiting my progress, roast by the fire of the Holy Spirit, in Jesus' name.

DREAM SURGERY 1

The dream world is a realm of reality. God can use our dreams to bring His plans and purposes to pass, while the devil can make use of the vehicle of the dream to attack men and women. Many people, who have battled with stubborn problems, have discovered that there is a link between their persistent problems and their dreams. Those who suffer failure, mysterious attacks, marital distress, failure at the edge of breakthroughs, incurable diseases, unexplainable tragedies, etc are often victims of satanic dream invasion. Most of the time, demonic infiltration begins in the realm of the dream. While the victims sleep, they are injected by evil surgeons from the realm of darkness. Such people need another kind of dream surgery.

You must go to the theatre of prayer and use the prayer points below to enable the Great Physician to thoroughly remove every poison of darkness from your life and destiny. This kind of dream surgery will enable you to get rid of evil deposits that are accumulated in your body and life over a long period of time.

This dream surgery will also keep dream criminals away from you.

Praise Worship

Confession: Job 5:12: He disappointeth the devices of the crafty, so that their hands cannot perform their enterprise.

1. I resist by fire the threat of death in my dreams, in Jesus' name.

2. Every evil dream, that other people have had about me, I cancel them in the astral world, in the name of Jesus.

3. Every image of satan in my dream, I curse you, wither now, in the name of Jesus.

4. Every dream of demotion, die, in Jesus' name.

5. Every arrow of death in my dream, come out now and go back to your sender, in the name of Jesus.

6. Every dream of poverty, sponsored by household wickedness against my life, vanish, in the name of Jesus.

7. I dash every poverty dream to the ground, in the name of Jesus.

8. I cancel the manipulation of every satanic dream, in Jesus' name.

9. You powers of the night, polluting my night dreams, be paralysed, in the name of Jesus.

10. Every anti-prosperity dream, die, in the mighty name of Jesus.

11. All satanic designs of oppression against me in my dreams and

visions, be frustrated, in Jesus' name.

12. I paralyse the spirits that bring bad dreams to me, in Jesus' name.

13. I cancel and wipe off all evil dreams, in the name of Jesus.

14. O Lord, let the blood of Jesus erase all evil dreams in my life, in Jesus' name.

15. My dreams, my joys and my breakthroughs that have been buried in the dark world, come alive and locate me, in Jesus' name.

16. Every serpent in my dreams, go back to your sender, in Jesus' name.

17. Every power, planting affliction into my life in the dream, be buried alive, in the name of Jesus.

18. Any evil plan, programmed into my life from my dream, be dismantled now, in the name of Jesus.

19. O Lord, deliver me from witchcraft dreams.

20. Satanic dreams, go back to your senders, in the name of Jesus.

21. I reject oppression; I claim liberty, in the name of Jesus.

22. I reject infirmity; I claim divine health, in the name of Jesus.

23. I reject curses; I claim God's blessings, in the name of Jesus.

24. I reject poverty; I claim wealth, in the name of Jesus.

25. I reject evil storm; I claim the peace of God, in the name of Jesus.

26. I reject tragedy; I claim goodness, in the name of Jesus.

27. I reject satanic dreams; I claim divine revelations, in Jesus'

name.

28. I reject failure; I claim good prospects, in the name of Jesus.

29. I reject frustration; I claim multiple promotions, in the name of Jesus.

30. You powers of the night, polluting my night dreams, be paralysed, in the name of Jesus.

31. Every dream of failure, sponsored by household wickedness against my life, vanish, in the name of Jesus.

32. I drink the blood of Jesus to neutralize every satanic food or drink taken in the dream, in the name of Jesus.

33. I cancel every evil dream by the blood of Jesus and the fire of the Holy Ghost, in the name of Jesus.

34. Every instrument of satanic retaliation, die, in the name of Jesus.

35. Every entrance of satanic influence on my life, die, in Jesus' name.

36. O Lord, kill every internal destiny killer.

37. Blood of Jesus, recover my stolen birthright, in the name of Jesus.

38. Every power of familiar spirits on my destiny, die, in Jesus' name.

39. I shall fulfil my divine agenda, in the name of Jesus.

40. Thank God for the victory He has given you.

DREAM SURGERY 2

The dream world is a realm of reality. God can use our dreams to bring His plans and purposes to pass, while the devil can make use of the vehicle of the dream to attack men and women. Many people, who have battled with stubborn problems, have discovered that there is a link between their persistent problems and their dreams. Those who suffer failure, mysterious attacks, marital distress, failure at the edge of breakthroughs, incurable diseases, unexplainable tragedies etc are often victims of satanic dream invasion. Most of the time, demonic infiltration begins in the realm of the dream. While the victims sleep, they are injected by evil surgeons from the realm of darkness. Such people need another kind of dream surgery.

You must go to the theatre of prayer and make use of the prayer points below in order to allow the Great Physician to thoroughly remove every poison of darkness from your life and destiny. This kind of dream surgery will enable you get rid of evil deposits that are accumulated in your body and life over a long period of time.

This dream surgery will also keep dream criminals away from you.

Praise Worship

Confession: Rev. 13:10: He that leadeth into captivity shall go into captivity: he that killeth with the sword must be killed with the sword. Here is the patience and the faith of the saints.

1. O Lord, stir up the Holy Ghost in my spirit, in the name of Jesus.

2. Every anti-testimony altar, die, in the name of Jesus.

3. Every power, that wants me to pray in vain, die, in Jesus' name

4. Stubborn witchcraft, I rub your pepper of affliction on your body, in the name of Jesus.

5. Amputators and emptiers, loose your hold upon my life and die, in the name of Jesus.

6. Evil birds, assigned against my mounting up, crashland and die, in the name of Jesus.

7. Every bat/vulture/dog, programmed into my dreams, die, in the name of Jesus.

8. I decree that nobody shall pluck my stars out of my hands, in the name of Jesus.

9. I decree that nobody shall pluck my stars out of my head, in the

name of Jesus.

10. My Glory shall not sink, in the name of Jesus.

11. Every friendly Judas in my life, be exposed and be disgraced, in the name of Jesus.

12. Evil hands, pointed at me, dry up, in the name of Jesus.

13. By the power that divided the Red Sea, let my problems die, in the name of Jesus.

14. Every river, in my place of birth, release my virtue, in Jesus' name.

15. I dismantle every satanic checkpoint, mounted against my success, in the name of Jesus.

16. O Lord, let deliverance take place in my dream, in the name of Jesus.

17. O Lord, find the dragon in my life and kill it, in the name of Jesus.

18. Every foundation of witchcraft in my family, be dismantled, in the name of Jesus.

19. O God, attack my ignorance, my lack and my mountains, in Jesus' name.

20. By the power that sank Pharaoh; by the power that disgraced Goliath; by the power that commanded worms on Herod, let my stubborn problems die, in the name of Jesus.

21. Every power, cursing my destiny, die, in the name of Jesus.

22. You my full-time enemies, I strike you with chaos and confusion, in the name of Jesus.

23. Every witchcraft incantation against my destiny, die, in Jesus' name.

24. I go back to Adam and Eve on both sides of my ancestors and I cut off every evil root, in the name of Jesus.

25. Every wicked spirit, assigned against my destiny, fail and fall by fire, in the name of Jesus.

26. Bitter water, flow out of my life by fire, in the name of Jesus.

27. Every evil tooth, biting my goodness, crack to pieces, in Jesus' name.

28. I decree that no contrary spirit within my family shall have peace, in Jesus' name.

29. Every satanic crowd, gathered to mock me, be disgraced, in the name of Jesus.

30. I break every covenant that strengthens my enemy, in Jesus' name.

31. I decree that my enemies shall become stepping stones to my higher ground, in the name of Jesus.

32. Evil mountains, get out of my situation, in the name of Jesus.

33. My cry, provoke angelic violence, in the name of Jesus.

34. O Lord, do everything in Your power to bring my victory.

35. Any pot, calling my name for destruction, scatter, in Jesus' name.

36. Every foundational barrier to my greatness, die, in the name of Jesus.

37. Every fountain of poverty, break, in the name of Jesus.

POWER AGAINST THE SPIRIT OF DEATH AND HELL

The spirit of death and hell is the spiritual personality charged with the responsibility of destroying the lives of men and women.

This wicked spirit has carried out its activities unchallenged, in many lives. The result is that many have experienced premature or untimely death, while others have died through mysterious circumstances. Unknown to some of the victims, they entered into the covenant of death without knowing what they were going into. The spirit of death and hell is so strong that individuals, families and communities should carry out this prayer programme aggressively.

When satanic agents decide to send the spirit of death and hell over a victim, even the best medical facilities will prove abortive.

Prayer against the spirit of death and hell must be done aggressively. When this spirit hovers around a victim, he *or she may pass away within the shortest possible time. These prayer points will help you barricade your life and that of your loved ones from every attack of the spirit of death and hell.*

Praise Worship

Confession: Psalm 118:17: I shall not die, but live, and declare the works of the Lord.

1. Thank God for the power of resurrection and life.

2. I release myself from every curse of untimely death, in the name of Jesus.

3. I break every unprofitable covenant of untimely death, in the name of Jesus.

4. I remove my life from every shadow of death, in Jesus' name

5. I bind and paralyse every strongman of death and hell, in the name of Jesus.

6. O Lord, strengthen my body, soul and spirit.

7. Every secret about battles against my spiritual life, be revealed, in the name of Jesus.

8. I release myself from the grip of the spirit of infirmity, in the name of Jesus.

9. I drink the blood of Jesus into the whole of my system.

10. O Lord, build the hedge of fire around me.

11. Spirit of life, replace the spirit of death in my life, in Jesus' name

12. Woe unto the demonic vessel, that the enemy would use to cause me spiritual injury, in the name of Jesus.

13. Father Lord, let Your glory

cover every aspect of my life, in Jesus' name.

14. Father Lord, let Your angels encamp around me, in Jesus' name.

15. I renounce and break every death covenant that I have made or which anyone has made on my behalf, in Jesus' name.

16. I remove the control of my life from the hands of any dead person, in the name of Jesus.

17. I stand against every covenant of sudden death, in Jesus' name.

18. Every blessing of mine that has been buried in the ground or under any water, be released by fire, in Jesus' name.

19. I cancel my name from every death register, in Jesus' name

20. I stand against every form of tragedy, in Jesus' name.

21. Every grave cloth over my life, be removed by fire, in Jesus' name.

22. All my potentials that have been destroyed, receive life now, in the name of Jesus.

23. I stand against all the powers that push people into hell fire, in the name of Jesus.

POWER AGAINST WOMB POLLUTERS

One of the greatest problems today is that of childless couples. The greater bulk of instances of childlessness, if viewed from the standpoint of spiritual warfare, can be traced to the activities of womb polluters.

Womb polluters pollute the womb and give women complicated problems. Moreover, womb polluters are responsible for spiritual poisoning. When people consume poison, the womb or stomach becomes caged. Problems like internal heat, incurable stomach problems, emitting odious substances and other problems are sponsored by womb polluters. When the womb or stomach is polluted, the entire body functions go into disarray: blood circulation is impaired, sound health becomes difficult to come by, while medication will avail for nothing. You need to wage war against womb polluters in order to put a stop to womb-related problems.

Praise Worship

Confessions: Mark 16:18: They shall take up serpents; and if they drink any deadly thing, it shall not hurt them; they shall lay hands on the sick, and they shall recover.

Isaiah 54:17: No weapon that is formed against thee shall prosper; and every tongue that shall rise against thee in judgment thou shalt condemn. This is the heritage of the servants of the Lord, and their righteousness is of me, saith the Lord.

Prayer warfare

1. I expel every strange material from my body, in Jesus' name.
2. My womb, reject every anti-conception material, in Jesus' name.
3. I uproot every plantation of darkness from my womb, in the name of Jesus.
4. I cut off every negative presence attached to my womb, in the name of Jesus.
5. Holy Ghost fire, purge my womb with the blood of Jesus.
6. Blood of Jesus, purge my womb, in the name of Jesus.
7. Every hidden darkness in my womb, be flushed out, in Jesus' name.

8. I push out every plantation of darkness in my womb, in Jesus' name.

9. Every deposit of darkness, loose your hold, in Jesus' name.

10. Every evil hand laid upon my womb, roast, in Jesus' name

11. Anything planted in my womb to drink my blood, come out now, in the name of Jesus.

12. I shall not incubate any property of darkness in my womb, in the name of Jesus.

13. Womb polluters, loose your hold, in the name of Jesus.

14. Anything planted in my life that is contrary to the will of God, be uprooted now, in the name of Jesus.

15. I bind and cast out any dark spirit, moving about in my womb, in the name of Jesus.

16. Fire of God, destroy every plantation of infirmity, in my womb, in the name of Jesus.

17. Every blood-drinking demon, assigned against my womb, I bind and cast you out, in the name of Jesus.

18. Every conspiracy against my vessel of reproduction, scatter, in the name of Jesus.

19. O God, arise and let every enemy of my marital bliss scatter, in the name of Jesus.

20. My womb, depart from the hold of every altar of darkness, in the name of Jesus.

21. Every burden in my womb, be dissolved, in the name of Jesus.

22. Every yoke in my womb, break, in the name of Jesus.

POWER AGAINST EATERS OF FLESH AND DRINKERS OF BLOOD

The devil hates you with perfect hatred. Incidentally, he does not hide his wickedness. In recent times, eaters of flesh and drinkers of blood have switched to the most dangerous gear. Some satanic agents openly admit the fact that they eat human flesh and drink human blood. They cause precious lives to perish like ants.

The rate at which people get murdered spiritually in broad day light has become worrisome. This is the time when you must exhibit holy anger. We must rise up and declare that eaters of flesh shall eat their own flesh and drinkers of blood shall drink their own blood. These prayer points will enable you to put a stop to the spate of premature deaths in homes, families, offices, churches and communities. What is more, the prayer points will enable you to convert your blood and your flesh into poison, hence, you will become too hot for the enemy to handle.

Praise Worship

Confession: Isaiah 49:25-26: But thus saith the Lord, Even the captives of the mighty shall be taken away, and the prey of the terrible shall be delivered: for I will contend with him that contendeth with thee, and I will save thy children. [26] And I will feed them that oppress thee with their own flesh; and they shall be drunken with their own blood, as with sweet wine: and all flesh shall know that I the Lord am thy Saviour and thy Redeemer, the mighty One of Jacob.

Prayer warfare

1. O God, be my light and salvation, in the name of Jesus.

2. O God, be the strength of my life, in the name of Jesus.

3. O God, I render my life safe by Your power, in Jesus' name.

4. Every power and activity of eaters of flesh and drinkers of blood, die, in the name of Jesus.

5. Eaters of flesh and drinkers of blood, drink your own blood and eat your own flesh, in the name of Jesus.

6. I bind and cast out every power of eaters of flesh and drinkers of blood, in the name of Jesus.

7. You eaters of flesh and drinkers of blood, release my virtues, in the name of Jesus.

8. You the captive of the mighty, be released, in Jesus' name.

9. You the captive of the terrible, be released, in Jesus' name.

10. I declare freedom upon my life, in the name of Jesus.

11. Every power of blood-thirsty demons, be dismantled, in the name of Jesus.

12. I remove my name from the book of eaters of flesh and drinkers of blood, in the name of Jesus.

13. I pull down the stronghold of eaters of flesh and drinkers of blood, in the name of Jesus.

14. Fire of God, burn to ashes the agenda of eaters of flesh and drinkers of blood, in the name of Jesus.

15. I break every covenant of the destruction of my health, in Jesus' name

16. Holy Ghost fire, enter into my blood stream and flush out the poison of darkness, in the name of Jesus.

17. My life, become too hot for witchcraft to handle, in Jesus' name.

18. I bind and cast out any deposit of darkness in any part of my body, in the name of Jesus.

19. I receive power to disgrace every blood-thirsty aggressor, in the name of Jesus.

20.   Arrows of death, backfire, in the name of Jesus.

POWER AGAINST SATANIC POISON

One problem medical science has not been able to tackle is the problem of spiritual poison. When some people develop certain strange sicknesses and go from one hospital to the other without any tangible diagnosis, they are often advised by medical doctors to seek help elsewhere.

Satanic poison cannot be detected by any medical gadget simply because it is spiritual in nature. The only solution is to attack the roots of such spiritual poison. The weapon of aggressive prayer will lay the divine axe to the root of such wicked poisons and their power will be rendered impotent. Healing and health will result from the experience.

You need this prayer programme, if you have battled with a congenital health problem. The so-called psychosomatic diseases can also be cured through a spiritual programme such as this one.

Those who have spent a fortune on seeking medical help will do well to declare war against every form of spiritual poison, by using these acidic prayer points. No poison from the pit of hell will remain in your life and body after this spiritual warfare.

Praise Worship

Confession: Job 5:12: He disappointeth the devices of the crafty, so that their hands, cannot perform their enterprise.

Prayer warfare

1. My body, reject every poisonous arrow, in Jesus' name.

2. Every spiritual poison, that has entered into my system, be neutralized by the blood of Jesus.

3. Holy Ghost fire, purge away every handwriting of wickedness, in the name of Jesus.

4. Fire of God, burn to ashes every power programmed into my life to poison me, in the name of Jesus.

5. Every evil plantation in my life: **come out with all your roots, in the name of Jesus!** *(Lay your hands on your stomach and keep repeating the emphasized area.)*

6. Evil strangers in my body, come out of your hiding places, in the name of Jesus.

7. I disconnect any conscious or unconscious link with demonic caterers, in the name of Jesus.

8. All avenues of eating or drinking spiritual poisons, be closed, in the

name of Jesus.

9. I cough and vomit any food eaten from the table of the devil, in the name of Jesus. *(Cough and vomit it by faith. Prime the expulsion).*

10. All negative materials, circulating in my blood stream, be evacuated, in the name of Jesus.

11. I drink the blood of Jesus. *(Physically swallow it by faith. Do this for some time.)*

12. All evil spiritual feeders, warring against me, drink your own blood and eat your own flesh, in the name of Jesus.

13. All demonic food utensils, fashioned against me, roast, in the name of Jesus.

14. Holy Ghost fire, circulate all over my body.

15. All physical poisons, inside my system, be neutralized, in the name of Jesus.

16. All evil assignments, fashioned against me through the mouth gate, be nullified, in the name of Jesus.

17. All spiritual problems, attached to any hour of the night, be cancelled, in the name of Jesus. *(Pick the period from midnight to 6:00 a.m.)*

18. Bread of heaven, fill me till I want no more.

19. All catering equipments of evil caterers, attached to me, be destroyed, in the name of Jesus.

20. My digestive system, reject every evil command, in the name of

Jesus.

21. All satanic designs of oppression against me in dreams and visions, be frustrated, in the name of Jesus.

22. With the blood of Jesus, I remove my name from the register of evil feeders.

23. My Father, let the habitation of evil caterers become desolate, in the name of Jesus.

WITCHCRAFT MUST DIE

Witchcraft is public enemy number one. Its activities are deadly, its influence is pervading and its impact is destructive, while its presence is ubiquitous.

Families are invaded by witchcraft agents; communities are turned upside down by witches and wizards. Nations are sold into slavery by witchcraft, the mother of harlots. No family setup will remain intact when witchcraft invasion is allowed. No community will remain intact where witches and wizards have a field day. Your dreams and destiny cannot be fulfilled as long as witchcraft is given a spot from which to land and operate. Witchcraft must die. Spiritually, its agents must be stoned to death. You must make your life too hot for any witchcraft operative to live in.

You need the aggressive prayer programme in this section to kill witchcraft. You must not suffer a witch to live in your life or environment. You must get baptized with the spirit of a warrior as you carry out this particular programme. Anyone who is in the valley cannot wage this war. Your life must be charged with fire and you must be on top of the mountain where your spiritual thermometer is at the highest scale.

Praise Worship

Confession: Exodus 22:18: Thou shalt not suffer a witch to live.

Rev. 12:11: And they overcame him by the blood of the Lamb, and by the word of their testimony; and they loved not their lives unto the death.

Prayer warfare

1. O Rock of Ages, smash every foundation of witchcraft in my family into pieces, in the name of Jesus. Thou foundation of witchcraft in my father's house / mother's house, die, in the name of Jesus.

2. O Lord, let witchcraft powers eat their own flesh and drink their own blood, in the name of Jesus.

3. Every seat of witchcraft, receive the thunder fire of God, in the name of Jesus.

4. Every habitation of witchcraft powers, become desolate, in the name of Jesus.

5. Every throne of witchcraft, be dismantled by fire, in Jesus' name.

6. Every stronghold of witchcraft powers, be pulled down by fire, in the name of Jesus.

7. Every refuge of witchcraft, be disgraced, in Jesus' name.

8. Every network of witchcraft, disintegrate, in Jesus' name.

9. Every communication system of witchcraft powers, be destroyed by fire, in the name of Jesus.

10. Every transportation system of witchcraft powers, be disrupted, in the name of Jesus.

11. O Lord, let the weapons of witchcraft powers turn against them, in the name of Jesus.

12. I withdraw my blessings from every bank or strongroom of the enemy, in the name of Jesus.

13. O altar of witchcraft, break, in the name of Jesus.

14. Every witchcraft padlock, fashioned against me, break by fire, in Jesus' name.

15. Every trap of witchcraft, catch your owners, in Jesus' name.

16. Every witchcraft utterance, and projection made against me, backfire, in the name of Jesus.

17. I reverse, every witchcraft burial fashioned against me, in Jesus' name.

18. I deliver my soul from every witchcraft bewitchment, in the name of Jesus.

19. I reverse the effect of every witchcraft summons to my spirit, in Jesus' name.

20. Every witchcraft identification mark, be wiped off by the blood of Jesus.

21. I frustrate every witchcraft exchange of my

virtues, in the name of Jesus.

22. Blood of Jesus, block the flying route of witchcraft powers, targeted at me.

23. Every witchcraft curse, break and be destroyed, in Jesus' name.

24. Every covenant of witchcraft, melt by the blood of Jesus.

25. I withdraw every organ of my body from any witchcraft altar, in the name of Jesus.

26. Anything planted in my life by witchcraft, come out now and die, in the name of Jesus.

27. Blood of Jesus, cancel every witchcraft initiation, fashioned against my destiny, in the name of Jesus.

28. Every witchcraft poison, be destroyed, in the name of Jesus.

29. I reverse every witchcraft pattern, fashioned against my destiny, in the name of Jesus.

30. Every witchcraft cage, fashioned against my life, be destroyed, in the name of Jesus.

31. Every problem in my life, that originated from witchcraft, receive divine and instant solution, in Jesus' name.

32. All the damages done to my life by witchcraft, be repaired, in the name of Jesus.

33. Every blessing, confiscated by witchcraft spirits, be released, in Jesus' name.

34. Every witchcraft power, assigned against my life and marriage, receive . . . (pick

from the under   name.
listed), in Jesus'

-the thunder and lightning of God

-hail and fire mingled with the blood of the Lamb

-unbearable heat

-concentrated acid

- destroying flood

-destruction

- raging fire

-continuous plagues

- failure

- confusion

35. I loose myself from any power of witchcraft, in Jesus' name.

36. Every camp of witchcraft, gathered against my prosperity, fall down and die, in Jesus' name.

37. Every witchcraft pot, working against me, I bring the judgment of God upon you, in the name of Jesus.

38. Every witchcraft pot, using remote control against my health, break into pieces, in Jesus' name.

39. Witchcraft opposition, receive the rain of affliction, in the name of Jesus.

40. Spirit of witchcraft, attack the familiar spirits fashioned against me, in Jesus' name.

41. I retrieve my integrity from

the hands of household witchcraft, in Jesus' name.

42. I break the power of the occult, witchcraft and familiar spirits, over my life, in Jesus' name.

43. In the name of Jesus, I break and loose myself from all evil curses, chains, spells, jinxes, bewitchments, witchcraft or sorcery, which may have been put upon me.

44. Thunder of God, locate and dismantle the throne of witchcraft in my household, in the name of Jesus.

45. Every seat of witchcraft in my household, roast by the fire of God, in Jesus' name.

46. Every altar of witchcraft in my household, roast, in the name of Jesus.

47. Thunder of God, scatter the foundation of witchcraft in my household beyond redemption, in Jesus' name.

48. Every stronghold or refuge of my household witches, be destroyed, in Jesus' name.

49. Every hiding place and secret place of witchcraft in my family, be exposed by fire, in the name of Jesus.

50. Every local and international witchcraft network of my household witches, shatter to pieces, in Jesus' name.

51. O Lord, let the communication system of my household witches be frustrated, in Jesus' name.

52. Terrible fire of God, consume the transportation of my household witchcraft, in the name of Jesus.

53. Every agent, ministering at the altar of witchcraft in my household, fall down and die, in the name of Jesus.

54. Thunder and the fire of God,

locate the storehouses and strongrooms of the household witchcraft harbouring my blessings and pull them down, in the name of Jesus.

55. Any witchcraft curse, working against me, be revoked, by the blood of Jesus.

56. Every decision, vow and covenant of household witchcraft, affecting me, be nullified by the blood of Jesus.

57. I destroy with the fire of God, every weapon of witchcraft used against me, in Jesus' name.

58. Any material, taken from my body and now placed on a witchcraft altar, roast by the fire of God, in Jesus' name.

59. I reverse every witchcraft burial, fashioned against me,

in the name of Jesus.

60. Every trap, set for me by witches, begin to catch your owners, in the name of Jesus.

61. Every witchcraft padlock, fashioned against any area of my life, roast, in Jesus' name.

62. Every wisdom of household witches, be converted to foolishness, in Jesus' name.

63. Every wickedness of household enemies, overtake them, in the name of Jesus.

64. I deliver my soul from every witchcraft bewitchment, in the name of Jesus.

65. Any witchcraft bird, flying for my sake, fall down, die and roast to ashes, in Jesus' name.

66. Any of my blessings, traded with by household witches, be returned to me, in Jesus'

name.

67. Any of my blessings and testimonies, swallowed by witches, be converted to hot coals of fire of God and be vomited, in the name of Jesus.

68. I break loose from every bondage of witchcraft covenants, in Jesus' name.

69. Any witchcraft coven, where any of my blessings is hidden, be roasted by the fire of God, in the name of Jesus.

70. (Lay your right hand on your head) Every witchcraft plantation, pollution, deposit and material in my body, melt by the fire of God and be flushed out, by the blood of Jesus.

71. Every evil ever done to me through witchcraft attack, be reversed, in the name of Jesus.

72. Every witchcraft hand, planting evil seeds in my life through dream attacks, wither and burn to ashes, in Jesus' name.

73. Every witchcraft obstacle, put on the road to my desired miracle and success, be removed by the east wind of God, in Jesus' name.

74. Every witchcraft chant, spell and projection made against me, I bind you and turn you against your owner, in Jesus' name.

75. I frustrate every plot, device, scheme and project of witchcraft, designed to affect any area of my life, in the name of Jesus.

76. Any witch, projecting herself into the body of any animal, in order to do me harm, be trapped in the body of such an animal forever, in Jesus' name.

77. Any drop of my blood, sucked by any witch, be vomited now, in the name of Jesus.

78. Any part of me, shared out among household/village witches, I recover you, in the name of Jesus.

79. Any organ of my body, that has been exchanged for another through witchcraft operation, be replaced now, in Jesus' name.

80. I recover any of my virtues/blessings, shared out among village / household witches, in the name of Jesus.

81. I reverse the evil effect of any witchcraft invocation or summon to my spirit, in the name of Jesus.

82. I loose my hands and feet from any witchcraft bewitchment or bondage, in Jesus' name.

83. Blood of Jesus, wash away every witchcraft identification mark on me or on any of my properties, in Jesus' name.

84. I forbid any re-union or re-grouping of household and village witches, against my life, in the name of Jesus.

85. O Lord, let the entire body system of my household witches begin to run amok until they confess all their wickedness, in Jesus' name.

86. O Lord, let the mercies of God be withdrawn from them, in Jesus' name.

87. O Lord, let them begin to grope in the daytime as if in the thickness of a dark night, in the name of Jesus.

88. O Lord, let everything that has ever worked for them begin to work against them, in Jesus' name.

89. O Lord, let them not have any garment to cover their shame, in Jesus' name.

90. O Lord, let as many of them as are stubbornly unrepentant be smitten by the sun in the day and by the moon at night, in Jesus' name.

91. O Lord, let each step they take lead them to greater destruction, in Jesus' name.

92. But as for me, O Lord, let me dwell in the hollow of Your hand, in the name of Jesus.

93. O Lord, let Your goodness and mercies overwhelm me now, in the name of Jesus.

94. Any witchcraft operation against my life, under any water, receive immediate judgment of fire, in Jesus' name

95. Every witchcraft power, that has introduced spirit husband/wife or an evil child into my dreams, roast by fire, in the name of Jesus.

96. Every agent of witchcraft power, posing as my husband/wife or child in my dreams, roast by fire, in Jesus' name.

97. Every agent of witchcraft power, physically attached to my marriage to frustrate it, fall down now and perish, in Jesus' name.

98. Every agent of witchcraft power, assigned to attack my finances through dreams, fall down and perish, in Jesus' name.

99. O Lord, let Your thunderbolts locate and destroy every witchcraft power coven, where deliberations and decisions were fashioned against me, in the name of Jesus.

100. Any water spirit from my village or place of birth, practising witchcraft against me and my family, be amputated by the word of God, in Jesus' name.

101. Any power of witchcraft, holding any of my blessings in bondage, receive the fire of God and release them, in the name of Jesus.

102. I loose my mind and soul from the bondage of marine witches, in the name of Jesus.

103. Any witchcraft chain, binding my hands and feet from prospering, shatter to pieces, in Jesus' name.

104. Every arrow, shot into my life from under any water through witchcraft, come out of me and go back to your sender, in the name of Jesus.

105. Any evil material, transferred into my body through contact with any witchcraft agent, roast by fire, in Jesus' name.

106. Any evil, done against me through witchcraft oppression or manipulation, be reversed by the blood of Jesus.

107. I bind every witchcraft control and mind-blinding spirit, in the name of Jesus.

108. I cast out every witchcraft arrow, affecting my senses (sight, smell, taste, hearing), in the name of Jesus.

109. Every witchcraft arrow,
     depart from my

     - spinal cord - spleen   -navel - heart - throat

     - eyes   - head,

in the name of Jesus.

110. Blood of Jesus, purge me of every witchcraft contaminating material, in the name of Jesus.

111. I destroy the hand of any witch-doctor, working against me, in the name of Jesus.

112. Every witchcraft spirit, attempting to build a wall against my destiny, fall down and die, in the name of Jesus.

113. I send the rain of affliction upon every witchcraft power, working against me, in the name of Jesus.

114. O sun, moon, stars, earth, water and other elements of creation, vomit every enchantment that is against me, in the name of Jesus

115. Every power, using the heavenlies against me, fall down and be disgraced, in Jesus' name.

116. Stars of heaven, begin to fight for me, in Jesus' name.

117. O God, arise and scatter every conspiracy against me in the heavenlies, in Jesus' name.

118. I break with the blood of Jesus, all evil soul-ties affecting my life, in the name of Jesus.

119. Spirit of the living God, come upon my life and place a shield of protection around me, in the name of Jesus.

120. Every chain of inherited witchcraft in my family, break, in the name of Jesus.

121. Every ladder, used by witchcraft against me, roast, in the name of Jesus.

122. Any door, that I have opened to witchcraft, in any area of my life, be closed for ever, by the blood of Jesus.

123. I revoke every witchcraft verdict on my marital life, in the name of Jesus.

124. I send confusion into the camp of household witchcraft, in the name of Jesus.

125. Stubborn witchcraft, release me, in the name of Jesus.

126. Every witchcraft power, working against my destiny, fall down and die, in Jesus' name.

127. Every incantation, ritual and witchcraft power against my destiny, fall down and die, in the name of Jesus.

128. I break the power of the occult, witchcraft and familiar spirits over my life, in Jesus' name.

129. Witchcraft opposition, receive the rain of affliction, in the name of Jesus.

130. I cancel every witchcraft verdict against my life, in Jesus' name.

131. Every arrow of witchcraft in my life, come out with all your roots, in the name of Jesus! (Lay your hands on your stomach and pray aggressively.)

132. Every witchcraft pot, using remote control against my health, break into pieces, in Jesus' name.

133. I revoke the spell of any witchcraft pot on my neck, in the name of Jesus.

134. I break every witchcraft pot over my life, in Jesus' name.

135. Every council of witchcraft, working against me, scatter, in the name of Jesus.

136. I disentangle my family and I from every witchcraft cage and pot, in the name of Jesus.

137. I retrieve my integrity from the hands of household witchcraft, in the name of Jesus.

138. Every witchcraft hand, planting evil seeds in my life, through dream attacks, wither and burn to ashes, in Jesus' name.

139. All friendly witchcraft powers, be exposed and be disgraced, in the name of Jesus.

140. O Lord, plant Your warring angels around me to dismantle and destroy evil stronghold of internal witchcraft.

141. I exercise my authority over stubborn witchcraft and I pull down its structures, in Jesus' name.

142. Every placenta witchcraft, targeted at my destiny, what are you

waiting for? Die, in the name of Jesus.

143. Placenta witchcraft, manipulating my destiny, die, in Jesus' name.

144. Every blessing that I have lost through placenta witchcraft, I repossess you, in Jesus' name.

145. Every witchcraft coven and marine bank, release my placenta, in Jesus' name.

146. Every cage of family witchcraft, release my divine partner, in Jesus' name.

147. Oh Lord, let my dreams and visions reject every witchcraft projection, in the name of Jesus.

148. Thank God for answers to your prayers.

POWER AGAINST FAMILIAR SPIRITS

Life is a battle. Even if you are not ready to fight, the devil will not spare you. He remains a restless fighter and a stubborn destroyer.

The realm of familiar spirits is a dangerous department in the dark kingdom. Familiar spirits generally enter into people's lives secretly and settle down to perpetrate all forms of wickedness. One of their tactics is to set up a spy network with which they gather information to be used for attacking their victims.

Familiar spirits litter the community like dust. They gain access into people's lives stealthily and by the time they complete their evil assignments, the victims are finished. You must chase them out today by making use of these prayer points.

Praise Worship

Confession: Deut. 18:10: There shall not be found among you any one that maketh his son or his daughter to pass through the fire, or that useth divination, or an observer of times, or an enchanter, or a witch,

Prayer warfare

1. Power of God, destroy every foundation of familiar spirits in my family, in the name of Jesus. Thou foundation of familiar spirits in my father's house / mother's house, die, in Jesus' name.

2. Every soul-tie with familiar spirits, break to pieces, in Jesus' name.

3. Every seat of familiar spirits, receive the thunder fire of God, in the name of Jesus.

4. O Lord, let the habitation of familiar spirits become desolate, in Jesus' name.

5. Every throne of familiar spirits, be dismantled by fire, in Jesus' name.

6. Every stronghold of familiar spirits, be pulled down by fire, in the name of Jesus.

7. Every diviner of familiar spirits, be rendered impotent, in Jesus' name.

8. Every network of familiar spirits, be dismantled, in Jesus' name.

9. Every communication system of familiar spirits, be destroyed by fire, in the name of Jesus.

10. Every transportation system of familiar spirits, be disrupted, in the name of Jesus.

11. O Lord, let the weapons of familiar spirits turn against them, in

the name of Jesus.

12. I withdraw my blessings from every bank or strongroom of familiar spirits, in the name of Jesus.

13. O altar of familiar spirits, break, in the name of Jesus.

14. Every familiar spirit's padlock, fashioned against me, break by fire, in the name of Jesus.

15. Every trap of familiar spirits, roast by the fire of God, in the name of Jesus.

16. Every familiar spirit's utterance and projection, made against me, be overthrown, in the name of Jesus.

17. I reverse every familiar spirit's burial, fashioned against me, in the name of Jesus.

18. I deliver my soul from every bewitchment of familiar spirit, in the name of Jesus.

19. I reverse the effect of every summon to my spirit, by familiar spirits, in the name of Jesus.

20. Every familiar spirit's identification mark, be wiped off, by the blood of Jesus.

21. I frustrate every familiar spirit's exchange of my virtues, in the name of Jesus.

22. Blood of Jesus, destroy every familiar spirit's manipulation,

fashioned against me, in the name of Jesus.

23. Every spell and enchantment, programmed against me by familiar spirits, be destroyed, in the name of Jesus.

24. Every covenant with familiar spirits, melt, by the blood of Jesus.

25. I withdraw every organ of my body from any altar of familiar spirits, in the name of Jesus.

26. Anything planted in my life, by familiar spirits, come out now and die, in the name of Jesus.

27. Blood of Jesus, cancel every initiation of familiar spirits against my destiny, in the name of Jesus.

28. Every spiritual marriage with familiar spirits, be destroyed, in the name of Jesus.

29. I reverse every evil pattern of familiar spirits for my destiny, in the name of Jesus.

30. Every cage of familiar spirits, caging my life, be destroyed, in the name of Jesus.

DELIVERANCE FROM THE BONDAGE OF MARINE SPIRITS

If there is an area where people desperately seek deliverance, it is that of the bondage of marine spirits. Marine spirits are wicked to the core. They hold multitudes captive. Those from riverine communities are often victims of this satanic bondage. They suffer oppression, manipulation, bondage and diversion of destiny. Ordinary prayers can be used as a weapon of dealing with satanic bondage, but the bondage of marine spirits requires serious deliverance prayers.

If your place of birth or domicile happens to be a riverine community, there is every possibility of the presence of marine bondage in your life and you should seek total deliverance. It is crystal clear that marine demons are persistent in their attacks. You need bombardment to pound them to submission. This prayer programme will burn to ashes every cobweb of marine bondage hanging over your life.

Praise Worship

Confession: 2 Tim. 4:18: And the Lord shall deliver me from every evil work, and will preserve me unto his heavenly kingdom: to whom be glory for ever and ever. Amen.

Prayer warfare

1. I challenge my body with the fire of the Holy Ghost, and command every marine spirit, residing in my body to manifest and die, in Jesus' name.

2. You spirit of Leviathan in my life, I challenge you with the blood of Jesus and the fire of Holy Ghost, come out now and die, in the name of Jesus.

3. Every evil covenant, binding me with water spirits, break by the blood of Jesus.

4. Every evil association between me and marine spirits, break by the blood of Jesus.

5. Every evil dedication, made by my parents on any satanic altar, blood of Jesus, destroy it now, in the name of Jesus.

6. I reject and renounce every satanic office given to me, in the marine kingdom, in the name of Jesus.

7. I reject and renounce every satanic crown given to me, in the marine kingdom, in the name of Jesus.

8. I reject and renounce every satanic property in my possession, in the name of Jesus.

9. I reject and renounce every satanic gift ever given to me, from the marine kingdom, in the name of Jesus.

10. Every satanic guard, assigned to my life from the marine kingdom, I reject you. Receive the fire of God and depart from me, in Jesus' name.

11. Every satanic instrument from the marine kingdom, planted inside my body, I reject you, receive the fire of God now and burn to ashes, in the name of Jesus.

12. Every serpent, hidden in my body, I challenge your habitation with the fire of God, come out and die, in the name of Jesus.

13. Every unconscious association with marine spirits, be destroyed by the blood of Jesus.

14. Every throne, set up for me in the marine kingdom, I reject and renounce you, I command the thunder fire of God to destroy you now, in the name of Jesus.

15. Every ordinance of the marine kingdom in my life, be blotted out by the blood of Jesus.

16. I bind and cast every marine spirit out of my life, in the name of Jesus.

17. Every foundation of marine spirit in my life, be uprooted by fire, in the name of Jesus.

18. Anything that has survived on the evil foundation of marine spirits in my life, be destroyed, in the name of Jesus.

19. I bind and cast every spirit of Leviathan witchcraft out of my life, in the name of Jesus.

20. Every trading ground of the queen of the coast in my life, receive destruction by the fire of God, in the name of Jesus.

21. I am married to Jesus, by His blood, you queen of the coast, loose your hold upon my life now, in the name of Jesus.

22. Every river, water or sea, monitoring my life, I strike you with chaos and confusion by the blood of Jesus.

23. Blood of Jesus, purge me of every satanic food, that I have ever eaten in the marine kingdom, in the name of Jesus.

24. I challenge every marine hair on my head with the fire of God and I command it to catch fire now, in the name of Jesus.

25. Every family serpent, assigned to the foundation of my life, fall down and die, in the name of Jesus.

26. Any evil deposit from the marine kingdom in any part of my body, be destroyed by the fire of God, in the name of Jesus.

27. I declare that I am forever married to Jesus, who is my Saviour and my Deliverer.

28. Henceforth, let no power from the marine kingdom trouble me, for I bear in my body the mark of the blood of Jesus.

29. Lord Jesus, baptise my life with Holy Ghost fire.

30. Thank God for answers to your prayers.

POWER AGAINST DEMONIC FOOD

Just as we have human caterers, there are spiritual caterers. Their responsibility is to prepare demonic food and feed their victims with it. People are fed with evil food, mostly through dreams. Eating in the dream is a serious problem that must be spiritually handled with urgency.

Those who are ignorant of the devices of the devil consume delicacies each night in their dreams. As soon as demonic food is consumed, all kinds of complicated physical and spiritual problems ensue. Every instance of eating in the dream is an invitation to satanic bondage.

Demonic foods, whether consumed in a demonic gathering or not, always produces negative result. You must pray against demonic food until its effect and power are rendered null and void. Aggressive prayers will prevent you

> from any further eating in the dream.

Praise Worship

Confession: Read Psalm 24 out loud.

Prayer warfare

1. Every demonic caterer in my dream, receive the fire of God and die, in the name of Jesus.

2. You demonic caterer in my dream, eat your evil food, in the name of Jesus.

3. Every satanic agent, serving me evil food in my dream, fall down and die, in the name of Jesus.

4. Every satanic hand, assigned to serve me evil food, in my dream, be cut off by the fire of God, in the name of Jesus.

5. Blood of Jesus, purge my system of demonic food, eaten in the dream, in the name of Jesus.

6. Every evil contamination introduced into my life through eating in the dream, be dissolved, by the blood of Jesus.

7. I receive divine power to reject demonic food, in my dreams, in the name of Jesus.

8. Blood of Jesus, frustrate every activity of familiar spirits in my dream, in the name of Jesus.

9. Every satanic agent on assignment to poison my life through eating in the dream, fall down and die, in the name of Jesus.

10. Every evil power, sitting on the seat of my life, be uprooted by fire, in the name of Jesus.

11. Every satanic agent, sent to harm me, destroy your senders and yourself, in the name of Jesus.

12. Every satanic plan to pollute the anointing of God upon my life through demonic food, be frustrated, in the name of Jesus.

13. Every legal ground for satan to be feeding me with demonic food, blood of Jesus, destroy them, in the name of Jesus.

14. Thank God for answers to your prayers.

POWER AGAINST UNTIMELY DEATH

One of the most frightening phenomena today is the rate at which people die untimely. The problem of untimely death has reached an epidemic dimension.

The spirits responsible for untimely death belong to a department that can be described as the hit-squad in the kingdom of darkness. Untimely death is one of the most destructive weapons of the enemy. It has led to the cutting away of precious lives in many families, communities and nations. You must wage war against it. If the problem is too common in your lineage, these prayer points are for you. You must fight this battle with the totality of your strength. You must refuse to be a candidate of untimely death.

Apply fire and fervency to these prayer points and your name will be removed from the list of victims of untimely death.

Praise Worship

Confession: Psalm 118:17: I shall not die but live, and declare the works of the Lord.

Prayer warfare

1. Every power, transforming into masquerades in the night in order to attack me in the dreams, be exposed and die, in the name of Jesus.

2. Every power, transforming into animals in the night in order to attack me in the dreams, fall down and die, in Jesus' name.

3. Every coffin, prepared by the agent of death for my life, catch fire and roast to ashes, in the name of Jesus.

4. Every pit, dug for my life by agents of death, swallow the agents, in the name of Jesus.

5. Every power, oppressing my life through dreams of death, fall down and die, in the name of Jesus.

6. Every witchcraft power, tormenting my life with the spirit of death, fall down and die, in the name of Jesus.

7. Every witchcraft power, assigned to my family for untimely death, scatter and die, in the name of Jesus.

8. Every satanic agent, monitoring my life for evil, fall down and die, in the name of Jesus.

9. Every unconscious gift of death that I have received, receive the fire of God, in the name of Jesus.

10. Every stubborn pursuer of my life, turn back and perish in your own Red Sea, in the name of Jesus.

11. Every arrow of terminal sickness, come out of my life and die, in the name of Jesus.

12. Every power, enforcing terminal sickness in my life, fall down and die, in the name of Jesus.

13. Every decree of untimely death hovering over my life, catch fire and die, in the name of Jesus.

14. Every evil link between me and the spirit of untimely death, be cut off by the blood of Jesus.

15. I reject and renounce every association with the spirit of death, in the name of Jesus.

16. Every inherited satanic glasses on my eyes, break by the blood of Jesus.

17. Every ancestral agreement with the spirit of untimely death, break by the blood of Jesus.

18. Every agreement and covenant of hell fire in my family line, be destroyed by the blood of Jesus.

19. Every agreement with the spirit of death in my family line, break by the blood of Jesus.

20. I shall not die but live. The number of my days shall be fulfilled, in the name of Jesus.

21. I cancel every activity of untimely death within, around and over my life, in the name of Jesus.

22. I speak life unto the organs in my body and command them not to malfunction, in the name of Jesus.

23. Every agent of the spirit of death, monitoring my life day and night, receive blindness and die, in the name of Jesus.

24. Every spirit, working to initiate me into evil covenants of untimely death, be frustrated, in the name of Jesus.

25. Every plantation of untimely death in my life, be uprooted by fire, in the name of Jesus.

26. My head, reject every manipulation and bewitchment of untimely death, in the name of Jesus.

27. Every bewitchment of witchcraft on my destiny and potentials, die, in the name of Jesus.

28. Every arrow of untimely death, fired at me in the dream, come out and go back to your senders, in Jesus' name.

29. Every satanic attack of untimely death, in the dream, die, in the name of Jesus.

30. Every satanic bird, crying out for the untimely death of my life, fall down and die, in the name of Jesus.

31. Every door, opened in my life for the attacks of untimely death, be closed by the blood of Jesus.

32. Oh Lord, let my life become too hot for any agent of untimely death, in the name of Jesus.

33. Every power, meeting to decide on untimely death for my life, scatter unto desolation, in the name of Jesus.

34. Every power, that does not want to see me around, your time is up. Fall down and die, in the name of Jesus.

35. Thank God for answers to your prayers.

DELIVERANCE FROM OCCULT ENTANGLEMENT

Occult entanglement is a prevalent problem today. Many in search of security, protection and power have been blindly initiated into the occult. Different occult groups come up with invitations to people to come and acquire knowledge, experience peace or safety or win prestige or contracts. At the end of the day, they lead innocent victims into deep bondage and entanglements of great dimensions.

Many have joined the occult, only to discover that the more they look, the less they see. This programme is designed by the Holy Ghost for those who want to get rid of occult entanglement and experience freedom once again. Remember that satan and his agents will not easily let their victims go. You must therefore remain persistent as you dismantle the complex entanglements of the occult through these prayer points.

Praise Worship

Confession: Col. 1:13: Who hath delivered us from the power of darkness, and hath translated us into the kingdom of his dear Son.

Prayer warfare

1. I confess and renounce every occult participation, in Jesus' name.

2. Every anti-Christ spirit, working against my life, die, in the name of Jesus.

3. Every covenant, made with family idols on my behalf, break by the blood of Jesus.

4. Every dedication of ancestral demons on my life, break by the blood of Jesus.

5. Every demonic mark and incisions on my body, be washed off by the blood of Jesus.

6. I nullify every covenant, oath and promise made in the occult houses and shrines, in the name of Jesus.

7. Blood of Jesus, close every doorway of demonic invasion into my life, in the name of Jesus.

8. Blood of Jesus, purge my soul, spirit and body of every occult property, in the name of Jesus.

9. I loose my destiny from every grip of occult demons, in the name of Jesus.

10. Every spirit of the bondwoman, working in my life, be cast out by fire, in the name of Jesus.

11. Every evil link and contact with demons over the years, break now, in the name of Jesus.

12. Every occult agreement and covenant, made with the powers of darkness, break by the blood of Jesus.

13. Every evil knowledge I acquired from occult association, be flushed out of my life, by the blood of Jesus.

14. I declare myself free from every occult entanglement, in the name of Jesus.

DELIVERANCE FROM REPEATED PROBLEMS

The devil is a technical game player who ensures that batons are passed from one hand to another to make problems persistent. His intention and plan are to make the end of a problem the beginning of another. By so doing, he uses some of the weapons of repeated problems to weary his victims. Thank God for spiritual warfare. There is a type of prayer to pray when problems are repeated, time and again. These prayer points will prevent the repetition of problems that are sponsored by the devil.

These prayer points will enable you to deal with repeated problems. They will break the covenants strengthening the problems and destroy the spirits behind them. You must delete your name from the list of candidates for repeated problems.

Praise Worship

Prayer warfare

1. Every household enemy, resisting my breakthroughs, fall down and die, in the name of Jesus.

2. Every unfriendly friend, delegated against my blessing, scatter, in the name of Jesus.

3. Every spirit of disobedience and rebellion in my life, die, in Jesus' name.

4. Every demon, propagating satanic covenants in my life, fall down and die, in the name of Jesus.

5. Any organ in my body, presently on any evil altar, roast, in Jesus' name.

6. By the stripes of Jesus, I curse the root of every sickness in my life, in the name of Jesus.

7. I destroy every anchor of any bondage in my life, in the name of Jesus.

8. Every spirit of hardship in my life, loose your hold, in the name of Jesus.

9. Every problem that defies solution in my life, blood of Jesus, destroy it, in the name of Jesus.

10. Every power, resisting the power of God in my life, I attack you with the thunder fire of God, in the name of Jesus.

11. Every mountain of stubborn problems in my life, fall down and die, in the name of Jesus.

12. Every invisible hand, working evil in my life, wither, in Jesus' name.

13. Every demon of frustration in my life, die, in the name of Jesus.

14. I reject every spirit of rejection and cancel its operations in my life, in the name of Jesus.

15. I reject and cast out of my life every deeply rooted failure, in the name of Jesus.

16. Every spirit of poverty in my family line, my life is not your candidate, die, in the name of Jesus.

17. Holy Ghost fire, burn every garment of poverty in my life, in the name of Jesus.

18. Every spirit of failure in my life, loose your hold and die, in the name of Jesus.

19. Every spirit of pocket-with-holes, wasting my finances, die, in the name of Jesus.

20. I decree that I shall not labour in vain. Another person shall not eat the fruit of my labour, in the name of Jesus.

21. Every ancestral spirit of anger, loose your hold upon my life, in the name of Jesus.

22. Every hold of unforgiving spirit in my life, break by the blood of Jesus.

23. Every hold of the spirit of prayerlessness in my life, die now, in the name of Jesus.

24. Every spirit, stealing from me, fall down and die, in the name of Jesus.

25. Every spirit of blindness in my life, die, in the name of Jesus.

26. Every spirit of poverty in my foundation, die, in the name of Jesus.

27. Every problem, planned for my future, you shall not see the daylight, in the name of Jesus.

28. Every warfare, against my breakthroughs in the heavenlies, scatter, in the name of Jesus.

29. Every circle of problems in my life ,die, in the name of Jesus.

30. By the blood of Jesus, I make my breakthroughs untouchable for any evil power, in the name of Jesus.

31. You powers, working against my treasures, fall down and die, in the name of Jesus.

32. Thank God for answers to your prayers.

DESTINY CHANGING AND RESTORATION PRAYER 1

To fulfil your destiny, there are two things you must do. You must pray to make power change from the hands of the enemy to the hands of the Holy Ghost. Additionally, you must seek the restoration of your destiny through aggressive prayer points.

Destiny can only be restored and fulfilled when it is handled with seriousness. The battle for destiny fulfilment is one which you must fight and win. The greatest problem today is the inability of multitudes to fulfil their destinies. Many people are living in the valley as a result of destiny diversion by the combination of forces of witchcraft and household enemies. This problem must be solved through a change of destiny. Stolen destinies must be restored for God's will and purpose to be fulfilled.

I recommend these prayer points for anyone who wants to succeed in life and make heaven. This is one prayer programme you cannot joke with. It is a must for anyone who has an idea of the type of damage which household witchcraft has perpetrated.

Confessions: Ps. 113:5-8: Who is like unto the Lord our God, who dwelleth on high? He raised up the poor out of the dust, and lifteth the needy out of the dunghill; that he may set him with princes, even with the princes of his people

Deut 28:13: And the LORD shall make thee the head, and not the tail; and thou shalt be above only, and thou shalt not be beneath; if that thou hearken unto the commandments of the LORD thy God, which I command thee this day, to observe and to do them:

Job 22:25-28: Yea, the Almighty shall be thy defence, and thou shalt have plenty of silver. For then shalt thou have thy delight in the Almighty, and shalt lift up thy face unto God. Thou shalt make thy prayer unto him, and he shall hear thee, and thou shalt pay thy vows. Thou shalt also decree a thing, and it shall be established unto thee: and the light shall shine upon thy ways.

Ps 27:6: And now shall mine head be lifted up above mine enemies round about me: therefore will I offer in his tabernacle sacrifices of joy; I will sing, yea, I will sing praises unto the LORD.

God is not a man that He should lie, nor the son of man

that He should repent of any of His pronouncements. Once has God spoken, twice have I heard this, that all power belongs to Him. Therefore, I believe every word of God, because the word of God is God Himself, and if God, it cannot lie. Every promise of God for my life will surely come to pass.

As I make these confessions, I declare to the devil that I am not ignorant of who I am in Christ. I am born again and I have been crucified with Christ. Now, I am seated with Him, far above all realms of darkness in heavenly places.

I am a saint. I belong to God. I am a king and a royal priest, called to the service of God. Jesus bought me with His own precious and blameless blood, and has translated my life from the kingdom of darkness to His kingdom of light, peace and abundant life.

I stand on the victory of Jesus over satan, and over death and hell, for it is written that Jesus first of all descended into the lower parts of the earth, and stripped the devil of all his power. He then ascended on high, leading captivity captive and gave gifts unto men. By this victory, let every gathering of the powers of darkness that is against my prayer life, my success and my breakthrough, be defeated by the blood of Jesus.

The day I wholeheartedly gave my life to Christ, I have submitted myself to the authority of the Lord of hosts. Therefore, satan, I have authority to resist you and your attacks against my sound relationship with my Maker, Jehovah God. Through my faith in Jesus Christ, I have become a seed of Abraham. The blessings of Abraham are mine.

The Scriptures say that I am blessed with the faithful Abraham. I am a partaker of all God's heavenly blessings. It is written that God has blessed all His children with all spiritual blessings in the heavenly places. The Lord God is a sun and a shield; He will give me grace and glory. No good thing, will He withhold from them that walk uprightly.

The scripture says that if I ask I will receive. I ask and by faith, I receive grace, glory and open heavens from God. Jehovah God is all-sufficient. The bible says He is more than sufficient. I ask for God's divine abundance in every area of my life and I receive it by faith. I confess and receive it by faith.

My prayers are sweet smelling savour in the presence of God. I ask, and I receive His grace and fire to incubate me. As it is written, I shall be a crown of glory in the hand of God, a royal diadem in the hand of my Maker. I begin to shine as a shining light. The light of God is in me. Darkness cannot abide in me and cannot overshadow me. The light of God shall be seen upon me and all eyes shall see it together.

Anywhere I go, I shall always stand out. Even when darkness shall cover the earth and tense darkness over all people, the Lord shall arise over me and His glory shall be seen upon me. I shall see and be radiant. My heart shall thrill and tremble with joy and be enlarged, because the abundance of the sea shall be turned to me. Unto me shall the nations come with their treasures. Foreigners shall build up walls for me and their kings shall minister to me. In God's wrath, He smote me, but in His favour, pleasure and goodwill, He has mercy and love for me. ∘

The sons of those who afflicted me shall come, bending low to me; and all those who despised me shall bow down at my feet. They shall call me the city of the Lord, the Zion of the Holy one of Israel. Whereas I have been forsaken and hated, so that no good thing passed through me, God will make me an eternal glory, a joy from age to age.

I shall eat the riches of the Gentiles and in their glory I shall boast myself, and all shall see and shall acknowledge that I am the seed which the Lord has blessed.

God has spoken to my life. I believe it and I begin to manifest it. I am not a failure, I shall operate at the head only and not beneath. I shall dwell on the mountain always and not in the valley. I shall no longer experience the activities of the spirit of mount Pisgah. I shall no longer be disappointed or fail at the edge of my desired miracles, success and victory; for the blood of the Lamb of God has cleansed every mark of witchcraft, hatred, jealousy, bewitchment and envy from my life.

I trample under my feet every serpent of treachery, evil report, accusation, machination and criticism. No counsel of the wicked shall stand against me. If God be for me, who can be against me. No weapon that is fashioned against me shall prosper and every tongue that rises up against me is already condemned. Therefore, I tear down in faith, every spiritual wall between me and my divinely appointed helpers and benefactors.

Right now, I stand in my position as a true child of Jehovah God, ordained to reign as a king on earth and I command the flavour of divine favour of God to fill me.
God has put His Word in my mouth as a weapon of destruction and restoration. I use that power to speak

destruction upon all devil's agents, assigned to hinder me and divert my blessings. I use the same weapon to decree restoration upon my life. It is written that I should discard the former things. God shall do a new thing in my life and it shall spring forth. Now, I ask that new things should begin to spring forth in my marriage, in my business, in my finances and in my spiritual life.

The Lord will make His face to shine upon me always and shall be gracious unto me. His light will shine on my path and His favour will encompass me all the days of my life.

PRAISE WORSHIP

PRAYER POINTS

1. O Lord, thank You for scattering the enemies of my divine destiny.

2. Every incantation, ritual and witchcraft powers against my destiny, fall down and die, in the name of Jesus.

3. I render null and void, the influence of destiny swallowers, in the name of Jesus.

4. Every household wickedness struggling to re-arrange my destiny, fall down and die, in the name of Jesus.

5. My destiny is attached to God, therefore, I decree that I can never fail, in the name of Jesus.

6. I refuse to be programmed against my divine destiny, in the name of Jesus.

7. I destroy every record of my destiny in the marine world, in the name of Jesus.

8. Every altar mounted against my destiny in the heavenlies, be dismantled, in the name of Jesus.

9. I reject every satanic alternative for my destiny, in Jesus' name.

10. Evil caldrons, you will not cook up my destiny, in Jesus' name.

11. I destroy every witchcraft cauldron and concoction against my destiny, in the name of Jesus.

12. Every power of the caldron raised to manipulate my destiny, release me, in the name of Jesus.

13. Destiny swallowers, vomit my destiny, in the name of Jesus.

14. I recover my stolen vehicle of destiny, in the name of Jesus.

15. Every conference of darkness against my destiny, scatter, in the name of Jesus.

16. O Lord, anoint my destiny afresh.

17. I decree that failure shall not slaughter my destiny, in the name of Jesus.

18. Every power waging war against my destiny, fall down and die, in the name of Jesus.

19. Destiny thieves, release me now, in the name of Jesus.

20. I overthrow every satanic re-arrangement programmed against my destiny, in the name of Jesus.

21. I have come to Zion, my destiny must change, in Jesus' name.

22. Every power derailing my destiny, fall down and die, in the name of Jesus.

23. I refuse to miss my destiny in life, in the name of Jesus.

24. I refuse to accept satanic substitute for my destiny, in the name of Jesus.

25. Anything programmed against my destiny in the heavenlies, be shaken down, in the name of Jesus.

26. Every. power, drawing powers from the heavenlies against my destiny, fall down and die, in the name of Jesus.

27. Every satanic altar, fashioned against my destiny, crack asunder, in the name of Jesus.

28. O Lord, take away my destiny from the hands of men.

29. I revoke every satanic ownership of my destiny, in Jesus' name.

30. Satan, you will not settle down on my destiny, in Jesus' name.

31. My destiny shall not suffer affliction, in the name of Jesus.

32. Every association of the emptiers against my destiny, scatter by the Word of God, in the name of Jesus.

33. Today, I raise the altar of continuous prosperity upon my destiny, in the name of Jesus.

34. You anchor of failures, keeping down my destiny, break, in Jesus' name.

35. Every evil bank, established against my destiny, liquidate by fire, in the name of Jesus.

36. I set judgment against every evil altar, erected against my destiny, in the name of Jesus.

37. My divine destiny, appear; my perverted destiny disappear, in the name of Jesus.

38. I reject every satanic rearrangement of my destiny, in the name of Jesus.

39. Every evil power with the awareness of my destiny, be impotent, in the name of Jesus.

40. I paralyse every destiny polluter, in the name of Jesus.

DESTINY CHANGING AND RESTORATION PRAYER 2

To fulfil your destiny, there are two things you must do. You must pray in order to make power change from the hands of the enemy to the hands of the Holy Ghost. Additionally, you must seek the restoration of your destiny through aggressive prayer points.

Destiny can only be restored and fulfilled when it is handled with seriousness. The battle for destiny fulfilment is one which you must fight and win. The greatest problem today is the inability of multitudes to fulfil their destinies. Many people are living in the valley as a result of destiny diversion by the combination of forces of witchcraft and household enemies. This problem must be solved through a change of destiny. Stolen destinies must be restored in order for God's will and purpose to be fulfilled.

I recommend these prayer points for anyone who wants to succeed in life and make heaven. This is one prayer programme you cannot joke with. It is a must for anyone

who has an idea of the type of damage which household
witchcraft has perpetrated.

Confessions: Ps. 113:5-8: Who is like unto the Lord our
God, who dwelleth on high? He raised up the poor out of
the dust, and lifteth the needy out of the dunghill; that
he may set him with princes, even with the princes of his
people

Deut 28:13: And the LORD shall make thee the head,
and not the tail; and thou shalt be above only, and thou
shalt not be beneath; if that thou hearken unto the
commandments of the LORD thy God, which I command
thee this day, to observe and to do them:

Job 22:25-28: Yea, the Almighty shall be thy defence,
and thou shalt have plenty of silver. For then shalt thou
have thy delight in the Almighty, and shalt lift up thy face
unto God. Thou shalt make thy prayer unto him, and he
shall hear thee, and thou shalt pay thy vows. Thou shalt
also decree a thing, and it shall be established unto thee:
and the light shall shine upon thy ways.

Ps 27:6: And now shall mine head be lifted up above mine
enemies round about me: therefore will I offer in his
tabernacle sacrifices of joy; I will sing, yea, I will sing
praises unto the LORD.

God is not a man that He should lie, nor the son of man that He should repent of any of His pronouncements. Once has God spoken, twice have I heard this, that all power belongs to Him. Therefore, I believe every word of God, because the word of God is God Himself, and if God, He cannot lie. Every promise of God for my life will surely come to pass.

As I make these confessions, I declare to the devil that I am not ignorant of who I am in Christ. I am born again and I have been crucified with Christ. Now, I am seated with Him, far above all realms of darkness in heavenly places.

I am a saint. I belong to God. I am a king and a royal priest, called to the service of God. Jesus bought me with His own precious and blameless blood, and has translated my life from the kingdom of darkness to His kingdom of light, peace and abundant life.

I stand on the victory of Jesus over satan, and over death and hell, for it is written that Jesus first of all descended into the lower parts of the earth, and stripped the devil of all his power. He then ascended on high, leading captivity captive and gave gifts unto men. By this victory, let every gathering of the powers of darkness that is against my prayer life, my success and my breakthrough, be defeated by the blood of Jesus.

The day I wholeheartedly gave my life to Christ, I have submitted myself to the authority of the Lord of hosts. Therefore, satan, I have authority to resist you and your attacks against my sound relationship with my Maker, Jehovah God. Through my faith in Jesus Christ, I have become a seed of Abraham. The blessings of Abraham are mine.

The Scriptures say that I am blessed with the faithful Abraham. I am a partaker of all God's heavenly blessings. It is written that God has blessed all His children with all spiritual blessings in the heavenly places. The Lord God is a sun and a shield; He will give me grace and glory. No good thing, will He withhold from them that walk uprightly.

The scripture says that if I ask I will receive. I ask and by faith, I receive grace, glory and open heavens from God. Jehovah God is all-sufficient. The bible says He is more than sufficient. I ask for God's divine abundance in every area of my life and I receive it by faith. I confess and receive it by faith.

My prayers are sweet smelling savour in the presence of God. I ask, and I receive His grace and fire to incubate me. As it is written, I shall be a crown of glory in the hand of God, a royal diadem in the hand of my Maker. I begin to shine as a shining light. The light of God is in me. Darkness cannot abide in me and cannot overshadow me. The light of God shall be seen upon me and all eyes shall see it together.

Anywhere I go, I shall always stand out. Even when darkness shall cover the earth and tense darkness over all people, the Lord shall arise over me and His glory shall be seen upon me. I shall see and be radiant. My heart shall thrill and tremble with joy and be enlarged, because the abundance of the sea shall be turned to me. Unto me shall the nations come with their treasures. Foreigners shall build up walls for me and their kings shall minister to me. In God's wrath, He smote me, but in His favour, pleasure and goodwill, He has mercy and love for me.

The sons of those who afflicted me shall come, bending low to me; and all those who despised me shall bow down at my feet. They shall call me the city of the Lord, the Zion of the Holy one of Israel. Whereas I have been forsaken and hated, so that no good thing passed through me, God will make me an eternal glory, a joy from age to age.

I shall eat the riches of the Gentiles and in their glory I

shall boast myself, and all shall see and shall acknowledge that I am the seed which the Lord has blessed.

God has spoken to my life. I believe it and I begin to manifest it. I am not a failure, I shall operate as the head only and not beneath. I shall dwell on the mountain always and not in the valley. I shall no longer experience the activities of the spirit of mount Pisgah. I shall no longer be disappointed or fail at the edge of my desired miracles, success and victory; for the blood of the Lamb of God has cleansed every mark of witchcraft, hatred, jealousy, bewitchment and envy from my life.

I trample under my feet every serpent of treachery, evil report, accusation, machination and criticism. No counsel of the wicked shall stand against me. If God be for me, who can be against me. No weapon that is fashioned against me shall prosper and every tongue that rises up against me is already condemned. Therefore, I tear down in faith, every spiritual wall between me and my divinely appointed helpers and benefactors.

Right now, I stand in my position as a true child of Jehovah God, ordained to reign as a king on earth and I command the flavour of divine favour of God to fill me. God has put His word in my mouth as a weapon of destruction and restoration. I use that power to speak destruction upon all devil's agents, assigned to hinder me and divert my blessings. I use the same weapon to decree restoration upon my life. It is written that I should discard the former things. God shall do a new thing in my life and it shall spring forth. Now, I ask that new things should begin to spring forth in my marriage, in my business, in my finances and in my spiritual life.

The Lord will make His face to shine upon me always and shall be gracious unto me. His light will shine on my path and His favour will encompass me all the days of my life.

PRAISE WORSHIP

PRAYER POINTS

1. Every damage done to my destiny, be repaired, in Jesus' name.

2. I decree that the enemy will not convert my destiny to rags, in Jesus' name.

3. O Lord, lay Your hands of fire upon my life and change upon my destiny.

4. I reject and renounce destiny- demoting names, and I nullify their evil effects upon my destiny, in Jesus' name.

5. Any evil record against my destiny in the heavenlies, as a result destiny-demoting names, be wiped off by the blood of Jesus.

6. I refuse to operate below my divine destiny, in Jesus' name.

7. Every power, contending with my divine destiny, scatter, in Jesus' name.

8. O Lord, change my destiny to the best that will dumbfound the enemies.

9. Satan, I resist and rebuke your efforts to change my destiny, in the name of Jesus.

10. Satan, I remove from you the right to rob me of my divine destiny, in the name of Jesus.

11. All powers of darkness, assigned to my destiny, leave and never return, in the name of Jesus.

12. The desire of my enemy, against my destiny, will not be granted in the heavenlies, in the name of Jesus.

13. The designs of my enemy, against my destiny, shall be destroyed, in the name of Jesus.

14. The deposits of my enemy in the heavenlies, against my destiny, shall be destroyed, in the name of Jesus.

15. The destiny of my enemy shall not be my lot, in Jesus' name.

16. Whether satan likes it or not, I wake to my destiny by fire, in the name of Jesus.

17. Oh Lord, give me new eyes to see into my destiny, in Jesus' name.

18. Conspiracy of darkness, against my destiny, scatter by fire, in the name of Jesus.

19. The fire of the enemy, against my destiny, shall backfire, in Jesus' name.

20. I decree that no weapon formed against my destiny shall prosper, in Jesus' name.

21. You evil strongman, attached to my destiny, be bound, in Jesus' name.

22. Every programme of failure, fashioned against my destiny, die, in the name of Jesus.

23. Every foothold of the enemy, on my destiny, be overthrown, in the name of Jesus.

24. O Lord, arise and sit over my life and let my destiny change.

25. By the power of God, the mouth of the wicked shall not speak against my destiny again, in the name of Jesus.

26. Every destiny, destroyed by polygamy, be reversed, in Jesus' name.

27. Every witchcraft power, working against my destiny, fall down and die, in the name of Jesus.

28. Every incantation and ritual, working against my destiny, be disgraced, in the name of Jesus.

29. Every power of darkness, assigned against my destiny, fall down and die, in the name of Jesus.

30. I reject every rearrangement of my destiny by household wickedness, in the name of Jesus

31. Every quencher of my destiny, fall down and die, in the name of Jesus.

32. O Lord, restore me to Your original design for my life.

33. O Lord, enlarge my coast.

34. Oh Lord, let the spirit of excellence come upon me, in Jesus' name.

35. I paralyse every satanic opportunity contending against my life, in the name of Jesus.

36. The rod of the wicked shall not rest upon my life, in the name of Jesus.

37. I refuse to be removed from the divine agenda, in the name of Jesus.

38. I dismantle spiritual devices, working against my destiny, in the name of Jesus.

39. Every coffin throat, swallowing my destiny, die, in the name of Jesus.

40. You workers of iniquity, depart from my destiny, in the name of Jesus.

DESTINY CHANGING AND RESTORATION PRAYER 3

To fulfil your destiny, there are two things you must do. You must pray in order to make power change from the hands of the enemy to the hands of the Holy Ghost. Additionally, you must seek the restoration of your destiny through aggressive prayer points.

Destiny can only be restored and fulfilled when it is handled with seriousness. The battle for destiny fulfilment is one which you must fight and win. The greatest problem today is the inability of multitudes to fulfil their destinies. Many people are living in the valley as a result of destiny diversion by the combination of forces of witchcraft and household enemies. This problem must be solved through a change of destiny. Stolen destinies must be restored in order for God's will and purpose to be fulfilled.

I recommend these prayer points for anyone who wants to succeed in life and make heaven. This is one prayer programme you cannot joke with. It is a must for anyone who has an idea of the type of damage which household witchcraft has perpetrated.

Confessions: Ps. 113:5-8: Who is like unto the Lord our God, who dwelleth on high? He raised up the poor out of the dust, and lifteth the needy out of the dunghill; that he may set him with princes, even with the princes of his people

Deut 28:13: And the LORD shall make thee the head, and not the tail; and thou shalt be above only, and thou shalt not be beneath; if that thou hearken unto the commandments of the LORD thy God, which I command thee this day, to observe and to do them:

Job 22:25-28: Yea, the Almighty shall be thy defence, and thou shalt have plenty of silver. For then shalt thou have thy delight in the Almighty, and shalt lift up thy face unto God. Thou shalt make thy prayer unto him, and he shall hear thee, and thou shalt pay thy vows. Thou shalt also decree a thing, and it shall be established unto thee: and the light shall shine upon thy ways.

Ps 27:6: And now shall mine head be lifted up above mine enemies round about me: therefore will I offer in his tabernacle sacrifices of joy; I will sing, yea, I will sing praises unto the LORD.

God is not a man that He should lie, nor the son of man that He should repent of any of His pronouncements. Once has God spoken, twice have I heard this, that all power belongs to Him. Therefore, I believe every word of God, because the word of God is God Himself, and if God, He cannot lie. Every promise of God for my life will surely come to pass.

As I make these confessions, I declare to the devil that I am not ignorant of who I am in Christ. I am born again and I have been crucified with Christ. Now, I am seated with Him, far above all realms of darkness in heavenly places.

I am a saint. I belong to God. I am a king and a royal priest, called to the service of God. Jesus bought me with His own precious and blameless blood, and has translated my life from the kingdom of darkness to His kingdom of light, peace and abundant life.

I stand on the victory of Jesus over satan, and over death and hell, for it is written that Jesus first of all descended into the lower parts of the earth, and stripped the devil of all his powers. He then ascended on high, leading captivity captive and gave gifts unto men. By this victory, let every gathering of the powers of darkness that is against my prayer life, my success and my breakthrough, be defeated by the blood of Jesus.

The day I wholeheartedly gave my life to Christ, I have submitted myself to the authority of the Lord of hosts. Therefore, satan, I have authority to resist you and your attacks against my sound relationship with my Maker, Jehovah God. Through my faith in Jesus Christ, I have become a seed of Abraham. The blessings of Abraham are mine.

The scriptures say that I am blessed with the faithful Abraham. I am a partaker of all God's heavenly blessings. It is written that God has blessed all His children with all spiritual blessings in the heavenly places. The Lord God is a sun and a shield; He will give me grace and glory. No good thing will He withhold from them that walk uprightly.

The scripture says that if I ask I will receive. I ask and by faith, I receive grace, glory and open heavens from God. Jehovah God is all-sufficient. The bible says He is more than sufficient. I ask for God's divine abundance in every area of my life and I receive it by faith. I confess and receive it by faith.

My prayers are sweet smelling savouries in the presence of God. I ask, and I receive His grace and fire to incubate me. As it is written, I shall be a crown of glory in the hand of God, a royal diadem in the hand of my Maker. I begin to shine as a shining light. The light of God is in me. Darkness cannot abide in me and cannot overshadow me. The light of God shall be seen upon me and all eyes shall see it together.

Anywhere I go, I shall always stand out. Even when darkness shall cover the earth and tense darkness over all people, the Lord shall arise over me and His glory shall be seen upon me. I shall see and be radiant. My heart shall thrill and tremble with joy and be enlarged, because the abundance of the sea shall be turned to me. Unto me shall the nations come with their treasures. Foreigners shall build up walls for me and their kings shall minister to me. In God's wrath, He smote me, but in His favour, pleasure and goodwill, He has mercy and love for me.

The sons of those who afflicted me shall come, bending low to me; and all those who despised me shall bow down at my feet. They shall call me the city of the Lord, the Zion of the Holy one of Israel. Whereas I have been forsaken and hated, so that no good thing passed through me, God will make me an eternal glory, a joy from age to age.

I shall eat the riches of the Gentiles and in their glory I

shall boast myself, and all shall see and shall acknowledge that I am the seed which the Lord has blessed.

God has spoken to my life. I believe it and I begin to manifest it. I am not a failure, I shall operate at the head only and not beneath. I shall dwell on the mountain always and not in the valley. I shall no longer experience the activities of the spirit of mount Pisgah. I shall no longer be disappointed or fail at the edge of my desired miracles, success and victory; for the blood of the Lamb of God has cleansed every mark of witchcraft, hatred, jealousy, bewitchment and envy from my life.

I trample under my feet every serpent of treachery, evil report, accusation, machination and criticism. No counsel of the wicked shall stand against me. If God be for me, who can be against me. No weapon that is fashioned against me shall prosper and every tongue that rises up against me is already condemned. Therefore, I tear down in faith, every spiritual wall between me and my divinely appointed helpers and benefactors.

Right now, I stand in my position as a true child of Jehovah God, ordained to reign as a king on earth and I command the flavour of divine favour of God to fill me. God has put His word in my mouth as a weapon of destruction and restoration. I use that power to speak destruction upon all devil's agents, assigned to hinder me and divert my blessings. I use the same weapon to decree restoration upon my life. It is written that I should discard the former things. God shall do a new thing in my life and it shall spring forth. Now, I ask that new things should begin to spring forth in my marriage, in my business, in my finances and in my spiritual life.

The Lord will make His face to shine upon me always and shall be gracious unto me. His light will shine on my path and His favour will encompass me all the days of my life.

PRAISE WORSHIP

PRAYER POINTS

1. Every gathering of destiny demoters, o Lord, shoot Your arrows and scatter them, in the name of Jesus.

2. I enter into my prophetic destiny, in the name of Jesus.

3. Dream animals, release my destiny, in the name of Jesus.

4. The Pharaoh of my destiny, die, in the name of Jesus.

5. I take authority over every witchcraft prayer, working against my destiny, in the name of Jesus.

6. You the leaf of my destiny, you shall not wither, in the name of Jesus.

7. I am a hot coal of fire, any herbalist that tampers with my destiny shall get burnt, in the name of Jesus.

8. You the power that moves people out of God's destiny, you shall not locate me, in the name of Jesus.

9. I reject and renounce destiny-demoting advices, in Jesus' name.

10. I silence every oracle, speaking against my destiny, in Jesus' name.

11. O Lord, kill every internal destiny killer.

12. Every power of familiar spirit on my destiny, die, in Jesus' name.

13. Every power, cursing my destiny, die, in the name of Jesus.

14. Every witchcraft incantation, against my destiny, die, in Jesus' name.

15. Every wicked spirit, assigned against my destiny, fail and fall by fire, in the name of Jesus.

16. Every serpent and scorpion, working against my destiny, dry up and die, in the name of Jesus.

17. Every altar, speaking against my divine destiny, be dismantled, in the name of Jesus.

18. Every attack, against my destiny when I was a child, be destroyed, in the name of Jesus.

19. Every evil arrow, fired against my destiny, fall down and die, in the name of Jesus.

20. Every satanic prayer, against my destiny, be reversed, in Jesus' name.

21. I withdraw satan's mandate against my destiny, in the name of Jesus.

22. You vulture of judgment, destroy the Pharaoh of my destiny, in the name of Jesus.

23. You my destiny, overshadow witchcraft envy, in Jesus' name.

24. Holy Ghost, let Your firing squad shoot down every evil bird working against my destiny, in the name of Jesus.

25. Every satanic investment upon my destiny, scatter, in Jesus' name.

26. You my destiny, reject poverty, in the name of Jesus.

27. I forbid evil hands to perform their enterprise upon my destiny, in the name of Jesus.

28. I silence every oracle, speaking against my destiny, in Jesus' name.

29. Every old prophet, misleading my destiny, I command destruction upon you, in the name of Jesus.

30. Every labour of the enemy on my destiny this year, receive double failure, in the name of Jesus.

31. Satanic hunters of my destiny, receive double frustration, in the name of Jesus.

32. Every hold of the power of familiar spirits on my destiny, break, in the name of Jesus.

33. Every stronghold of amputators and emptiers, fashioned against my destiny this year, be destroyed, in Jesus' name.

34. Any evil hand that will point against my destiny this year shall dry up, in the name of Jesus.

35. Every satanic check-point, mounted against my destiny this year, scatter by fire, in the name of Jesus.

36. Every poison of darkness, in my destiny, dry up and die, in Jesus' name.

37. Every switch, designed to put on the light of my destiny, operate by fire, in the name of Jesus.

38. I destroy the gates of violent spirits, that are working against my destiny, in the name of Jesus.

39. Every demonic chain, holding my destiny, break, in the name of Jesus.

40. You grave clothes, fighting my destiny, I tear you off, in Jesus' name.

41. Thou contrary king, reigning in my destiny, die, in Jesus' name.

42. Thou Lion of Judah, pursue affliction out of my destiny, in Jesus' name.

43. Thou eagle of my destiny, fly, in the name of Jesus.

44. Every tree of affliction, growing in my destiny, die, in Jesus' name.

45. I scatter every sacrifice, made against my destiny, in Jesus' name.

46. O Lord, reschedule my destiny, for uncommon breakthroughs, in the name of Jesus.

47. Every power, cursing my destiny, die, in the name of Jesus.

48. Every spiritual parent, assigned against my destiny, die, in Jesus' name.

49. Any satanic statement, programmed into the sun, moon and stars against my destiny, I revoke you by fire, in Jesus' name.

50. Any power, pressing suckers of blood against my destiny, fall down and die, in the name of Jesus.

51. My divine destiny, come out now, in the name of Jesus.

52. You this month, you must cooperate with my destiny, in Jesus' name

53. I overturn and destroy any wicked pattern of dream pollution attached to my destiny, in the name of Jesus.

54. Every satanic prayer, against my destiny, be reversed, in Jesus' name.

55. O God, arise and dismantle the obstacle against my destiny, in the name of Jesus.

56. Every seed of dream pollution, attacking my destiny, be uprooted by fire, in the name of Jesus.

57. Angels of God, scatter all those plotting against my destiny, in the name of Jesus.

58. I render all evil attacks against my potentials and destiny impotent, in the name of Jesus.

59. Thank God, for answers to your prayers.

SUCCESS IN THE MINISTRY

Ministerial success goes beyond the acquisition of theological knowledge or hard work.

A good number of spiritual factors determine the level of success which anyone in the ministry would achieve. A typical minister has lots of hostile powers to contend with. The devil has assigned hindering forces to each minister to programme failure into the work of the ministry. To succeed therefore, you need a great deal of prayer. Since the work of the ministry is spiritual in nature, the minister must fight and win certain battles in the spiritual realm to achieve success in the ministry.

You will achieve success in the ministry as a minister if you will take time to handle this prayer programme with uncommon aggression. This is the secret of success in the ministry.

Scriptures: John 12:24; 2Cor. 6; 1Cor. 9:16; Deut. 28:13; Rom. 8:35-

Confessions: Psalm 27:2: When the wicked, even mine enemies and my foes, came upon me to eat up my flesh, they stumbled and fell.

Matthew 3:11: I indeed baptize you with water unto repentance: but he that cometh after me is mightier than I, whose shoes I am not worthy to bear: he shall baptize you with the Holy Ghost, and with fire:

Galatians 3:13-14 : Christ hath redeemed us from the curse of the law, being made a curse for us: for it is written, Cursed is every one that hangeth on a tree: That the blessing of Abraham might come on the Gentiles through Jesus Christ; that we might receive the promise of the Spirit through faith.

2 Tim. 4:18: And the Lord shall deliver me from every evil work, and will preserve me unto his heavenly kingdom: to whom be glory for ever and ever. Amen.

Col. 1:13 : Who hath delivered us from the power of darkness, and hath translated us into the kingdom of his dear Son:

Col. 2:15: And having spoiled principalities and powers, he made a shew of them openly, triumphing over them in it.

Hebrews 2:15: And deliver them who through fear of

death were all their lifetime subject to bondage.

Praise worship

1. Thank God for the privilege of your calling.

2. Thank God for providing deliverance from any form of bondage.

3. Confess your sins and those of your ancestors, especially those sins linked to evil powers.

4. Ask the Lord for forgiveness.

5. I cover myself with the blood of Jesus.

6. You the power in the blood of Jesus, separate me from the sins of my ancestors.

7. Blood of Jesus, remove any unprogressive label from every aspect of my life.

8. O Lord, create in me a clean heart by Your power.

9. O Lord, renew a right spirit within me.

10. O Lord, teach me to die to self.

11. O Lord, ignite my calling with Your fire.

12. O Lord, anoint me to pray without ceasing.

13. O Lord, establish me a holy person unto You.

14. O Lord, restore my spiritual eyes and ears, in the name of Jesus.

15. O Lord, let the anointing to excel in my spiritual and physical life fall on me.

16. O Lord, produce in me the power of self-control and gentleness.

17. O Lord, let the anointing of the Holy Spirit break every yoke of backwardness in my life.

18. Holy Spirit, control my ability to frame my words, in the name of Jesus.

19. Holy Ghost, breathe on me now, in the name of Jesus.

20. Holy Ghost fire, ignite me to the glory of God.

21. Every form of rebellion, flee from my heart, in the name of Jesus.

22. Every spiritual contamination in my life, receive cleansing by the blood of Jesus.

23. You the brush of the Lord, scrub out every dirtiness in my spiritual pipe, in the name of Jesus.

24. Every rusted spiritual pipe in my life, receive wholeness, in the name of Jesus.

25. Every power, eating up my spiritual pipe, roast, in Jesus' name.

26. I renounce any evil dedication placed upon my life, in Jesus' name.

27. I break every evil edict and ordination, in the name of Jesus.

28. I renounce and loose myself from every negative dedication placed upon my life, in Jesus' name.

29. All demons, associated with negative dedication, leave now, in the name of Jesus Christ.

30. I loose myself from any inherited bondage, in the name of Jesus.

31. I break loose from every inherited evil covenant, in the name of Jesus.

32. I break loose from every inherited evil curse, in the name of Jesus.

33. All foundational strongmen, attached to my life, be paralysed, in the name of Jesus.

34. I cancel the consequences of any evil local name, attached to my person, in the name of Jesus.

35. I bind all principalities and powers of . . . operating over and within my life, in the name of Jesus.

36. I bind every power, pulling anything in my body towards evil by means of energy drawn from the sun, the moon and the stars, in Jesus' name.

37. I bind every power, pulling anything in my body towards evil by means of energy drawn from the planets, constellations and the earth, in the name of Jesus.

38. I bind every power, pulling anything in my body towards evil, by means of energy drawn from the . . ., in the name of Jesus.

    - air - wind - fire - water - light - darkness-elements

39. I forbid any transfer of spirit into my life from my family, friends and associates, in the name of Jesus.

40. Every altar, speaking against my divine destiny, be dismantled, in the name of Jesus.

41. Every chain of inherited witchcraft in my family, be destroyed, in the name of Jesus.

42. Every evil plantation in my life: **Come out with all your roots in the name of Jesus!** (*Lay your hands on your stomach and keep repeating the emphasised area.*)

43. (*Lay one hand on your head, and the other on your stomach or navel, and begin to pray like this*): Holy Ghost fire, burn from the top of my head to the sole of my feet. *Begin to mention every organ of your body; your kidney, liver, intestines, etc. You must not rush at this level, because the fire will actually come and you may start feeling the heat.*

44. I cut myself off from every spirit of . . . (*mention the name of your place of birth*), in the name of Jesus.

45. I cut myself off from every tribal spirit and curse, in Jesus' name.

46. I cut myself off from every territorial spirit and curse, in Jesus' name.

47. Every evil spiritual padlock and evil chain, hindering my spiritual growth, roast, in the name of Jesus.

48. I rebuke every spirit of spiritual deafness and blindness in my life, in the name of Jesus.

49. I send the fire of God to my eyes and ears to melt away satanic deposits, in the name of Jesus.

50. You my spiritual sight and eardrum, receive healing, in Jesus' name.

51. You spirit of confusion, loose your hold over my life, in Jesus' name.

52. By the power of God, I will not loose my calling, in the name of Jesus.

53. I reject the spirit of the tail; I choose the spirit of the head, in the name of Jesus.

54. I reject any demonic limitation on my progress, in the name of Jesus.

55. I reject the anointing of non-achievement in my handiwork, in the name of Jesus.

56. I declare that I am called of God. No evil power shall cut me down, in the name of Jesus.

57. O Lord, give me the power to be faithful to my calling, in Jesus' name.

58. I receive the anointing to remain steady, committed and consistent in my ministerial life, in the name of Jesus.

59. I shall not be lured into politics, church rivalry or rebellion, in the name of Jesus.

60. O Lord, give me the wisdom to respect my teachers and seniors, who have trained me, in the name of Jesus.

61. O Lord, give me the heart of a servant, so that I can experience Your blessings everyday, in the name of Jesus.

62. I receive power to rise up with wings as eagles, in the name of Jesus.

63. The enemy will not waste my calling, in the name of Jesus.

64. The devil will not swallow my ministerial destiny, in the name of Jesus.

65. Power for effective development in my calling, come upon me now, in the name of Jesus.

66. I declare war against spiritual ignorance, in the name of Jesus.

67. I bind and cast out every unteachable spirit, in the name of Jesus.

68. I receive the anointing for success in my ministry, in Jesus' name.

69. I shall not be an enemy of integrity, in the name of Jesus.

70. I shall not steal God's money, in the name of Jesus.

71. I shall not disgrace the call of God upon my life, in the name of Jesus.

72. I shall work in holiness everyday, in the name of Jesus.

73. I bind the spirit of sexual immorality, in the name of Jesus.

74. I receive the culture of loyalty in my ministry, in the name of Jesus.

75. I shall not become an old king that is resistant to advice, in the name of Jesus.

76. I shall not live a wasteful or extravagant life, in Jesus' name.

77. I shall not serve my wonderful Saviour for filthy financial gain, in the name of Jesus.

78. I bind every spirit of quarrels and opposition from my wife/husband, in the name of Jesus.

79. My wife/husband shall not scatter my church members, in Jesus' name.

80. Every Judas in my ministry, fall into your own trap, in Jesus' name.

81. My ministry will not destroy my marriage, in the name of Jesus.

82. My marriage will not destroy my ministry, in the name of Jesus.

83. My children will not be misfired arrows in my ministry, in Jesus' name

84. I claim progress and excellence for my ministry, in the name of Jesus.

85. My church shall experience prosperity, in the name of Jesus.

86. O Lord, let my ministry reach the unreached, in the name of Jesus.

87. Multitude of people will go to heaven because of my ministry, in the name of Jesus.

88. I kill every attack on my ministry; I shall prevail, in the name of Jesus.

89. I shall not bite the fingers that fed me, in the name of Jesus.

90. I shall not engage in rebellion, in the name of Jesus.

91. Every power of my father's house, working against my calling, die, in the name of Jesus.

92. Anointing for excellence, fall upon me, in the name of Jesus.

93. Oh Lord, break me and re-mould me, in the name of Jesus.

94. I will not surrender to the enemy, in the name of Jesus.

95. I shall not die before my time, in the name of Jesus.

96. I shall not desire the prosperity of Naaman, in the name of Jesus.

97. Oh God arise and let every enemy of my calling scatter, in Jesus' name.

98. I receive fresh fire and fresh anointing, in the name of Jesus.

99. Holy fire of revival, fall upon my branch, in the name of Jesus.

100. Thank God, for answers to your prayers.

NOTE: These prayer points are to be said from midnight to 3:00 a.m. for 3 days. At least one day dry fast is recommended.

Victory is yours, in Jesus' name.

PRAYERS FOR THE MIRACLE OF SUPERNATURAL CONCEPTION AND DIVINE PROTECTION

Conception is the work of God. Every expectant mother or couple will do well to carry out this all-important prayer programme.

When you pray for the miracle of supernatural conception, you are placing your trust in the unfailing power of God, while waging war against every power that has decreed that your conception will be an aborted dream. This prayer programme will make conception possible, as well as safeguard your pregnancy. It is a spiritual insurance for the fruit of the womb. You must take the prayer points by faith, while making sure that spiritual aggression is added to it to make God's plan for becoming a joyful mother a glorious reality. Whether you are in an environment where medical facilities are poor or you are being attended to in an environment where there are state-of-the art medical facilities, you need this prayer programme. Use these prayer points and your testimony will gladden your heart.

Confessions: 1 John 5:14-15: And this is the confidence that we have in him, that, if we ask any thing according to his will, he heareth us: And if we know that he hear us, whatsoever we ask, we know that we have the petitions that we desired of him.

2 Cor 1:20: For all the promises of God in him are yea, and in him Amen, unto the glory of God by us.

Num 23:19: God is not a man, that he should lie; neither the son of man, that he should repent: hath he said, and shall he not do it? or hath he spoken, and shall he not make it good?

Isa 55:11: So shall my word be that goeth forth out of my mouth: it shall not return unto me void, but it shall accomplish that which I please, and it shall prosper in the thing whereto I sent it.

1. Praise worship.

2. Father, I thank You for entrusting these children to me.

3. O God, perfect your gifts in me, in the name of Jesus.

4. My babies and I are fearfully and wonderfully made, in Jesus' name.

5. O God, arise and guide me through this childbearing journey with ease, grace and loving-kindness, in the name of Jesus.

6. Oh Lord, as I experience biological and emotional changes, let Your joy be my strength, in the name of Jesus.

7. Oh Father, be glorified in my life, in the name of Jesus.

8. O God, arise according to Jeremiah 29:11 and give me the expected end of safety and joy, in the name of Jesus.

9. I shield myself with the envelope of divine fire, away from evil observers and evil monitors, in Jesus' name.

10. O God, give me heavenly care and proper development for my baby, in the name of Jesus.

11. O God, direct throughout this process of pregnancy, in the name of Jesus.

12. By Your mercy, o God, deliver me and my babies from any harvest of the seeds of iniquity, sown in the past, in the name of Jesus.

13. O God, let my case stand out for dumbfounding success, in Jesus' name.

14. Oh Lord, you who cause me to conceive, cause me to bring forth, in the name of Jesus (Isa. 66:9).

15. I decree that all things must work together for my good, in Jesus' name.

16. I bind every spirit of error, in the name of Jesus.

17. As a spiritual child of Abraham, I am fruitful and will multiply, in the name of Jesus.

18. My fruit (babies/pregnancy) shall be firmly established and I shall not miscarry, in the name of Jesus (Exod. 23:26).

19. These children shall serve God's purpose for me to multiply and subdue the earth, in the name of Jesus.

20. O God, deliver me from morning sickness and any complication, in the name of Jesus.

21. I stand against any birth defect in my babies and claim perfection for them, in the name of Jesus.

22. O God, frustrate any action You do not want me to take, in the name of Jesus.

23. O God, bring the good work You have started in me to a glorious conclusion, in the name of Jesus.

24. I claim proper growth and development for the babies in the womb, and safety for us during childbirth, in the name of Jesus.

25. My expectations shall not be cut off, in the name of Jesus.

26. Make the following confessions:

Gen 1:28: And God blessed them, and God said unto them, Be fruitful, and multiply, and replenish the earth, and subdue it: and have dominion over the fish of the sea, and over the fowl of the air, and over every living thing that moveth upon the earth.

Gen 9:1: And God blessed Noah and his sons, and said unto them, Be fruitful, and multiply, and replenish the earth.

Gen 9:7: And you, be ye fruitful, and multiply; bring forth abundantly in the earth, and multiply therein.

Gen 17:6: And I will make thee exceeding fruitful, and I will make nations of thee, and kings shall come out of thee.

Ex 1:12: But the more they afflicted them, the more they multiplied and grew. And they were grieved because of the children of Israel.

Ex 23:26: There shall nothing cast their young, nor be barren, in thy land: the number of thy days I will fulfil.

Deut 7:13-14: And he will love thee, and bless thee, and multiply thee: he will also bless the fruit of thy womb, and the fruit of thy land, thy corn, and thy wine, and thine oil, the increase of thy kine, and the flocks of thy sheep, in the land which he sware unto thy fathers to give thee. [14] Thou shalt be blessed above all people: there shall not be male or female barren among you, or among your cattle.

Ps 113:9: He maketh the barren woman to keep house, and to be a joyful mother of children. Praise ye the Lord.

Ps 127:3-5: Lo, children are an heritage of the LORD: and the fruit of the womb is his reward. As arrows are in the hand of a mighty man; so are children of the youth. Happy is the man that hath his quiver full of them: they shall not be ashamed, but they shall speak with the enemies in the gate.

Ps 128:3,6: Thy wife shall be as a fruitful vine by the sides of thine house: thy children like olive plants round about thy table. Yea, thou shalt see thy children's children, and peace upon Israel.

1 Tim 2:15: Notwithstanding she shall be saved in childbearing, if they continue in faith and charity and holiness with sobriety.

27. I receive divine mandate to enforce my right of conception, in the name of Jesus.

28. Any abnormality in my organs of conception, receive divine correction, in the name of Jesus.

29. Every negative medical report, be converted to positive result, in the name of Jesus.

30. Blood of Jesus, flush out any satanic deposit in my womb, in the name of Jesus.

31. I cover every drug or injection given to me with the blood of Jesus.

32. You my womb, become an expressway to conception, in Jesus' name.

33. I charge every hand that treats me, every bed I lie on and every test conducted on me with the blood of Jesus and the fire of the Holy Ghost, in the name of Jesus.

34. Every satanic road-block, mounted against pregnancy development, be dismantled by fire, in the name of Jesus.

35. Anything on my way to the miracle of supernatural conception and birth, clear away by the blood of Jesus.

36. You my womb and breasts, begin to function as ordained by God, in the name of Jesus.

37. Thou creative power of God, move in my womb by Your fire, in the name of Jesus.

38. I withdraw my womb from every evil altar, in the name of Jesus.

39. Every seed of pregnancy failure in my foundation, die, in Jesus' name.

40. Every satanic transfer or exchange of my womb, die, in Jesus' name.

41. I bind and cast out every spirit of failure in all stages of the pregnancy, in the name of Jesus.

42. Every word, spoken by the enemy against my conception, backfire, in the name of Jesus.

43. Any evil tree, growing in our family that is working against my conception, die, in the name of Jesus.

44. Any curse, strengthening the enemy of my pregnancy, die by the blood of Jesus.

45. Every strongman, supervising my womb to arrest my babies, die, in the name of Jesus.

46. By the power that divided the Red Sea, I obtain my babies by fire, in the name of Jesus.

47. Holy Spirit, make my womb super-conducive for pregnancy, in the name of Jesus.

48. I bind and arrest every infection, in the name of Jesus.

49. Blood of Jesus, nullify the after-effect of any drug administered to me, in the name of Jesus.

50. Holy Spirit, by Your power that incubated the womb of Elizabeth and Sarah, bind my egg and the sperm of my husband together in conception, in the name of Jesus.

I declare, according to the word of God, that the Lord shall perfect everything concerning me. The Lord, who has started His good work of creation in me will complete it (Phil. 1:6).

By the power in the blood of the Lord Jesus Christ, I confess that my pregnancy is perfect, in the name of Jesus. Every part of my body shall function perfectly for the formation of the baby, in Jesus' name. My blood shall circulate effectively. Everything that passes from me to the baby for its development shall be perfect, in Jesus' name. I confess that I am strong. Weakness is not my lot, in the name of Jesus. I will not have morning sickness or vomiting in my pregnancy, in the name of Jesus. I reject cramps, varicose veins, piles and backaches, because Jesus Christ has borne all my sicknesses. I refuse constipation, anaemia, vitamin and mineral deficiencies, swollen hands and feet, hypertension, convulsion and diabetes in the mighty name of Jesus. My urine will remain normal in the name of Jesus (Psalm 103: 3-5). I confess that the activities of eaters of flesh and drinkers of blood will not prosper in my life, in the name of Jesus. I refuse and reject all negative dreams, visions, prophecies and imaginations, in the name of Jesus.

I confess God's Word in Exodus 23:26, that I shall not have a miscarriage or any form of abnormal bleeding or malformation of the baby, in Jesus' name. I shall be a joyous mother of children. My womb is fruitful. I am a fruitful vine by the side of our house. My children are like olive plants round about our table. As the baby grows, every aspect of its growth, formation and development, shall be perfect, in Jesus' name.

I also confess that I shall not suffer any sickness like nausea, irritation, headache, internal or external pain, because by the stripes of Jesus, I am healed. I tread on sickness and upon all the powers of the devil. My body is the temple of the Holy Spirit. I have the life and health of Christ in me. The Sun of Righteousness has arisen, having conquered sickness, pains and satan. There is healing in His wings for me. God's will for me and my baby is to prosper and be in good health. God is at work in me now to will and to do His good pleasure. The power of the Holy Spirit is at work in me right now. It is flowing in me and perfecting all that pertains to my baby's formation, in Jesus' name.

I declare that every disease and germ should die now, in Jesus' name. Nothing I take into my body through the mouth shall harm me or my baby, in Jesus' name. God's word says, "If I drink any deadly thing, it shall not harm me." I confess that as I go to deliver my baby, the Lord shall direct those taking the delivery on what care suits me and the baby, in Jesus' name.

My pregnancy is established in righteousness. I am far from oppression, therefore, I shall not fear, because no terror shall come near me. No evil shall befall me or my baby, and no plague shall come near my dwelling place and my family.

As the pregnancy progresses, the Lord shall fulfil the number of my days. I shall not have a premature baby but a fully grown baby. My baby shall come out alive, strong and healthy because nothing shall harm my young ones. I am fearfully and wonderfully made. My pelvis is wide enough to allow my baby to pass through, in the name of Jesus.

I also confess, according to Isaiah 43, that when I pass

through the water, the Lord will be with me, if through the rivers, it shall not overflow me and if I walk through the fire, I shall not be burnt nor shall the flame scorch me. Therefore, I confess that I shall pass through the child-delivery without any pain or hurt, in Jesus' name.

The Lord shall take away from me every sickness of pregnancy and child bearing and those that accompany complication, according to Deut. 7:14,15. Therefore, I shall not fear because I have been redeemed from the curse of the law - the curse of bringing forth in agony (Galatians 4).

I boldly confess Isaiah 66:7, that before I travail, I will give birth and before any pain comes, I will be delivered of my baby. Moreover, according to 1 Tim. 2:15, I will be delivered of my baby. Also, according to 1 Tim. 2:15, I will be saved in child-bearing because I continue in faith, love and holiness with self-control.

I confess that I shall go to the delivery room confidently, in Jesus' name. The Lord has given me perfect peace, because my mind rests on Him. My trust is in the Lord and Jehovah God is my everlasting strength.

According to Psalm 118:17, I confess that I shall neither die at child-birth nor shall my baby suffer death. We shall both live to declare the works of the Lord, in Jesus' name.

My cervix shall be fully dilated, and the passage big and open enough to allow the baby pass through with ease. The delivery shall be perfect, in Jesus' name. No evil shall befall me or my baby. No weapon of the devil that is fashioned against me or against my baby shall prosper, in Jesus' name.

The Lord is the strength of my life, of whom shall I be afraid. He is my Deliverer, my God, my Buckler and the Horn of my Salvation. The Lord is all I need to take through on that day. He will strengthen the bars of my gate. He has blessed my children within me. Therefore, through the Lord, I shall do valiantly. I will live to be the happy mother of my baby. None of us shall see death, in Jesus' name. I refuse prolonged labour and reject all pains from the devil, during labour and afterwards.

I look forward to the rearing of the children after birth. I confess that we shall bring them up in the way of the Lord. The children shall grow up to know and love the Lord from their youth. I also confess that the Lord shall supply all our needs during pregnancy and the needs of the babies after their delivery, in Jesus' name.

Glory be to the name of the Lord, because I shall have what I say, in Jesus' name.

PRAYERS FOR THE MIRACLE OF SUPERNATURAL CONCEPTION AND DIVINE PROTECTION 1

This programme is specially tailored and vomited by the Holy Ghost for women and couples who want to lay a good foundation for the fruit of the womb. It will enable them to enjoy protection throughout the period of pregnancy.

Getting pregnant is one thing, while keeping the state full-term is another. Many women who have struggled with bouts of miscarriages would find this prayer programme comforting and helpful. These prayer points will enable you to set a divine watch over your pregnancy from the beginning to the end. You will be spared the trauma of satanic attacks that can threaten your pregnancy. This is a divine immunity against all forms of demonic attacks against pregnancy.

Confessions: 1 John 5:14-15: And this is the confidence that we have in him, that, if we ask any thing according to his will, he heareth us: And if we know that he hear us, whatsoever we ask, we know that we have the petitions that we desired of him.

2 Cor 1:20: For all the promises of God in him are yea, and in him Amen, unto the glory of God by us.

Num 23:19: God is not a man, that he should lie; neither the son of man, that he should repent: hath he said, and shall he not do it? or hath he spoken, and shall he not make it good?

Isa 55:11: So shall my word be that goeth forth out of my mouth: it shall not return unto me void, but it shall accomplish that which I please, and it shall prosper in the thing whereto I sent it.

---

1. Praise worship.

2. I confess and repent of the sin of bloodshed, committed in my days of ignorance, in Jesus' name.

3. Lord Jesus, wash away my sins of the past and their consequences.

4. Father, I thank You for entrusting these children to me.

5. O God, perfect these gifts in me, in the name of Jesus.

6. My babies and I are fearfully and wonderfully made, in the name of Jesus.

7. O God, arise and guide me through this childbearing journey with ease, grace and loving-kindness, in the name of Jesus.

8. As I experience biological and emotional changes, let Your joy be my strength, in the name of Jesus.

9. Father, be glorified in my life, in the name of Jesus.

10. O God, arise according to Jeremiah 29:11, and give me the

expected end of safety and joy, in Jesus' name.

11. I shield myself with the envelop of divine fire, away from evil observers and evil monitors, in Jesus' name.

12. O God, give me heavenly care and proper development for my baby, in the name of Jesus.

13. O God, always direct me throughout this process of pregnancy, in the name of Jesus.

14. By Your mercy, O God, deliver me and my babies from any harvest of the seeds of iniquity sown in the past, in the name of Jesus.

15. O God, let my case stand out for dumbfounding success, in the name of Jesus.

16. You who caused me to conceive, cause me to bring forth, in the name of Jesus (Isa. 66:9).

17. I prophesy that all things must work together for my good, in the name of Jesus.

18. I bind every spirit of error, in the name of Jesus.

19. As a spiritual child of Abraham, I am fruitful and will multiply, in the name of Jesus.

20. My fruit (babies/pregnancy) shall be firmly established and shall not miscarry before the normal delivery time, in the name of Jesus (Exod. 23:26).

21. These children shall serve God's purpose for me to multiply and subdue the earth, in the name of Jesus.

22. O God, deliver me from morning sickness and any complication, in the name of Jesus.

23. I stand against any birth defect in my babies and claim perfection for them, in the name of Jesus.

24. O God, frustrate any action You do not want me to take, in the name of Jesus.

25. O God, bring the good work You have started in me to a glorious conclusion, in the name of Jesus.

26. I claim proper growth and development for the babies in the womb, and safety for the child and I during childbirth, in the name of Jesus.

27. My expectations shall not be cut off, in the name of Jesus.

28. Make the following confessions:

Gen 1:28: And God blessed them, and God said unto them, Be fruitful, and multiply, and replenish the earth, and subdue it: and have dominion over the fish of the sea, and over the fowl of the air, and over every living thing that moveth upon the earth.

Gen 9:1: And God blessed Noah and his sons, and said unto them, Be fruitful, and multiply, and replenish the earth.

Gen 9:7: And you, be ye fruitful, and multiply; bring forth abundantly in the earth, and multiply therein.

Gen 17:6: So shall my word be that goeth forth out of my mouth: it shall not return unto me void, but it shall accomplish that which I please, and it shall prosper in the thing whereto I sent it.

Ex 1:12: But the more they afflicted them, the more they multiplied and grew. And they were grieved because of the children of Israel.

Ex 23:26: There shall nothing cast their young, nor be barren, in thy land: the number of thy days I will fulfil.

Deut 7:13-14: And he will love thee, and bless thee, and multiply thee: he will also bless the fruit of thy womb, and the fruit of thy land, thy corn, and thy wine, and thine oil, the increase of thy kine, and the flocks of thy sheep, in the land which he sware unto thy fathers to give thee. Thou shalt be blessed above all people: there shall not be male or female barren among you, or among your cattle.

Ps 113:9: He maketh the barren woman to keep house, and to be a joyful mother of children. Praise ye the Lord.

Ps 127:3-5: Lo, children are an heritage of the LORD: and the fruit of the womb is his reward. As arrows are in the hand of a mighty man; so are children of the youth. Happy is the man that hath his quiver full of them: they shall not be ashamed, but they shall speak with the enemies in the gate.

Ps 128:3,6: Thy wife shall be as a fruitful vine by the sides of thine house: thy children like olive plants round about thy table. Yea, thou shalt see thy children's children, and peace upon Israel.

1 Tim 2:15: Notwithstanding she shall be saved in childbearing, if they continue in faith and charity and holiness with sobriety.

29. I receive a divine mandate to enforce my right of conception, in the name of Jesus.

29. Any abnormality in my organs of conception and pregnancy, receive divine correction, in Jesus' name.

30. Every negative medical report, be converted to positive results, in the name of Jesus.

31. Blood of Jesus, flush out any satanic deposit in my womb, in the name of Jesus.

32. I cover every drug or injection given to me with the blood of Jesus.

33. My womb, become an expressway to conception, in the name of Jesus.

34. I charge every hand, every bed and every test with the blood of Jesus, and the fire of the Holy Ghost, in the name of Jesus.

35. Every satanic road-block, mounted against pregnancy development, be dismantled by fire, in the name of Jesus.

36. Anything on my way to the miracle of supernatural conception and birth, clear away by the blood of Jesus.

37. My womb and breast, begin to function as ordained by God, in the

name of Jesus.

38. Thou creative power of God, move in my womb by Your fire, in the name of Jesus.

39. I withdraw my womb from every evil altar, in the name of Jesus.

40. Every seed of pregnancy failure in my foundation, die, in Jesus' name.

41. Every satanic transfer or exchange of my womb, die, in Jesus' name.

42. I bind and cast out every spirit of failure in all procedures, in the name of Jesus.

43. Every word, spoken by the enemy against my conception, backfire, in the name of Jesus.

44. Any evil tree, growing in our family that is working against my conception, die, in the name of Jesus.

45. Any curse, strengthening the enemy of my pregnancy, die by the blood of Jesus.

46. Every strongman, supervising my womb to arrest babies, die, in the name of Jesus.

47. By the power that divided the Red Sea, I obtain my babies by fire, in the name of Jesus.

48. Holy Spirit, make my womb super-conducive for pregnancy, in the name of Jesus.

49. I bind and arrest every infection, in the name of Jesus.

50. Blood of Jesus, nullify the after-effect of any drug administered on me, in the name of Jesus.

51. Holy Spirit, by Your power that incubated the womb of Elizabeth and Sarah, bind my egg and the sperm of my husband together in conception, in the name of Jesus.

I declare, according to the word of God, that the Lord shall perfect everything concerning me. The Lord who has started His good work of creation in me will complete it (Phil. 1:6).

By the power in the blood of the Lord Jesus Christ, I confess that my pregnancy is perfect, in the name of Jesus. Every part of my body shall function perfectly for the formation of the baby, in Jesus' name. My blood shall circulate effectively. Everything that passes from me to the baby for its development shall be perfect, in Jesus' name. I confess that I am strong. Weakness is not my lot, in the name of Jesus. I will not have morning sickness or vomiting in my pregnancy, in the name of Jesus. I reject cramps, varicose veins, piles and backaches, because Jesus Christ has borne all my sicknesses. I refuse constipation, anaemia, vitamin and mineral deficiencies, swollen hands and feet, hypertension, convulsion and diabetes, in the mighty name of Jesus. My urine will remain normal, in the name of Jesus (Psalm 103: 3-5). I confess that the activities of eaters of flesh and drinkers of blood will not prosper in my life, in the name of Jesus. I refuse and reject all negative dreams, visions, prophecies and imaginations, in the name of Jesus.

I confess God's word in Exodus 23:26, that I shall not have a miscarriage, any form of abnormal bleeding or malformation of the baby, in Jesus' name. I shall be a joyous mother of children. My womb is fruitful. I am a fruitful vine by the side of our house. My children are like olive plants round about our table. As the baby grows, every aspect of its growth, formation and development shall be perfect, in Jesus' name.

I also confess that I shall not suffer from any sickness like nausea, irritation, headache, internal or external pain because by the stripes of Jesus, I am healed. I tread on sickness and upon all the powers of the devil. My body is the temple of the Holy spirit. I have the life and health of Christ in me. The Sun of Righteousness has arisen, having conquered sickness, pains and satan. There is healing in His wings for me. God's will for me and my baby is to prosper and be in good health. God is at work in me now to will and to do His good pleasure. The power of the Holy Spirit is at work in me right now. It is flowing in me and perfecting all that pertains to my baby's formation, in Jesus' name.

I declare that every disease and germ should die now, in Jesus' name. Nothing I take into my body through the mouth shall harm me or my baby, in Jesus' name. God's word says, "If I drink any deadly thing, it shall not harm me." I confess that as I go to deliver my baby, the Lord shall direct those taking the delivery on what care suits me and the baby, in Jesus'

name.

My pregnancy is established in righteousness. I am far from oppression. Therefore, I shall not fear, because no terror shall come near me. No evil shall befall me or befall my baby, and no plague shall come near my dwelling place and my family.

As the pregnancy progresses, the Lord shall fulfil the number of my days. I shall not have a premature baby, but a fully grown baby. My baby shall come out alive, strong and healthy, because nothing shall harm my young. I am fearfully and wonderfully made. My pelvis is wide enough to allow my baby to pass through, in the name of Jesus.

I also confess, according to Isaiah 43, that when I pass through the water, the Lord will be with me; if through the rivers, it shall not overflow me and if I walk through the fire, I shall neither be burnt nor shall the flame scorch me. Therefore, I confess that I shall pass through child-delivery without any pain or hurt, in Jesus' name.

The Lord shall take away from me every sickness of pregnancy and childbearing and those accompanying complications according to Deut. 7:14,15. Therefore, I shall not fear because I have been redeemed from the curse of the law - the curse of bringing forth in agony (Galatians 4).

I boldly confess Isaiah 66:7 that before I travail, I will give birth and before any pain comes, I will be delivered of my baby. Also, according to 1 Tim. 2:15, I will be delivered of my baby. Moreover, according to 1 Tim. 2:15, I will be saved in child bearing because I continue in faith, love and holiness with self-control.

I confess that I shall go to the delivery room confidently, in Jesus' name. The Lord has given me perfect peace because my mind rests on Him. My trust is in the Lord and Jehovah God is my everlasting strength.

According to Psalm 118:17, I confess that I shall neither die at child-birth nor shall my baby suffer death. We shall both live to declare the works of the Lord, in Jesus' name. My cervix shall be fully dilated, and the passage big and open enough to allow the baby to pass through with ease. The delivery shall be perfect, in Jesus' name. No evil shall befall me or my baby. No weapon of the devil that is fashioned against me or against my baby shall prosper, in Jesus' name.

The Lord is the strength of my life, of whom shall I be afraid? He is my Deliverer, my God, my Buckler and the Horn of my Salvation. The Lord is all I need to take through delivery on that day. He will strengthen the bars of my gate. He has blessed my children within me. Therefore, through the Lord I shall do valiantly. I will live to be the happy mother of my baby. None of us shall see death, in Jesus' name. I refuse prolonged labour, and reject all pains from the devil during labour and afterwards.

I look forward to the rearing of the children after birth. I confess that we shall bring them up in the way of the Lord. The children shall grow up to know and love the Lord from their youth. I also confess that the Lord shall supply all our needs during pregnancy and those of the babies after their delivery in Jesus' name.

Glory be to the name of the Lord because I shall have what I say, in Jesus' name.

52. Lord Jesus, let every sword depart from my marriage, in Jesus' name.

53. O Lord, make ways for me where there is no way, in Jesus' name.

54. I break any covenant between me and every evil husband or wife, in the name of Jesus.

55. Any of my clothes, that the enemy has set aside to afflict my conception, roast, in Jesus' name.

56. Every bow of the mighty, contending with my fruitfulness, break, break, break, in the name of Jesus.

57. Any decoration in my apartment that is bewitched, o Lord, reveal it to me.

58. I destroy every evil stone or goat destroying my children in pregnancy, in the name of Jesus.

59. Any garment, that the enemy is using to destroy my pregnancy, roast, in the name of Jesus.

60. O Lord, let Your strong east wind blow against the Red Sea in my womb now, in the name of Jesus.

61. Every demonic instrument of operation, set aside to abort my

pregnancy, break to pieces, in the name of Jesus.

62. O Lord, fight against the destroyer, working against my increase and fruitfulness, in the name of Jesus.

63. Every demonic doctor/nurse, delegated by satan to destroy my pregnancy, inject yourself to death, in Jesus' name.

64. Blood of Jesus, wash me and show me mercy, in the name of Jesus.

65. Every evil remote control gadget, being used to manipulate my pregnancy, roast by fire, in Jesus' name.

66. Thou Man of war, save me out of the hands of wicked midwives, in the name of Jesus.

67. I render every weapon fashioned against my pregnancy impotent, in the name of Jesus.

68. O Lord, overthrow every Egyptian working against me, in the midst of the sea, in the name of Jesus.

69. I close down every satanic broadcasting station, fashioned against my pregnancy, in the name of Jesus.

70. I will see, the great work of the Lord, as I deliver my children safely, in the name of Jesus.

71. I refuse to harbour any pregnancy killer in any department of my life, in the name of Jesus.

72. Every horse and its rider in my womb, family or office, be thrown into the sea of forgetfulness, in the name of Jesus.

73. I bind every spirit of error assigned against my pregnancy, in the name of Jesus.

74. O Lord, send Your light before me to drive miscarriages from my womb and life, in the name of Jesus.

75. I bind the spirit of almost there; you will not operate in my life, in the name of Jesus.

76. I cast out every power casting out my children, in the name of Jesus.

77. I break every grip and hold of witchcraft over my pregnancy, in the name of Jesus.

78. From today, I shall not cast my young, in the name of Jesus.

79. I paralyse every opposition to my pregnancy, in the name of Jesus.

80. I prophesy that I will fulfil the number of the days of this pregnancy, in the name of Jesus.

81. Any member of my family, reporting my pregnancy to the evil ones, receive the slap of the angels of God, in Jesus' name.

82. I shall not cast out my pregnancy before delivery, in Jesus' name.

83. Every territorial demon, working against my marriage, receive the thunder fire of God, in Jesus' name.

84. Every spirit of stillbirth and threatened abortion, be consumed by fire, in the name of Jesus.

85. I nullify every satanic threat against my pregnancy, in Jesus' name.

86. I shall not bring forth to murderers, in the name of Jesus.

87. Every power/spirit, visiting me at night or in the dream in order to terminate my pregnancy, fall down and die, in the name of Jesus.

88. Every power of murderers, shatter, in the name of Jesus.

89. I nullify every evil influence of satanic visitation upon my pregnancy, in the name of Jesus.

90. O Lord, deliver me from the womb that miscarries, in Jesus' name.

91. You the plug of my womb, receive the power of the Holy Spirit to carry my pregnancy to the point of delivery, in the name of Jesus.

92. Every violence of miscarriage, stop permanently, in the name of Jesus.

93. I reject every manifestation of fever during my pregnancy, in the name of Jesus.

94. Every evil power, appearing through a dog, a man or a woman, be destroyed by fire, in Jesus' name.

95. I reject every satanic stress during my pregnancy, in Jesus' name.

96. You evil children, causing abortion, die, in the name of Jesus. I am loosed from your oppression, in the name of Jesus.

97. I decree death of every spirit husband or spirit wife, killing my children, in the name of Jesus.

98. O earth, help me to conquer the power of miscarriage, in Jesus' name.

99. O Lord, give me wings of a great eagle to escape from miscarriage, in the name of Jesus.

100. O Lord, give me a male-child, in the name of Jesus.

101. I declare that I am fruitful and I will bring forth in peace, in the name of Jesus.

102. I overcome miscarriage by the power of the Lord, in Jesus' name.

103. My Father, cover me with Your shield and put me under Your banner, in the name of Jesus.

104. Every power, that has swallowed my children, vomit them now, in the name of Jesus.

105. Every foundation of miscarriage, receive the judgment of God, in the name of Jesus.

106. I command fibroid, drop off my womb, in the name of Jesus.

107. Every low sperm count, be converted to full sperm count, in the name of Jesus.

108. Throughout the period of the pregnancy, I shall not be stressed. I receive angelic ministration, in the name of Jesus.

109. My body, be strong to labour, in the name of Jesus.

110. O Lord, send Your heavenly nurse to minister to me throughout the period of this pregnancy, in the name of Jesus.

111. I shall bring forth a normal child to the glory of God, in Jesus' name.

112. O Lord, deliver me from the spirit of error, in the name of Jesus.

113. I judge the hold of mismanagement through wrong medical advice or wrong medication, in Jesus' name.

114. My cervix, close up, let there be no contraction or dilation before the nine months period, in the name of Jesus.

115. I receive power from on high to bring forth, in the name of Jesus.

116. I break the horn of the wicked exercising evil against me, in the name of Jesus.

117. Holy Spirit, envelop me and overshadow me throughout the period of this pregnancy, in the name of Jesus.

118. I will neither labour in vain, nor bring forth for trouble, in Jesus' name.

119. As I build, I will inhabit; and as I plant, I shall eat, in Jesus' name.

120. I and the children that God has given me are for signs and wonders, in the name of Jesus.

121. Thank God, for answers to your prayers

PRAYERS FOR THE MIRACLE OF SUPERNATURAL CONCEPTION AND DIVINE PROTECTION 2

This programme is specially tailored and vomited by the Holy Ghost for women and couples who want to lay a good foundation for the fruit of the womb. It will enable them to enjoy protection throughout the period of pregnancy.

Getting pregnant is one thing, while keeping the state full-term is another. Many women who have struggled with bouts of miscarriages would find this prayer programme comforting and helpful. These prayer points will enable you to set a divine watch over your pregnancy from the beginning to the end. You will be spared the trauma of satanic attacks that can threaten your pregnancy. This is a divine immunity against all forms of demonic attacks against pregnancy.

Confessions: 1 John 5:14-15: And this is the confidence that we have in him, that, if we ask any thing according to his will, he heareth us: And if we know that he hear us, whatsoever we ask, we know that we have the petitions that we desired of him.

2 Cor 1:20: For all the promises of God in him are yea, and in him Amen, unto the glory of God by us.

Num 23:19: God is not a man, that he should lie; neither the son of man, that he should repent: hath he said, and shall he not do it? or hath he spoken, and shall he not make it good?

Isa 55:11: So shall my word be that goeth forth out of my mouth: it shall not return unto me void, but it shall accomplish that which I please, and it shall prosper in the thing whereto I sent it.

1. Praise worship.

2. I confess and repent of the sin of bloodshed, committed in my days of ignorance, in Jesus' name.

3. Lord Jesus, wash away the sins of the past and their and consequences.

4. Father, I thank You for entrusting these children to me.

5. O God, perfect these gifts in me, in the name of Jesus.

6. My babies and I are fearfully and wonderfully made, in the name of Jesus.

7. O God, arise and guide me through this childbearing journey with

ease, grace and loving-kindness, in the name of Jesus.

8. As I experience biological and emotional changes, let Your joy be my strength, in the name of Jesus.

9. Father, be glorified in my life, in the name of Jesus.

10. O God, arise according to Jeremiah 29:11, and give me the expected end of safety and joy, in Jesus' name.

11. I shield myself with the envelope of divine fire away from evil observers and evil monitors, in Jesus' name.

12. O God, give me heavenly care and proper development for my baby, in the name of Jesus.

13. O God, always direct me throughout the process of this pregnancy, in the name of Jesus.

14. By Your mercy, O God, deliver me and my babies from any harvest of the seeds of iniquity sown in the past, in the name of Jesus.

15. O God, let my case stand out for dumbfounding success, in the name of Jesus.

16. You, who cause me to conceive, cause me to bring forth, in the name of Jesus (Isa. 66:9).

17. All things must work together for my good, in the name of Jesus.

18. I bind every spirit of error, in the name of Jesus.

19. As a spiritual child of Abraham, I am fruitful and will multiply, in the name of Jesus.

20. My fruit (babies/pregnancy) shall be firmly established and shall not miscarry before the normal delivery time, in the name of Jesus (Exod. 23:26).

21. These children shall serve God's purpose for me to multiply and subdue the earth, in the name of Jesus.

22. O God, deliver me from morning sickness and any complication, in the name of Jesus.

23. I stand against any birth defect in my babies and claim perfection for them, in the name of Jesus.

24. O God, frustrate any action You do not want me to take, in the name of Jesus.

25. O God, bring the good work You have started in me to a glorious conclusion, in the name of Jesus.

26. I claim proper growth and development for the babies in the womb, and safety for the children and I during childbirth, in the name of Jesus.

27. My expectations shall not be cut off, in the name of Jesus.

28. Make the following confessions:

Gen 1:28: And God blessed them, and God said unto them, Be fruitful, and multiply, and replenish the earth, and subdue it: and have dominion over the fish of the sea, and over the fowl of the air, and over every living thing that moveth upon the earth.

Gen 9:1: And God blessed Noah and his sons, and said unto them, Be fruitful, and multiply, and replenish the earth.

Gen 9:7: And you, be ye fruitful, and multiply; bring forth abundantly in the earth, and multiply therein.

Gen 17:6: And I will make thee exceeding fruitful, and I will make nations of thee, and kings shall come out of thee.

Ex 1:12: But the more they afflicted them, the more they multiplied and grew. And they were grieved because of the children of Israel.

Ex 23:26: There shall nothing cast their young, nor be barren, in thy land: the number of thy days I will fulfil.

Deut 7:13-14: And he will love thee, and bless thee, and multiply thee: he will also bless the fruit of thy womb, and the fruit of thy land, thy corn, and thy wine, and thine oil, the increase of thy kine, and the flocks of thy sheep, in the land which he sware unto thy fathers to give thee. Thou shalt be blessed above all people: there shall not be male or female barren among you, or among your cattle.

Ps 113:9: He maketh the barren woman to keep house, and to be a joyful mother of children. Praise ye the Lord.

Ps 127:3-5: Lo, children are an heritage of the LORD: and the fruit of the womb is his reward. As arrows are in the hand of a mighty man; so are children of the youth. Happy is the man that hath his quiver full of them: they shall not be ashamed, but they shall speak with the enemies in the gate.

Ps 128:3,6: Thy wife shall be as a fruitful vine by the sides of thine house: thy children like olive plants round about thy table. Yea, thou shalt see thy children's children, and peace upon Israel.

1 Tim 2:15: Notwithstanding she shall be saved in childbearing, if they continue in faith and charity and holiness with sobriety.

29. I receive a divine mandate to enforce my right of conception, in the name of Jesus.

30. Any abnormality in my organs of conception and pregnancy, receive divine correction, in Jesus' name.

31. Every negative medical report, be converted to positive result, in the name of Jesus.

32. Blood of Jesus, flush out any satanic deposit in my womb, in the name of Jesus.

33. My womb, become an expressway to conception, in the name of Jesus.

34. I charge every hand that would treat me, every bed I would lie on and every test to be conducted on me with the blood of Jesus and the fire of the Holy Ghost, in the name of Jesus.

35. Every satanic road-block, mounted against pregnancy development, be dismantled by fire, in the name of Jesus.

36. Anything on my way to the miracle of supernatural conception

and birth, clear away by the blood of Jesus.

37. My womb and breasts, begin to function as ordained by God, in the name of Jesus.

38. Thou creative power of God, move in my womb by Your fire, in the name of Jesus.

39. I withdraw my womb from every evil altar, in the name of Jesus.

40. Every seed of the pregnancy of failure in my foundation, die, in the name of Jesus.

41. Every satanic transfer or exchange of my womb, die, in the name of Jesus.

42. I bind and cast out every spirit of failure in all stages, in the name of Jesus.

43. Every word, spoken by the enemy against my conception, backfire, in the name of Jesus.

44. Any evil tree, growing in our family that is working against my conception, die, in the name of Jesus.

45. Any curse, strengthening the enemy of my pregnancy, die by the blood of Jesus.

46. Every strongman, supervising my womb to arrest my babies, die, in the name of Jesus.

47. By the power that divided the Red Sea, I obtain my babies by fire, in the name of Jesus.

48. Holy Spirit, make my womb super-conducive for pregnancy, in the name of Jesus.

49. I bind and arrest every infection, in the name of Jesus.

50. Holy Spirit, by Your power that incubated the womb of Elizabeth and Sarah, bind my egg and the sperm of my husband together in conception, in the name of Jesus.

I declare, according to the word of God, that the Lord shall perfect everything concerning me. The Lord, who has started His good work of creation in me, will complete it (Phil. 1:6).

By the power in the blood of the Lord Jesus Christ, I confess that my pregnancy is perfect, in the name of Jesus. Every part of my body shall function perfectly for the formation of the baby, in Jesus' name. My blood shall circulate effectively. Everything that passes from me to the baby for its development shall be perfect, in Jesus' name. I confess that I am strong. Weakness is not my lot, in the name of Jesus. I will not have morning sickness or vomiting in my pregnancy, in the name of Jesus. I reject cramps, varicose veins, piles and backaches, because Jesus Christ has borne all my sicknesses. I refuse constipation, anaemia, vitamin and mineral deficiencies, swollen hands and feet, hypertension, convulsion and diabetes, in the mighty name of Jesus. My urine will remain normal, in the name of Jesus (Psalm 103: 3-5). I confess that the activities of eaters of flesh and drinkers of blood will not prosper in my life, in the name of Jesus. I refuse and reject all negative dreams, visions, prophecies and imaginations, in the name of Jesus.

I confess God's word in Exodus 23:26, that I shall not experience miscarriage, any form of abnormal bleeding or malformation of the baby, in Jesus' name. I shall be a joyous mother of children. My womb is fruitful. I am a fruitful vine by the side of our house. My children are like olive plants round about our table. As the baby grows, every aspect of its growth, formation and development shall be perfect, in Jesus' name.

I also confess that I shall not suffer from any sickness like nausea, irritation, headache, internal or external pain because by the stripes of Jesus, I am healed. I tread on sickness and upon all the power of the devil. My body is the temple of the Holy spirit. I have the life and health of Christ in me. The Sun of Righteousness has arisen, having conquered sicknesses and pains. There is healing in His wings for me. God's will for me and my baby is to prosper and be in good health. God is at work in me now to will and to do His good pleasure. The power of the Holy Spirit is at work in me right now. It is flowing in me and perfecting all that pertains to my baby's formation, in Jesus' name.

I declare that every disease and germ should die now, in Jesus' name. Nothing I take into my body through the mouth shall harm me or my baby, in Jesus' name. God's word says, "If I drink any deadly thing, it shall not harm me." I confess that as I go to deliver my baby, the Lord shall direct those taking the delivery on what care suits me and the baby, in Jesus'

name.

My pregnancy is established in righteousness. I am far from oppression. Therefore, I shall not fear because terror shall not come near me. No evil shall befall me or befall my baby, and no plague shall come near my dwelling place and my family.

As the pregnancy progresses, the Lord shall fulfil the number of my days. I shall not have a premature baby, but a fully grown baby. My baby shall come out alive, strong and healthy because nothing shall harm my young. I am fearfully and wonderfully made. My pelvis is wide enough to allow my baby to pass through, in the name of Jesus.

I also confess, according to Isaiah 43, that when I pass through the water, the Lord will be with me; if through the rivers, it shall not overflow me and if I walk through the fire, I shall neither be burnt nor shall the flame scorch me. Therefore, I confess that I shall pass through child-delivery without any pain or hurt, in Jesus' name.

The Lord, shall take away from me, every sickness of pregnancy and childbearing and those that accompany complications according to Deut. 7:14,15. Therefore, I shall not fear because I have been redeemed from the curse of the law - the curse of bringing forth in agony (Galatians 4).

I boldly confess Isaiah 66:7, that before I travail, I will give birth and before any pain comes, I will be delivered of my baby. Moreover, according to 1 Tim. 2:15, I will be delivered of my baby. Also, according to 1 Tim. 2:15, I will be saved in child bearing because I continue in faith, love and holiness with self-control.

I confess that I shall go to the delivery room confidently, in Jesus' name. The Lord has given me perfect peace because my mind rests on Him. My trust is in the Lord and Jehovah God is my everlasting strength.

According to Psalm 118:17, I confess that I shall neither die at child-birth nor shall my baby suffer death. We shall both live to declare the works of the Lord, in Jesus' name. My cervix shall be fully dilated, and the passage big and open enough to allow the baby to pass through with ease. The delivery shall be perfect, in Jesus' name. No evil shall befall me or my baby. No weapon of the devil that is fashioned against me or against my baby shall prosper, in Jesus' name.

The Lord is the strength of my life, of whom shall I be afraid? He is my Deliverer, my God, my Buckler and the Horn of my Salvation. The Lord is all I need to take through delivery on that day. He will strengthen the bars of my gate. He has blessed my children within me. Therefore, through the Lord I shall do valiantly. I will live to be the happy mother of my baby. None of us shall see death, in Jesus' name. I refuse prolonged labour, and reject all pains from the devil during labour and afterwards.

I look forward to the rearing of the children after birth. I confess that we shall bring them up in the way of the Lord. The children shall grow up to know and love the Lord from their youth. I also confess that the Lord shall supply all our needs during pregnancy and those of the babies after their delivery in Jesus' name.

Glory be to the name of the Lord, because I shall have what I say, in Jesus' name.

51. Lord Jesus, let every sword depart from my marriage, in Jesus' name.

52. O Lord, make ways for me where there is no way, in Jesus' name.

53. I break any covenant between me and every evil husband or wife, in the name of Jesus.

54. Any of my clothes, that the enemy has set aside to afflict my conception, roast, in Jesus' name.

55. Every bow of the mighty, contending with my fruitfulness, break, break, break, in the name of Jesus.

56. Any decoration in my apartment that is bewitched, o Lord, reveal it to me.

57. I destroy, every evil stone or goat, destroying my children in pregnancy, in the name of Jesus.

58. Any garment, that the enemy is using to destroy my pregnancy, roast.

59. O Lord, let Your strong east wind blow against the Red Sea in my womb now, in the name of Jesus.

60. Every demonic instrument of operation, set aside to abort my pregnancy, break to pieces, in the name of Jesus.

61. O Lord, fight against the destroyer, working against my increase and fruitfulness, in the name of Jesus.

62. Every demonic doctor /nurse, delegated by satan to destroy my pregnancy, inject yourself to death, in Jesus' name.

63. Blood of Jesus, wash me and show me mercy, in the name of Jesus.

64. Every evil remote control gadget being used to manipulate my pregnancy, roast by fire, in Jesus' name.

65. Thou Man of war, save me out of the hands of wicked midwives, in the name of Jesus.

66. I render every weapon fashioned against my pregnancy impotent, in the name of Jesus.

67. Oh Lord, overthrow every Egyptian working against me in the midst of the sea, in the name of Jesus.

68. I close down every satanic broadcasting station, fashioned against my pregnancy, in the name of Jesus.

69. I prophesy that I will see the great work of the Lord as I deliver my children safely, in the name of Jesus.

70. I refuse to harbour any pregnancy killer, in any department of my life, in the name of Jesus.

71. Every horse and its rider in my womb, family or office, be thrown into the sea of forgetfulness, in the name of Jesus.

72. I bind every spirit of error assigned to my pregnancy, in the name of Jesus.

73. O Lord, send Your light before me to drive miscarriages away from my womb and life, in the name of Jesus.

74. I bind the spirit of almost there; You will not operate in my life, in the name of Jesus.

75. I cast out every power casting out my children, in the name of Jesus.

76. I break every grip and hold of witchcraft over my pregnancy, in the name of Jesus.

77. From today, I shall not cast away my young, in the name of Jesus.

78. I prophesy, that I paralyse every opposition to my pregnancy, in the name of Jesus.

79. I will fulfil the number of the days of this pregnancy, in the name of Jesus.

80. Any member of my family, reporting my pregnancy to the evil ones, receive the slap of the angels of God, in Jesus' name.

81. I shall not cast out my pregnancy before delivery, in Jesus' name.

82. Every territorial demon, working against my marriage, receive the thunder fire of God, in the name of Jesus.

83. Every spirit of stillbirth and threatened abortion, be consumed by fire, in the name of Jesus.

84. I nullify every satanic threat against my pregnancy, in the name of Jesus.

85. I shall not bring forth to murderers, in the name of Jesus.

86. Every power/spirit visiting me at night or in the dream, in order to terminate my pregnancy, fall down and die, in the name of Jesus.

87. Every power of murderers, shatter, in the name of Jesus.

88. I nullify every evil influence of satanic visitation upon my pregnancy, in the name of Jesus.

89. O Lord, deliver me from the womb that miscarries, in the name of Jesus.

90. You the plug of my womb, receive the power of the Holy Spirit to carry my pregnancy to the point of delivery, in the name of Jesus.

91. Every violence of miscarriage, stop permanently, in the name of Jesus.

92. I reject every manifestation of fever during my pregnancy, in the name of Jesus.

93. Every evil power, appearing through a dog, a man or a woman, be destroyed by fire, in Jesus' name.

94. I reject every satanic stress during my pregnancy, in the name of Jesus.

95. You evil children, causing abortion, die, in the name of Jesus. I am loosed from your oppression, in the name of Jesus.

96. I decree death of every spirit husband or spirit wife, killing my children, in the name of Jesus.

97. O earth, help me to conquer the power of miscarriages, in the name of Jesus.

98. O Lord, give me wings of a great eagle to escape from miscarriage, in the name of Jesus.

99. O Lord, give me a male-child, in the name of Jesus.

100. I declare that I am fruitful and I will bring forth in peace, in the name of Jesus.

101. I overcome miscarriage by the power of the Lord, in Jesus' name.

102. My Father, cover me with Your shield and put me under Your banner, in the name of Jesus.

103. Every power, that has swallowed my children, vomit them now, in the name of Jesus.

104. Every foundation of miscarriage, receive the judgment of God, in the name of Jesus.

105. I command fibroid, drop off my womb, in the name of Jesus.

106. Every low sperm count, be converted to full sperm count, in the name of Jesus.

107. Throughout the period of the pregnancy, I shall not be stressed. I receive angelic ministration, in the name of Jesus.

108. My body, be strong to labour, in the name of Jesus.

109. O Lord, send Your heavenly nurse to minister to me throughout the period of this pregnancy, in the name of Jesus.

110. I shall bring forth a normal child to the glory of God, in Jesus' name.

111. O Lord, deliver me from the spirit of error, in Jesus' name.

112. I judge the hold of mismanagement through wrong medical advice or wrong medication, in Jesus' name.

113. My cervix, close up, let there be no contraction or dilation before the nine months period, in the name of Jesus.

114. I receive power from on high to bring forth, in the name of Jesus.

115. I break the horn of the wicked exercising evil against me, in the name of Jesus.

116. Holy Spirit, envelop me and overshadow me throughout the period of this pregnancy, in the name of Jesus.

117. I will neither labour in vain nor bring forth for trouble, in Jesus' name.

118. As I build, I will inhabit; and as I plant, I shall eat, in Jesus' name.

119. I and the children that God has given me are for signs and wonders, in the name of Jesus.

120. Thank God for answers to your prayers.

PRAYERS FOR THE MIRACLE OF SUPERNATURAL CONCEPTION AND DIVINE PROTECTION 3

12 KEYS TO SUCCESS IN THIS PRAYER PROGRAMME

1. Husband and wife should participate in this programme and be serious with it.

2. It is assumed that couples have undergone deliverance, if not, consult the book 'How To Obtain Personal Deliverance'.

3. Make sure you are free from all forms of anxiety, agitation, depression, bitterness, feelings of frustration, and shame. Confess and renounce these things.

4. Understand that there is nothing impossible unto God.

5. Understand that God has the final say on all things and not Doctors or specialists, or consultants.

6. Give God sincere and deep praise and worship before beginning the prayers each day.

7. Forgive anyone who has offended you and also forgive yourself.

8. This programme must include at least, seven days of two hour vigil.

9. Anoint your womb or underneath the belly before this prayer programme.

10. During and after this prayer programme, there must be no bitterness, anger, strife, argument, debate, quarrel, of any form between couples.

11. All sins must be confessed, particularly, sexual sins.

12. All the words of God must also be confessed loud and clear.

Confessions: 1 John 5:14-15: And this is the confidence that we have in him, that, if we ask any thing according to his will, he heareth us: And if we know that he hear us, whatsoever we ask, we know that we have the petitions that we desired of him.

---

2 Cor 1:20: For all the promises of God in him are yea, and in him Amen, unto the glory of God by us.

Num 23:19: God is not a man, that he should lie; neither the son of man, that he should repent: hath he said, and shall he not do it? or hath he spoken, and shall he not make it good?

Isaiah 55:11: So shall my word be that goeth forth out of my mouth: it shall not return unto me void, but it shall accomplish that which I please, and it shall prosper in the thing whereto I sent it.

Genesis 1:28: And God blessed them, and God said unto them, Be fruitful, and multiply, and replenish the earth, and subdue it: and have dominion over the fish of the sea, and over the fowl of the air, and over every living thing that moveth upon the earth.

Genesis 9:1: And God blessed Noah and his sons, and said unto them, Be fruitful, and multiply, and replenish the earth.

Genesis 9:7: And you, be ye fruitful, and multiply; bring forth abundantly in the earth, and multiply therein.

Genesis 17:6: And I will make thee exceeding fruitful, and I will make nations of thee, and kings shall come out of thee.

Exodus 1:12: But the more they afflicted them, the more they multiplied and grew. And they were grieved because of the children of Israel.

Exodus 23:26: There shall nothing cast their young, nor be barren, in thy land: the number of thy days I will fulfil.

Deut. 7:13-14: And he will love thee, and bless thee, and multiply thee: he will also bless the fruit of thy womb, and the fruit of thy land, thy corn, and thy wine, and thine oil, the increase of thy kine, and the flocks of thy sheep, in the land which he sware unto thy fathers to give thee. [14] Thou shalt be blessed above all people: there shall not be male or female barren among you, or among your cattle.

Psalm 113:9: He maketh the barren woman to keep house, and to be a joyful mother of children. Praise ye the Lord.

Psalm 127:3-5: Lo, children are an heritage of the Lord: and the fruit of the womb is his reward. [4] As arrows are in the hand of a mighty man; so are children of the youth. [5] Happy is the man that hath his quiver full of them: they shall not be ashamed, but they shall speak with the enemies in the gate.

Psalm 128:3: Thy wife shall be as a fruitful vine by the sides of thine house: thy children like olive plants round about thy table.

Psalm 128:6: Yea, thou shalt see thy children's children, and peace upon Israel.

1 Tim. 2:15: Notwithstanding she shall be saved in childbearing, if they continue in faith and charity and holiness with sobriety.

PRAYER POINTS

1. Lord Jesus, have mercy on me. If there is anything the devil still holds against me, to block my child-bearing, forgive me and cleanse me by Your blood.

2. Before this time next year, I will have my own child/children, in the mighty name of Jesus.

3. All weapons fashioned against my child-bearing shall not prosper, in the name of Jesus.

4. You devil, loose your hold upon my child-bearing, in the name of Jesus.

5. From now on, let no man trouble me, for I bear in my body the marks of the Lord Jesus Christ.

6. From now on, let no ancestral power trouble me, and let no power from my father's house disturb my conception, in Jesus' name.

7. From now on, let no marine power trouble my womb, and let no disease trouble my womb, in the name of Jesus.

8. By the bulldozing power of the Holy Ghost, I command every hindrance to conception in my life to die, in the name of Jesus.

9. Every disturbance and blockage, physical or spiritual, in the womb, or any where in my system, get out in the name of Jesus.

10. Every power behind my delayed child-bearing, get out now, in the name of Jesus.

11. O God, arise, and open the door of fruitfulness for me today, in the name of Jesus.

12. Every conscious and unconscious evil covenant regarding child-bearing, be broken, in the name of Jesus.

13. I apply the blood of Jesus to my reproductive organs, in Jesus' name.

14. My body, hear the word of the Lord, I command you now, multiply, reproduce yourself, come alive, in the name of Jesus.

15. Every miracle that I desire to make me fruitful, manifest in my life now, in the name of Jesus.

16. Every curse working against child-bearing in my life, break, in the name of Jesus.

17. My Father, carry out the necessary surgical operation in our bodies tonight by Your mercy and Your grace, in the name of Jesus.

18. Every contrary hand-writing assigned against my child-bearing, wither, in the name of Jesus.

19. Thou power of infertility and fear in my life, die, in Jesus' name.

20. Every curse issued against me by satanic agent, backfire, in the name of Jesus.

21. I release myself from any inherited problem, in the name of Jesus.

22. Every bewitchment assigned against my reproductive organ, die, in the name of Jesus.

23. O God, arise and send Your angels to retrieve my children from every satanic hiding places, in the name of Jesus.

24. By the power that establishes the heaven and the earth, let this month be my month of breakthrough, in the name of Jesus.

25. You serpent that attacks babies, and causes miscarriages, release me, in the name of Jesus.

26. Thou power of pregnancy wastage, loose your hold, in Jesus' name.

27. You eaters of flesh and drinkers of blood, that swallow conception, I bind you and cast you out, in the name of Jesus.

28. Every spirit behind impotency, low sperm count, ovulation failure, hormonal problems, and other anti-pregnancy weapons, scatter, in the name of Jesus.

29. Every problem, introduced into my life, by my past sexual sins, vanish, in the name of Jesus.

30. All the consequences of sexual relationship with demonised partners, be removed from my life, in the name of Jesus.

31. All the consequences of bewitched menstrual pads and lost of under-wear, be cancelled, in the name of Jesus.

32. Any material in my body, present in the dark kingdom, that is being used against my conception, cash fire, in the name of Jesus.

33. Every ungodly soul-ties with all sexual partners of the past, break, in the name of Jesus.

34. This year, all those who have looked down on me because of my condition, shall laugh with me, in the name of Jesus.

35. I receive deliverance from the spirit of monthly anxiety and nervousness, in the name of Jesus.

36. By the power in the blood of Jesus, my expectation shall not be cut off, in the name of Jesus.

37. Thou power of threatening miscarriage, loose your hold, in the name of Jesus.

38. Every power assigned to cause miscarriage or missed abortion, I bind you and cast you out, in the name of Jesus.

39. I retrieve my original reproductive organ by force, in the name of Jesus.

40. I recover my normal womb from where it is hidden by witches and wizards, household wickedness, occult powers, in Jesus' name.

41. Every non-functioning part of my reproductive organ, perform normally, in the name of Jesus.

42. My Father, remove every anxiety of my age from me, in the name of Jesus.

43. My Father, as I grow older in age, let there be a proportional increase in my chances of getting pregnant, in the name of Jesus.

44. I refuse to consider the Doctors' negative report, in the name of Jesus.

45. Every deadness in my reproductive organ, come alive, in the name of Jesus.

46. Every negative report of low sperm count or total absence of sperms, be cancelled, in the name of Jesus.

47. Every contrary spiritual and physical verdict, pertaining to child-birth in my life, I cancel and neutralise you, in the name of Jesus.

48. O Lord, transform my sperm to the ones that will supernaturally achieve a successful conception, in the name of Jesus.

49. My Father, replace every abnormal sperm with a normal sperm, in the name of Jesus.

50. O God, arise and let my sperm be the type that would achieve instant conception, the moment I meet my spouse, in Jesus' name.

51. I retrieve my semen by fire, in the name of Jesus.

52. O Lord, let the womb of my spouse be supernaturally receptive to my sperm and result to conception, in the name of Jesus.

53. Thou power of hormonal imbalance, die, in the name of Jesus.

54. Thou power of hormonal failure, die, in the name of Jesus.

55. Every abnormality in my reproductive organs, be corrected by fire, in the name of Jesus.

56. I refuse to consider or be discouraged by previous occurrence of miscarriage, in the name of Jesus.

57. I soak my reproductive organs in the blood of Jesus.

58. I break every witchcraft curse and spell concerning my womb, in the name of Jesus.

59. O God, arise and convert my womb to a fertile womb, in Jesus' name.

60. Say this loud and clear for 21 times: I reverse the effect of the aging process on my reproductive structures, in Jesus' name.

61. Every power stealing conception from my womb, I bind and cast you out, in the name of Jesus.

62. Let Your creative anointing restore my sperms, in Jesus' name.

63. O doors of conception, open unto me, in the name of Jesus.

64. The anointing that openeth the doors of the womb, fall upon me, in the name of Jesus.

65. Every strongman, attached to the gate of the womb, fall down and die, in the name of Jesus.

66. Let the doors of my womb become the passage of death for every enemy of conception, in the name of Jesus.

67. Let the doors of my womb become an expressway to conception, in the name of Jesus.

68. Let every virtue of conception transferred or stolen from my womb by anti-conception forces, be restored seven-fold, in the name of Jesus.

69. Fire of the God of Elijah, pass through my reproductive organs and burn to ashes everything that is contrary to conception, in Jesus' name.

70. My Father, where my womb has aged, renew and refurbrished it unto conception, in the name of Jesus.

71. By the power that directed Angel Gabriel to Zachariah, let the angel of my miracle baby locate me now, in the name of Jesus.

72. Thank You, Lord, because I know You have done it.

73. Thank You, Lord, because I know that satan cannot continue his work in my life.

74. Thank You, Lord, because I know that I am free by the blood of Jesus.

75. Thank You, Lord, because the power of delayed child-bearing and barrenness are dead in my life, in the name of Jesus.

I declare according to the word of God that the Lord shall perfect everything concerning me. The Lord who has started His good work of creation in me will complete it (Phil. 1:6).

By the power in the blood of the Lord Jesus Christ, I confess that my pregnancy is perfect in the name of Jesus. Every part of my body shall function perfectly for the formation of the baby in Jesus' name. My blood shall circulate effectively. Everything that passes from me to the baby shall be perfect in Jesus' name for the development of the baby. I confess I am strong. Weakness is not my lot in the name of Jesus. I will not have morning sickness or vomiting in my pregnancy in the name of Jesus. I reject cramps, varicose veins, piles and backaches because Jesus Christ has borne all my sicknesses. I refuse constipation, anaemia, vitamin and mineral deficiencies, swollen hands and feet, hypertension, convulsion and diabetes in the mighty name of Jesus. My urine will remain normal in the name of Jesus (Psalm 103: 3-5). I confess that the activities of eaters of flesh and drinkers of blood will not prosper in my life in the name of Jesus. I refuse and reject all negative dreams, visions, prophecies and imaginations in the name of Jesus.

I confess God's Word in Exodus 23:26, that I shall not have a miscarriage, any form of abnormal bleeding or malformation of the baby in Jesus' name. I shall be a joyous mother of children. My womb is fruitful. I am a fruitful vine by the sides of our house. My children are like olive plants round about our table. As the baby grows, every aspect of its growth, formation and development shall be perfect in Jesus' name.

I also confess that I shall not suffer any sickness like nausea, irritation, headache, internal or external pain because by the stripes of Jesus, I am healed. I tread on sickness and upon all the power of the devil. My body is the temple of the Holy spirit. I have the life and health of Christ in me. The Sun of Righteousness has arisen, having conquered sickness and pains, and satan. There is healing in His wings for me. God's will for me and my baby is to prosper and be in good health. God is at work in me now to will and to do His good pleasure. The power of the Holy Spirit is at work in me right now. It is flowing in me and perfecting all that pertains to my baby's formation in Jesus' name.

I declare that every disease and germ should die now in Jesus' name. Nothing I take into my body through the mouth shall harm me nor my baby in Jesus' name. God's Word says, if I drink any deadly thing, it shall not harm me. I confess that as I go to deliver my baby, that the Lord shall direct those taking the delivery what care suits me and the baby in Jesus' name.

My pregnancy is established in righteousness. I am far from oppression. Therefore, I shall not fear, and from terror, because it shall not come near me. No evil shall befall me nor befall my baby, and no plague shall come near my dwelling place and my family.

As the pregnancy progresses, the Lord shall fulfil the number of my days. I shall not have a premature baby but a fully grown baby. My baby shall come out alive, strong and healthy, because nothing shall harm my young. I am fearfully and wonderfully made. My pelvis is wide enough to allow my baby to pass through in the name of Jesus.

I also confess, according to Isaiah 43, that when I pass through the water, the Lord will be with me, if through the rivers, it shall not overflow me and if I walk through the fire, I shall not be burnt nor shall the flame scorch me. Therefore, I confess that I shall pass through the child-delivering without any pain nor hurt in Jesus' name.

The Lord shall take away from me every sickness of pregnancy and child bearing and those that accompany complication according to Deut. 7:14,15. Therefore, I shall not fear because I have been redeemed from the curse of the law - the curse of bringing forth in agony (Galatians 4).

I boldly confess Isaiah 66:7 that before I travail, I will give birth and before any pain comes, I will be delivered of my baby. Moreover, according to 1 Tim. 2:15, I will be delivered of my baby. Moreover, according to 1 Tim. 2:15, I will be saved in child bearing because I continue in faith, love and holiness with self-control.

I confess I shall go to the delivery room confidently in Jesus' name. The Lord has given me perfect peace because my mind rests on Him. My trust is in the Lord and Jehovah God is my everlasting strength.

According to Psalm 118:17, I confess that I shall not die at child-birth, nor shall my baby suffer death. We shall both live to declare the works of the Lord in Jesus' name. My cervix shall be fully dilated and the passage big and open enough to allow the baby pass through with ease. The delivery shall be perfect in Jesus' name. No evil shall befall me nor my baby. No weapon of the devil that is fashioned against me nor against my baby shall prosper in Jesus' name.

The Lord is the strength of my life, of whom shall I be afraid. He is my Deliverer, my God, my Buckler and the Horn of my Salvation. The Lord is all I need to take through on that day. He will strengthen the bars of my gate. He has blessed my children within me. Therefore, through the Lord I shall do valiantly. I will live to be the happy mother of my baby. None of us shall see death in Jesus' name. I refuse prolonged labour and reject all pains from the devil during labour and afterwards.

I look forward to the rearing of the children after birth. I confess we shall bring them up in the way of the Lord. The children shall grow up to know and love the Lord from their youth. I also confess that the Lord shall supply all our needs during pregnancy and for the babies after their delivery in Jesus' name.

Glory be to the name of the Lord, because I shall have what I say in Jesus' name.

PRAYERS FOR THE MIRACLE OF SUPERNATURAL CONCEPTION AND DIVINE PROTECTION 4

THESE PRAYER POINTS ARE FOR MARRIED MEN AND WOMEN:

☞ Who are desiring the fruit of the womb

☞ Who have cases of miscarriages

☞ Whose systems / organs have been damaged or removed

☞ Who have been classified as impotent or having low sperm count

☞ Who medical science have written off for one reason or the other

☞ Who are unable to give birth as a result of curses (known or hidden) operating in their lives

☞ Who are under direct satanic bondage

PRAISE WORSHIP

PRAYER POINTS

1. O Lord, send Your fire to the foundation of my problems, in the name of Jesus.

2. Let every evil planting in my womb be destroyed by the blood of Jesus, in the name of Jesus.

3. I retrieve by fire and the blood of Jesus, every personal effect in the camp of the wicked being used to manipulate my life and marriage, in the name of Jesus.

4. O Lord, replace every damaged organ in my body, in the name of Jesus.

5. In the name of Jesus, I declare that my reproductive system is in a perfect working condition.

6. I reject, reverse and revoke every curse of barrenness and unfruitfulness in my life and marriage, in the name of Jesus.

7. I evacuate by fire, every evil deposit and planting upon my womb, in the name of Jesus.

8. I reverse and revoke every covenant of barrenness in my life through sex, abortion, incisions, in the name of Jesus.

9. I flush my womb, organs and reproductive system with the blood of Jesus.

10. I command restoration to any damaged or malfunctioning cell, tissue, tube, organ, in the name of Jesus.

11. I loose my womb and reproductive organs from every witchcraft bag and chain, in the name of Jesus.

12. Let the fire of God melt and consume every evil padlock, chain and cord used to tie my womb, in the name of Jesus.

13. Let the fire of God destroy every witchcraft bag used to tie my womb, in the name of Jesus.

14. Let the fire of God destroy all evil altars and priests sitting upon my womb, children, marriage and home, in the name of Jesus.

15. I cannot be barren, in the name of Jesus.

16. I command all my children to come to me now, by fire, in Jesus' name.

17. O Lord, take away every shame, reproach, confusion and frustration from me and heap it upon all my enemies, in the name of Jesus.

18. O Lord, turn my sorrows to joy, and my pains to gain and my mockery to rejoicing, in the name of Jesus.

19. I reject still birth, I will not labour in vain and will not die at child birth, in the name of Jesus.

20. I cancel with the blood of Jesus, every evil blood covenant entered into by myself, parents, ancestors, in the name of Jesus.

21. I refuse that my child be used as a sacrifice material to the devil, in the name of Jesus.

22. Every evil marriage covenant in my life, break now, in Jesus' name.

23. Let the fire of God destroy every evil consumption and contamination through food and sex, in the name of Jesus.

24. I terminate the appointment of the spirits of barrenness and miscarriage in my life and marriage, in the name of Jesus.

25. Let the fire of God roast every agent of darkness and their monitoring system against my life and marriage, in the name of Jesus.

26. It is written 'at the mention of the name of Jesus Christ, every knee must bow', therefore, I command all that is working against the manifestation of my miracle in the heavenlies, on earth, underneath the earth, and in the water, to bow now, in the name of Jesus.

27. I command every blessing confiscated by principalities, powers, rulers of darkness, and spiritual wickedness in high places, be released, in the name of Jesus.

28. I command every blessing confiscated by familiar / ancestral spirits and envious enemies be released, in the name of Jesus.

29. Every evil altar where my name has been mentioned for evil, be destroyed, in the name of Jesus.

30. Let every tree/pot planted over my umbilical cord and foreskin be rooted out, in the name of Jesus.

31. Children are the heritage of the Lord and the fruit of the womb is His reward. Therefore, everything contesting against my children, what are you waiting for, die, in the name of Jesus.

32. Let every dead organ in my life receive life now, in the name of Jesus.

33. I break the power of impotence and low sperm count in my life, in the name of Jesus.

34. I command every manipulation of darkness over my manhood to be destroyed, in the name of Jesus.

35. You spirit of impotence and low sperm count, I terminate your appointments over my life, in the name of Jesus.

36. I nullify every manipulation of darkness over my life and body systems, in the name of Jesus.

37. I neutralise every high sugar content in my body with the blood of Jesus, and command my nervous and muscular systems to receive strength, in the name of Jesus.

38. I destroy and reprogramme every evil programming against my fruitfulness, in the name of Jesus.

39. Every problem in my life resisting solution be consumed by the fire of God, in the name of Jesus.

40. O Lord, turn my shame to glory, in the name of Jesus.

PRAYERS TO DEFEAT ANTI-CONCEPTION WITCHCRAFT

This programme is specially tailored and vomited by the Holy Ghost for women and couples who want to lay a good foundation for the fruit of the womb. It will enable them to enjoy protection throughout the period of pregnancy.

Getting pregnant is one thing, while keeping the state full-term is another. Many women who have struggled with bouts of miscarriages would find this prayer programme comforting and helpful. These prayer points will enable you to set a divine watch over your pregnancy from the beginning to the end. You will be spared the trauma of satanic attacks that can threaten your pregnancy. This is a divine immunity against all forms of demonic attacks against pregnancy.

Praise worship

Confessions: Psalm 35:1-8: Plead my cause, O Lord, with them that strive with me: fight against them that fight against me. Take hold of shield and buckler, and stand up for mine help. Draw out also the spear, and stop the way against them that persecute me: say unto my soul, I am thy salvation. Let them be confounded and put to shame that seek after my soul: let them be turned back and brought to confusion that devise my hurt. Let them be as chaff before the wind: and let the angel of the Lord chase them. Let their way be dark and slippery: and let the angel of the Lord persecute them. For without cause have they hid for me their net in a pit, which without cause they have digged for my soul. Let destruction come upon him at unawares; and let his net that he hath hid catch himself: into that very destruction let him fall.

1. Every witchcraft power, hindering my fruitfulness, be arrested, in the name of Jesus.

2. According to the word of God in Exodus 23:25-26, I shall not be barren, in the name of Jesus.

3. Every evil power and satanic conspiracy against my conception, scatter, in the name of Jesus.

4. Everything satan has set into motion to make me barren, scatter, in the name of Jesus.

5. Every satanic hand against my ability to have children, be cut off, in the name of Jesus.

6. Every seed of witchcraft inside my reproductive organs, hindering my conception, come out, in the name of Jesus.

7. Every witchcraft power, manipulating my menstrual cycle, loose

your hold, in the name of Jesus.

8. Every satanic heat in my womb and waist, die, by the blood of Jesus.

9. Witchcraft spirit of barrenness of my father's house, release me, in the name of Jesus.

10. Every witchcraft power, monitoring the success of my conception, be arrested, in the name of Jesus.

11. Every witchcraft spirit, assigned to prevent pregnancy in my life, die, in the name of Jesus.

12. Witchcraft spirit, assigned against the sperm count of my husband, loose your hold, in the name of Jesus.

13. Every witchcraft power, causing erection failure, weakness of my husband's organ and impotency, loose your hold, in the name of Jesus.

14. You witchcraft power in charge of watery sperm, loose your hold, in the name of Jesus.

15. Every evil vow of the evil powers of my father's house against my child-bearing, be revoked by the blood of Jesus.

16. Every witchcraft power, responsible for miscarriages of pregnancies in my life, be arrested, in the name of Jesus.

17. Every record of my name in the register of childless couples, be wiped off by the blood of Jesus.

18. Every covenant of spiritual marriage, be cancelled by the blood of Jesus.

19. Every evil hold of the spirit husband upon my life, break by the blood of Jesus.

20. Every remnant of the sperm of the spirit husband in my reproductive system, be flushed out by the blood of Jesus.

21. Every anti-conception curse from spiritual partner upon my life, be cancelled by the blood of Jesus.

22. Every demonic object, moving around in my reproductive systems, come out now, in the name of Jesus.

23. Every witchcraft point of contact in my reproductive system, die, in the name of Jesus.

24. Every witchcraft curse of barrenness upon my life, die, by the blood of Jesus.

25. Every curse of barrenness upon my life as a result of past abortions, be cancelled by the blood of Jesus.

26. Every anti-conception curse, placed upon my life by former partners, be cancelled by the blood of Jesus.

27. Every ancestral witchcraft curse of barrenness upon my life, loose your hold, in the name of Jesus.

28. Ancestral evil powers of my father's house, causing barrenness in my family line, my life is not your candidate, release my conception, in the name of Jesus.

29. Every concoction and charm I used in the past that is now hindering my childbearing, I vomit by fire, in the name of Jesus.

30. I release my life, the success of my conception, my reproductive organs and my children from every power that operates in the air, water, sun, moon, stars, forests, stones and ground, in Jesus' name.

31. O God, arise and deliver my marriage from the spirit of childlessness, in the name of Jesus.

32. I release my babies from every witchcraft cage, in the name of Jesus.

33. Every covenant of barrenness with any water spirit, break, by the blood of Jesus.

34. Every spirit that is against childbearing in my family line, loose your hold, in the name of Jesus.

35. Every witchcraft hand, holding my reproductive system, loose your hold, in the name of Jesus.

36. I renounce every spiritual home with all its associated properties, in the name of Jesus.

37. Every witchcraft cage, holding my womb, die, in the name of Jesus.

38. Every witchcraft cage, holding my marriage, die, in the name of Jesus.

39. Every witchcraft blanket, holding my children, die, in Jesus' name.

40. Every witchcraft gate, barricade and checkpoint, set up against my marriage, scatter, in the name of Jesus.

41. Every witchcraft chain of stagnancy, holding me to one spot, die, break, in the name of Jesus.

42. Every witchcraft dominion over my life as a result of my past encounter with any native doctor, scatter, in the name of Jesus.

43. Every witchcraft altar, raised against my conception, be pulled down, in the name of Jesus.

44. Every witchcraft cobweb upon my life, burn to ashes by the fire of God, in the name of Jesus.

45. Every witchcraft burial against my marriage, die, in the name of Jesus.

46. Every witchcraft burial against my conception, die, in Jesus' name.

47. Every witchcraft summon to manipulate my conception, scatter, in the name of Jesus.

48. Every witchcraft case file on my marriage and conception, catch fire, in the name of Jesus.

49. Every witchcraft coven, set up against my marriage and conception, die, in the name of Jesus.

50. Every witchcraft gun-shot in the dream, backfire, in the name of Jesus.

51. Every witchcraft injection in the dream, die, in the name of Jesus.

52. Every witchcraft food in the dream, die, in the name of Jesus.

53. Every witchcraft attack in the dream, die, in the name of Jesus.

54. Every witchcraft family altar, catch fire, in the name of Jesus.

55. You witchcraft strongman in my family line, loose your hold upon my life, in the name of Jesus.

56. Every witchcraft cellophane, covering my womb, catch fire, in the name of Jesus.

57. Every witchcraft kingdom in my family line, be overthrown by fire, in the name of Jesus.

58. I release my marriage and conception from the dominion of witchcraft powers, in the name of Jesus.

59. Every witchcraft pot, prepared for me and my family, catch fire, in the name of Jesus.

60. Every witchcraft hand, feeding my babies in the womb, be cut off, in the name of Jesus.

61. Every witchcraft deposit, in my reproductive organs, be flushed out by the blood of Jesus.

62. Every witchcraft injection, in my reproductive organs, be flushed out by the blood of Jesus.

63. Every sexual witchcraft deposit, in my body, be flushed out by the blood of Jesus.

64. Every witchcraft tree, carrying the fruit of my womb, catch fire, in the name of Jesus.

65. Every witchcraft mark of failure, upon my life, be wiped off by the blood of Jesus.

66. Every witchcraft desire for my marriage, die, in the name of Jesus.

67. Every witchcraft incantation and divination, against my marriage and conception, die, in the name of Jesus.

68. Every witchcraft power, using the weapon of the dust against my marriage and conception, die, in the name of Jesus.

69. Every witchcraft-induced sickness, preventing my conception, die, in the name of Jesus.

70. O Lord, let my life become a no-go-area for witchcraft powers in the dream, in the name of Jesus.

71. Every witchcraft stronghold, causing barrenness in my marriage, be pulled down by fire, in the name of Jesus.

72. Any power, spirit or personality that has entered into witchcraft covenants against my life, scatter, in the name of Jesus.

73. Every power, spirit and personality that has entered into witchcraft covenants against my conception, scatter, in the name of Jesus.

74. Every witchcraft monitoring gadget, set up against the success of my conception, catch fire, in the name of Jesus.

75. Every witchcraft foundation, in the foundation of my life, catch fire and die, in the name of Jesus.

76. Blood of Jesus, blot out every witchcraft handwriting and ordinances that is working against my life in the heavenlies, in Jesus' name.

77. Every witchcraft time, agenda and calendar for my life, catch fire, in the name of Jesus.

78. Every evil power, monitoring the progress of evil in my family line, be arrested, in the name of Jesus.

79. By the blood of Jesus, let evil seasons in my family line stop, in the name of Jesus.

80. Every witchcraft altar, ministering barrenness into my marriage, scatter, in the name of Jesus.

81. Let confusion baptise the camp of witchcraft powers, assigned against my life, in the name of Jesus.

82. Every witchcraft-induced tongue, speaking evil into my marriage, die, in the name of Jesus.

83.   Let the dwelling place of witchcraft powers in my family line become desolate by the blood of Jesus.

84.   You heavens, rain snares, fire and brimstone on the witchcraft powers, depriving me of conception, in the name of Jesus.

85.   By the blood of Jesus, let every witchcraft association against my marriage scatter, in the name of Jesus.

86.   Every evil word by witchcraft powers against my life, fall to the ground and die, in the name of Jesus.

87.   Every witchcraft horn, raised against my life, be cut off, in the name of Jesus.

88.   Every evil flow of ancestral witchcraft powers into my life, dry up, in the name of Jesus.

89.   O God, arise and scatter every witchcraft judgment against my life, in the name of Jesus.

90.   Begin to thank God for answers to your prayers.

MARITAL BREAKTHROUGHS 1

In this programme, you are offered the type of prayers to pray when you are stepping into marriage. "Prevention," they say, "is better than cure." Many people have suffered marital distress due to their inability to lay a good foundation for their marriage.

The foundation of a building goes a long way to determine the stability and strength of the building. When the foundation is started on a good note, you will succeed as a couple. This programme is a must for men and women contemplating marriage. It is an insecticide for killing every spiritual insect that has the potentials for eating up the fibre of the marriage. You must take cognizance of the fact that, just as you are planning to succeed in a marriage, the devil is secretly laying land mines to blow up your marriage. Therefore, you must painstakingly pray these prayer points to safe-guard your marriage now and in the years ahead.

Confessions: **Gal. 3:13-14** - Christ hath redeemed us from the curse of the law, being made a curse for us: for it is written, Cursed is every one that hangeth on a tree: That the blessing of Abraham might come on the Gentiles through Jesus Christ; that we might receive the promise of the Spirit through faith.

Col 2:14-15 - Blotting out the handwriting of ordinances that was against us, which was contrary to us, and took it out of the way, nailing it to his cross; And having spoiled principalities and powers, he made a shew of them openly, triumphing over them in it.

2 Tim 4:18: And the Lord shall deliver me from every evil work, and will preserve me unto his heavenly kingdom: to whom be glory for ever and ever. Amen.

Praise worship

1. Thank the Lord, because this year is your year of dumbfounding miracles.

2. I confess the sins of my ancestors (list them).

3. Ask the Lord for forgiveness.

4. Lord, make known to me the secrets needed for my marital breakthrough.

5. Help me Lord to discover my real self.

6. Every imagination of the enemy against my marital life, be rendered impotent, in the name of Jesus.

7. Thou power in the blood of Jesus, separate me from the sins of my ancestors, in the name of Jesus.

8. I renounce any evil dedication placed upon my life, in Jesus' name.

9. I break every evil edict and ordination, in the name of Jesus.

10. I renounce and loose myself from every negative dedication placed upon my life, in the name of Jesus.

11. All demons, associated with the dedication, leave now, in the name of Jesus Christ.

12. I take authority over all the associated curses, in Jesus' name.

13. Oh Lord, cancel the evil consequences of any broken demonic promises or dedications, in the name of Jesus.

14. I take authority over all the curses, emanating from broken dedication, in the name of Jesus.

15. All demons, associated with any broken evil parental vow and dedication, depart from me now, in the name of Jesus.

16. I bind all principalities and powers of . . . . , operating over and within my life, in the name of Jesus.

17. I bind all wickedness in high places and evil thrones of . . . . , operating over and within my life, in the name of Jesus.

18. I bind all evil dominions and strongmen of . . . . . operating over and within my life, in the name of Jesus.

19. I bind every witchcraft control and mind-blinding spirit, in the name of Jesus.

20. I strip each spirit off the power and rank of . . . . . and separate them from one another, in the name of Jesus.

21. I cast out every witchcraft arrow, affecting my senses (sight, smell, taste, hearing), in the name of Jesus.

22. Every witchcraft arrow, depart from my (pick from the underlisted), in the name of Jesus.

    - spinal cord - spleen   - navel   - heart

    - throat   - between the eyes - top of the head.

23. I bind every evil presence in my (pick from the underlisted), system, in the name of Jesus.

    - reproductive   - digestive   - respiratory

    - nervous   - skeletal   - muscular

    - circulatory - endocrine   - excretory

24. I break the backbone and destroy the root of every evil spirit speaking against me, in the name of Jesus.

25. Every astral projection against me, I frustrate you, in Jesus' name.

26. Every complicated evil network against me, be eaten up by the elements, in the name of Jesus.

27. I bind every power, pulling anything in my body towards evil by means of energy drawn from the sun, the moon and the stars, in the name of Jesus.

28. I bind every power, pulling anything in my body towards evil by means of energy drawn from the planets, the constellations and the earth, in the name of Jesus.

29. I bind every power, pulling anything in my body towards evil by means of energy drawn from the (pick from the underlisted), in the name of Jesus.

   - air   - wind - fire - water- light- darkness   -elements

30. Any power of . . . . . . drawing energy against me from evil lines and circles, fall down and die, in the name of Jesus.

31. I forbid any transference of spirit into my life from my family, friends and associates, in the name of Jesus.

32. Every altar, speaking against my divine destiny, be dismantled, in the name of Jesus.

33. I bring the blood of Jesus over the spirit that does not want to let me go, in the name of Jesus.

34. Blood of Jesus, purge me of every witchcraft contaminating material, in the name of Jesus.

35. I destroy the hand of the witch-doctor, working against me, in the name of Jesus.

36. Every witchcraft spirit, attempting to build wall against my destiny, fall down and die, in the name of Jesus.

37. I send the rain of affliction upon every marine witchcraft, working against me, in the name of Jesus.

38. O sun, moon, stars, earth, water and the elements, vomit every enchantment that is against me, in the name of Jesus

39. Every power, using the heavenlies against me, fall down and be disgraced, in the name of Jesus.

40. Stars of heaven, begin to fight for me, in the name of Jesus.

41. O God, arise and scatter every conspiracy against me in the heavenlies, in the name of Jesus.

42. I break with the blood of Jesus, all evil soul-ties affecting my life, in the name of Jesus.

43. Spirit of the living God, come upon my life and place a shield of protection around me, in the name of Jesus.

44. Every chain of inherited witchcraft in my family, be destroyed, in the name of Jesus.

45. Every ladder, used by witchcraft against me, roast, in the name of Jesus.

46. Any door that I have opened to witchcraft in any area of my life, be closed for ever by the blood of Jesus.

47. I release myself from every ancestral demonic pollution, in the name of Jesus.

48. I release myself from every demonic pollution, emanating from my parents' religion, in the name of Jesus.

49. I release myself from demonic pollution, emanating from my past involvement in any demonic religion, in the name of Jesus.

50. I break loose from every idol and related association, in Jesus' name.

51. I release myself from every dream pollution, in Jesus' name.

52. Every satanic attack, against my life in my dreams, be converted to victory, in the name of Jesus.

53. All rivers, trees, forests, evil companions, evil pursuers, pictures of dead relatives, snakes, spirit husbands, spirit wives and masquerades manipulated against me in the dream, be completely destroyed by the power in the blood of the Lord Jesus.

54. Every evil plantation in my life: **Come out with all your roots, in the name of Jesus!** (*Lay your hands on your stomach and keep repeating the emphasised area.*)

55. Evil strangers in my body, come out of your hiding places, in the name of Jesus.

56. I disconnect any conscious or unconscious link with demonic caterers, in the name of Jesus.

57. All avenues of eating or drinking spiritual poisons, close, in the name of Jesus.

58. I cough and vomit any food eaten from the table of the devil, in the name of Jesus. (*Cough and vomit them in faith. Prime the expulsion.*)

59. All negative materials, circulating in my blood stream, be evacuated, in the name of Jesus.

60. I drink the blood of Jesus. (*Physically swallow and drink it in faith. Keep doing this for some time.*)

61. (*Lay one hand on your head, and the other on your stomach or navel and begin to pray like this*): Holy Ghost Fire, burn from the top of my head to the sole of my feet. (*Begin to mention every organ of your body; your kidney, liver, intestines, blood, etc. You must not rush at this level, because the fire will actually come and you may start feeling the heat*).

62. I cut myself off from every spirit of . . . (*mention the name of your place of birth*), in the name of Jesus.

63. I cut myself off from every tribal spirit and curse, in Jesus' name.

64. I cut myself off from every territorial spirit and curse, in the name of Jesus.

65. Holy Ghost fire, purge my life.

66. I claim my complete deliverance from the spirit of . . . (*mention those things you do not desire in your life*), in the name of Jesus.

67. I break the hold of any evil power over my life, in Jesus' name.

68. I refuse to co-operate with any anti-marriage spell and curse, in the name of Jesus.

69. I cancel every bewitchment, fashioned against my settling down in marriage, in the name of Jesus.

70. Every force, magnetizing the wrong people to me, be paralysed, in the name of Jesus.

71. I break every covenant of marital failure and late marriage, in the name of Jesus.

72. I cancel every spiritual wedding, conducted consciously or unconsciously on my behalf, in Jesus' name.

73. I remove the hand of household wickedness from my marital life, in the name of Jesus.

74. Every incantation, incision and other spiritually harmful activities, working against my marriage, be completely neutralized, in the name of Jesus.

75. All forces of evil, manipulating, delaying or hindering my marriage, be completely paralysed, in the name of Jesus.

76. All evil, anti-marriage covenants, break, in the name of Jesus.

77. Oh Lord, restore me to the perfect way You created me if, I have been altered.

78. Father, let Your fire destroy every satanic weapon fashioned against my marriage, in the name of Jesus.

79. I forsake any personal sin that has given ground to the enemy, in the name of Jesus.

80. I reclaim all the grounds I have lost to the enemy, in the name of Jesus.

81. Blood of Jesus, speak against every power working against my marriage.

82. I apply the blood of Jesus to remove all the consequences of evil operations and oppression, in Jesus' name.

83. I break the binding effect of anything evil, ever put upon me from any source, in the name of Jesus.

84. I remove the right of the enemy to afflict my plan to get married, in the name of Jesus.

85. I break every bondage of inherited marital confusion, in the name of Jesus.

86. I bind and plunder the goods of every strongman attached to my marriage, in the name of Jesus.

87. Oh Lord, let the angels of the living God roll away the stone blocking my marital breakthroughs, in Jesus' name.

88. Oh God arise and let all the enemies of my marital breakthrough scatter, in the name of Jesus.

89. Thou fire of God, melt away the stones hindering my marital blessings, in the mighty name of Jesus.

90. You the cloud, blocking the sunlight of my marital breakthrough, clear away, in Jesus' name.

91. All evil spirits, masquerading in order to trouble my marital life, be bound, in the name of Jesus.

92. Oh Lord, let wonderful changes be my lot this year.

93. Oh Lord, turn away all that would jilt, disappoint or fail me, in the name of Jesus.

94. Thank God, for the victory.

PRAYERS FOR MARITAL BREAKTHROUGHS 2

This section contains the types of prayers to pray when you want to save your marriage from collapse. If you have failed to lay a good foundation in prayer for your marriage, and the unity and stability of the marriage is now threatened, this prayer programme is for you. No matter the problem or the threats you are facing in your marriage, you need a prayer programme that will give you the miracle of marital breakthroughs.

God will use this prayer programme to restore your marriage. You must take these prayer points with every strength and fire in you. They will bring marital breakthroughs, heaven into your home, honey into your marriage and divine peace into your relationship. Pray persistently until there is definite change in your marriage.

Meditation Points

☞ **Spiritual maturity.**

☞ **Psychological and emotional maturity.**

☞ **Financial independence.**

☞ **Readiness to serve and share what you have with others.**

Confessions: Genesis 2:10-19: And a river went out of Eden to water the garden; and from thence it was parted, and became into four heads. The name of the first is Pison: that is it which compasseth the whole land of Havilah, where there is gold; And the gold of that land is good: there is bdellium and the onyx stone. And the name of the second river is Gihon: the same is it that compasseth the whole land of Ethiopia. And the name of the third river is Hiddekel: that is it which goeth toward the east of Assyria. And the fourth river is Euphrates. And the Lord God took the man, and put him into the garden of Eden to dress it and to keep it. And the Lord God commanded the man, saying, Of every tree of the garden thou mayest freely eat: But of the tree of the knowledge of good and evil, thou shalt not eat of it: for in the day that thou eatest thereof thou shalt surely die. And the Lord God said, It is not good that the man should be alone; I will make him an help meet for him. And out of the ground the Lord God formed every beast of the field, and every fowl of the air; and brought them unto Adam to see what he would call them: and whatsoever Adam called every living creature, that was the name thereof.

Deut. 32:30: How should one chase a thousand, and two put ten thousand to flight, except their Rock had sold them, and the Lord had shut them up?

Proverbs 31:10-11: Who can find a virtuous woman? for her price is far above rubies. The heart of her husband doth safely trust in her, so that he shall have no need of spoil.

Eccles. 4:9-12: Two are better than one; because they have a good reward for their labour. For if they fall, the one will lift up his fellow: but woe to him that is alone when he falleth; for he hath not another to help him up. Again, if two lie together, then they have heat: but how can one be warm alone? And if one prevail against him, two shall withstand him; and a threefold cord is not quickly broken.

Isaiah 62:4-6: Thou shalt no more be termed Forsaken; neither shall thy land any more be termed Desolate: but thou shalt be called Hephzi-bah, and thy land Beulah: for the Lord delighteth in thee, and thy land shall be married. For as a young man marrieth a virgin, so shall thy sons marry thee: and as the bridegroom rejoiceth over the bride, so shall thy God rejoice over thee. I have set watchmen upon thy walls, O Jerusalem, which shall never hold their peace day nor night: ye that make mention of the Lord, keep not silence,

Malachi 2:10-16: Have we not all one father? hath not one God created us? why do we deal treacherously every man against his brother, by profaning the covenant of our fathers?

Judah hath dealt treacherously, and an abomination is committed in Israel and in Jerusalem; for Judah hath profaned the holiness of the Lord which he loved, and hath married the daughter of a strange god. The Lord will cut off the man that doeth this, the master and the scholar, out of the tabernacles of Jacob, and him that offereth an offering unto the Lord of hosts. And this have ye done again, covering the altar of the Lord with tears, with weeping, and with crying out, insomuch that he regardeth not the offering any more, or receiveth it with good will at your hand. Yet ye say, Wherefore? Because the Lord hath been witness between thee and the wife of thy youth, against whom thou hast dealt treacherously: yet is she thy companion, and the wife of thy covenant. And did not he make one? Yet had he the residue of the spirit. And wherefore one? That he might seek a godly seed. Therefore take heed to your spirit, and let none deal treacherously against the wife of his youth. For the Lord, the God of Israel, saith that he hateth putting away: for one covereth violence with his garment, saith the Lord of hosts: therefore take heed to your spirit, that ye deal not treacherously.

Galatians 2:14-15: But when I saw that they walked not uprightly according to the truth of the gospel, I said unto Peter before them all, If thou, being a Jew, livest after the manner of Gentiles, and not as do the Jews, why compellest thou the Gentiles to live as do the Jews? We who are Jews by nature, and not sinners of the Gentiles,

Col. 2:14-15: Blotting out the handwriting of ordinances that was against us, which was contrary to us, and took it out of the way, nailing it to his cross; And having spoiled principalities and powers, he made a shew of them openly, triumphing over them in it.

2 Tim. 4:18: And the Lord shall deliver me from every evil work, and will preserve me unto his heavenly kingdom: to whom be glory for ever and ever. Amen.

Praise worship

1. Thank the Lord because this year is your year of dumbfounding miracles.

2. Lord, I give You thanks for making me perfect.

3. Lord, I give You thanks for Your plan for my marriage.

4. Father, I worship You for the partner You have chosen for me from the beginning of creation.

5. I confess and repent of any act of sexual sins.

6. I confess the sins of my ancestors (list them).

7. Ask the Lord for forgiveness.

8. O Lord, make known to me the secrets needed for my marital breakthroughs.

9. Help me Lord to discover my real self.

10. Every imagination of the enemy, against my marital life, be rendered impotent, in the name of Jesus.

11. I renounce any covenant existing between me and any spirit husband or wife, in the name of Jesus.

12. Thou power in the blood of Jesus, separate me from the sins of my ancestors, in the name of Jesus.

13. I divorce my marriage to the king or queen of the coast, in Jesus' name.

14. I renounce any evil dedication, placed upon my life, in the name of Jesus.

15. I receive freedom from satanic marriage by fire, in the name of Jesus.

16. I break every evil edict and ordination, in the name of Jesus.

17. O Lord, wash me from blood contamination, in the name of Jesus.

18. I renounce and loose myself from every negative dedication placed upon my life, in the name of Jesus.

19. Holy Ghost, prepare me for my marriage partner, in the name of Jesus.

20. All demons, associated with evil dedication, leave me now, in the name of Jesus Christ.

21. O Lord, see my need for marriage and establish me, in the name of Jesus.

22. I take authority over all associated curses, in the name of Jesus.

23. O Lord, cancel the evil consequences of any broken demonic promise or dedication, in the name of Jesus.

24. I take authority over all the curses, emanating from broken dedication, in the name of Jesus.

25. All demons, associated with any broken evil parental vow and dedication, depart from me now, in the name of Jesus.

26. I bind all principalities and powers of . . . . . operating over and within my life, in the name of Jesus.

27. I bind all wickedness in high places and evil thrones of . . . . . operating over and within my life, in the name of Jesus.

28. I bind all evil dominions and strongmen of . . . . . operating over and within my life, in the name of Jesus.

29. I overthrow every satanic middle-man or middle-woman opposing my engagement and marriage, in the name of Jesus.

30. I bind every witchcraft control and mind-blinding spirit, in the name of Jesus.

31. I strip each spirit off the power and rank of . . . . . and separate them from one another, in the name of Jesus.

32. I receive release from family captivity in marriage, in the name of Jesus.

33. I cast out every witchcraft arrow, affecting my senses (sight, smell, taste, hearing), in the name of Jesus.

34. Every witchcraft arrow, depart from my (pick from the underlisted), in the name of Jesus.

- spinal cord - spleen   - navel   - heart - throat

- between the eyes - top of the head.

35. I bind every evil presence in my (pick from the underlisted), system, in the name of Jesus.

- reproductive   - digestive   - respiratory - nervous

- skeletal   - muscular   - circulatory - endocrine

- excretory

36. I break the backbone and destroy the root of every spirit speaking against me, in the name of Jesus.

37. Every evil mark on my family, be erased by the blood of Jesus.

38. Every astral projection against me, I frustrate you, in Jesus' name.

39. Holy Ghost, bring me in contact with the one You have chosen for me as my partner, in the name of Jesus.

40. Holy Ghost, let our paths cross and never to part again, in the name of Jesus.

41. Every complicated evil network against me, be eaten up by the elements, in the name of Jesus.

42. I bind every power, pulling anything in my body towards evil by means of energy drawn from the sun, the moon and the stars, in the name of Jesus.

43. I bind every power, pulling anything in my body towards evil by means of energy drawn from the planets, the constellations and the earth, in the name of Jesus.

44. I bind every power, pulling anything in my body towards evil by means of energy drawn from the (pick from the underlisted), in the name of Jesus.

- air - wind - fire - water - light - darkness -

elements

45. Any power of . . . . . . drawing energy against me from evil lines and circles, fall down and die, in the name of Jesus.

46. I forbid any transfer of spirit into my life from my family, friends and associates, in the name of Jesus.

47. Every altar, speaking against my divine destiny, be dismantled, in the name of Jesus.

48. I bring the blood of Jesus over the spirit that does not want to let me go, in the name of Jesus.

49. Blood of Jesus, purge me of every witchcraft contaminating material, in the name of Jesus.

50. I destroy the hand of the witch-doctor, working against me, in the name of Jesus.

51. Every witchcraft spirit, attempting to build a wall against my destiny, fall down and die, in the name of Jesus.

52. I send the rain of affliction upon every marine witchcraft, working against me, in the name of Jesus.

53. O sun, moon, stars, earth, water and the elements, vomit every enchantment that is against me, in the name of Jesus.

54. Every power, using the heavenlies against me, fall down and be disgraced, in the name of Jesus.

55. You the stars of heaven, begin to fight for me, in the name of Jesus.

56. O God, arise and scatter every conspiracy against me in the heavenlies, in the name of Jesus.

57. I break with the blood of Jesus, all evil soul-ties affecting my life, in the name of Jesus.

58. Spirit of the living God, come upon my life and place a shield of protection around me, in the name of Jesus.

59. Every chain of inherited witchcraft in my family, be destroyed, in the name of Jesus.

60. Every ladder, used by witchcraft against me, roast, in the name of Jesus.

61. Holy Ghost, destroy any marriage certificate, binding me to any a spirit husband or wife, in the name of Jesus.

62.   Any door that I have opened to witchcraft in any area of my life, close forever by the blood of Jesus.

63.   I release myself from every ancestral demonic pollution, in the name of Jesus.

64.   I release myself from every demonic pollution, emanating from my parents' religion, in the name of Jesus.

65.   I release myself from demonic pollution, emanating from my past involvement in any demonic religion, in the name of Jesus.

66.   I break loose from every idol and related association, in the name of Jesus.

67.   I release myself from every dream pollution, in the name of Jesus.

68.   Every satanic attack against my life in my dreams, be converted to victory, in the name of Jesus.

69.   All rivers, trees, forests, evil companions, evil pursuers, pictures of dead relatives, snakes, spirit husbands, spirit wives and masquerades, manipulated against me in the dream, be completely destroyed by the power in the blood of the Lord Jesus.

70.   Every evil plantation in my life: **Come out with all your roots, in the name of Jesus!** (*Lay your hands on your stomach and keep repeating the emphasised area.*)

71. Evil strangers in my body, come out of your hiding places, in the name of Jesus.

72. I disconnect any conscious or unconscious link with demonic caterers, in the name of Jesus.

73. O Lord, let all avenues of eating or drinking spiritual poisons close, in the name of Jesus.

74. I cough and vomit any food eaten from the table of the devil, in the name of Jesus. (*Cough and vomit them in faith. Prime the expulsion.*)

75. All negative materials, circulating in my blood stream, come out and die, in the name of Jesus.

76. I drink the blood of Jesus. (*Physically swallow and drink it in faith. Keep doing this for some time.*)

77. (*Lay one hand on your head and the other on your stomach or navel and begin to pray like this*): Holy Ghost fire, burn from the top of my head to the sole of my feet. (*Begin to mention every organ of your body: your kidney, liver, intestines, etc. You must not rush at this level, because the fire will actually come and you may start feeling the heat*).

78. I cut myself off from every spirit of . . . (*mention the name of your place of birth*), in the name of Jesus.

79. I cut myself off from every tribal spirit and curse, in the name of Jesus.

80. I cut myself off from every territorial spirit and curse, in the name of Jesus.

81. Holy Ghost fire, purge my life.

82. I claim my complete deliverance, from the spirit of ... (*mention those things you do not desire in your life*), in Jesus' name.

83. I break the hold of any evil power over my life, in the name of Jesus.

84. I refuse to co-operate with any anti-marriage spell and curse, in the name of Jesus.

85. I cancel every bewitchment fashioned against my settling down in marriage, in the name of Jesus.

86. Every force, magnetizing the wrong people to me, be paralysed, in the name of Jesus.

87. I break every covenant of marital failure and late marriage, in the name of Jesus.

88. I cancel every spiritual wedding, conducted consciously or unconsciously on my behalf, in Jesus' name.

89. I remove the hand of household wickedness from my marital life, in the name of Jesus.

90. Every incantation, incision, hex and other spiritually harmful activities, working against my marriage, be completely neutralized, in the name of Jesus.

91. All forces of evil, manipulating, delaying or hindering my marriage, be completely paralysed, in the name of Jesus.

92. All evil anti-marriage covenants, break, in the name of Jesus.

93. O Lord, restore me to the perfect way You created me if I have been altered.

94. Father, let Your fire destroy every satanic weapon fashioned against my marriage, in the name of Jesus.

95. I forsake any personal sin that has given ground to the enemy, in the name of Jesus.

96. I reclaim all the grounds I have lost to the enemy, in the name of Jesus.

97. Blood of Jesus, speak against every power working against my marriage.

98. I apply the blood of Jesus to remove all consequences of evil operations and oppressions, in Jesus' name.

99. I break the binding effect of anything evil, ever put upon me from any source, in the name of Jesus.

100. I remove the right of the enemy to afflict my plan to get married, in the name of Jesus.

101. I break every bondage of inherited marital confusion, in the name of Jesus.

102. I bind and plunder the goods of every strongman attached to my marriage, in the name of Jesus.

103. You angels of the living God, roll away the stone blocking my marital breakthroughs, in Jesus' name.

104. O God arise and let all the enemies of my marital breakthrough scatter, in the name of Jesus.

105. Thou fire of God, melt away the stones hindering my marital blessings, in the mighty name of Jesus.

106. Every cloud, blocking the sunlight of my marital breakthrough, clear away, in Jesus' name.

107. All evil spirits, masquerading in order to trouble my marital life, be bound, in the name of Jesus.

108. O Lord, let wonderful changes be my lot this year.

109. O Lord, turn away all who would jilt, disappoint or fail me, in the name of Jesus.

110. Any power, standing against my marriage, be consumed by fire, in the name of Jesus.

111. Father, reveal to me Your choice for my life, in the name of Jesus.

112. Father, introduce me to my partner, in the name of Jesus.

113. Holy Ghost, dress me and make me acceptable to my partner, in the name of Jesus.

114. I confess that I am loveable, in the name of Jesus.

115. I declare that I am honourable and undefiled among my peers, in the name of Jesus.

116. Holy Ghost, crown my head and life with divine glory, in the name of Jesus.

117. Any tongue, speaking evil against me when I am being considered by my partner, be silenced now, in Jesus' name.

118. I declare that I shall not miss my season of marriage, in the name of Jesus.

119. I prophesy that I am the delight of my partner, in Jesus' name.

120. Holy Ghost, shut up the mouth of anyone speaking against me now, in the name of Jesus.

121. I prophesy that my courtship will lead to marriage; and I shall be fruitful, in the name of Jesus.

122. I close any door that I have opened to the devil through my confessions and past actions, in the name of Jesus.

123. Lord Jesus, wash me from the impurity and stigma of the past, in the name of Jesus.

124. You gates and everlasting doors, resisting my marital breakthrough, be lifted and be uprooted, in the name of Jesus.

125. I lay hold on my covenant right of marriage; therefore, I shall be happily married, in the name of Jesus.

126. Thank God, for the victory.

PRAYERS FOR MARITAL BREAKTHROUGHS 3

Meditation Points

☞ Spiritual maturity.

☞ Psychological and emotional maturity.

☞ Financial independence.

☞ Readiness to serve and share what you have with others.

Confessions: Genesis 2:10-19: And a river went out of Eden to water the garden; and from thence it was parted, and became into four heads. The name of the first is Pison: that is it which compasseth the whole land of Havilah, where there is gold; And the gold of that land is good: there is bdellium and the onyx stone. And the name of the second river is Gihon: the same is it that compasseth the whole land of Ethiopia. And the name of the third river is Hiddekel: that is it which goeth toward the east of Assyria. And the fourth river is Euphrates. And the Lord God took the man, and put him into the garden of Eden to dress it and to keep it. And the Lord God commanded the man, saying, Of every tree of the garden thou mayest freely eat: But of the tree of the knowledge of good and evil, thou shalt not eat of it: for in the day that thou eatest thereof thou shalt surely die. And the Lord God said, It is not good that the man should be alone; I will make him an help meet for him. And out of the ground the Lord God formed every beast of the field, and every fowl of the air; and brought them unto Adam to see what he would call them: and whatsoever Adam called every living creature, that was the name thereof.

Deut. 32:30: How should one chase a thousand, and two put ten thousand to flight, except their Rock had sold them, and the Lord had shut them up?

Proverbs 31:10-11: Who can find a virtuous woman? for her price is far above rubies. The heart of her husband doth safely trust in her, so that he shall have no need of spoil.

Eccles. 4:9-12: Two are better than one; because they have a good reward for their labour. For if they fall, the one will lift up his fellow: but woe to him that is alone when he falleth; for he hath not another to help him up. Again, if two lie together, then they have heat: but how can one be warm alone? And if one prevail against him, two shall withstand him; and a threefold cord is not quickly broken.

Isaiah 62:4-6: Thou shalt no more be termed Forsaken;

neither shall thy land any more be termed Desolate: but thou shalt be called Hephzi-bah, and thy land Beulah: for the Lord delighteth in thee, and thy land shall be married. For as a young man marrieth a virgin, so shall thy sons marry thee: and as the bridegroom rejoiceth over the bride, so shall thy God rejoice over thee. I have set watchmen upon thy walls, O Jerusalem, which shall never hold their peace day nor night: ye that make mention of the Lord, keep not silence.

Malachi 2:10-16: Have we not all one father? hath not one God created us? why do we deal treacherously every man against his brother, by profaning the covenant of our fathers? Judah hath dealt treacherously, and an abomination is committed in Israel and in Jerusalem; for Judah hath profaned the holiness of the Lord which he loved, and hath married the daughter of a strange god. The Lord will cut off the man that doeth this, the master and the scholar, out of the tabernacles of Jacob, and him that offereth an offering unto the Lord of hosts. And this have ye done again, covering the altar of the Lord with tears, with weeping, and with crying out, insomuch that he regardeth not the offering any more, or receiveth it with good will at your hand. Yet ye say, Wherefore? Because the Lord hath been witness between thee and the wife of thy youth, against whom thou hast dealt treacherously: yet is she thy companion, and the wife of thy covenant. And did not he make one? Yet had he the residue of the spirit. And wherefore one? That he might seek a godly seed. Therefore take heed to your spirit, and let none deal treacherously against the wife of his youth. For the Lord, the God of Israel, saith that he hateth putting away: for one covereth violence with his garment, saith the Lord of hosts: therefore take heed to your spirit, that ye deal not treacherously.

Galatians 2:14-15: But when I saw that they walked not uprightly according to the truth of the gospel, I said unto Peter before them all, If thou, being a Jew, livest after the manner of Gentiles; and not as do the Jews, why compellest thou the Gentiles to live as do the Jews? We who are Jews by nature, and not sinners of the Gentiles,

Col. 2:14-15: Blotting out the handwriting of ordinances that was against us, which was contrary to us, and took it out of the way, nailing it to his cross; And having spoiled principalities and powers, he made a shew of them openly, triumphing over them in it.

2 Tim. 4:18: And the Lord shall deliver me from every evil work, and will preserve me unto his heavenly kingdom: to whom be glory for ever and ever. Amen.

Praise worship

1. Thank the Lord because this year is your year of dumbfounding miracles.

2. Lord, I give You thanks for making me perfect.

3. Lord, I give You thanks for Your plan for my marriage.

4. Father, I worship You for the partner You have chosen for me from the beginning of creation.

5. I confess and repent of any act of sexual sins.

6. I confess the sins of my ancestors (list them).

7. Ask the Lord for forgiveness.

8. O Lord, make known to me the secrets needed for my marital breakthroughs.

9. Help me Lord to discover my real self.

10. Every imagination of the enemy, against my marital life, be rendered impotent, in the name of Jesus.

11. I renounce any covenant, existing between me and a spirit husband or a spirit wife, in the name of Jesus.

12. Thou power in the blood of Jesus, separate me from the sins of my ancestors, in the name of Jesus.

13. I divorce my marriage to the king or queen of the coast, in the name of Jesus.

14. I renounce any evil dedication placed upon my life, in the name of Jesus.

15. I receive freedom from satanic marriage by fire, in the name of Jesus.

16. I break every evil edict and ordination, in the name of Jesus.

17. O Lord, wash me from blood contamination, in the name of Jesus.

18. I renounce and loose myself from every negative dedication placed upon my life, in the name of Jesus.

19. Holy Ghost, prepare me for my marriage partner, in the name of Jesus.

20. All demons, associated with evil dedication, leave me now, in the name of Jesus Christ.

21. O Lord, see my need for marriage and establish me, in the name of Jesus.

22. I take authority over all associated curses, in Jesus' name.

23. O Lord, cancel the evil consequences of any broken demonic promise or dedication, in the name of Jesus.

24. I take authority over all the curses emanating from broken dedication, in the name of Jesus.

25. All demons, associated with any broken evil parental vow and dedication, depart from me now, in the name of Jesus.

26. I bind all principalities and powers of . . . . . . operating over and within my life, in the name of Jesus.

27. I bind all wickedness in high places and evil thrones of . . . . . . operating over and within my life, in the name of Jesus.

28. I bind all evil dominions and strongmen of . . . . . . operating over and within my life, in the name of Jesus.

29. I overthrow every satanic middle-man or middle-woman opposing my engagement and marriage, in the name of Jesus.

30. I bind every witchcraft control and mind-blinding spirit, in the name of Jesus.

31. I strip each spirit off the power and rank of . . . . . and I separate them from one another, in the name of Jesus.

32. I receive release from family captivity in marriage, in the name of Jesus.

33. I cast out every witchcraft arrow affecting my senses (sight, smell, taste, hearing), in the name of Jesus.

34. Every witchcraft arrow, depart from my (Pick from the underlisted), in the name of Jesus.

    - spinal cord - spleen   - navel   - heart   - throat

    - between the eyes   - top of the head.

35. I bind every evil presence in my (Pick from the underlisted) system, in the name of Jesus.

    - reproductive   - digestive   - respiratory - nervous

    - skeletal   - muscular

    - circulatory   - endocrine   - excretory

36. I break the backbone and destroy the root of every spirit speaking against me, in the name of Jesus.

37. Every evil mark on my family, be erased by the blood of Jesus.

38. Every astral projection against me, I frustrate you, in the name of Jesus.

39. Holy Ghost, bring me in contact with the one You have chosen for me as my partner, in the name of Jesus.

40. Holy Ghost, let our path cross and never to part again, in the name of Jesus.

41. Every complicated evil network against me, be eaten up by the elements, in the name of Jesus.

42. I bind every power, pulling anything in my body towards evil by means of energy drawn from the sun, the moon and the stars, in the name of Jesus.

43. I bind every power, pulling anything in my body towards evil by means of energy drawn from the planets, constellations and the earth, in the name of Jesus.

44. I bind every power, pulling anything in my body towards evil by means of energy drawn from the . . . in the name of Jesus.

    - air - wind - fire - water   - light - darkness - elements

45. Any power of . . . . . . drawing energy against me from evil lines and circles, fall down and die, in the name of Jesus.

46. I forbid any transfer of spirit into my life from my family, friends and associates, in the name of Jesus.

47. Every altar, speaking against my divine destiny, be dismantled, in the name of Jesus.

48. I bring the blood of Jesus over the spirit that does not want to let me go, in the name of Jesus.

49. Blood of Jesus, purge me of every witchcraft contaminating material, in the name of Jesus.

50. I destroy the hands of the witch-doctors, working against me, in the name of Jesus.

51. Every witchcraft spirit, attempting to build a wall against my destiny, fall down and die, in the name of Jesus.

52. I send the rain of affliction upon every marine witchcraft, working against me, in the name of Jesus.

53. O sun, moon, stars, earth, water and the elements, vomit every enchantment that is working against me, in the name of Jesus

54. Every power, using the heavenlies against me, fall down and be disgraced, in the name of Jesus.

55. You the stars of heaven, begin to fight for me, in the name of Jesus.

56. O God, arise and scatter every conspiracy against me in the heavenlies, in the name of Jesus.

57. I break with the blood of Jesus, all evil soul-ties affecting my life, in the name of Jesus.

58. Spirit of the living God, come upon my life and place a shield of protection around me, in the name of Jesus.

59. Every chain of inherited witchcraft in my family, be destroyed, in the name of Jesus.

60. Every ladder, used by witchcraft against me, roast, in the name of Jesus.

61. Holy Ghost, destroy any marriage certificate, binding me to a spirit husband or a spirit wife, in the name of Jesus.

62. Any door, that I have opened to witchcraft in any area of my life, close forever, by the blood of Jesus.

63. I release myself from every ancestral demonic pollution, in the name of Jesus.

64. I release myself from every demonic pollution, emanating from my parents' religion, in the name of Jesus.

65. I release myself from demonic pollution, emanating from my past involvement in any demonic religion, in the name of Jesus.

66. I break loose from every idol and related association, in the name of Jesus.

67. I release myself from every dream pollution, in the name of Jesus.

68. Every satanic attack, against my life in my dreams, be converted to victory, in the name of Jesus.

69. All rivers, trees, forests, evil companions, evil pursuers, pictures of dead relatives, snakes, spirit husbands/spirit wives, and masquerades, manipulated against me in the dream, be completely destroyed by the power in the blood of the Lord Jesus.

70. Every evil plantation in my life: **Come out with all your roots, in the name of Jesus!** (*Lay your hands on your stomach and keep repeating the emphasised area.*)

71. Evil strangers in my body, come out of your hiding places, in the name of Jesus.

72. I disconnect any conscious or unconscious link with demonic caterers, in the name of Jesus.

73. O Lord, let all avenues of eating or drinking spiritual poisons be closed, in the name of Jesus.

74. I cough and vomit any food eaten from the table of the devil, in the name of Jesus. (*Cough and vomit them in faith. Prime the expulsion.*)

75. All negative materials, circulating in my blood stream, come out by fire, in the name of Jesus.

76. I drink the blood of Jesus. (*Physically swallow and drink it in faith. Keep doing this for some time.*)

77. *(Lay one hand on your head, and the other on your stomach or navel and begin to pray like this):* Holy Ghost Fire, burn from the top of my head to the sole of my feet. *(Begin to mention every organ of your body; your kidney, liver, intestines, blood, etc. You must not rush at this level, because the fire will actually come and you may start feeling the heat).*

78. I cut myself off from every spirit of ... *(mention the name of your place of birth)*, in the name of Jesus.

79. I cut myself off from every tribal spirit and curse, in the name of Jesus.

80. I cut myself off from every territorial spirit and curse, in the name of Jesus.

81. Holy Ghost fire, purge my life.

82. I claim my complete deliverance, from the spirit of ... *(mention those things you do not desire in your life)*, in Jesus' name.

83. I break the hold of any evil power over my life, in the name of Jesus.

84. I refuse to co-operate with any anti-marriage spell and curse, in the name of Jesus.

85. I cancel every bewitchment, fashioned against my settling down in marriage, in the name of Jesus.

86. Every force, magnetizing the wrong people to me, be paralysed, in the name of Jesus.

87. I break every covenant of marital failure and late marriage, in the name of Jesus.

88. I cancel every spiritual wedding, conducted consciously or unconsciously on my behalf, in Jesus' name.

89. I remove the hand of household wickedness from my marital life, in the name of Jesus.

90. Every incantation, incision, hex and other spiritually harmful activities, working against my marriage, be completely neutralized, in the name of Jesus.

91. All forces of evil, manipulating, delaying or hindering my marriage, be completely paralysed, in the name of Jesus.

92. All evil anti-marriage covenants, break, in the name of Jesus.

93. O Lord, restore me to the perfect way in which You created me, if I have been altered.

94. Father, let Your fire destroy every satanic weapon, fashioned against my marriage, in the name of Jesus.

95. I forsake any personal sin that has given ground to the enemy, in the name of Jesus.

96. I reclaim all the ground that I have lost to the enemy, in the name of Jesus.

97. Blood of Jesus, speak against every power, working against my marriage.

98. I apply, the blood of Jesus to remove all consequences of evil operations and oppression, in Jesus' name.

99. I break the binding effect of anything evil ever put upon me from any source, in the name of Jesus.

100. I remove the right of the enemy to afflict my plan to get married, in the name of Jesus.

101. I break every bondage of inherited marital confusion, in the name of Jesus.

102. I bind and plunder the goods of every strongman attached to my marriage, in the name of Jesus.

103. Angels of the living God, roll away the stones, blocking my marital breakthroughs, in Jesus' name.

104. O God arise and let all the enemies of my marital breakthrough scatter, in the name of Jesus.

105. Fire of God, melt away the stones, hindering my marital blessings, in the mighty name of Jesus.

106. You cloud, blocking the sunlight of my marital breakthrough, disperse, in Jesus' name.

107. All evil spirits, masquerading to trouble my marital life, be bound, in the name of Jesus.

108. O Lord, let wonderful changes be my lot this year.

109. O Lord, turn away all that would jilt, disappoint or fail me, in the name of Jesus.

110. Any power, standing against my marriage, be consumed by fire, in the name of Jesus.

111. Father, reveal to me Your choice for my life, in the name of Jesus.

112. Father, introduce me to my partner, in the name of Jesus.

113. Holy Ghost, dress me and make me acceptable to my partner, in the name of Jesus.

114. I confess that I am loveable, in the name of Jesus.

115. I declare that I am honourable and undefiled among my peers, in the name of Jesus.

116. Holy Ghost, crown my head and life with divine glory, in the name of Jesus.

117. Any tongue, speaking against me when I am being considered by my partner, be silenced now, in the name of Jesus.

118. I declare that I shall not miss my season of marriage, in the name of Jesus.

119. I prophesy that I am the delight of my partner, in the name of Jesus.

120. Holy Ghost, shut up the mouth of anyone, speaking against me now, in the name of Jesus.

121. I prophesy that my courtship will lead to marriage and I shall be fruitful, in the name of Jesus.

122. I close any door that I have opened to the devil through my confessions and past actions, in the name of Jesus.

123. Lord Jesus, wash me from the impurity and stigma of the past, in the name of Jesus.

124. You gates and everlasting doors, resisting my marital breakthrough, be lifted up and be uprooted, in Jesus' name.

125. I lay hold on my covenant right of marriage. Therefore, I shall be happily married, in the name of Jesus.

126. Every household enemy, resisting my breakthroughs, fall down and die, in the name of Jesus.

127. Every unfriendly friend, delegated against my blessing, scatter, in the name of Jesus.

128. Every spirit of disobedience and rebellion in my life, die, in the name of Jesus.

129. Every demon, propagating satanic covenants in my life, fall down and die, in the name of Jesus.

130. Any organ in my body, presently on any evil altar, locate me by fire, in the name of Jesus.

131. By the stripes of Jesus, I curse the root of every sickness in my life, in the name of Jesus.

132. I destroy every anchor of any bondage in my life, in the name of Jesus.

133. Every spirit of hardship in my life, loose your hold, in the name of Jesus.

134. Every problem that defies solution in my life, blood of Jesus, destroy it, in the name of Jesus.

135. Every power, resisting the power of God in my life, I attack you with the thunder fire of God, in the name of Jesus.

136. Every mountain of stubborn problems in my life, fall down and die, in the name of Jesus.

137. Every invisible hand, working evil in my life, wither, in the name of Jesus.

138. Every demon of frustration in my life, die, in the name of Jesus.

139. I reject every spirit of rejection and cancel its operations in my life, in the name of Jesus.

140. I reject and cast out of my life, every deeply rooted failure, in the name of Jesus.

141. Every spirit of abject poverty in my family line, my life is not your candidate, die, in the name of Jesus.

142. Holy Ghost fire, burn every garment of poverty in my life, in the name of Jesus.

143. Every spirit of monument in my life, loose your hold and die, in the name of Jesus.

144. Every spirit of pocket-with-holes, wasting my finances, die, in the name of Jesus.

145. I shall not labour in vain; another person shall not eat the fruit of my labour, in the name of Jesus.

146. Every ancestral spirit of anger, loose your hold upon my life, in the name of Jesus.

147. Every hold of unforgiving spirit in my life, break by the blood of Jesus.

148. Every hold of the spirit of prayerlessness in my life, die now, in the name of Jesus.

149. Every spirit, stealing from me, fall down and die, in the name of Jesus.

150. Every spirit of blindness in my life, die, in the name of Jesus.

151. Every spirit of poverty in my foundation, die, in the name of Jesus.

152. Every problem, planned for my future, you shall not see the daylight, in the name of Jesus.

153. Every warfare, against my breakthroughs in the heavenlies, scatter, in the name of Jesus.

154. Every circle of problems in my life, die, in the name of Jesus.

155. By the blood of Jesus, I make my breakthroughs untouchable for any evil power, in the name of Jesus.

156. You powers, working against my treasures, fall down and die, in the name of Jesus.

157. Thank God, for the victory.

PRAYERS FOR MARITAL BREAKTHROUGHS 4

In this programme, you are offered the type of prayers to pray when you are stepping into marriage. "Prevention," they say, "is better than cure." Many people have suffered marital distress due to their inability to lay a good foundation for their marriage.

The foundation of a building goes a long way to determine the stability and strength of the building. When the foundation is started on a good note, you will succeed as a couple. This programme is a must for men and women contemplating marriage. It is an insecticide for killing every spiritual insect that has the potentials for eating up the fibre of the marriage. You must take cognizance of the fact that, just as you are planning to succeed in a marriage, the devil is secretly laying land mines to blow up your marriage. Therefore, you must painstakingly pray these prayer points to safe-guard your marriage now and in the years ahead.

Confessions: Genesis 2:10-19: And a river went out of

Eden to water the garden; and from thence it was parted, and became into four heads. The name of the first is Pison: that is it which compasseth the whole land of Havilah, where there is gold; And the gold of that land is good: there is bdellium and the onyx stone. And the name of the second river is Gihon: the same is it that compasseth the whole land of Ethiopia. And the name of the third river is Hiddekel: that is it which goeth toward the east of Assyria. And the fourth river is Euphrates. And the Lord God took the man, and put him into the garden of Eden to dress it and to keep it. And the Lord God commanded the man, saying, Of every tree of the garden thou mayest freely eat: But of the tree of the knowledge of good and evil, thou shalt not eat of it: for in the day that thou eatest thereof thou shalt surely die. And the Lord God said, It is not good that the man should be alone; I will make him an help meet for him. And out of the ground the Lord God formed every beast of the field, and every fowl of the air; and brought them unto Adam to see what he would call them: and whatsoever Adam called every living creature, that was the name thereof.

Deut. 32:30: How should one chase a thousand, and two put ten thousand to flight, except their Rock had sold them, and the Lord had shut them up?

Proverbs 31:10-11: Who can find a virtuous woman? for her

price is far above rubies. The heart of her husband doth safely trust in her, so that he shall have no need of spoil.

Eccles. 4:9-12: Two are better than one; because they have a good reward for their labour. For if they fall, the one will lift up his fellow: but woe to him that is alone when he falleth; for he hath not another to help him up. Again, if two lie together, then they have heat: but how can one be warm alone? And if one prevail against him, two shall withstand him; and a threefold cord is not quickly broken.

Isaiah 62:4-6: Thou shalt no more be termed Forsaken; neither shall thy land any more be termed Desolate: but thou shalt be called Hephzi-bah, and thy land Beulah: for the Lord delighteth in thee, and thy land shall be married. For as a young man marrieth a virgin, so shall thy sons marry thee: and as the bridegroom rejoiceth over the bride, so shall thy God rejoice over thee. I have set watchmen upon thy walls, O Jerusalem, which shall never hold their peace day nor night: ye that make mention of the Lord, keep not silence,

Malachi 2:10-16: Have we not all one father? hath not one God created us? why do we deal treacherously every man against his brother, by profaning the covenant of our fathers? Judah hath dealt treacherously, and an abomination is committed in Israel and in Jerusalem; for Judah hath profaned the holiness of the Lord which he loved, and hath married the daughter of a strange god. The Lord will cut off the man that doeth this, the master and the scholar, out of the tabernacles of Jacob, and him that offereth an offering unto the Lord of hosts. And this have ye done again, covering the altar of the Lord with tears, with weeping, and with crying out, insomuch that he regardeth not the offering any more, or receiveth it with good will at your hand. Yet ye say, Wherefore? Because the Lord hath been witness between thee and the wife of thy youth, against whom thou hast dealt treacherously: yet is she thy companion, and the wife of thy covenant. And did not he make one? Yet had he the residue of the spirit. And wherefore one? That he might seek a godly seed. Therefore take heed to your spirit, and let none deal treacherously against the wife of his youth. For the Lord, the God of Israel, saith that he hateth putting away: for one covereth violence with his garment, saith the Lord of hosts: therefore take heed to your spirit, that ye deal not treacherously.

Galatians 2:14-15: But when I saw that they walked not uprightly according to the truth of the gospel, I said unto Peter before them all, If thou, being a Jew, livest after the manner of Gentiles, and not as do the Jews, why compellest thou the Gentiles to live as do the Jews? We who are Jews by nature, and not sinners of the Gentiles,

Col. 2:14-15: Blotting out the handwriting of ordinances that was against us, which was contrary to us, and took it out of the way, nailing it to his cross; And having spoiled principalities and powers, he made a shew of them openly, triumphing over them in it.

2 Tim. 4:18: And the Lord shall deliver me from every evil work, and will preserve me unto his heavenly kingdom: to whom be glory for ever and ever. Amen.

PRAYER POINTS

1. Thank the Lord because this year is your year of dumbfounding miracles.

2. Lord, I give thanks to You for Your plan for my marriage.

3. Confess these Scriptures out loud: Philippians 2:9; Colossians 2:13; Rev. 12:12; Luke 1:37.

4. O Lord, make known to me the secrets needed for my marital breakthrough.

5. Help me Lord to discover my real self.

6. Every imagination of the enemy against my marital life, be rendered impotent, in the name of Jesus.

7. I refuse to co-operate with any anti-marriage spell and curse, in the name of Jesus.

8. I cancel every bewitchment, fashioned against my settling down in marriage, in the name of Jesus.

9. Every force, magnetizing the wrong people to me, be paralysed, in the name of Jesus.

10. I break every covenant of marital failure and late marriage, in the name of Jesus.

11. I cancel every spiritual wedding, conducted consciously or unconsciously on my behalf, in Jesus' name.

12. I remove the hand of household wickedness from my marital life, in the name of Jesus.

13. Every incantation, incision, hex and other spiritually harmful activities, working against my marriage, be completely neutralized, in the name of Jesus.

14. All forces of evil, manipulating, delaying or hindering my marriage, be completely paralysed, in the name of Jesus.

15. All evil anti-marriage covenants, break, in the name of Jesus.

16. O Lord, restore me to the perfect way You created me, if I have been altered.

17. Father, let Your fire destroy every satanic weapon, fashioned against my marriage, in the name of Jesus.

18. I forsake any personal sin that has given ground to the enemy, in the name of Jesus.

19. I reclaim all the ground I have lost to the enemy, in the name of Jesus.

20. Blood of Jesus, speak against every power, working against my marriage.

21. I apply the blood of Jesus to remove all consequences of evil operations and oppression, in Jesus' name.

22. I break the binding effect of anything evil, ever put upon me from any source, in the name of Jesus.

23. I remove the right of the enemy to afflict my plan to get married, in the name of Jesus.

24. I break every bondage of inherited marital confusion, in the name of Jesus.

25. I bind and plunder the goods of every strongman attached to my marriage, in the name of Jesus.

26. Angels of the living God, roll away the stone blocking my marital breakthrough, in Jesus' name.

27. O God arise and let all the enemies of my marital breakthrough, scatter, in the name of Jesus.

28. Fire of God, melt away the stones hindering my marital blessings, in the mighty name of Jesus.

29. You evil cloud, blocking the sunlight of my marital breakthrough, disperse, in Jesus' name.

30. All evil spirits, masquerading to trouble my marital life, be bound, in the name of Jesus.

31. O Lord, let wonderful changes be my lot this year.

32. O Lord, turn away all who would jilt, disappoint or fail me, in the name of Jesus.

33. Any power, standing against my marriage, be consumed by fire, in the name of Jesus.

34. Father, reveal to me Your choice for my life, in Jesus' name.

35. Father, introduce me to my partner, in the name of Jesus.

36. Holy Ghost, dress me and make me acceptable to my partner, in the name of Jesus.

37. I confess that I am loveable, in the name of Jesus.

38. I declare that I am honourable and undefiled among my peers, in the name of Jesus.

39. Holy Ghost, crown my head and life with divine glory, in the name of Jesus.

40. Any tongue, speaking against me when I am being considered by my partner, be silenced now, in the name of Jesus.

41. I declare that I shall not miss my season of marriage, in the name of Jesus.

42. I prophesy that I am the delight of my partner, in Jesus' name.

43. Holy Ghost, shut up the mouth of anyone speaking against me now, in the name of Jesus.

44. I prophesy that my courtship will lead to marriage and I shall be fruitful, in the name of Jesus.

45. I close any door that I have opened to the devil, through my confessions and past actions, in the name of Jesus.

46. Lord Jesus, wash me from the impurity and stigma of the past, in the name of Jesus.

47. You gates and everlasting doors, resisting my marital breakthrough, be lifted up and be uprooted, in the name of Jesus.

48. I lay hold on my covenant right of marriage, therefore, I shall be happily married, in the name of Jesus.

49. Every household enemy, resisting my breakthrough, fall down and die, in the name of Jesus.

50. Every unfriendly friend, delegated against my blessing, scatter, in the name of Jesus.

51. Every spirit of disobedience and rebellion in my life, die, in the name of Jesus.

52. Every demon, propagating satanic covenants in my life, fall down and die, in the name of Jesus.

53. Thank God, for the victory.

PRAYERS AGAINST COLLECTIVE CAPTIVITY

The problem of collective captivity is a stubborn one. One must know the kind of prayers to pray. When captivity comes upon a community, group of people or family, everyone under the umbrella will be affected. To be free from the results or the effects of collective captivity, you must pray certain prayers that are centred on affecting the overall umbrella under which all the victims are placed. Family members, inhabitants of the community and the entire citizenry of a nation will go along the same pattern and suffer the same problems until the yoke of collective captivity is broken.

These prayer points are targeted at setting you free from collective bondage, removing your life from underneath the evil umbrella, as well as erasing every evil writing affecting your life negatively. They will enable you to rise above your roots.

Scripture: 2Tim. 4:18

1. Praise the Lord for the power in His name at which every knee must bow.

2. Thank God for providing deliverance from any form of bondage.

3. I cover myself with the blood of Jesus.

4. Confess any sin that can hinder answers to your prayers and ask God to forgive you.

5. Stand against any power already organised against this prayer.

6. I destroy the power of every satanic arrest in my life, in Jesus' name.

7. All satanic-arresting agents, release me, in the mighty name of our Lord Jesus Christ.

8. Everything that is representing me in the demonic world against my career, be destroyed by the fire of God, in the name of Jesus.

9. Spirit of the living God, quicken my whole being, in the name of Jesus.

10. O God, smash me and renew my strength, in the name of Jesus.

11. Holy Spirit, open my eyes to see beyond the visible to the invisible, in the name of Jesus.

12. O Lord, ignite my career with Your fire.

13. O Lord, liberate my spirit to follow the leading of the Holy Spirit.

14. Holy Spirit, teach me to pray through problems, instead of praying about them, in the name of Jesus.

15. O Lord, deliver me from the lies I tell to myself.

16. Every evil spiritual padlock and evil chain, hindering my success, roast, in the name of Jesus.

17. I rebuke every spirit of spiritual deafness and blindness in my life, in the name of Jesus.

18. O Lord, empower me to resist satan so that he would flee from me.

19. I chose to believe the report of the Lord and no other, in the name of Jesus.

20. O Lord, anoint my eyes and my ears so that they may see and hear wondrous things from heaven.

21. O Lord, anoint me to pray without ceasing.

22. In the name of Jesus, I capture every power behind any career failure.

23. Holy Spirit, rain on me now, in the name of Jesus.

24. Holy Spirit, uncover my darkest secrets, in the name of Jesus.

25. You spirit of confusion, loose your hold over my life, in Jesus' name.

26. In the power of the Holy Spirit, I defy satan's power upon my career, in the name of Jesus.

27. Water of life, flush out every unwanted stranger in my life, in the name of Jesus.

28. You the enemies of my career, be paralyzed, in the name of Jesus.

29. O Lord, begin to clear away from my life all that does not reflect You.

30. Holy Spirit fire, ignite me to the glory of God, in the name of Jesus.

31. Oh Lord, let the anointing of the Holy Spirit break every yoke of backwardness in my life.

32. I frustrate every demonic arrest of my spirit-man, in Jesus' name.

33. Blood of Jesus, remove any unprogressive label from every aspect of my life, in Jesus' name.

34. Anti-breakthrough decrees, be revoked, in the name of Jesus.

35. Holy Ghost fire, destroy every satanic garment in my life, in the name of Jesus.

36. Oh Lord, give unto me the key to good success, so that anywhere I go, the doors of good success will open unto me.

37. Every wicked house, constructed against me and my career, be demolished, in the name of Jesus.

38. Oh Lord, establish me a holy person unto You, in Jesus' name.

39. Oh Lord, let the anointing to excel in my career fall on me, in the name of Jesus.

40. I shall not serve my enemies; my enemies shall bow down to me, in the name of Jesus.

41. I bind every desert and poverty spirit in my life, in Jesus' name.

42. I reject the anointing of non-achievement in my career, in the name of Jesus.

43. I pull down all the strongholds erected against my progress, in the name of Jesus.

44. I recall all my blessings thrown into the water, forest and satanic bank, in the name of Jesus.

45. I cut down all the roots of problems in my life, in Jesus' name.

46. O Lord, let satanic scorpions be rendered stingless in every area of my life, in the name of Jesus.

47. O Lord, let demonic serpents be rendered venom-less in every area of my life, in the name of Jesus.

48. I declare with my mouth that nothing shall be impossible with me, in the name of Jesus.

49. O Lord, let the camp of the enemy be put in disarray, in the name of Jesus.

50. Spiritual parasites in my life, be disgraced, in the name of Jesus.

51. O Lord, let all my Herods receive spiritual decay, in Jesus' name.

52. Oh Lord, in my career, let Your favour and that of man encompass me this year, in the name Jesus.

53. I reject any demonic limitation on my progress, in the name of Jesus.

54. All evil handwriting against me, be paralyzed, in Jesus' name.

55. I reject the spirit of the tail; I choose the spirit of the head, in the name of Jesus.

56. All those circulating my name for evil, be disgraced, in the name of Jesus.

57. All evil friends, make mistakes that would expose you, in Jesus' name.

58. O Lord, let the strongmen from both sides of my family that are attacking my career destroy themselves, in the name of Jesus.

59. I refuse to wear the garment of tribulation and sorrow, in the name of Jesus.

60. O Lord, let every rebellion flee from my heart, in Jesus' name.

61. O Lord, let the spirit that flees from sin incubate my life.

62. I claim all my rights now, in the name of Jesus.

63. Holy Ghost, grant me a glimpse of Your glory now, in Jesus' name.

64. Holy Ghost, quicken me, in the name of Jesus.

65. I release myself from any inherited bondage that is negatively affecting my career, in Jesus' name.

66. O Lord, send Your axe of fire to the foundation of my life and destroy every evil plantation, attacking the success of my career.

67. Blood of Jesus, flush every inherited satanic deposit out of my system, in Jesus' name.

68. All foundational strongmen, attached to my life, be paralyzed, in the name of Jesus.

69. Any rod of the wicked, rising up against my career, be rendered impotent for my sake, in the name of Jesus.

70. I cancel the consequences of any evil local name, attached to my person, in the name of Jesus.

71. I release myself from every evil domination and control, in the name of Jesus.

72. Every evil imagination against my career, wither from the source, in the name of Jesus.

73. O Lord, let the destructive plan of the enemies aimed at my career blow up in their faces, in the name of Jesus.

74. O lord, let my point of ridicule be converted to a source of miracle, in Jesus' name.

75. All powers, sponsoring evil decisions against me, be disgraced, in the name of Jesus.

76. You stubborn strongman, delegated against me and my career, fall down to the ground and become impotent, in Jesus' name.

77. O Lord, let the stronghold of every spirit of Korah, Dathan and Abiram, militating against me, be smashed to pieces, in the name of Jesus.

78. Every spirit of Balaam, hired to curse me, fall after the order of Balaam, in the name of Jesus.

79. Every spirit of Sanballat and Tobiah, planning evil against me, receive the stones of fire, in the name of Jesus.

80. Every spirit of Egypt, fall after the order of Pharaoh, in the name of Jesus.

81. Every spirit of Herod, be disgraced, in the name of Jesus.

82. Every spirit of Goliath, receive the stones of fire, in Jesus' name.

83. Every spirit of Pharaoh, fall into your Red Sea, in the name of Jesus.

84. All satanic manipulations, aimed at changing my destiny, be frustrated, in the name of Jesus.

85. All unprofitable broadcasters of my goodness, be silenced, in Jesus' name.

86. All evil monitoring eyes, fashioned against me and my career, become blind, in the name of Jesus.

87. All demonic reverse gears, installed to hinder the progress of my career, be roasted, in the name of Jesus.

88. Any evil sleep, undertaken to harm me and my career, be converted to dead sleep, in Jesus' name.

89. All weapons, and devices of oppressors and tormentors, be rendered impotent, in Jesus' name.

90. Fire of God, destroy the power operating any spiritual vehicle, working against me and my career, in the name of Jesus.

91. All evil advice, given against my favour, crash and disintegrate, in the name of Jesus.

92. O Lord, let the wind, the sun and the moon run contrary to every demonic presence, militating against my career in my environment, in the name of Jesus.

93. O Lord, let those laughing me to scorn witness my testimony, in the name of Jesus.

94. Every wicked pot, cooking my affairs, catch fire, in Jesus' name.

95. Every witchcraft pot, working against me, I bring the judgment of God upon you, in Jesus' name.

96. You My place of birth, you will not be my caldron, in the name of.Jesus.

97. This city where I live will not be my caldron, in the name of Jesus.

98. Every pot of darkness, assigned against my life, be destroyed by fire, in the name of Jesus.

99. Every witchcraft pot, using remote control against my health, break into pieces, in the name of Jesus.

100. Every power, calling my name into any caldron, fall down and die, in the name of Jesus.

101. Every caldron, making noise against me and monitoring my life, disintegrate, in the name of Jesus.

102. Every power, cooking my progress in an evil pot, receive the fire of judgment, in the name of Jesus.

103. Every satanic programme, emanating from the caldron of darkness, be reversed, in the name of Jesus.

104. Any evil fire, boiling any satanic programme in my life, be quenched, in the name of Jesus.

105. The counsels of the wicked against my life in this city shall not stand and I command them to perish, in the name of Jesus.

106. O Lord, let Your counsel for my life prosper, in Jesus' name.

107. Every power, cooking my flesh and my health in any evil caldron, receive the fire of God, in the name of Jesus.

108. Every evil bird of satanic programme, emanating from any caldron of darkness, fall down and die, in the name of Jesus.

109. Every pot, cooking my affairs, the Lord rebuke you, in Jesus' name.

110. I rebuke the spell of any witchcraft pot over my neck, in the name of Jesus.

111. I break every witchcraft pot over my life, in Jesus' name.

112. O Lord, let every evil pot hunt its owners, in the name of Jesus.

113. Mention the names of the items listed below one by one and pray in this format: **I release my life from your caldron, in the name of the Lord Jesus Christ.**

- blood hunters   - eaters of flesh and drinkers of blood

- household witchcraft   - star hunters

- mischief planners   - blood polluters

- envious witchcraft   - destiny killers

- health destroyers   - priests, operating on evil altars

114. Every evil caldron or pot, be judged from heaven, in Jesus' name.

115. No evil caldron will cook up my life, in the name of Jesus.

116. Every counsel of witchcraft, working against me, you will not prosper, in the name of Jesus.

117. Every agreement with satan over my life, I cancel you now, in Jesus' name.

118. Every astral projection against me, I frustrate you, in Jesus' name.

119. I disentangle myself and my family from every witchcraft cage and pot, in the name of Jesus.

120. Every enemy that will not let me go easily, I bring the judgment of death against you, in Jesus' name.

121. This year, my blessings will not sink, in the name of Jesus.

122. You the spirit of salvation, fall upon my family, in Jesus' name.

123. Every grip of the evil consequences of the ancestral worship of my forefathers' gods over my life and ministry, break by fire, in Jesus' name.

124. Every covenant with water spirits, desert spirits, witchcraft spirits, spirits in evil sacred trees, spirits inside / under sacred rocks / hills, family gods, evil family guardian spirits, family / village serpentine spirits, masquerade spirits and inherited spirit husbands / wives, break by the blood of Jesus.

125. Every unconscious evil soul-tie and covenant with the spirits of my dead grandfather, grandmother, occultic uncles, aunties and custodian of family gods/oracles/shrines, break by the blood of Jesus.

126. Every decision, vow or promise made by my forefathers contrary to my divine destiny, loose your hold by fire, in the name of Jesus.

127. Every legal ground, that ancestral/guardian spirits have in my life, be destroyed by the blood of Jesus.

128. Every generational curse of God, resulting from the sin of idolatry of my forefathers, loose your hold, in Jesus' name. .

129. Every ancestral evil altar, prospering against me, be dashed against the Rock of Ages, in the name of Jesus.

130. Every ancestral placenta manipulation of my life, be reversed, in the name of Jesus.

131. Every evil ancestral life pattern, designed for me through vows, promises and covenants, be reversed, in the name of Jesus.

132. Every hold of any sacrifice ever offered in my family or on my behalf, I break your power in my life, in the name of Jesus.

133. Any ancestral blood shed of animals or human beings affecting me, loose your hold by the blood of Jesus.

134. Any curse, placed on my ancestral line by anybody cheated, maltreated or at the point of death, break now, in Jesus' name.

135. Every garment of ancestral infirmity, disease, sickness, untimely death, poverty, disfavour, dishonour, shame and failure at the edge of miracles passed down to my generation, roast by fire, in the name of Jesus.

136. Every evil ancestral river, flowing down to my generation, I cut you off, in the name of Jesus.

137. Every evil ancestral habit and weakness of moral failures, manifesting in my life, loose your grip and release me now, in Jesus' name.

138. Any power from my family background, seeking to make a shipwreck of my life and ministry, be destroyed by the fire of God, in the name of Jesus.

139. Every rage and rampage of ancestral and family spirits, resulting from my being born again, quench by the liquid fire of God, in Jesus' name.

140. Any ancestral power, frustrating any area of my life in order to discourage me from following Christ, receive multiple destruction, in the name of Jesus.

141. Every ancestral chain of slavery, binding my people from prospering in life, you are broken in my life by the hammer of God, in the name of Jesus.

142. I will reach the height nobody has attained in my generation, in Jesus' name.

143. I recover every good thing, stolen by ancestral evil spirits from my forefathers, my immediate family and myself, in the name of Jesus.

144. Every ancestral embargo, lift up; and let good things begin to break forth in my life and in my family, in the name of Jesus.

145. I release myself from any inherited bondage, in Jesus' name.

146. O Lord, send Your axe of fire to the foundation of my life and destroy every evil plantation there.

147. Blood of Jesus, flush every inherited satanic deposit out of my system, in Jesus' name.

148. I release myself from the grip of any problem, transferred into my life from the womb, in Jesus' name.

149. I break loose from every inherited evil covenant, in Jesus' name.

150. I break loose from every inherited evil curse, in Jesus' name.

151. I vomit every evil thing that I have been fed with as a child, in the name of Jesus.

152. All foundational strongmen, attached to my life, be paralysed, in the name of Jesus.

153. Any rod of the wicked, rising up against my family line, be rendered impotent for my sake, in the name of Jesus.

154. I cancel all the consequences of any evil local name, attached to my person, in the name of Jesus.

155. You evil foundational plantations, come out of my life with all your roots, in the name of Jesus.

156. I break loose from every form of demonic bewitchment, in the name of Jesus.

157. I release myself from every evil domination and control, in Jesus' name.

158. Every gate, opened to the enemy by my foundation, close forever with the blood of Jesus.

159. Lord Jesus, walk back into every second of my life, deliver me where I need deliverance, heal me where I need healing and transform me where I need transformation.

160. Every evil imagination against me, wither from the source, in the name of Jesus.

161. O Lord, let all those laughing me to scorn witness my testimony, in Jesus' name.

162. O Lord, let all the destructive plans of the enemies aimed at me blow up in their faces, in Jesus' name.

163. O Lord, let my point of ridicule be converted to a source of miracle, in Jesus' name.

164. O Lord, let all powers, sponsoring evil decisions against me, be disgraced, in the name of Jesus.

165. You stubborn strongman, delegated against me, fall down to the ground and become impotent, in the name of Jesus.

166. You stronghold of every spirit of Korah, Dathan and Abiram, militating against me, be smashed to pieces, in the name of Jesus.

167. Every spirit of Balaam, hired to curse me, fall after the order of Balaam, in the name of Jesus.

168. Every spirit of Sanballat and Tobiah, planning evil against me, receive the stones of fire, in the name of Jesus.

169. Every spirit of Egypt, fall after the order of Pharaoh, in Jesus' name.

170. Every spirit of Herod, be disgraced, in the name of Jesus.

171. Every spirit of Goliath, receive the stones of fire, in Jesus' name.

172. Every spirit of Pharaoh, fall into your Red Sea and perish, in the name of Jesus.

173. All satanic manipulations, aimed at changing my destiny, be frustrated, in the name of Jesus.

174. All unprofitable broadcasters of my goodness, be silenced, in the name of Jesus.

175. All leaking bags and pockets, be sealed up, in Jesus' name.

176. All evil monitoring eyes, fashioned against me, become blind, in Jesus' name.

177. Every evil effect of any strange touch, be removed from my life, in the name of Jesus.

178. All demonic reverse gears, installed to hinder my progress, roast, in Jesus' name.

179. Any evil sleep, undertaken to harm me, be converted to dead sleep, in Jesus' name.

180. All weapons and devices of the oppressors and tormentors, be rendered impotent, in Jesus' name.

181. Thou fire of God, destroy every power, operating any spiritual vehicle working against me, in the name of Jesus.

182. All evil advice given against my favour, crash and disintegrate, in the name of Jesus.

183. O Lord, let the wind, the sun and the moon run contrary to every demonic presence in my environment, in the name of Jesus.

184. O you devourers, vanish from my labour, in the name of Jesus.

185. Every tree, planted by fear in my life, dry up from the roots, in the name of Jesus.

186. I cancel all the enchantments, curses and spells that are against me, in Jesus' name.

187. All iron-like curses, break, in the name of Jesus.

188. You divine tongues of fire, roast any evil tongue that is against me, in Jesus' name.

189. O Lord, I thank You very much for everything You have done for me through these prayer points.

PRAYERS TO HEAL HYPERTENSION

Medical experts and sufferers of hypertension have agreed that this disease is a chronic one.

However, there is a spirit behind this dreaded, terminal disease. It is on record that those who are hypertensive often wait hopelessly for death, after they have obtained medical treatment to no avail. The spirit behind hypertension can be addressed, disgraced and sent packing. It must be addressed from the roots. The power of aggressive prayer must be used to combat the dreaded killer disease. You can get rid of it by praying with spiritual force until every symptom dries from the roots. These prayer points will break its spiritual backbone.

Confessions: Psalm 103:3: Who forgiveth all thine iniquities; who healeth all thy diseases;

Psalm 107:20: He sent his word, and healed them, and delivered *them* from their destructions.

Psalm 138:1-8: I will praise thee with my whole heart: before the gods will I sing praise unto thee. ²I will worship toward thy holy temple, and praise thy name for thy lovingkindness and for thy truth: for thou hast magnified thy word above all thy name. ³In the day when I cried thou answeredst me, *and* strengthenedst me *with* strength in my soul. ⁴All the kings of the earth shall praise thee, O LORD, when they hear the words of thy mouth. ⁵Yea, they shall sing in the ways of the LORD: for great *is* the glory of the LORD. ⁶Though the LORD *be* high, yet hath he respect unto the lowly: but the proud he knoweth afar off. ⁷Though I walk in the midst of trouble, thou wilt revive me: thou shalt stretch forth thine hand against the wrath of mine enemies, and thy right hand shall save me. ⁸The LORD will perfect *that which* concerneth me: thy mercy, O LORD, *endureth* for ever: forsake not the works of thine own hands.

Proverbs 12:18: There is that speaketh like the piercings of a sword: but the tongue of the wise *is* health.

Jeremiah 17:14: Heal me, O LORD, and I shall be healed; save me, and I shall be saved: for thou *art* my praise.

Jeremiah 33:6: Behold, I will bring it health and cure, and I will cure them, and will reveal unto them the abundance of peace and truth.

1Peter 3:12: For the eyes of the Lord *are* over the righteous, and his ears *are open* unto their prayers: but the face of the Lord *is* against them that do evil.

James 5:16: Confess *your* faults one to another, and pray one for another, that ye may be healed. The effectual fervent prayer of a righteous man availeth much.

3John 2: Beloved, I wish above all things that thou mayest prosper and be in health, even as thy soul prospereth.

Praise worship

1. Every power, planning to kill, steal and destroy my body, release me by fire, in the name of Jesus.

2. Every spirit of tiredness, release me, in the name of Jesus.

3. Every spirit of hypertension, come out of my body with all your roots, in the name of Jesus.

4. Every bondage of diabetic spirits, break by fire, in Jesus' name.

5. Any evil power, running through my body, loose your hold, in the name of Jesus.

6. Every evil power, hooking on to my brain, release me, in Jesus' name.

7. Every spirit with tentacles moving about in my body, come out by fire, in the name of Jesus.

8. Every spirit of migraine and headache, come out by fire, in the name of Jesus.

9. Every dark spirit, working against the kingdom of God in my life, come out by fire, in the name of Jesus.

10. Every power, working on my eyes and reducing my vision, be eliminated completely, in the name of Jesus.

11. Every demon of insulin deficiency, depart from me by fire, in Jesus' name.

12. Every spirit of hypertension, release my liver, in Jesus' name.

13. Every evil power, planning to amputate my leg, I bury you alive, in the name of Jesus.

14. Every spirit of hypertension, release my bladder, in Jesus' name.

15. Every spirit of excessive urination, release me, in Jesus' name.

16. Every spirit of hypertension, release my skin and ears, in the name of Jesus.

17. Every spirit of itching, depart from me, in the name of Jesus.

18. Every spirit of hypertension, release my lungs, in Jesus' name.

19. Every spirit of hypertension, release my reproductive areas, in the name of Jesus.

20. I release myself from every spirit of drowsiness, tiredness and impaired vision; I bind you and cast you out, in Jesus' name.

21. Every spirit of infirmity, generating tiredness, loose your hold, in the name of Jesus.

22. Every spirit of excessive thirst and hunger, I bind you and cast you out, in the name of Jesus.

23. I bind every spirit of weight loss, in the name of Jesus.

24. I bind every spirit of rashes, in the name of Jesus.

25. I bind every spirit of slow healing of cuts and bruises, in the name of Jesus.

26. I bind every spirit of bed-wetting, in the name of Jesus.

27. I bind every spirit of enlargement of the liver, in Jesus' name.

28. I bind every spirit of kidney disease, in the name of Jesus.

29. I bind every spirit of blockage, in the name of Jesus.

30. I bind every spirit of hardening of the arteries, in Jesus' name.

31. I bind every spirit of confusion, in the name of Jesus.

32. I bind every spirit of convulsion, in the name of Jesus.

33. I bind every spirit of loss of consciousness, in the name of Jesus.

34. You spirit of fear of death, depart from my life, in Jesus' name.

35. You evil doorkeeper of insulin, loose your hold, inJesus' name.

36. Every power, destroying insulin in my body, I bind you and cast you out, in the name of Jesus.

37. Every power, hindering the co-ordination between my brain and my mouth, I bind you and cast you out, in the name of Jesus.

38. Every spirit of torment, release me, in the name of Jesus.

39. Every power, attacking my blood sugar, loose your hold, in the name of Jesus.

40. I break every curse of eating and drinking blood from ten generations backward on both sides of my family line, in the name of Jesus.

41. Every door, opened to diabetic spirits, close by the blood of Jesus.

42. Every inherited blood disease, loose your hold, in Jesus' name.

43. All bloodline curses, break, in the name of Jesus.

44. Every curse of breaking my skin unrighteously, break, in the name of Jesus.

45. I bind and cast out every demon in my pancreas, in Jesus' name.

46. Any power, affecting my vision, I bind you, in Jesus' name.

47. Every satanic arrow in my blood vessel, come out by fire, in the name of Jesus.

48. Every demon of stroke, come out of my life with all your roots, in the name of Jesus.

49. Every spirit of confusion, loose your hold over my life, in the name of Jesus.

50. Anything inhibiting my ability to read and meditate on the word of God, be uprooted, in the name of Jesus.

51. I bind and cast out every spirit of (convulsion - abdominal problems - fear - guilt - hopelessness - impotence - palsy- animal - candor - swelling - stress - worry - anxiety - deafness - high blood pressure - nerve destruction - kidney destruction), in Jesus' name.

52. I bind and cast out, familiar spirits travelling through family bloodlines to afflict me with hypertension and other sickness, in Jesus' name.

53. Every evil plantation in my life: **Come out with all your roots in the name of Jesus!** (*Lay your hands on your stomach and keep repeating the emphasised area.*)

54. I cough and vomit any food eaten from the table of the devil, in the name of Jesus. (*Cough and vomit them in faith. Prime the expulsion.*)

55. All negative materials, circulating in my blood stream, be evacuated, in the name of Jesus.

56. I drink the blood of Jesus. (*Physically swallow and drink it in faith. Keep doing this for some time.*)

57. *(Lay one hand on your head and the other on your stomach or navel and begin to pray like this):* Holy Ghost Fire, burn from the top of my head to the sole of my feet. *(Begin to mention every organ of your body; your kidney, liver, intestines, etc. You must not rush at this level, because the fire will actually come, and you may start feeling the heat).*

58. Blood of Jesus, be transfused into my blood vessels, in the name of Jesus.

59. Every agent of disease in my blood and body organs, die, in the name of Jesus.

60. My blood, reject every evil foreign entity, in Jesus' name.

61. Holy Spirit, speak deliverance and healing into my life, in the name of Jesus.

62. Blood of Jesus, speak disappearance unto every infirmity in my life.

63. I hold the blood of Jesus against you spirit of . . . (mention what is troubling you). You have to flee.

64. O Lord, let Your healing hand be stretched out upon my life now.

65. O Lord, let Your miracle hand be stretched out upon my life now.

66. O Lord, let Your deliverance hand be stretched out upon my life now.

67. I annul every engagement with the spirit of death, in Jesus' name.

68. I rebuke every refuge of sickness, in the name of Jesus.

69. I destroy the grip and operation of sickness upon my life, in the name of Jesus.

70. Every knee of infirmity in my life, bow, in Jesus' name.

71. O Lord, let my negativity be converted to positivity.

72. I command death upon any sickness in any area of my life, in the name of Jesus.

73. I shall see my sickness no more, in the name of Jesus.

74. Father Lord, let the whirlwind of God scatter every vessel of infirmity fashioned against my life, in the name of Jesus.

75. Every spirit, hindering my perfect healing, fall down and die now, in the name of Jesus.

76. Father Lord, let all death contractors begin to kill themselves, in the name of Jesus.

77. Father Lord, let every germ of infirmity in my body die, in the name of Jesus.

78. Father Lord, let every agent of sickness working against my health disappear, in the name of Jesus.

79. Every fountain of discomfort in my life, dry up now, in the name of Jesus.

80. Every dead organ in my body, receive life now, in the name of Jesus.

81. Father Lord, let my blood be transfused with the blood of Jesus to effect my perfect health, in the name of Jesus.

82. Every internal disorder, receive order, in the name of Jesus.

83. Every infirmity, come out with all your roots, in the name of Jesus.

84. I withdraw every conscious and unconscious cooperation with sickness, in the name of Jesus.

85. O Lord, let the whirlwind of God blow every wind of infirmity away.

86. I release my body from every curse of infirmity, in the name of Jesus.

87. O Lord, let the blood of Jesus flush out every evil deposit from my blood.

88. I recover every organ of my body from every evil altar, in Jesus' name.

89. I withdraw my body from the manipulation of every caldron of darkness, in the name of Jesus.

90. Holy Ghost fire, destroy every stubborn agent of disease in my body, in the name of Jesus.

91. I arrest every demon of terminal disease, in Jesus' name.

92. I cancel every clinical prophecy concerning my life, in the name of Jesus.

93. Holy Ghost fire, boil every infirmity out of my system, in the name of Jesus.

94. I cancel every witchcraft verdict on my life, in Jesus' name.

95. O earth, vomit anything that has been buried inside you against my health, in the name of Jesus.

96. Every tree that infirmity has planted in my blood, be uprooted by fire, in the name of Jesus.

97. Every witchcraft arrow, depart from my _ _ _ (spinal cord - spleen - navel - heart - throat -eyes - nose - head), in the name of Jesus.

98. I bind every evil presence in my (reproductive, digestive, respiratory, nervous, skeletal, muscular, circulatory, endocrine, excretory) system, in the name of Jesus.

99. I break the backbone and destroy the root of every spirit speaking against me, in the name of Jesus.

100. Begin to thank God for your healing.

RELEASE ME BY FIRE

This prayer programme is for those who seek prompt release from captivity. It is for those who are ready to bid bye bye to bondage or slavery. You need these prayer points when you are tired of languishing in the dungeon of slavery. They will enable you to order the enemy to release you by fire and let you go.

This is a prayer programme which will grant sweet liberty to the captives. It requires holy anger and persistent bombardment. With it, you can send signals to the kingdom of darkness and make them release you.

This programme will make you to say goodbye to bondage.

Praise Worship

Scripture Reading: Exodus 6:10-11: And the Lord spake unto Moses, saying, Go in, speak unto Pharaoh king of Egypt, that he let the children of Israel go out of his land.

Exodus 7:1-4: And the Lord said unto Moses, See, I have made thee a god to Pharaoh: and Aaron thy brother shall be thy prophet. Thou shalt speak all that I command thee: and Aaron thy brother shall speak unto Pharaoh, that he send the children of Israel out of his land. And I will harden Pharaoh's heart, and multiply my signs and my wonders in the land of Egypt. But Pharaoh shall not hearken unto you, that I may lay my hand upon Egypt, and bring forth mine armies, and my people the children of Israel, out of the land of Egypt by great judgments.

Psalm 71:7: I am as a wonder unto many; but thou art my strong refuge.

Exodus 8:28: And Pharaoh said, I will let you go, that ye may sacrifice to the Lord your God in the wilderness; only ye shall not go very far away: intreat for me.

Exodus 10:8: And Moses and Aaron were brought again unto Pharaoh: and he said unto them, Go, serve the Lord your God: but who are they that shall go?

1. Thou power of God, penetrate my spirit, soul and body, in the name of Jesus.

2. Association of demons, gathered against my progress, roast by the thunder fire of God, in the name of Jesus.

3. Blood of Jesus, redeem me, in the name of Jesus.

4. Every satanic decision, taken against my progress, be nullified, in the name of Jesus.

5. Every evil deposit in my spirit, soul and body, be flushed out by the blood of Jesus, in the name of Jesus.

6. Oh Lord my God, promote me in the spiritual and in the physical, in the name of Jesus.

7. Every stranger in my body (ministry, life and calling), jump out, in the name of Jesus.

8. Any satanic arrow, fired at me, go back, locate and destroy your sender, in the name of Jesus.

9. Holy Ghost, arise and destroy the habitation and works of the wicked in my life (home, finances, ministry), in the name of Jesus.

10. Every serpentine spirit, spitting on my breakthrough, roast, in the name of Jesus.

11. Every enemy of the perfect will of God for my life, die, in the name of Jesus.

12. The anointing of joy and peace, replace heaviness and sorrow in my life, in the name of Jesus.

13. O Lord, let abundance replace lack and insufficiency in my life, in the name of Jesus.

14. Every Pharaoh in my life, destroy yourself, in the name of Jesus.

15. Garment of Pharaoh that is upon my life, be removed by fire, in the name of Jesus.

16. Thou power of impossibility in my destiny, die, in the name of Jesus.

17. Every task master, assigned against me, somersault and die, in the name of Jesus.

18. I refuse to continue eating the crumbs from the task master's table, in the name of Jesus.

19. Any man or woman, who wouldn't let me prosper, oh Lord, write his/her obituary, in the name of Jesus.

20. Oh Lord, give me a new inner man, if I have been altered, in the name of Jesus.

21. Oh Lord, activate Your high call on my life, in the name of Jesus.

22. Oh Lord, anoint me to recover the wasted years in every area of my life, in the name of Jesus.

23. Oh Lord, if I have fallen behind in many areas of my life, empower me to recover all lost opportunities and wasted years, in the name of Jesus.

24. Any power, that says I will not go forward, be arrested, in the name of Jesus.

25. Any power, that wants to keep me in want in the midst of plenty, die, in the name of Jesus.

26. Any power, that wants to draw me away from the presence of the Lord to destroy me, die, in the name of Jesus.

27. I will get to my promised inheritance, in the name of Jesus.

28. Any power, that wants me to fulfil my destiny only partially, die, in the name of Jesus.

29. Oh Lord, anoint me with power to destroy all foundational covenants, in the name of Jesus.

30. Oh Lord, use my substance for the furtherance of the gospel, in the name of Jesus.

31. Oh Lord, arise and bless my inheritance, in the name of Jesus.

32. All my stolen virtues, be returned to me, in the name of Jesus.

33. O Lord, let my release bring revival, in the name of Jesus.

34. Oh Lord, reveal all ignorant ways in me by Your Holy Spirit, in the name of Jesus.

35. Today, you my spirit man, you will not bewitch me, in the name of Jesus.

36. Power in the blood of Jesus, redeem my destiny, in the name of Jesus.

37. Every satanic weapon, formed against my destiny, backfire, in the name of Jesus.

38. Arrows of deliverance, locate my destiny, in the name of Jesus.

39. Every spiritual cobweb on my destiny, burn, in the name of Jesus.

40. Every serpent in my foundation, swallowing my destiny, die, in the name of Jesus.

41. Every red candle, burning against my destiny, catch fire, in the name of Jesus.

42. Song: "God of deliverance, send down fire..." (sing for about 15 minutes clapping your hands).

43. Every lid the enemy has put on my destiny, jump up, die, in the name of Jesus.

44. Every serpent in my blood, die, in the name of Jesus.

45. Every serpent, caging my destiny, die, in the name of Jesus.

46. Every power of darkness, following me about, die, in the name of Jesus.

47. Evil cord of wickedness, sin or iniquity, blocking my communication with heaven and God, be cut off, in the name of Jesus.

48. Every power, spirit or personality, listening to my prayers in order to report them to the demonic world, Father, scatter them, in the name of Jesus.

49. Every authority of darkness upon which wealth and blessings are based, crumble suddenly in one day, in the name of Jesus.

50. Father, expose and destroy the workers of iniquity, in Jesus'

name.

51. Father, let the mystery and secret of my fulfilment be revealed, in the name of Jesus.

52. O Lord, let the heaven open, let the anointing speak, let my hidden blessings be revealed and released, in Jesus' name.

53. Oh Lord, forgive me, where I have judged others out of ignorance and pride, in the name of Jesus.

54. Oh Lord, remove the penalty of judgment upon my life and calling, in the name of Jesus.

55. Oh heavens, fight for me today, in Jesus' name.

56. Oh Lord, increase me so that Your name may be glorified, in the name of Jesus.

57. Any power, diverting the will of God out of my life, somersault and die, in Jesus' name.

58. Oh Lord, arise and let every poison in my life be arrested, in Jesus' name.

59. I declare the obituary of all the opposition powers, attacking my glory and calling, in Jesus' name.

60. Holy Spirit, activate the will of God in my life and calling, in the name of Jesus.

61. I decree the will of my enemies against me to backfire, in the name of Jesus.

62. Every plot of the enemy against me, be reversed, in Jesus' name.

63. I command the confidence of my enemies to be dashed to pieces, in Jesus' name.

64. Every spiritual manipulation, against my glory and calling, fail, in Jesus' name.

65. Oh Lord, destroy the personalities of all those who live to destroy my personality, in Jesus' name.

66. Oh Lord, vindicate my position in this city (company, country, nation, etc.), in Jesus' name.

67. Oh Lord, reveal to me what You have called me to be in life (in this city, country, company), in Jesus' name.

68. Every strange god, assigned to attack my destiny, personality, glory or calling, attack your sender, in Jesus' name.

69. Ark of God, pursue every dragon assigned against me, in Jesus' name.

70. You hosts of heaven, pursue those who are raging against me, in Jesus' name.

71. Ark of God, come into my house today to locate and fight the power of the opposition against me, in the name of Jesus.

72. Ark of God, wherever I have been accepted in the past and they are now rejecting me, arise and fight for me, in Jesus' name.

73. Lion of Judah, devour every opposition, raging against me now, in Jesus' name.

74. Wherever they have rejected me, let my spirit man be accepted now, in Jesus' name.

75. I resist and refuse the sale of my glory and calling for a pair of shoes or for silver, in the name of Jesus.

76. Wine of condemnation, drunk against me, become poison for my enemies, in Jesus' name.

77. Oh Lord, let the mighty among my enemies flee from me naked, in Jesus' name.

78. Every power of darkness, that has arrested my ministry and calling, release me now, in the name of Jesus.

79. I am coming out of captivity, in the name of the Lord Jesus.

80. Holy Ghost, arise and promote me, in the name of Jesus.

81. Every association of demons, cooperating with workers of iniquity from my father's house, scatter unto desolation, in Jesus' name.

82. Vehicle of my destiny, be repaired and put back on the road, in the name of Jesus.

83. Holy Ghost, arise and send me divine help, in the name of Jesus.

84. Oh Lord my God, pour blessings upon me now from Your reservoir of blessings and power, in Jesus' name.

85. Holy Ghost, arise and activate my ministry and calling, in Jesus' name.

86. All roadblocks and impediments to the fulfilment of my life and calling, be removed, in Jesus' name.

87. Thou yoke of frustration, failure and unfulfilment over my life, be destroyed by fire, in the name of Jesus.

88. Thou siege of the wicked over my life, be lifted by the hand of God, in Jesus' name

PRAYERS TO DISMANTLE MARITAL JERICHO

This prayer is for singles believing God for Godly spouses, but are beginning to notice inexplicable hindrances.

Note: Prayers to dismantle marital Jericho are to be said with holy anger, holy stubbornness, holy madness, violent faith and violent praises.

Confession: Psalm 65:2: O thou that hearest prayer, unto thee shall all flesh come.

Aggressive Praise Worship

1. O thou that troubleth my Israel, my God shall trouble you today, in the name of Jesus.

2. Thou rain of blessing, fall upon the marital life of . . ., in the name of Jesus.

3. Magnets of favour, in the life of . . ., arise and shine, in the name of Jesus.

4. Powers of spiritual dowry in the life of . . . , die, in the name of Jesus.

5. O Lord, let divine beauty settle upon the life of . . . , in the name of Jesus.

6. Evil twin substitute in the spirit, die, in the name of Jesus.

7. Evil spiritual parents, die, in the name of Jesus.

8. O God, make the life of . . . an amazement to my enemies, in Jesus' name.

9. Before the cock crows, let the sun of . . . rise, in the name of Jesus.

10. O God, give . . . the very best You can do for him/her, in the name of Jesus.

11. Every cage of family witchcraft, release the divine partner of . . ., in Jesus' name.

12. Satanic substitutes, go away from his/her life, in the name of Jesus.

13. The God-given partner of . . ., appear and locate him/her by fire, in the name of Jesus.

14. Arrows of permanent loneliness, come out of the life of . . ., in the name of Jesus.

15. O Lord, let the glory of . . . reject evil exchange and evil transfer, in the name of Jesus.

16. Holy Ghost, arise and re-arrange the life of ... for breakthroughs, in Jesus' name.

17. Satanic spiritual wedding garments and rings, roast, in the name of Jesus

18. Thou power of evil marriage, die, in the name of Jesus.

19. All unrepentant friends of darkness in my family, be exposed and disgraced, in the name of Jesus.

20. O God, arise and sink all my Pharaohs in the Red Sea, in the name of Jesus.

21. Every satanic pregnancy in the life of . . ., be aborted, in the name of Jesus.

22. O heavens, open over the marital life of . . ., in Jesus' name.

23. Every mention of the marriage of . . . by the enemy, become poison, in the name of Jesus.

24. O Lord, make known to . . . the secrets needed for his marital breakthrough.

25. Every imagination of the enemy, against the marital life of ... be rendered impotent, in the name of Jesus.

26. Every force, magnetizing the wrong people to . . ., be paralysed, in Jesus' name.

27. Every incantation, incision, hex and other spiritually harmful activities, working against the marriage of . . ., be completely neutralized, in the name of Jesus.

28. All forces of evil, manipulating, delaying or hindering the marriage of . . ., be completely paralysed, in the name of Jesus.

29. Blood of Jesus, speak against every power, working against the marriage of . . ..

30. I remove the right of the enemy to affect his/her plan to get married, in the name of Jesus.

31. I break every bondage of inherited marital confusion over his/her life, in the name of Jesus.

32. I bind and plunder the goods of every strongman attached to his/her marriage, in the name of Jesus.

33. Angels of the living God, roll away the stones blocking the marital breakthrough of . . ., in the name of Jesus.

34. O God arise and let all the enemies of the marital breakthrough of . . . scatter, in the name of Jesus.

35. You the cloud, blocking the sunlight of the marital breakthrough of . . ., be dispersed, in Jesus' name.

36. All masquerading evil spirits, troubling the marital life of. . . , be bound, in the name of Jesus.

37. O Lord, turn away all who would jilt, disappoint or fail . . . , in the name of Jesus.

38. I destroy the power of every satanic arrest in the life of . . ., in the name of Jesus.

39. All satanic arresting-agents, release . . ., in the mighty name of our Lord Jesus Christ.

40. Spirit of the living God, quicken the whole being of . . ., in the name of Jesus.

41. O Lord, liberate the spirit of . . ., to follow the leading of the Holy Spirit.

42. I rebuke every spirit of spiritual deafness and blindness, in the life of . . ., in the name of Jesus.

43. I choose to believe the report of the Lord and none other, in the name of Jesus.

44. You spirit of confusion, loose your hold over the life of . . . , in the name of Jesus.

45. I frustrate every demonic arrest over the spirit-man of . . ., in the name of Jesus.

46. I cut down all the roots of problems in the life of . . ., in the name of Jesus.

47. I reject any demonic limitation on the marriage of . . ., in the name of Jesus.

48. I refuse to wear the garment of tribulation and sorrow, in the name of Jesus.

49. Every rebellion, depart from the heart of . . ., in the name of Jesus.

50. O Lord, let wonderful changes be the lot of . . ., this year.

51. Lord, I pray that . . ., will not find peace until he returns in repentance to his Creator.

52. Let every way of all unfriendly friends confusing . . . ., become dark and slippery, in the name of Jesus.

53. You angels of God, arise and block the path of . . ., with thorns after the order of Balaam until he runs back to the Saviour, in the name of Jesus.

54. All strange lovers, begin to avoid . . . as from today, in the name of Jesus.

55. O Lord, ordain terrifying noises against all evil collaborators confusing . . .

56. O Lord, build a wall of hindrance around . . . ., so that he will be unable to carry out any ungodly activity.

57. All the good things that . . . is enjoying, which are hardening his heart to the truth, be withdrawn, in the name of Jesus.

58. I break every curse of the vagabond spirit upon the life of . . ., in the mighty name of Jesus.

59. Angels of the living God, begin to pursue all strange lovers caging . . . ., in the name of Jesus.

60. Every gadget of marriage destruction, be frustrated in my home, in the name of Jesus.

61. Every evil anti-marriage link with our parents, be dashed to pieces, in the name of Jesus.

62. Every evil power, trying to re-draw the marriage map of . . ., be put to shame, in the name of Jesus.

63. Father, in the name of Jesus, give unto . . . ., the spirit of wisdom and revelation in Your knowledge.

64. Every stronghold of the enemy, barricading the mind of . . ., from receiving the Lord, be pulled down, in the name of Jesus.

65. All hindrances, coming between the heart of . . . ., and the gospel, melt away by the fire of the Holy Spirit.

66. Lord, build a hedge of thorns around . . . ., so that he turns to You.

67. You spirit of death and hell, release . . . ., in the name of Jesus.

68. Every desire of the enemy on the soul of . . . ., will not prosper, in the name of Jesus.

69. I bind every spirit of mind blindness in the life of . . . ., in the name of Jesus.

70. Spirit of bondage, lukewarmness and perdition, release . . ., in the name of Jesus.

71. Father, let spiritual blindness be erased from the life of . . ., in the name of Jesus.

72. I tear down and smash every stronghold of deception, keeping . . ., in the enemy's camp, in Jesus' name.

73. O Lord, let . . ., come from the kingdom of darkness into the kingdom of light, in the name of Jesus.

74. O Lord, let Your plan and purpose for the life of . . . prevail.

75. I prophesy that those laughing me to scorn shall witness my testimony, in the name of Jesus.

76. O Lord, let my point of ridicule be converted to a source of miracle, in the name of Jesus.

77. All powers, sponsoring evil decisions against me, be disgraced, in the name of Jesus.

78. All satanic manipulations, aimed at changing the destiny of ..., be frustrated, in the name of Jesus.

79. All unprofitable broadcasters of my goodness, be silenced, in the name of Jesus.

80. All evil monitoring eyes, fashioned against me, become blind, in the name of Jesus.

81. All demonic reverse gears, installed to hinder my progress, roast, in the name of Jesus.

82. By the blood of Jesus, I loose . . . ., from the bondage that powers of darkness are putting on him.

83. I bind the god of this age and declare that it can no longer blind . . . in darkness, in the name of Jesus.

84. Father Lord, let Your power draw . . . out of every trap, in the name of Jesus.

85. You powers of darkness, seeking after . . . , be confounded and put to shame in the name of Jesus.

86. Father Lord, grant . . ., open eyes and ears, understanding heart and grace to be converted and healed, in the name of Jesus.

87. O Lord, bring all of . . .'s thoughts captive to the obedience of Christ.

88. O Lord, let the hedge of thorns be built around . . . and let it repel all the workers of darkness in his life, in Jesus' name.

89. O Lord, grant . . . conviction of sin with godly sorrow to repentance.

90. Thank God, for the victory.

BRING THE JUDGEMENT OF GOD UPON THEM

This prayer must be prayed with holy anger. You must rise up in holy bitterness against anyone who has vowed that your spouse or your loved ones will experience deadly attacks of the devil.

There are mild satanic agents and there are deadly ones. You must be ready to destroy destructive agents and attack the attackers who want to make you shed tears by attacking your loved ones. You are not meant to parley with those who want to sentence you to sorrow and mourning. You are expected to order them to fall into their own traps. If some enemies should have their way, they will wipe out a whole lineage. These wicked agents must be dragged to the court of God where they are made to drink from the cup of God's indignation. Pray with anger until the enemies are made to hang in the same gallows that they constructed for your loved ones.

Praise worship

Scriptures

Jeremiah 7:18: The children gather wood, and the fathers kindle the fire, and the women knead *their* dough, to make cakes to the queen of heaven, and to pour out drink offerings unto other gods, that they may provoke me to anger.

Jeremiah 44:17-19: But we will certainly do whatsoever thing goeth forth out of our own mouth, to burn incense unto the queen of heaven, and to pour out drink offerings unto her, as we have done, we, and our fathers, our kings, and our princes, in the cities of Judah, and in the streets of Jerusalem: for *then* had we plenty of victuals, and were well, and saw no evil. [18]But since we left off to burn incense to the queen of heaven, and to pour out drink offerings unto her, we have wanted all *things,* and have been consumed by the sword and by the famine. [19]And when we burned incense to the queen of heaven, and poured out drink offerings unto her, did we make her cakes to worship her, and pour out drink offerings unto her, without our men?

Jeremiah 44:25: Thus saith the LORD of hosts, the God of Israel, saying; Ye and your wives have both spoken with your mouths, and fulfilled with your hand, saying, We will surely perform our vows that we have vowed, to burn incense to the queen of heaven, and to pour out drink offerings unto her: ye will surely accomplish your vows, and surely perform your vows.

Isaiah 49:24-25: Shall the prey be taken from the mighty, or the lawful captive delivered? [25]But thus saith the LORD, Even the captives of the mighty shall be taken away, and the prey of the terrible shall be delivered: for I will contend with him that contendeth with thee, and I will save thy children.

Psalm 124:7: Our soul is escaped as a bird out of the snare of the fowlers: the snare is broken, and we are escaped.

Psalm 56:9: When I cry *unto thee,* then shall mine enemies turn back: this I know; for God *is* for me.

Psalm 91:13: Thou shalt tread upon the lion and adder: the young lion and the dragon shalt thou trample under feet.

Psalm 18:37-40: I have pursued mine enemies, and overtaken them: neither did I turn again till they were consumed. [38]I have wounded them that they were not able to rise: they are fallen under my feet. [39]For thou hast girded me with strength unto the battle: thou hast subdued under me those that rose up against me. [40]Thou hast also given me the necks of mine enemies; that I might destroy them that hate me.

Psalm 35:4-6: Let them be confounded and put to shame

that seek after my soul: let them be turned back and brought to confusion that devise my hurt. [5]Let them be as chaff before the wind: and let the angel of the LORD chase *them*. [6]Let their way be dark and slippery: and let the angel of the LORD persecute them.

Psalm 11:6-7: Upon the wicked he shall rain snares, fire and brimstone, and an horrible tempest: *this shall be* the portion of their cup. [7]For the righteous LORD loveth righteousness; his countenance doth behold the upright.

Psalm 129:4: The LORD *is* righteous: he hath cut asunder the cords of the wicked.

Psalm 6:8-10: Depart from me, all ye workers of iniquity; for the LORD hath heard the voice of my weeping. [9]The LORD hath heard my supplication; the LORD will receive my prayer. [10]Let all mine enemies be ashamed and sore vexed: let them return *and* be ashamed suddenly.

Psalm 140:9-10: *As for* the head of those that compass me about, let the mischief of their own lips cover them. [10]Let burning coals fall upon them: let them be cast into the fire; into deep pits, that they rise not up again.

Psalm 58:6-7: Break their teeth, O God, in their mouth: break out the great teeth of the young lions, O LORD. [7]Let them melt away as waters *which* run continually: *when* he bendeth *his bow to shoot* his arrows, let them be as cut in pieces.

Psalm 118:7: The LORD taketh my part with them that help me: therefore shall I see *my desire* upon them that hate me.

Psalm 118:12: They compassed me about like bees; they are quenched as the fire of thorns: for in the name of the LORD I will destroy them.

Psalm 31:17-18: Let me not be ashamed, O LORD; for I have called upon thee: let the wicked be ashamed, *and* let them be silent in the grave. [18]Let the lying lips be put to silence; which speak grievous things proudly and contemptuously against the righteous.

Psalm 92:9-11: For, lo, thine enemies, O LORD, for, lo, thine enemies shall perish; all the workers of iniquity shall be scattered. [10]But my horn shalt thou exalt like *the horn of* an unicorn: I shall be anointed with fresh oil. [11]Mine eye also shall see *my desire* on mine enemies, *and* mine ears shall hear *my desire* of the wicked that rise up against me.

Matthew 4:10: Then saith Jesus unto him, Get thee hence, Satan: for it is written, Thou shalt worship the Lord thy God, and him only shalt thou serve.

Matthew 28:18: And Jesus came and spake unto them, saying, All power is given unto me in heaven and in earth.

Luke 10:19: Behold, I give unto you power to tread on serpents and scorpions, and over all the power of the enemy: and nothing shall by any means hurt you.

Luke 11:21-22: When a strong man armed keepeth his palace, his goods are in peace: [22]But when a stronger than he shall come upon him, and overcome him, he taketh from him all his armour wherein he trusted, and divideth his spoils.

John 12:31: Now is the judgment of this world: now shall the prince of this world be cast out.

John 16:11: Of judgment, because the prince of this world is judged.

Romans 16:20: And the God of peace shall bruise Satan under your feet shortly. The grace of our Lord Jesus Christ *be* with you. Amen.

---

2 Cor. 10:3-5: For though we walk in the flesh, we do not war after the flesh: [4](For the weapons of our warfare *are* not carnal, but mighty through God to the pulling down of strong holds;) [5]Casting down imaginations, and every high thing that exalteth itself against the knowledge of God, and bringing into captivity every thought to the obedience of Christ;

Col. 2:15: *And* having spoiled principalities and powers, he made a shew of them openly, triumphing over them in it.

Hebrews 2:14-15: Forasmuch then as the children are partakers of flesh and blood, he also himself likewise took part of the same; that through death he might destroy him that had the power of death, that is, the devil; [15]And deliver them who through fear of death were all their lifetime subject to bondage.

James 4:7: Submit yourselves therefore to God. Resist the devil, and he will flee from you.

1 John 3:8: He that committeth sin is of the devil; for the devil sinneth from the beginning. For this purpose the Son of God was manifested, that he might destroy the works of the devil.

1 John 4:4: Ye are of God, little children, and have overcome them: because greater is he that is in you, than he that is in the world.

Rev. 12:11: And they overcame him by the blood of the Lamb, and by the word of their testimony; and they loved not their lives unto the death.

Rev. 20:10: And the devil that deceived them was cast into the lake of fire and brimstone, where the beast and the false prophet *are,* and shall be tormented day and night for ever and ever.

Matthew 25:41: Then shall he say also unto them on the left hand, Depart from me, ye cursed, into everlasting fire, prepared for the devil and his angels:

1. Every jinx upon my _ _ _, break, in the name of Jesus.

2. Every spell upon my _ _ _,break, in the name of Jesus.

3. You rod of the wrath of the Lord, come upon every enemy of my _ _ _, in Jesus' name.

4. Angels of God, invade them and lead them into darkness, in the name of Jesus.

5. You hand of the Lord, turn against them, day by day, in the name of Jesus.

6. O Lord, let their flesh and skin become old and let their bones be broken, in Jesus' name.

7. O Lord, let them be compassed with gall and travail, in the name of Jesus.

8. O Lord, let Your angels hedge them about and block their paths, in the name of Jesus.

9. O Lord, make their chains heavy.

10. When they cry, shut out their cries, in Jesus' name.

11. O Lord, make their paths crooked.

12. O Lord, make their ways

to be hewed with sharp stones.

13. O Lord, let the power of their own wickedness fall upon them, in Jesus' name.

14. O Lord, turn them aside and pull them into pieces.

15. O Lord, make their ways desolate.

16. O Lord, fill them with bitterness and let them be drunk with wormwood.

17. O Lord, break their teeth with gravel.

18. O Lord, cover them with ashes.

19. O Lord, remove their souls far from peace and let them forget prosperity.

20. I crush under my feet, all the evil powers trying to imprison me, in Jesus' name.

21. O Lord, let their mouths be buried in the dust, in the name of Jesus.

22. O Lord, let there be civil war in the camp of the enemies of my _ _ _, in Jesus' name.

23. Power of God, pull down the stronghold of the enemies of my _ _ _, in Jesus' name.

24. O Lord, persecute and destroy them in Your anger, in the name of Jesus.

25. Every blockage in my way of _ _ _ , clear away by fire, in the name of Jesus.

26. Every demonic claim of the earth over my life, be dismantled, in Jesus' name.

27. I refuse to be chained to my place of birth, in Jesus'

name.

28. Any power, pressing the sand against me, fall down and die, in the name of Jesus.

29. I receive my breakthroughs, in the name of Jesus.

30. I release my money from the house of the strongman, in the name of Jesus.

31. Blood of Jesus and the fire of the Holy Ghost, cleanse every organ in my body, in the name of Jesus.

32. I break loose from every inherited evil covenant of the earth, in the name of Jesus.

33. I break loose from every inherited evil curse of the earth, in the name of Jesus.

34. I break loose from every form of demonic bewitchment of the earth, in the name of Jesus.

35. I release myself from every evil domination and control from the earth, in the name of Jesus.

36. Blood of Jesus, be transfused into my blood vessel.

37. I release panic upon my full-time enemies, in Jesus' name.

38. O Lord, let stubborn confusion come upon the headquarters of my enemies, in the name of Jesus.

39. I loose confusion upon the plans of my enemies, in the

name of Jesus.

40. Every stronghold of darkness, receive acidic confusion, in Jesus' name.

41. I loose panic and frustration on satanic orders issued against me, in Jesus' name.

42. Every evil plan against my life, receive confusion, in the name of Jesus.

43. All curses and demons, programmed against me, I neutralise you by the blood of Jesus. ·

44. Every warfare, prepared against my peace, I command panic upon you, in the name of Jesus.

45. Every warfare, prepared against my peace, I command havoc upon you, in the name of Jesus.

46. Every warfare, prepared against my peace, I command chaos upon you, in the name of Jesus.

47. Every warfare, prepared against my peace, I command pandemonium upon you, in the name of Jesus.

48. Every warfare, prepared against my peace, I command disaster upon you, in the name of Jesus.

49. Every warfare, prepared against my peace, I command confusion upon you, in the name of Jesus.

50. Every warfare, prepared against my peace, I command spiritual acid upon you, in the name of Jesus.

51. Every warfare, prepared

against my peace, I command destruction upon you, in the name of Jesus.

52. Every warfare, prepared against my peace, I command hornets of the Lord upon you, in Jesus' name.

53. Every warfare, prepared against my peace, I command brimstone and hailstone upon you, in the name of Jesus.

54. I frustrate every satanic verdict, issued against me, in the name of Jesus.

55. Thou finger, vengeance, terror, anger, fear, wrath, hatred and burning judgment of God, be released against my full-time enemies, in the name of Jesus.

56. Every power, preventing the perfect will of God from being done in my life, receive failure and defeat, in the name of Jesus.

57. You warring angels and Spirit of God, arise and scatter every evil gathering sponsored against me, in the name of Jesus.

58. I disobey any satanic order programmed by inheritance into my life, in Jesus' name.

59. I bind and cast out every power causing internal warfare, in Jesus' name.

60. Every demonic doorkeeper, locking out good things from me, be paralysed by fire, in the name of Jesus.

61. I command every evil power, fighting against me to fight against and destroy each other, in Jesus' name.

62. Every demon, hindering, delaying, preventing or destroying breakthrough, receive confusion, in the name of Jesus.

63. Thou divine power and control, attack the spirits of violence and torture, in the name of Jesus.

64. You the spirit of witchcraft, attack familiar spirits fashioned against me, in the name of Jesus.

65. O Lord, let there be a civil war in the kingdom of darkness, in Jesus' name.

66. O Lord, loose Your judgment and destruction upon all stubborn, disobedient and reluctant spirits who fail to obey my commands promptly.

RELEASE FROM DESTRUCTIVE COVENANTS

This prayer programme is meant for those who seek release from destructive covenants. Destructive covenants are meant to destroy. As long as they are in place, destruction is inevitable. The kind of covenants referred to here may be inherited or entered into consciously. As long as they are destructive, you must release yourself from their binding powers. To obtain release from such covenants, you will have to renounce them either for yourself or in respect of your ancestors.

You must be thorough as you take these prayer points. Note the fact that some of the destructive covenants must have been in place for a very long time. To get rid of such deeply entrenched ones, you need to pray with fervency and aggression. With this prayer, their power will be rendered null and void.

Praise worship

Confessions: Col. 2:14-15: Blotting out the handwriting of ordinances that was against us, which was contrary to us, and took it out of the way, nailing it to his cross; And having spoiled principalities and powers, he made a shew of them openly, triumphing over them in it.

Galatians 3:13-14: Christ hath redeemed us from the curse of the law, being made a curse for us: for it is written, Cursed is every one that hangeth on a tree: That the blessing of Abraham might come on the Gentiles through Jesus Christ; that we might receive the promise of the Spirit through faith.

1. I take back, all the grounds given to satan by my ancestors, in the name of Jesus.

---

2. I curse you spirit enforcing evil covenants in my life and I command you to release me, in Jesus' name. (When you have said this three times, begin to say, 'Release me', in the name of Jesus).

---

3. Everything that has been transferred into my life by demonic laying on of hands, loose your hold right now, in the name of Jesus.

---

4. Every serpentine poison that has been passed into my life, get out now, in the name of Jesus. I flush you out with the blood of Jesus.

---

5. O Lord, let fire fall on every spirit of death and hell, fashioned against my life, in the name of Jesus.

---

6. I break the head and crush the tail of every serpentine spirit, in the name of Jesus.

---

7. You spiritual bat and spiritual lizard that have been introduced into my head, receive the fire of God, in the name of Jesus.

8. Sword of fire, begin to cut off every evil parental attachment, in the mighty name of Jesus.

9. Father Lord, reveal to me any hidden covenant that the devil might have arranged for me, in the name of Jesus.

10. Every tree, that the Father did not plant in my life, be uprooted, in the name of Jesus.

11. Father Lord, I electrify the ground of this place now and let every covenant with the feet begin to shatter now, in Jesus' name.

12. Let every evil hidden covenant, break, in the mighty name of Jesus.

13. I apply the blood of Jesus to break all curses.

14. Sing this song: "There is power mighty in the blood (x2). There is power mighty in the blood of Jesus Christ. There is power mighty in the blood."

15. I apply the blood of Jesus to break all consequences of parental sins.

16. O Lord, turn all the evils directed at me to good.

17. All powers of evil, directed at me, return directly to your sender, in the name of Jesus.

18. O God, make everything the enemy has said is impossible in my life possible, in the name of Jesus.

19. I release myself from the umbrella of any collective captivity, in the name of Jesus.

20. I release myself from any inherited bondage, in Jesus' name.

21. O Lord, send Your axe of fire to the foundation of my life and destroy every evil plantation therein.

22. Blood of Jesus, flush out of my system, every inherited satanic deposit, in the name of Jesus.

23. I release myself from the grip of any problem, transferred into my life from the womb, in the name of Jesus.

24. Blood of Jesus and fire of the Holy Ghost, cleanse every organ in my body, in the name of Jesus.

25. I break loose from every collective evil covenant, in the name of Jesus.

26. I break loose from every collective curse, in the name of Jesus.

27. I vomit every evil food that I have been fed with as a child, in the name of Jesus.

28. All foundational strongmen, attached to my life, be paralysed, in the name of Jesus.

29. Any rod of the wicked, rising up against my family line, be rendered impotent for my sake, in the name of Jesus.

30. I cancel the consequences of any evil local name, attached to my person, in the name of Jesus.

31. Pray aggressively against the following roots of collective captivity. Pray as follows: Every effect of . . . (*pick from the under listed one by one*), upon my life, come out with all your roots, in the name of Jesus.

   - Evil physical design   - Evil dedication   - Parental curses

   - Demonic marriage   - Envious rivalry   - Demonic sacrifice

   - Demonic incisions   - Inherited infirmity - Dream pollution

   - Laying on of evil hands   - Demonic initiations

   - Wrong exposure to sex   - Demonic blood transfusion

   - Exposure to evil diviners   - Demonic alteration of destiny

   - Fellowship with local idols   - Fellowship with family idols

   - Fellowship with demonic consultants

   - Unscriptural manner of conception

   - Destructive effect of polygamy

32. I refuse to drink from the fountain of sorrow, in Jesus' name.

33. I take authority over all curses pronounced against my life, in the name of Jesus.

34. Ask God to remove any curse He has placed on your life as a result of disobedience.

35. Any demon, attached to any curse, depart from me now, in the mighty name of our Lord Jesus Christ.

36. All curses, issued against me, be converted to blessings, in the name of Jesus.

37. When you mention any of the under-listed curses, you will aggressively say, "break, break, break, in the name of Jesus. I release myself from you, in the name of Jesus."

   - Every curse of mental and physical sickness

   - Every curse of failure and defeat

   - Every curse of poverty

   - Every curse of family break-up

   - Every curse of oppression

   - Every curse of bad reputation

   - Every curse of personal destruction or suicide

   - Every curse of chronic sickness

   - Every curse of witchcraft

   - Every curse of corruption of the reproductive organ

   - Every curse of family strife

   - Every curse of profitless hard work

   - Every curse of evil dedication

   - Every curse of sickness and infirmity

38. You will now place blessings on yourself by saying, "There shall be no more poverty, sickness, etc in my life, in Jesus' name."

39. I release myself from the bondage of evil altars, in the name of Jesus. Say this once, then be repeating, "I release myself, in the name of Jesus." Spend some time on this.

40. I vomit every satanic poison that I have swallowed, in the name of Jesus.

41. I cancel every demonic dedication, in the name of Jesus. Be repeating, "I cancel you, in the name of Jesus."

42. (Place your two hands on your head.) I break every evil authority over my life, in the name of Jesus. Be repeating, "I break you, in the name of Jesus."

43. Mention the underlisted with authority and say, "Break, in the name of Jesus." Repeat it seven hot times.

    - Every evil authority of family shrine or idol

    - Every evil authority of witchcraft and family spirits

    - Every evil authority of remote control powers

    - Every evil authority of the strongman

44. Every owner of evil load, carry your load, in the name of Jesus. (If it is sickness or bad luck, let them carry it.)

45. I render every aggressive altar impotent, in the name of Jesus.

46. Every evil altar, erected against me, be disgraced, in Jesus' name.

47. Anything done against my life under demonic anointing, be nullified, in the name of Jesus.

48. I curse every local altar, fashioned against me, in Jesus' name.

49. You hammer of the Almighty God, smash every evil altar erected against me, in Jesus name.

50. O Lord, send Your fire to destroy every evil altar fashioned against me, in the name of Jesus.

51. Every evil priest, ministering against me at any evil altar, receive the sword of God, in the name of Jesus.

52. Thou thunder of God, smite every evil priest working against me on the evil altar and burn them to ashes, in the name of Jesus.

53. Every satanic priest, ministering against me at evil altars, fall down and die, in the name of Jesus.

54. Any hand that wants to retaliate or arrest me because of all these prayers I am praying, dry up and wither, in the name of Jesus.

55. Every stubborn evil altar priest, drink your own blood, in the name of Jesus.

56. I possess my possession, stolen by the evil altar, in Jesus' name.

57. I withdraw my name from every evil altar, in the name of Jesus.

58. (Transfer the hand to your chest.) I withdraw my blessings, from every evil altar, in the name of Jesus.

59. (Take the hand back to your head.) I withdraw my breakthroughs from every evil altar, in the name of Jesus.

60. I withdraw my glory from every evil altar, in the name of Jesus.

61. (Transfer the hand to your chest.) I withdraw my prosperity from every evil altar, in the name of Jesus.

62. (One hand on the head, the other one on the chest.) I withdraw anything representing me from every evil altar, in Jesus' name.

63. Mention the organ that you know is not behaving the way it should. When you have done this begin to say: "I withdraw you from every evil altar." Say this seven hot times.

64. Put one hand on the head and the other on the stomach. All prayers to renounce covenants, whether consciously or unconsciously entered into are to be said aggressively, vigorously and loudly because you may be fighting a battle that is two thousand years old. The Bible says, "*My people are destroyed for lack of knowledge*" (Hosea 4:6). Say this with holy aggression:

65. "Holy Ghost fire, boil spiritual contamination out of my blood. (Boiling purifies water. As the water boils, vapour condenses and becomes pure water.). Say this once and repeat, "Holy Ghost fire boil it out."

66. I release myself from every satanic blood covenant, in the name of Jesus.

67. Grip your head with your two hands and pray very aggressively, "I release my head from every evil blood covenant, in the name of Jesus."

68. (Still gripping your head with your two hands,) "I dismantle every stronghold of evil covenants, in the name of Jesus."

69. When somebody enters into an evil covenant, a curse is issued on him. As he is breaking the covenant, he is bombarded with two different things: the covenant and the curse. So, pray like this; "I release myself from every covenanted curse, in Jesus' name."

70. Blood of Jesus, speak against every unconscious evil covenant.

71. I speak destruction unto the fruits of unclean spirits in my life, in the name of Jesus.

72. I break every evil covenant link, in the name of Jesus.

73. I dismantle every stronghold of evil blood covenants, in the name of Jesus.

74. I nullify the effects of evil access to my blood, in Jesus' name.

75. I release myself from every covenanted-curse ,in Jesus' name.

76. I release every organ in my body from the grip of evil blood covenant, in the name of Jesus.

77. I dissociate myself and my family from every territorial blood covenant, in the name of Jesus.

78. I dissociate myself from every tribal blood covenant, in the name of Jesus.

79. I dissociate myself from every inherited blood covenant, in the name of Jesus.

80. I withdraw my blood from every evil altar, in the name of Jesus.

81. I withdraw my blood from every satanic blood bank, in the name of Jesus.

82. I break every unconscious evil blood covenant, in Jesus' name.

83. O Lord, let the blood of any animal shed on my behalf loose its covenant power, in the name of Jesus.

84. Every drop of blood, speaking evil against me, be silenced by the blood of Jesus.

85. I release myself from every collective blood covenant captivity, in the name of Jesus.

86. I release myself from every conscious or unconscious evil blood covenant, in the name of Jesus.

87. O Lord, let the blood of every evil covenant loose its power over me, in the name of Jesus.

88. I defy and destroy every evil covenant agreement, in Jesus' name.

89. Blood of the new-covenant, speak against the blood of any evil covenant militating against me, in the name of Jesus.

90. I receive, the mandate, to disqualify the right of all evil blood covenants, in the name of Jesus.

91. Every evil blood covenant, formed with any organ of my body, be nullified, by the blood of Jesus.

92. I recover, all the good things stolen through evil covenants by the enemies, in the name of Jesus.

93. Every evil blood covenant, along my blood-line, be neutralised, in the name of Jesus.

94. I release myself from every curse, attached to evil covenants, in the name of Jesus.

95. I release myself from the grip of curse-covenant breakers, in the name of Jesus.

96. Every repercussion of breaking unconscious covenants, be washed away by the blood of Jesus.

PRAYERS FOR DIVINE GUIDANCE

This prayer is meant for those who seek God's guidance over important matters. You need to pray it seriously if you want to be guided during crucial moments in life. The program will open up the tap of divine revelation and you will be led aright by God. Nobody can deceive God. So, you need to prepare your heart and thoroughly give Him undivided attention while you seek His face for guidance. Prayer for divine guidance must be persistent until you receive total guidance in every area in which you seek God's face.

Confessions: Deut 29:29: The secret things belong unto the LORD our God: but those things which are revealed belong unto us and to our children for ever, that we may do all the words of this law.

Ps 5:8: Lead me, O LORD, in thy righteousness because of mine enemies; make thy way straight before my face.

Ps 25:14: The secret of the LORD is with them that fear him; and he will shew them his covenant.

Dan 2:22: He revealeth the deep and secret things: he knoweth what is in the darkness, and the light dwelleth with him.

Eph 1:17: That the God of our Lord Jesus Christ, the Father of glory, may give unto you the spirit of wisdom and revelation in the knowledge of him.

PRAYER POINTS

1. Praise worship.

2. Thank God for the revelational power of the Holy Spirit.

3. Thank God for the purifying power of the Holy Ghost fire.

4. I cover myself with the blood of the Lord Jesus.

5. Father, let Your fire that burns away every deposit of the enemy fall upon me, in the name of Jesus.

6. Holy Ghost fire, incubate me, in the name of the Lord Jesus Christ.

7. I reject any evil stamp or seal, placed upon me by ancestral spirits, in the name of Jesus.

8. I release myself from every negative anointing, in the name of Jesus.

9. Every door of spiritual leakage, close, in the name of Jesus.

10. I challenge every organ of my body with the fire of the Holy

Spirit. (Lay your right hand on various parts of your body, beginning from the head), in the name of Jesus.

11. Every human spirit, attacking my spirit, release me, in the name of Jesus.

12. I reject every spirit of the tail, in the name of Jesus.

13. Sing the song: "Holy Ghost fire, fire fall on me."

14. All evil marks on my body, burn off by the fire of the Holy Spirit, in the name of Jesus.

15. The anointing of the Holy Ghost, fall upon me and break every negative yoke, in the name of Jesus.

16. Every garment of hindrance and dirtiness, be dissolved by the fire of the Holy Ghost, in the name of Jesus.

17. All my chained blessings, be unchained, in the name of Jesus.

18. All spiritual cages, inhibiting my progress, roast by the fire of the Holy Spirit, in Jesus' name.

19. O Lord, give unto me the spirit of revelation and wisdom in the knowledge of You.

20. O Lord, make Your way plain before my face on this issue.

21. O Lord, remove spiritual cataract from my eyes.

22. O Lord, forgive me of every false motive or thought that has ever been formed in my heart since the day I was born.

23. O Lord, forgive me of any lie that I have ever told against any

person, system or organisation.

24. O Lord, deliver me from the bondage and sin of spiritual laziness.

25. O Lord, open my eyes to see all I should see on this issue.

26. O Lord, teach me deep and secret things.

27. O Lord, reveal to me every secret behind any problem that I have.

28. O Lord, bring to light every thing planned against me in darkness.

29. O Lord, ignite and revive my beneficial potentials.

30. O Lord, give me divine wisdom to operate my life.

31. O Lord, let every veil preventing me from having plain spiritual vision be removed.

32. O Lord, give unto me the spirit of revelation and wisdom in the knowledge of You.

33. O Lord, open my spiritual understanding.

34. O Lord, let me know all I should know about this issue.

35. O Lord, reveal to me every secret behind this particular issue whether beneficial or not.

36. O Lord, remove from me any persistent buried grudge, enmity against anyone and every other thing that can block my spiritual vision.

37. O Lord, teach me to know what is worth knowing, and love what

is worth loving and to dislike whatsoever is not pleasing to You.

38. O Lord, make me a vessel capable of knowing Your secret things.

39. Father, in the name of Jesus, I ask to know Your mind, about . .
. (*slot in the appropriate situation*) situation.

40. You spirit of prophecy and revelation, fall upon the totality of my
being, in the name of Jesus.

41. Holy Spirit, reveal deep and secret things to me about . . ., in the
name of Jesus.

42. I bind every demon polluting my spiritual vision and dreams, in
the name of Jesus.

43. Every dirt, blocking my communication pipe with the living God,
be washed clean with the blood of Jesus, in the name of Jesus.

44. I receive power to operate with sharp spiritual eyes that cannot
be deceived, in the name of Jesus.

45. You glory and the power of the Almighty God, fall upon my life in
a mighty way, in the name of Jesus.

46. I remove my name from the book of those who grope and stumble
in darkness, in the name of Jesus.

47. Divine revelations, spiritual visions, dreams and information will
not become a scarce commodity in my life, in the name of Jesus.

48. I drink to the full from the well of salvation and anointing, in the
name of Jesus.

49. O God to whom no secret is hidden, make known unto me whether or not... (*mention the name of the thing*) is Your choice for me, in the name of Jesus.

50. Every idol, present in my heart consciously or unconsciously concerning this issue, melt away by the fire of the Holy Spirit, in the name of Jesus.

51. I refuse to fall under the manipulation of the spirits of confusion, in the name of Jesus.

52. I refuse to make foundational mistakes in my decision-making, in the name of Jesus.

53. Father Lord, guide and direct me in knowing Your mind on this particular issue, in the name of Jesus.

54. I stand against all satanic attachments that may want to confuse my decision, in the name of Jesus.

55. If ... (*mention the name of the thing*) is not for me, O Lord, redirect my steps.

56. I bind the activities of ... (*pick from the list below*) in my life, in the name of Jesus.

    (i)   lust (ii) ungodly infatuation (iii) ungodly family pressure

    (iv) demonic manipulation in dreams and visions

    (v)   attachment to the wrong choice

    (vi) confusing revelations

(vii) spiritual blindness and deafness

(viii) unprofitable advice

(ix) ungodly impatience

57. O God, You who reveals secret things, make known unto me Your choice for me on this issue, in the name of Jesus.

58. Holy Spirit, open my eyes and help me to take the right decision, in the name of Jesus.

59. Thank You Jesus for Your presence and the good testimonies that will follow.

60. Pray in the spirit for at least 15 minutes before going to bed.

LET NOT MY ENEMIES TRIUMPH OVER ME

The Bible clearly explains that there are enemies in life. No matter how good or godly you may be, you will surely have enemies who hate to see you make progress and enjoy the blessings of God.

Enemies generally wage war against all sorts of people. When an enemy rises up and comes up with wicked plots, you need to rise up and make him bow in defeat. As a child of God, you should not allow your enemies to triumph over you.

When you are armed with the weapons of aggressive prayers (the type used by the Psalmist) and fight fervently, your enemies will not be able to overcome you.

To experience victory and triumph over your enemies, you need to take the prayer points below. No matter how you are attacked by the enemies, you can use these prayer points as your weapon to make the enemies submit

themselves unto you.

Confessions:

> **Psalm 27:6:** And now shall mine head be lifted up above mine enemies round about me: therefore will I offer in his tabernacle sacrifices of joy; I will sing, yea, I will sing praises unto the Lord.

> **Deut 28:13:** And the LORD shall make thee the head, and not the tail; and thou shalt be above only, and thou shalt not be beneath; if that thou hearken unto the commandments of the LORD thy God, which I command thee this day, to observe and to do them.

> **Prov. 21:1:** The king's heart is in the hand of the LORD, as the rivers of water: he turneth it whithersoever he will.

> **Jeremiah 7:18:** The children gather wood, and the fathers kindle the fire, and the women knead *their* dough, to make cakes to the queen of heaven, and to pour out drink offerings unto other gods, that they may provoke me to anger.

> **Jeremiah 44:17-19:** But we will certainly do whatsoever thing goeth forth out of our own mouth, to burn incense unto the queen of heaven, and to pour out drink offerings unto her, as we have done, we, and our fathers, our kings, and our princes, in the cities of Judah, and in the streets of Jerusalem: for *then* had we plenty of victuals, and were well, and saw no evil. [18]But since we left off to burn incense to the queen of heaven,

and to pour out drink offerings unto her, we have wanted all *things,* and have been consumed by the sword and by the famine. [19]And when we burned incense to the queen of heaven, and poured out drink offerings unto her, did we make her cakes to worship her, and pour out drink offerings unto her, without our men?

Jeremiah 44:25: Thus saith the LORD of hosts, the God of Israel, saying; Ye and your wives have both spoken with your mouths, and fulfilled with your hand, saying, We will surely perform our vows that we have vowed, to burn incense to the queen of heaven, and to pour out drink offerings unto her: ye will surely accomplish your vows, and surely perform your vows.

Isaiah 49:24-25: Shall the prey be taken from the mighty, or the lawful captive delivered? [25]But thus saith the LORD, Even the captives of the mighty shall be taken away, and the prey of the terrible shall be delivered: for I will contend with him that contendeth with thee, and I will save thy children.

Psalm 124:7: Our soul is escaped as a bird out of the snare of the fowlers: the snare is broken, and we are escaped.

Psalm 56:9: When I cry *unto thee,* then shall mine enemies turn back: this I know; for God *is* for me.

Psalm 91:13: Thou shalt tread upon the lion and adder: the young lion and the dragon shalt thou trample under feet.

Psalm 18:37-40: I have pursued mine enemies, and overtaken

them: neither did I turn again till they were consumed. [38]I have wounded them that they were not able to rise: they are fallen under my feet. [39]For thou hast girded me with strength unto the battle: thou hast subdued under me those that rose up against me. [40]Thou hast also given me the necks of mine enemies; that I might destroy them that hate me.

Psalm 35:4-6: Let them be confounded and put to shame that seek after my soul: let them be turned back and brought to confusion that devise my hurt. [5]Let them be as chaff before the wind: and let the angel of the LORD chase *them.* [6]Let their way be dark and slippery: and let the angel of the LORD persecute them.

Psalm 11:6-7: Upon the wicked he shall rain snares, fire and brimstone, and an horrible tempest: *this shall be* the portion of their cup. [7]For the righteous LORD loveth righteousness; his countenance doth behold the upright.

Psalm 129:4: The LORD *is* righteous: he hath cut asunder the cords of the wicked.

Psalm 6:8-10: Depart from me, all ye workers of iniquity; for the LORD hath heard the voice of my weeping. [9]The LORD hath heard my supplication; the LORD will receive my prayer. [10]Let all mine enemies be ashamed and sore vexed: let them return *and* be ashamed suddenly.

Psalm 140:9-10: *As for* the head of those that compass me about, let the mischief of their own lips cover them. [10]Let burning coals fall upon them: let them be cast into the fire; into deep pits, that they rise not up again.

Psalm 58:6-7: Break their teeth, O God, in their mouth: break out the great teeth of the young lions, O LORD. 7Let them melt away as waters *which* run continually: *when* he bendeth *his bow to shoot* his arrows, let them be as cut in pieces.

Psalm 118:7: The LORD taketh my part with them that help me: therefore shall I see *my desire* upon them that hate me.

Psalm 118:12: They compassed me about like bees; they are quenched as the fire of thorns: for in the name of the LORD I will destroy them.

Psalm 31:17-18: Let me not be ashamed, O LORD; for I have called upon thee: let the wicked be ashamed, *and* let them be silent in the grave. 18Let the lying lips be put to silence; which speak grievous things proudly and contemptuously against the righteous.

Psalm 92:9-11: For, lo, thine enemies, O LORD, for, lo, thine enemies shall perish; all the workers of iniquity shall be scattered. 10But my horn shalt thou exalt like *the horn of* an unicorn: I shall be anointed with fresh oil. 11Mine eye also shall see *my desire* on mine enemies, *and* mine ears shall hear *my desire* of the wicked that rise up against me.

Matthew 4:10: Then saith Jesus unto him, Get thee hence, Satan: for it is written, Thou shalt worship the Lord thy God,

and him only shalt thou serve.
Matthew 28:18: And Jesus came and spake unto them, saying, All power is given unto me in heaven and in earth.
Luke 10:19: Behold, I give unto you power to tread on serpents and scorpions, and over all the power of the enemy: and nothing shall by any means hurt you.
Luke 11:21-22: When a strong man armed keepeth his palace, his goods are in peace: ^{22}But when a stronger than he shall come upon him, and overcome him, he taketh from him all his armour wherein he trusted, and divideth his spoils.
John 12:31: Now is the judgment of this world: now shall the prince of this world be cast out.
John 16:11: Of judgment, because the prince of this world is judged.
Romans 16:20: And the God of peace shall bruise Satan under your feet shortly. The grace of our Lord Jesus Christ *be* with you. Amen.
2 Cor. 10:3-5: For though we walk in the flesh, we do not war after the flesh: ^{4}For the weapons of our warfare *are* not carnal, but mighty through God to the pulling down of strong holds; ^{5}Casting down imaginations, and every high thing that exalteth itself against the knowledge of God, and bringing into captivity every thought to the obedience of Christ;

Col. 2:15: *And* having spoiled principalities and powers, he made a shew of them openly, triumphing over them in it.

Hebrews 2:14-15: Forasmuch then as the children are partakers of flesh and blood, he also himself likewise took part of the same; that through death he might destroy him that had the power of death, that is, the devil; [15]And deliver them who through fear of death were all their lifetime subject to bondage.

James 4:7: Submit yourselves therefore to God. Resist the devil, and he will flee from you.

1 John 3:8: He that committeth sin is of the devil; for the devil sinneth from the beginning. For this purpose the Son of God was manifested, that he might destroy the works of the devil.

1 John 4:4: Ye are of God, little children, and have overcome them: because greater is he that is in you, than he that is in the world.

Rev. 12:11: And they overcame him by the blood of the Lamb, and by the word of their testimony; and they loved not their lives unto the death.

Rev. 20:10: And the devil that deceived them was cast into the lake of fire and brimstone, where the beast and the false prophet *are*, and shall be tormented day and night for ever and ever.

> **Matthew 25:41: Then shall he say also unto them on the left hand, Depart from me, ye cursed, into everlasting fire, prepared for the devil and his angels:**

Praise Worship

Prayer Points

1. Thou King of glory, arise, visit me and turn around my captivity, in the name of Jesus.

2. I shall not regret; I will become great, in the name of Jesus.

3. Every habitation of humiliation and demotion, fashioned against me, be battered, shattered and swallowed up by the power of God.

4. O Lord, station and establish me in Your favour.

5. God of restoration, restore my glory, in the name of Jesus.

6. As darkness gives up before light, o Lord, let all my problems give up before me, in the name of Jesus.

7. Thou power of God, destroy every trouble in my life, in Jesus' name.

8. O God, arise and attack every lack in my life, in the name of Jesus.

9. Thou power of liberty and dignity, manifest in my life, in the name of Jesus.

10. Every chapter of sorrow and slavery in my life, close forever, in the name of Jesus.

11. Thou power of God, usher me out of the balcony of disgrace by fire, in the name of Jesus.

12. Every obstacle in my life, give way to miracles, in Jesus' name

13. Every frustration in my life, become a bridge to my miracles, in the name of Jesus.

14. Every enemy, exploring devastating strategies against my progress in life, be disgraced, in the name of Jesus.

15. Every residential permit for me to stay in the valley of defeat, be revoked, in the name of Jesus.

16. I prophesy that bitter life shall not be my portion;   better life shall be my testimony, in the name of Jesus.

17. Every habitation of cruelty, fashioned against my destiny, become desolate, in the name of Jesus.

18. All my trials, become gateways to my promotions, in the name of Jesus.

19. You anger of God, write the obituary of all my oppressors, in the name of Jesus.

20.   O Lord, let Your presence begin a glorious story in my life.

21.   Every strange god, attacking my destiny, scatter and die, in the name of Jesus.

22.   Every horn of satan, fighting against my destiny, scatter, in the name of Jesus.

23. Every altar, speaking hardship into my life, die, in the name of Jesus.

24. Every inherited battle in my life, die, in Jesus' name.

25. All my blessings, that have been buried with dead relatives, come alive and locate me, in Jesus' name.

26. All my blessings, that are presently not in this country, arise and locate me, in the name of Jesus.

27. Every stronghold of my father's house, be dismantled, in Jesus' name.

28. Father, let all my proposals find favour in the sight of . . . in the name of Jesus.

29. O Lord, let me find favour, compassion and loving-kindness with . . . concerning this matter.

30. All demonic obstacles, that have been established in the heart of . . . against this matter, be destroyed, in Jesus' name.

31. O Lord, show . . . dreams, visions and restlessness, that would advance my cause.

32. My money, being caged by the enemy, be released, in Jesus' name.

33. O Lord, give me supernatural breakthroughs, in all my present proposals.

34. I bind and put to flight, all the spirits of fear, anxiety and discouragement, in the name of Jesus.

35. O Lord, let divine wisdom fall upon all who are supporting me, in these matters.

36. I break the backbone of any further spirit of conspiracy and treachery, in the name of Jesus.

37. O Lord, hammer my matter into the mind of those who will assist me so that they do not suffer from demonic loss of memory.

38. I paralyse the handiwork of household enemies and envious agents in this matter, in the name of Jesus.

39. You devil, take your legs away from the top of my finances, in the mighty name of Jesus.

40. Fire of the Holy Spirit, purge my life from any evil mark put upon me, in the name of Jesus.

41. Every jinx upon my _ _ _, break, in the name of Jesus.

42. Every spell upon my _ _ _, break, in the name of Jesus.

43. You rod of the wrath of the Lord, come upon every enemy of my _ _ _, in the name of Jesus.

44. Angels of God, invade them and lead them into darkness, in the name of Jesus.

45. Thou hand of the Lord, turn against them day by day, in the name of Jesus.

46. O Lord, let their flesh and skin become old, and let their bones break, in the name of Jesus.

47. O Lord, let them be compassed with gall and travail, in the name of Jesus.

48. O Lord, let Your angels hedge them about and block their paths, in the name of Jesus.

49. O Lord, make their chains heavy.

50. When they cry, o Lord, shut out their cries, in the name of Jesus.

51. O Lord, make their paths crooked.

52. O Lord, make their ways to be strewn with sharp stones.

53. O Lord, let the power of their own wickedness fall upon them, in the name of Jesus.

54. O Lord, turn them aside and pull them into pieces.

55. O Lord, make their ways desolate.

56. O Lord, fill them with bitterness and let them be drunk with wormwood.

57. O Lord, break their teeth with gravel.

58. O Lord, cover them with ashes.

59. O Lord, remove their souls far from peace and let them forget prosperity.

60. I crush under my feet, all the evil powers trying to imprison me, in the name of Jesus.

61. O Lord, let their mouths be buried in the dust, in the name of Jesus.

62. O Lord, let there be civil war in the camp of the enemies of my _ _ _, in the name of Jesus.

63. Power of God, pull down the stronghold of the enemies of my _ _ _, in the name of Jesus.

64. O Lord, persecute and destroy them in anger, in the name of Jesus.

65. Every blockage, in my way of _ _ _ clear away by fire, in the name of Jesus.

66. Every demonic claim of the earth over my life, be dismantled, in the name of Jesus.

67. I refuse to be chained to my place of birth, in Jesus' name.

68. Any power, pressing the sand against me, fall down and die, in the name of Jesus.

69. I receive my breakthroughs, in the name of Jesus.

70. I release my money from the house of the strongman, in Jesus' name.

71. Blood of Jesus and the fire of the Holy Ghost, cleanse every organ in my body, in the name of Jesus.

72. I break loose from every inherited evil covenant of the earth, in the name of Jesus.

73. I break loose from every inherited evil curse of the earth, in the name of Jesus.

74. I break loose from every form of demonic bewitchment of the earth, in the name of Jesus.

75. I release myself from every evil domination and control from the earth, in the name of Jesus.

76. Blood of Jesus, be transfused into my blood vessel.

77. I release panic upon my full-time enemies, in the name of Jesus.

78. O Lord, let stubborn confusion come upon the headquarters of my enemies, in the name of Jesus.

79. I loose confusion upon the plans of my enemies, in the name of Jesus.

80. Every stronghold of darkness, receive acidic confusion, in the name of Jesus.

81. I loose panic and frustration on satanic orders issued against me, in the name of Jesus.

82. Every evil plan against my life, receive confusion, in the name of Jesus.

83. All curses and demons, programmed against me, I neutralise you by the blood of Jesus.

84. Every warfare, prepared against my peace, I command panic upon you, in the name of Jesus.

85. Every warfare, prepared against my peace, I command havoc upon you, in the name of Jesus.

86. Every warfare, prepared against my peace, I command chaos upon you, in the name of Jesus.

87. Every warfare, prepared against my peace, I command pandemonium upon you, in the name of Jesus.

88. Every warfare, prepared against my peace, I command disaster upon you, in the name of Jesus.

89. Every warfare, prepared against my peace, I command confusion upon you, in the name of Jesus.

90. Every warfare, prepared against my peace, I command spiritual acid upon you, in the name of Jesus.

91. Every warfare, prepared against my peace, I command destruction upon you, in the name of Jesus.

92. Every warfare, prepared against my peace, I command hornets of the Lord upon you, in Jesus' name.

93. Every warfare, prepared against my peace, I command brimstone and hailstone upon you, in the name of Jesus.

94. I frustrate every satanic verdict issued against me, in Jesus' name.

95. You the finger, vengeance, terror, anger, fear, wrath, hatred and burning judgment of God, be released against my full-time enemies, in the name of Jesus.

96. Every power, preventing the perfect will of God from being done in my life, receive failure, in the name of Jesus.

97. You warring angels and Spirit of God, arise and scatter every evil gathering sponsored against me, in the name of Jesus.

98. I disobey any satanic order, programmed by inheritance into my life, in the name of Jesus.

99. I bind and cast out every power causing internal warfare, in the name of Jesus.

100. Every demonic doorkeeper, locking out good things from me, be paralysed by fire, in the name of Jesus.

101. Every evil power, fighting against me, fight and destroy yourselves, in Jesus' name.

102. Every breakthrough hindering, delaying, preventing, destroying and breaking demons, receive confusion, in the name of Jesus.

103. O Lord, let divine power and control attack the spirits of violence and torture, in the name of Jesus.

104. O Lord, let the spirit of witchcraft attack familiar spirits fashioned against me, in the name of Jesus.

105. O Lord, let there be a civil war, in the kingdom of darkness, in the name of Jesus.

106. O Lord, loose judgment and destruction upon all stubborn, disobedient and reluctant spirits who fail to follow my commands promptly.

107. Thank the Lord, for answered prayers.

POWER AGAINST PYTHON SPIRIT 1

This is a prayer to deal with the powers of the serpents in all it's ramifications. These prayers should be done at night, when

1. Your ancestors worship serpents

2. When you have regular serpentine attacks in your dreams

3. When you notice objects moving around your body

4. When you exhibit negative reactions whenever you come across anything having to do with serpent

5. When you need deliverance from religious spirits

6. When you want to trample upon serpents of darkness.

This prayer programme is designed for those who desire victory over serpentine enemies. The python, being the king of the spiritual serpentine kingdom, stands for the totality of the power of the serpent, the devil. When problems are programmed into people's life by spiritual serpents, the victim may go from place to place in search of help without any solution in sight. Until the spirit or the python is roasted by fire, the manifestations will become recurrent experiences. Attacks from the python are deadly. The poison of serpentine spirits have sent many to untimely graves, sentenced many to destiny diversion and made many become casualties on the field of battle. To experience victory over the spirit of the python, you need to take the battle to its gates and keep bombarding the powers of the evil serpent until you experience resounding victory.

Confessions: Isaiah 54:17: No weapon that is formed against thee shall prosper; and every tongue that shall rise against thee in judgment thou shalt condemn. This is the heritage of the servants of the Lord, and their righteousness is of me, saith the Lord.

Luke 10:19: Behold, I give unto you power to tread on serpents and scorpions, and over all the power of the enemy: and nothing shall by any means hurt you.

Rev. 12:11: And they overcame him by the blood of the Lamb, and by the word of their testimony; and they loved not their lives unto the death.

Job 5:12: He disappointeth the devices of the crafty, so that *their hands cannot perform their enterprise.*

Psalm 18:44-45: As soon as they hear of me, they shall obey me: the strangers shall submit themselves unto me. The strangers shall fade away, and be afraid out of their close places.

Aggressive Praise Worship

Prayer Points

1. I cover everything within me, everything around me and everything over me now with the blood of Jesus.

2. You demonic serpents, be rendered venom-less in every area of my life, in the name of Jesus.

3. Thou serpent of impossibility, die, in the name of Jesus.

4. Thou serpent and scorpion of affliction, die, in the name of Jesus.

5. Every serpent and scorpion, anointed against my destiny, dry up and die, in the name of Jesus.

6. Every serpentine spirit and poison, depart from my tongue, in the name of Jesus.

7. I break every egg, that the serpent has laid in every department of my life, in the name of Jesus.

8. Every serpentine and scorpion power, militating against my life, be disgraced, in the name of Jesus.

9. O Lord, let all the serpents and scorpions assigned against me

10. Every serpent, sent to destroy me, return to your sender in anger, in the name of Jesus.

11. Any of my spiritual strength, sapped by the serpent, receive divine touch of God and be revived, in Jesus' name.

12. You serpent, loose your grip upon my spiritual strength, in Jesus' name.

13. Every pollution of my spiritual life and health by the serpent, be cleansed by the blood of Jesus.

14. Every serpentine manipulation of my health, be frustrated and be rendered impotent, in the name of Jesus.

15. All you serpents, vomit my prosperity, health, marriage, finances and spiritual strength that you have swallowed, in the mighty name of our Lord Jesus Christ.

16. I tread upon all serpents and scorpions; they cannot harm me, in the name of Jesus.

17. You the bullet from heaven, kill every serpent of death, in the name of Jesus.

18. I cut off every soul-tie with any serpent spirit, in the name of Jesus.

19. I excise the poison and venom of scorpions and serpents from my flesh, in Jesus' name.

20. I cut myself off from all cobra, serpent and ancestral worship, in the name of Jesus.

21. I repent of all serpent worship, and the worship of animal deities and forces of the air, fire, water, the nether world and nature, in the name of Jesus.

22. All serpent and scorpion spirits, depart from me now, in Jesus' name.

23. I release myself from every serpent bite and poison, in the name of Jesus.

24. Every scorpion, set in motion against me, be rendered stingless, in the name of Jesus.

25. Every serpent, set in motion against my spiritual progress, be rendered venomless, in the name of Jesus.

26. Satanic serpents, dispatched against me, receive madness, in the name of Jesus.

27. Satanic serpents, dispatched against my family, be paralyzed and roast, in the name of Jesus.

28. I trample upon every problematic serpent and scorpion, in Jesus' name.

29. I receive shoes of iron and trample upon serpents and scorpions, in the name of Jesus.

30. You stubborn problems, I trample upon your serpents and scorpions, in the name of Jesus.

31. Every spirit-serpent, delegated against me, run into the desert and be buried in the hot sand, in the name of Jesus.

32. I smash the head of poverty-serpents on the wall of fire, in Jesus' name.

33. I trample upon every serpent and scorpion, monitoring the progress of my life, in the name of Jesus.

34. I cast all serpents of infirmity into the fire of judgment, in the name of Jesus.

35. I cut myself free from the hands of serpents and scorpions, in the name of Jesus

36. I remove the portion of the serpent from my own life, in Jesus' name.

37. Every serpent-spirit, unwind and depart from my life, in Jesus' name.

38. Thou serpent of the Lord, swallow the serpent of my Pharaoh, in the name of Jesus.

39. Thou serpent of the Lord, bite every hidden enemy of my life, in the name of Jesus.

40. Every crocodile and serpent spirit, I kill you with the hook of the Lord, in the name of Jesus.

41. Holy Ghost fire, kill every serpent and scorpion targeted at my Israel, in the name of Jesus.

42. As a child of the Lion of Judah, I chase out serpents from my life, in the name of Jesus.

43. Every serpent and scorpion of poverty, die, in the name of Jesus.

44. Every poison of serpents and scorpions, come out of me, in the name of Jesus.

45. Every crooked serpent, be destroyed, in the name of Jesus.

46. My life, reject every serpent and scorpion, in the name of Jesus.

47. O God, arise and grind foundational serpents to ashes, in Jesus' name.

48. You serpent of impossibility, be dissolved by the fire of the God of Elijah, in the name of Jesus.

49. Every serpent in my dreams, go back to your sender, in Jesus' name.

50. Every serpent and scorpion, working against my destiny, dry up and die, in the name of Jesus.

51. Every dream-serpent, die, in the name of Jesus.

52. Every serpent in my foundation, die, in the name of Jesus.

53. You serpent of the Lord, bite every serpent in my family line, in the name of Jesus

54. Every serpent in my foundation, die, in the name of Jesus.

55. Every scorpion in my foundation, die, in the name of Jesus.

56. You serpent, loose your grip upon my spiritual strength, in the name of Jesus.

57. Every serpentine manipulation of my health, be frustrated and be rendered impotent, in the name of Jesus.

58. Every serpent that has refused to let me go, Holy Ghost fire, dry it up, in the name of Jesus.

59. Every serpent idol in my family, I break your link with my family, in the name of Jesus.

60. I decree that no serpent shall control my life, in Jesus' name.

61. Every serpent, fired into my life, go back to your sender, in the name of Jesus.

62. Every dream-serpent, go back to your sender, in the name of Jesus.

63. Every serpent, working in the root of my life, die, in the name of Jesus.

64. You serpent and scorpion of darkness, delegated against my victory, die, in the name of Jesus.

65. I smash and scatter the heads of serpent spirits, in the name of Jesus.

66. Thank God, for answers to your prayers.

POWER AGAINST PYTHON SPIRIT 2

This is a prayer to deal with the powers of the serpents in all it's ramifications. These prayers should be done at night, when

1. *Your ancestors worship serpents*

2. *When you have regular serpentine attacks in your dreams*

3. *When you notice objects moving around your body*

4. *When you exhibit negative reactions whenever you come across anything having to do with serpent*

5. *When you need deliverance from religious spirits*

6. *When you want to trample upon serpents of darkness.*

This prayer programme is designed for those who desire victory over serpentine enemies. The python, being the king of the spiritual serpentine kingdom, stands for the totality of the power of the serpent, the devil. When problems are programmed into people's life by spiritual serpents, the victim may go from place to place in search of help without any solution in sight. Until the spirit or the python is roasted by fire, the manifestations will become recurrent experiences. Attacks from the python are deadly. The poison of serpentine spirits have sent many to untimely graves, sentenced many to destiny diversion and made many become casualties on the field of battle. To experience victory over the spirit of the python, you need to take the battle to its gates and keep bombarding the powers of the evil serpent until you experience resounding victory.

Confessions: Isaiah 54:17: No weapon that is formed against thee shall prosper; and every tongue that shall rise against thee in judgment thou shalt condemn. This is the heritage of the servants of the Lord, and their righteousness is of me, saith the Lord.

Luke 10:19: Behold, I give unto you power to tread on serpents and scorpions, and over all the power of the enemy: and nothing shall by any means hurt you.

Rev. 12:11: And they overcame him by the blood of the Lamb, and by the word of their testimony; and they loved not their lives unto the death.

Job 5:12: He disappointeth the devices of the crafty, so that their hands cannot perform their enterprise.

Psalm 18:44-45: As soon as they hear of me, they shall obey

me: the strangers shall submit themselves unto me. The strangers shall fade away, and be afraid out of their close places.

Aggressive Praise Worship

Prayer Points

1. I cover everything within me, everything around me, and everything over me now with the blood of Jesus.

2. You demonic serpents, be rendered venom-less in every area of my life, in the name of Jesus.

3. Thou serpent of impossibility, die, in the name of Jesus.

4. Thou serpent and scorpion of affliction, die, in the name of Jesus.

5. Every serpent and scorpion, anointed against my destiny, dry up and die, in the name of Jesus.

6. Every serpent spirit and poison, depart from my tongue, in the name of Jesus.

7. I break every egg that the serpent has laid in every department of my life, in the name of Jesus.

8. Every serpentine and scorpion power, militating against my life, be disgraced, in the name of Jesus.

9. O Lord, let all the serpents and scorpions assigned against me begin to fight themselves, in the name of Jesus.

10. Every serpent, sent to destroy me, return to your sender in anger, in the name of Jesus.

11. Any of my spiritual strength, sapped by the serpent, receive divine touch of God and be revived, in Jesus' name.

12. You serpent, loose your grip upon my spiritual strength, in the name of Jesus.

13. Every pollution of my spiritual life and health by the serpent, be cleansed by the blood of Jesus.

14. Every serpentine manipulation of my health, be frustrated and be rendered impotent, in the name of Jesus.

15. All you serpents, vomit my prosperity, health, marriage, finances and spiritual strength that you have swallowed, in the mighty name of our Lord Jesus Christ.

16. I tread upon all serpents and scorpions; they cannot harm me, in the name of Jesus.

17. You the bullet from heaven, kill every serpent of death, in Jesus' name.

18. I cut every soul-tie with any serpent spirit, in the name of Jesus.

19. I excise the poison and venom of scorpions and serpents from my flesh, in Jesus' name.

20. I cut myself off from all cobra, serpent and ancestral worship, in the name of Jesus.

21. I repent of all serpent worship, and the worship of animal deities and forces of the air, fire, water, the nether world and nature, in the name of Jesus.

22. All serpent and scorpion spirits, depart from me now, in the name of Jesus.

23. I release myself from every serpent bite and poison, in the name of Jesus.

24. Every scorpion, set in motion against me, be rendered sting-less, in the name of Jesus.

25. Every serpent, set in motion against my spiritual progress, be rendered venom-less, in the name of Jesus.

26. Satanic serpents, dispatched against me, receive madness, in the name of Jesus.

27. Satanic serpents, dispatched against my family, be paralyzed and roast, in the name of Jesus.

28. I trample upon every problematic serpent and scorpion, in Jesus' name.

29. I receive shoes of iron and trample upon serpents and scorpions, in the name of Jesus.

30. You stubborn problems, I trample upon your serpents and scorpions, in the name of Jesus.

31. Every spirit-serpent, delegated against me, run into the desert and be buried in the hot sand, in the name of Jesus.

32. I smash the head of poverty-serpents on the wall of fire, in Jesus' name.

33. I trample upon every serpent and scorpion, monitoring the progress of my life, in the name of Jesus.

34. I cast all serpents of infirmity into the fire of judgment, in the name of Jesus.

35. I cut myself free from the hands of serpents and scorpions, in the name of Jesus

36. I remove the portion of the serpent from my own life, in the name of Jesus.

37. Every serpent-spirit, unwind and depart from my life, in Jesus' name.

38. Thou serpent of the Lord, swallow the serpent of my Pharaoh, in the name of Jesus.

39. Thou serpent of the Lord, bite every hidden enemy of my life, in the name of Jesus.

40. Every crocodile and serpent spirit, I kill you with the hook of the Lord, in the name of Jesus.

41. Holy Ghost fire, kill every serpent and scorpion targeted at my Israel, in the name of Jesus.

42. As a child of the Lion of Judah, I chase out serpents from my life, in the name of Jesus.

43. Every serpent and scorpion of poverty, die, in the name of Jesus.

44. Every poison of serpents and scorpions, come out of me, in the name of Jesus.

45. Every crooked serpent, be destroyed, in the name of Jesus.

46. My life, reject every serpent and scorpion, in the name of Jesus.

47. O God, arise and grind foundational serpents to ashes, in Jesus' name.

48. You serpent of impossibility, be dissolved by the fire of the God of Elijah, in the name of Jesus.

49. Every dream-serpent, go back to your sender, in Jesus' name.

50. Every serpent and scorpion, working against my destiny, dry up and die, in the name of Jesus.

51. Every dream-serpent, die, in the name of Jesus.

52. Every serpent in my foundation, die, in the name of Jesus.

53. You serpent of the Lord, bite every serpent in my family line, in the name of Jesus

54. Every serpent in my foundation, die, in the name of Jesus.

55. Every scorpion in my foundation, die, in the name of Jesus.

56. You serpent, lose your grip upon my spiritual strength, in Jesus' name.

57. Every serpentine manipulation of my health, be frustrated and be rendered impotent, in the name of Jesus.

58. Every serpent that has refused to let me go, Holy Ghost fire, dry it up, in the name of Jesus.

59. Every serpent idol in my family, I break your link with my family, in the name of Jesus.

60. I decree that no serpent shall control my life, in the name of Jesus.

61. Every serpent, fired into my life, go back to your sender, in the name of Jesus.

62. Every dream-serpent, go back to your sender, in the name of Jesus.

63. Every serpent, working in the root of my life, die, in the name of Jesus.

64. You serpent and scorpion of darkness, delegated against my victory, die, in the name of Jesus.

65. I smash and scatter the heads of serpent spirits, in the name of Jesus.

66. I break every covenant with the spirit of the python, in the name of Jesus.

67. Every serpent, attached to my life, roast by fire, in the name of Jesus.

68. Every attraction of the serpent spirit to my life, be washed off by the blood of Jesus.

69. Every consultation with the powers of divination against my life, end in confusion, in the name of Jesus.

70. Every power of divination, manipulating my destiny, be destroyed, in the name of Jesus.

71. Every evil oracle with my name, be consumed by fire, in the name of Jesus.

72. Every altar of the serpent, erected against me, burn to ashes, in the name of Jesus.

73. I withdraw my name from every evil register and record file, in the name of Jesus.

74. Every link between the python spirit and my life, break into pieces, in the name of Jesus.

75. Every covenant, formed on my behalf with serpent spirit by my ancestors / parents, break by the blood of Jesus.

76. I loose myself from every hold of the serpent, in the name of Jesus.

77. Every poison of the serpent in my life, come out, in the name of Jesus.

78. Every egg of the serpent in the vessel of my life, be smashed into pieces by the hammer of fire, in Jesus' name.

79. Every property of the serpent in my possession, vanish and return no more, in the name of Jesus.

80. Every resting place of the serpent in my life, receive the unbearable heat of the Almighty, in the name of Jesus.

81. Every strongroom of the serpent in my life, be destroyed by the fire of God, in the name of Jesus.

82. You the head of the serpent, be smashed to pieces by Holy Ghost fire, in the name of Jesus.

83. Fire of God, enter into my life and consume every stranger there, in the name of Jesus.

84. Every poison of sexual immorality in my life, be paralysed, in the name of Jesus.

85. Every activity of seduction in any area of my life, be paralysed, in the name of Jesus.

86. Every invisible programme of the serpent in my life, be destroyed, in the name of Jesus.

87. Every ancestral altar of the serpent spirit in my family, burn to ashes, in the name of Jesus.

88. Every unrepentant snake worshipper in my family, fall down and die, in the name of Jesus.

89. Every habitation of the power of the serpent in (name your village river), be consumed by fire, in the name of Jesus.

90. Holy Ghost, fill the vacuum of the serpent spirit in my life, in the name of Jesus.

91. Thank God, for answers to your prayers.

DEALING WITH NIGHT RAIDERS

A lot of havoc is done under the cover of darkness by members of the dark kingdom. To wage war against night raiders, you need prayer points vomited by the Holy Ghost. This is what this programme offers. Since it is targeted at evil night raiders, you will need to carry it out with aggression. You must overpower the agents of darkness if you want to put a stop to their activities. The task of terminating the appointments of night raiders must be carried out persistently, powerfully and with holy anger.

Confessions: Psalm 91:1-16: He that dwelleth in the secret place of the most High shall abide under the shadow of the Almighty. I will say of the Lord, He is my refuge and my fortress: my God; in him will I trust. Surely he shall deliver thee from the snare of the fowler, and from the noisome pestilence. He shall cover thee with his feathers, and under his wings shalt thou trust: his truth shall be thy shield and buckler. Thou shalt not be afraid for the terror by night; nor for the arrow that flieth by day; Nor for the pestilence that walketh in darkness; nor for the destruction that wasteth at noonday. A thousand shall fall at thy side, and ten thousand at thy right hand; but it shall not come nigh thee. Only with thine eyes shalt thou behold and see the reward of the wicked. Because thou hast made the Lord, which is my refuge, even the most High, thy habitation; There shall no evil befall thee, neither shall any plague come nigh thy dwelling. For he shall give his angels charge over thee, to keep thee in all thy ways. They shall bear thee up in their hands, lest thou dash thy foot against a stone. Thou shalt tread upon the lion and adder: the young lion and the dragon shalt thou trample under feet. Because he hath set his love upon me, therefore will I deliver him: I will set him on high, because he hath known my name. He shall call upon me, and I will answer him: I will be with him in trouble; I will deliver him, and honour him. With long life will I satisfy him, and shew him my salvation.

SING SONGS OF WORSHIP AND WARFARE

Prayer Points

1. Every doorway and ladder to satanic invasion in my life, be abolished forever by the blood of Jesus.

2. I loose myself from curses, hexes, spells, bewitchments and evil domination, directed against me through dreams, in the name of Jesus.

3. You ungodly powers, release me by fire, in the name of Jesus.

4. All past satanic defeats in the dream, be converted to victory, in the name of Jesus.

5. All tests in the dream, be converted to testimonies, in Jesus' name.

6. All trials in the dream, be converted to triumphs, in Jesus' name.

7. All failures in the dream, be converted to success, in Jesus' name.

8. All scars in the dream, be converted to stars, in Jesus' name.

9. All bondage in the dream, be converted to freedom, in Jesus' name.

10. All losses in the dream, be converted to gains, in Jesus' name.

11. All oppositions in the dream, be converted to victory, in Jesus' name.

12. All weaknesses in the dream, be converted to strength, in Jesus' name.

13. All negative situations in the dream, be converted to positive situations, in Jesus' name.

14. I release myself from every infirmity introduced into my life through dreams, in the name of Jesus.

15. All attempts by the enemy to deceive me through dreams, fail woefully, in the name of Jesus.

16. I reject evil spiritual husband, wife, children, marriage, engagement, trade, pursuit, ornament, money, friend, relative, etc., in the name of Jesus.

17. Lord Jesus, wash my spiritual eyes, ears and mouth with Your blood.

18. The God, who answereth by fire; answer by fire whenever any spiritual attacker comes against me.

19. Lord Jesus, replace all satanic dreams with heavenly visions and divinely-inspired dreams.

20. Wonderful Lord, I reverse any defeat that I have ever suffered in the dream, in the name of Jesus.

21. Any dream that I have dreamt that is good and from God, I receive it; and those that are satanic, I reject them, in the name of Jesus.

22. Every night and dream attack and its consequences, be nullified, in Jesus' name.

23. I claim freedom from satanic and restless dreams, in Jesus' name.

24. I claim freedom from importing anxiety and shameful thoughts into my dreams, in Jesus' name.

25. I stand against every dream of defeat and its effects, in the name of Jesus.

26. All satanic designs of oppression against me in dreams and visions, be frustrated, in the name of Jesus.

27. Every demonic influence, targeted at destroying my vision, dream and ministry, receive total disappointment, in the name of Jesus.

28. Every witchcraft hand, planting evil seeds in my life through dream attacks, wither and burn to ashes, in the name of Jesus.

29. By the blood of Jesus, I rebuke every frightening dream, in the name of Jesus.

30. O Lord, let the evil vision and dream about my life evaporate in the camp of the enemy, in the name of Jesus.

31. Every curse of demotion in my life through dream, be nullified by the blood of Jesus.

32. Every curse of confused and unprogressive dream in my life, be nullified by the blood of Jesus.

33. Every curse of harassment in my life through dreams by familiar faces, be nullified by the blood of Jesus.

34. I send the bullets of any gun shot in the dream back to sender, in the name of Jesus.

35. I paralyse all the night caterers and I forbid their food in my dream, in the name of Jesus.

36. All pursuers in my dreams, begin to pursue yourselves, in Jesus' name.

37. All the contamination in my life through dreams, be cleansed by the blood of Jesus.

38. I cancel every dream of backwardness, in the name of Jesus.

39. Every dream of demotion to junior school, be dismantled. I shall go from glory to glory, in the name of Jesus.

40. By the power in the blood of Jesus, I cancel the maturity dates of all evil dreams in my life.

41. You God of promotion, promote me beyond my wildest dreams, in the name of Jesus.

42. Every sickness, planted in the dream into my life, get out now and go back to your sender, in the name of Jesus.

43. O Lord, let life be squeezed out of my dream attackers, in Jesus' name.

44. By the power in the blood of Jesus, all my buried good dreams and visions, come alive.

45. By the power in the blood of Jesus, all my polluted good dreams and visions, receive divine solution.

46. By the power in the blood of Jesus, let all dream and vision killers that are working against the manifestation of my good dreams and visions be paralysed.

47. By the power in the blood of Jesus, let every good dream and vision that has been stolen be restored with fresh fire.

48. By the power in the blood of Jesus, every good dream and vision, that has been transferred, be restored with fresh fire.

49. By the power in the blood of Jesus, let every good dream and vision that has been poisoned be neutralised.

50. By the power in the blood of Jesus, let every good dream and vision that has been amputated receive divine strength.

51. All the contamination in my life, through dreams, be cleansed by the blood of Jesus.

52. Any anti-progress arrow, fired into my life through dreams, be nullified, in the name of Jesus.

53. I resist the threat of death in my dreams by fire, in Jesus' name.

54. Every evil dream, that other people have had about me, I cancel it in the astral world, in the name of Jesus.

55. Every image of satan in my dream, I curse you, catch fire now, in the name of Jesus.

56. Every dream of demotion, backfire, in Jesus' name.

57. Every arrow of death in the dream, come out and go back to your sender, in the name of Jesus.

58. Every sponsored dream of poverty against my life by household wickedness, vanish, in the name of Jesus.

59. I dash every poverty dream to the ground, in the name of Jesus.

60. I cancel the manipulation of every satanic dream, in the name of Jesus.

61. You powers of the night, polluting my night dreams, be paralysed, in the name of Jesus.

62. Every anti-prosperity dream, die, in the mighty name of Jesus.

63. All satanic designs of oppression against me in dreams and visions, be frustrated, in Jesus' name.

64. I paralyse the spirits who bring bad dreams to me, in the name of Jesus.

65. I cancel and wipe off all evil dreams, in the name of Jesus.

66. Blood of Jesus, erase all evil dreams in my life, in the name of Jesus.

67. My dreams, my joys and my breakthroughs that have been buried in the dark world, come alive and locate me now, in Jesus' name.

68. Every dream serpent, go back to your sender, in Jesus' name.

69. Every power, planting affliction into my life in the dream, be buried alive, in the name of Jesus.

70. Any evil programme, positioned into my life from my dream, be dismantled now, in the name of Jesus.

71. Every altar of witchcraft, despising my prayer and my prayer life, receive the attack of divine thunder, in the name of Jesus.

72. Every invisible satanic remote control, affecting my prayers and my prayer life, be consumed by pure divine fire, in the name of Jesus.

73. You evil foundational bondage, connecting my life to internal and external destruction, be consumed by fire, in the name of Jesus.

74. You family foundational bondage, affecting and disgracing my life, I terminate and destroy your activities by the blood of Jesus, in the name of Jesus.

75. Any invisible and visible satanic material in my environment and my house, attracting demonic invasion, roast, in the name of Jesus.

76. You my prayer altar, receive Holy Ghost revival fire and power, in the name of Jesus.

77. Every dead personal prayer altar, receive the touch of fire and come alive, in the name of Jesus.

78. Every physical and spiritual disturbance, contributing to my prayerlessness, die sudden death by fire, in the name of Jesus.

79. Every pathway of witchcraft into my life, overturn by the blood of Jesus, in the name of Jesus.

80. Every arrow of evil consumption, fired into my life, come out and go back to your sender by fire, in Jesus' name.

81. Any organ of my body, under the influence of evil consumption, be released by fire, in Jesus' name.

82. O Lord, let divine arrows of destruction be roasted with fire and be released against the camp of night caterers, in the name of Jesus.

83. You my mouth, I fortify you with the blood of Jesus, reject satanic food, in the name of Jesus.

84. Every evil deception being used to feed me in my dream, I destroy you by fire, in the name of Jesus.

85. Every association of night caterers, targeting my life for evil, scatter by thunder, in the name of Jesus.

86. O Lord, let the pathway of witchcraft spirit and operations into my life be closed by the blood of Jesus.

87. Anything in my life, house and environment, attracting the activities of night caterers to me, be consumed by fire, in the name of Jesus.

88. Every stubborn cause of failure in my life, I bury and destroy you by fire, in the name of Jesus.

89. Any member of my family, empowering external enemies against me, die by thunder, in the name of Jesus.

90. Every weapon of operation of night caterers, bombarding my life day and night, turn against your owners, in the name of Jesus.

91. Every seat of witchcraft in my family/marriage/home, catch fire, in the name of Jesus.

GO FORWARD BY FIRE

The Bible clearly teaches us that God's people are meant to make progress, rather than struggle with stagnancy or backwardness. A lot of people go through such acute stagnancy and retrogression that they wonder why nothing is working for them. Much as they desire to go forward, they find an invisible hand pulling them backward. Such a situation requires a drastic solution.

When the powers behind your problems are recalcitrant, you must use the artillery of aggressive prayer. If you want to move forward by fire, you need to make use of the prayer points in this section. These prayer points are vomited by the Holy Ghost to make you go forward. You need them when you are tired of doing a merry-go- round on the same spot. You need the prayer points when you want to go beyond the boundaries of limitation. You need them when you desire extraordinary progress in life

Confessions: Deut 28:13: *And the LORD shall make thee the*

head, and not the tail; and thou shalt be above only, and thou shalt not be beneath; if that thou hearken unto the commandments of the LORD thy God, which I command thee this day, to observe and to do them.

Prov 21:1: The king's heart is in the hand of the LORD, as the rivers of water: he turneth it whithersoever he will.

1 Sam 17:45-46: Then said David to the Philistine, Thou comest to me with a sword, and with a spear, and with a shield: but I come to thee in the name of the LORD of hosts, the God of the armies of Israel, whom thou hast defied. This day will the LORD deliver thee into mine hand; and I will smite thee, and take thine head from thee; and I will give the carcases of the host of the Philistines this day unto the fowls of the air, and to the wild beasts of the earth; that all the earth may know that there is a God in Israel.

Deut 33:25-27: Thy shoes shall be iron and brass; and as thy days, so shall thy strength be. There is none like unto the God of Jeshurun, who rideth upon the heaven in thy help, and in his excellency on the sky. The eternal God is thy refuge, and underneath are the everlasting arms: and he shall thrust out the enemy from before thee; and shall say, Destroy them.

Jer 1:19 :And they shall fight against thee; but they shall not prevail against thee; for I am with thee, saith the LORD, to deliver thee.

Nahum 1:7-8: The LORD is good, a strong hold in the day of trouble; and he knoweth them that trust in him. But with an *overrunning flood he will make an utter end of the place thereof, and darkness shall pursue his enemies.*

Ps 75:6: *For promotion cometh neither from the east, nor from the west, nor from the south.*

Ps 113:5,7-8: *Who is like unto the LORD our God, who dwelleth on high, He raiseth up the poor out of the dust, and lifteth the needy out of the dunghill; That he may set him with princes, even with the princes of his people.*

Phil 4:13,19: *I can do all things through Christ which strengtheneth me. But my God shall supply all your need according to his riches in glory by Christ Jesus.*

Gal 6:17: *From henceforth let no man trouble me: for I bear in my body the marks of the Lord Jesus.*

As I make this confession of the word of God into my life, I believe and I receive the power that is in it into my spirit, soul and body, in the name of Jesus Christ – Amen.

In my mouth is the power of life and death. I speak life unto myself, and I speak destruction unto all my enemies and all their weapons against me, in Jesus' name – Amen.

With my heart, I believe unto righteousness and with my mouth confession is made unto salvation, in Jesus' name – Amen.

The name of Jesus is my authority over all the powers of darkness, including satan, in Jesus' name – Amen.

As I begin to make this confession, I command that at the name of

Jesus Christ, every knee should bow; of things in heaven, things on earth and things under the earth, in Jesus' name – Amen.

As I speak the word of God right now, I send it to run swiftly and become operational, to manifest and fulfil the purpose for which I send it, in Jesus' name – Amen.

Right now, I command the word to go forth, in Jesus' name – Amen.

I am a child of God, I believe in the Father, I believe in the Son and I believe in the Holy Ghost, in Jesus' name.

I believe that Jesus Christ came in the flesh and laid down His life and shed His blood for me on the cross of Calvary, in Jesus' name – Amen.

I believe that Jesus has defeated satan, and delivered me from this present evil world and satan, in Jesus' name – Amen.

I have accepted Jesus Christ as my personal Saviour; I belong to the Lord Jesus Christ. I am a new creature. Old things have passed away; my old life is done away with, I am now living a new life. The life I now live is in Christ Jesus. Jesus Christ has paid the price for me with His blood and set me free. Satan and all his demons have no more power or dominion over my life, in Jesus' name – Amen.

For whomsoever Jesus has set free, is free indeed. I am free indeed, in Jesus' name – Amen.

Jesus has delivered me from all the powers of darkness. I am delivered from principalities, powers, dominions and all the forces of darkness, in the name of Jesus Christ – Amen.

The devil has no more dominion over me, in Jesus' name – Amen.

I submit myself unto the mighty hand of God and I command satan and all his demons to release me, and to flee from me right now, in the name of Jesus Christ – Amen.

In the name of Jesus Christ, there is no condemnation for those who are in Christ Jesus; there is no condemnation for me being in Christ Jesus, in Jesus' name – Amen.

The Spirit of Life in Christ Jesus that dwells inside me has delivered me from the law of sin and death, in Jesus' name – Amen.

On the authority in the name of Jesus Christ, I break, damage, destroy and uproot right now, all covenants, agreements, statements, names and requests of any kind, promises of any kind and all links of any type made with the kingdom of darkness; including everything that the enemy is holding against me. I break them, cast them down, cancel and reject all of them, Amen.

I break any association with the kingdom of darkness, entered into knowingly or unknowingly; whether done in my sleep or when I was awake. I dissociate myself from all of them, in the name of Jesus Christ – Amen.

In the name of Jesus Christ, I command right now a total destruction of all yokes, burdens, fears, oppressions and terrors of any kind, invoked by the enemy against me. I reject and cancel them,

I also command the total destruction of all enchantments, witchcraft, divinations, spells, curses, ordinances and hand writings by the enemy against me, a child of God, in the name of Jesus Christ - Amen.

I command all these things that I have spoken to be destroyed, all - together, leaving nothing. I break them down, I blot them out by the blood of Jesus Christ, shed for my redemption, I nail them to the Cross, in Jesus' name - Amen.

I declare that all the devilish acts of the enemy in my life are erased and finished with, in Jesus' name - Amen.

Right now, I cut myself loose from all the links with the kingdom of darkness, in Jesus' name - Amen.

All their works against me are now damaged, wiped away and forgotten forever, in the name of Jesus Christ - Amen.

Jesus Christ has set me free from all the captivity of satan and all his demons, in Jesus' name - Amen.

When Jesus Christ ascended, He led captivity captive. The Lord has broken down the gates of brass, cut asunder the bars of iron and delivered me from the imprisonment of the devil, in Jesus' name.

Jesus has broken down and scattered all the powers of the enemy against me, in Jesus' name - Amen.

All powers in heaven and on earth are given unto me by Christ Jesus on the authority in His name. I have the keys to the kingdom of heaven. Whatsoever I loose on earth is loosed in heaven. Right now, I loose myself from every imprisonment of the devil and his followers, in Jesus' name – Amen.

Whatsoever I bind on earth is bound in heaven. Right now, I bind and put a stop to all the numerous activities of the devil, made against me, in Jesus' name – Amen.

I ask the vengeance of the Lord upon all my enemies: for vengeance is the Lord's.

In the name of Jesus Christ, I send the wrath of God to pour like water upon all my enemies. I conquer and lock them up, for God is for me and no one can rise up or be against me, in Jesus' name – Amen.

Jesus Christ is the fighter of all my battles against the attacks of my enemies, in Jesus' name – Amen.

I do not trust in my own arrow, and I do not trust in my own sword; I do not fight for myself. It is not by might, nor by power, but by the Spirit of the Lord, in the name of Jesus Christ- Amen.

In the name of Jesus Christ, I hand over all my battles to the Lord Jesus Christ. The Lord fights for me and I hold my peace, in Jesus' name – Amen.

I am an overcomer, through the name of Jesus Christ, I am victorious in all circumstances and situations, in the name of Jesus – Amen.

I do not need to fight in this battle nor in any other battle. I stand still, I put my trust in God and I shall see the salvation of the Lord, in the name of Jesus Christ. Jesus Christ has defeated all my enemies, and they have fallen and brought down under my feet, in Jesus' name. Right now, I crush them to the ground and I command them to begin to lick up the dust of the earth under my feet; for at the name of Jesus, every knee must bow, in Jesus' name - Amen.

God has equipped me, and made me a danger and a terror to all my enemies, in Jesus' name. The Lord has sent the fear and the dread of me upon all my enemies. My report or information shall cause them to fear, tremble and be in anguish, in Jesus' name - Amen.

I am a soldier for Christ. I am wearing the whole armour of God, in the name of Jesus Christ - Amen.

The armour of God gives me power against principalities, against powers, against rulers of darkness of this world, against spiritual wickedness and against all the powers of darkness, even against satan himself, in Jesus' name - Amen.

I am God's power house, the power of God resides inside me and is manifested outside me, in Jesus' name - Amen.

The glory of God is a covering round about me, in Jesus' name. In the name of Jesus Christ and by the presence of God in my life, I command the wicked to perish before me and melt away like wax in fire. None shall be able to stand before me all the days of my life, in Jesus' name - Amen.

I am built up in Christ Jesus. As Jesus is, so am I on the face of this earth, in the name of Jesus Christ - Amen.

I know who I am in Christ. I am a royal priesthood, a holy nation, a chosen generation and a peculiar person, delivered from the kingdom of darkness into the marvellous light of Christ Jesus, in Jesus' name, Amen.

I know who I am in Christ. All demons, even satan, are subject to me, in Jesus' name, Amen. By the name of Jesus, I pull down all my enemies. They cannot hurt me, in Jesus' name - Amen.

As I make this confession, I send forth a mighty destruction to scatter, destroy and break into pieces, every gathering or association of my enemies against me, in Jesus' name. No plot, device or counsel of the wicked against me shall stand and every tongue that shall rise up against me in judgment I condemn, in Jesus' name - Amen.

Jesus Christ saves me from all those who rise up against me. Jesus is my Defender, Jesus is my Rock, Jesus is my Deliverer, Jesus is my Strength, Jesus is my Fortress and my High Tower, in Jesus' name - Amen.

No weapon that is formed against me shall prosper, in Jesus' name - Amen.

If the enemy comes against me, the Spirit of the Lord will lift up a standard against him and he cannot pass through, in Jesus' name - Amen.

The Lord Jesus Christ has set a boundary round about me. There is a strong hedge of protection round about me, a powerful hedge that all the demons in hell, including satan, can never cross to reach me in Jesus' name – Amen.

I am a child of God, I am dwelling in the secret place of the Most High God. I am protected and covered under the shadow of the wings of Jehovah, in Jesus' name – Amen.

The word of God is the power of God, and the entrance of the word of God into my life has brought His light into my life and darkness cannot comprehend it, in Jesus' name. I send forth this light that is in me as a two-edged sword to destroy all the kingdoms of darkness, in Jesus' name – Amen.

The word of God is quick and powerful, in my mouth. God has put the power of His word in my mouth, in Jesus' name. I trust in the word of God. The word stands sure when I speak it. It will accomplish the purpose for which I have spoken it, in Jesus' name Amen.

Right now, I send the word of God as a missile to destroy all principalities, powers, thrones, rulers of darkness and all wicked spirits, in Jesus' name – Amen.

I receive the word of God as a shield and cover over my life, in Jesus' name – Amen.

My God is the God that answers by fire. He has fully armed me with His fire for the destruction of all my enemies, including satan, in Jesus' name – Amen.

My body is The temple of the Holy Spirit; the Spirit of God dwells inside me, in Jesus' name – Amen.

I am a container for the fire of the Holy Ghost. The power of God resides in me, in Jesus' name – Amen.

As I speak the word of God, I send it to go forth as flames of unquenchable fire to consume all my enemies, in the name of Jesus – Amen.

I receive it to encircle me and protect me from all my enemies, in Jesus' name – Amen.

I am fire-proof to all the enemies' fire and weapons of war, in Jesus' name – Amen.

I am a danger to the whole kingdom of darkness. I am as a live wire, anyone that touches me shall be electrocuted and set ablaze forever, in Jesus' name – Amen.

The word of God says, "Never touch or try to harm a child of God." I am the apple of God's eye. Anyone that intends to or plots evil against me, God shall destroy him, in Jesus' name – Amen

I receive the blood of Jesus Christ that was shed for me on the cross of Calvary, I am redeemed by the blood of Jesus. Right now, I take out the blood of Jesus Christ, and I use it to set a boundary round about me, in Jesus' name – Amen.

I receive the blood of Jesus Christ upon me and upon my house where I live, in Jesus' name – Amen.

When the enemy sees the blood, he shall pass over. The destroyers will not be able to enter because of the blood. If my enemies seek me, they shall not be able to find me, for my life is hidden in the blood of Jesus, in Jesus' name – Amen.

The blood of Jesus Christ is a cover and hiding place for me from all my enemies, including satan, in Jesus' name – Amen.

The angels of God hearken to the word of God. They hear and obey the word of God because the word of God is God speaking to them. As I speak the word of God out of my mouth, it goes forth to execute the purpose for which I send it, in Jesus' name – Amen.

I receive the ammunition of angelic guidance and operations in my life right now, in Jesus' name – Amen.

The angels have been ordered by God to take charge of me in all my ways and I receive them, in Jesus' name. They go ahead of me wherever I go and they go ahead of me in whatever I do. They go forth and make my crooked ways straight, in Jesus' name – Amen.

The angels of God watch over me in the day time; they watch over me at night. They make sure that no evil, whatsoever, befalls me, in Jesus' name – Amen.

Right now, I send the angels to pursue all my enemies and make them like chaff in the wind. I also send a destructive whirlwind to hit them, destroy them and cast them into the bottomless pit, in Jesus' name' – Amen.

The mighty hand of God is upon my life, upholding and protecting me from all those who rise up against me, in Jesus' name – Amen.

Jesus Christ has made His grace available to me. I ask for the grace and I receive it by faith, in Jesus' name – Amen.

When I call upon the name of the Lord, He shall stretch forth His mighty hand and lift me up above all my enemies and deliver me from all of them, in Jesus' name – Amen.

In the name of Jesus, I am inscribed in the palm of God's mighty hand. I am neatly tucked away and hidden from all the evils and troubles of this present world - Amen.

No one, whomsoever, be it the principalities, powers, dominions, all the powers of darkness, or even satan himself, can pluck me out of the mighty hand of God. For my God is stronger than all, in Jesus' name – Amen.

I am armed with the shoes of the gospel of the Lord Jesus Christ which is the power of God; and I wear them and use them to trample on all the powers of darkness. I tread on all snakes and scorpions and destroy them, in Jesus' name – Amen.

My feet are like the deer's feet; my appearance is like that of a horse. So I run like horses and chariots. I go forth conquering and I conquer all my enemies. I am more than a conqueror through Christ Jesus, in Jesus' name – Amen.

I move faster than the speed of light, in Jesus' name – Amen.

I pursue my enemies; I overtake them and destroy them, in Jesus' name - Amen.

The Lord has lifted me up and I am seated with Him in heavenly places, in Christ Jesus, far above principalities, powers and dominions. The Lord has put all things under my feet and I use my feet to bruise and destroy all my enemies, even satan, in Jesus' name - Amen.

Anywhere the soles of my feet shall tread upon, the Lord has given unto me, in Jesus' name - Amen.

I tread upon and completely destroy all strongholds, walls, foundations and barriers of the enemy against me, in Jesus' name - Amen.

I tread on them with the shoes of the gospel of the Lord Jesus Christ. I make an utter ruin of them and an utter end of all their possessions, kingdoms, thrones, dominions, palaces and everything in them, in Jesus' name - Amen.

I erase them all and I make them completely desolate, in Jesus' name - Amen.

My strength is in the Lord Jesus Christ. Jesus is my strength. I receive strength from the Lord, in Jesus' name - Amen.

There is no weakness in me for I have received the might of God. I am strong; I can do all things through Christ who strengthens me. I walk and I do not faint, I run and I am not weary in Jesus' name - Amen.

The Spirit of Christ that dwells inside me strengthens my physical body, in Jesus' name – Amen.

I have prayer power, in Jesus' name – Amen.

I pray without ceasing, I am fortified with strength to pray, in Jesus' name – Amen.

Jesus Christ has given me His peace and I receive it, in Jesus' name – Amen.

I have the peace of God that surpasses all understanding; the peace of God that keeps my heart and my mind, through Christ Jesus, in Jesus' name – Amen.

My mind is renewed day by day by the word of God, in Jesus' name – Amen.

My mind is stayed on Christ Jesus. I control my thoughts from thinking evil, in Jesus' name, I cast down every imagination and high thing that exalts itself against the word of God in my life. I command my thoughts and mind to be in obedience to Christ, in Jesus' name – Amen.

I am full of faith in God, I do not doubt. I do not operate in unbelief, I believe and trust God as my helper. I do not fear anything, for God has not given me the spirit of fear. I have the Spirit of power, and I have a sound mind through Christ, in Jesus' name – Amen.

In the name of Jesus Christ, my body is healed; by the stripes of Jesus Christ I receive my healing, in Jesus' name – Amen.

Sickness and disease of any kind have no place in my body, in Jesus' name, Jesus has taken all my sicknesses and pains to the cross of Calvary, in Jesus' name – Amen.

And if I eat or drink any deadly or harmful thing, it cannot hurt me, in Jesus' name – Amen.

Right now, in the name of Jesus Christ, I curse every sickness and I curse every disease that has attacked or intends to attack my body. I curse it, in the name of Jesus and I command it to die and disappear from my body right now, in the name of Jesus Christ – Amen.

The Spirit of God is my guide, in Jesus' name – Amen.

I am led by the Spirit for those who are led by the Spirit of God are the sons of God. I acknowledge God as my Father, therefore He will order my footsteps and direct my path, in Jesus' name – Amen.

I am not lazy and I am not slack to follow the leadings of the Spirit of God. I am energetic at all times, always yielding and ready to be in obedience to God, in Jesus' name – Amen.

Right now, I reject, I refuse and I bind, every voice or leading of the devil, in Jesus' name – Amen.

I say, I reject, I refuse and I bind every voice or leading of the devil in my life today and always, in Jesus' name – Amen.

The voice of a stranger I will not hear; the leading of a stranger I will not follow. The Lord is my shepherd and it is Him I will hear. It is Him I will follow forever, for Jesus is my Anchor, in Jesus' name – Amen.

Today, right now, as I conclude this confession, I also cancel all negative confessions that I have made at anytime in my life, in Jesus' name. I agree with the will of God for my life. I come against all negative confessions spoken by me or anyone against me. As I speak, I send the power in the word of God to change every negative confession to positive, in Jesus' name – Amen.

Against my health - I am healed, in Jesus' name – Amen.

Against my finances   - I am rich, I shall lack nothing, in Jesus' name – Amen.

Against my marriage - My marriage is stable, I have peace in my marriage, in Jesus' name – Amen.

Against my children - My children shall prosper in every area and have peace, in Jesus' name – Amen.

Against my calling - What God has purposed for my life must be accomplished, in Jesus' name – Amen.

Against my safety - No accident or evil shall befall me, I do not fear anything, in Jesus' name – Amen.

Against my life   - God has satisfied me with long life, in Jesus' name – Amen.

I erase all negative words spoken, all evil statements, all doubtful statements and unbelief, and all statements that glorify the devil. I wipe them away with the blood of Jesus Christ, in Jesus' name – Amen.

I have total control over my speech, in Jesus' name – Amen.

I ask the Lord to help me and set a guard over my lips, in Jesus' name – Amen.

Right now, as I enter into prayer warfare, I submit myself to God completely, in Jesus' name – Amen.

I cast out the devil. I rebuke the devil and I command him to flee from me right now, in the name of Jesus Christ – Amen.

I bind the devil from stealing, killing or destroying anything belonging to me, be it life or possession, in Jesus' name – Amen.

As I enter into warfare prayer, I bind the devil and his followers from being a hindrance to my prayers, in Jesus' name – Amen.

I also bind the enemy from firing any arrow or other weapon against me, as I pray, in Jesus' name – Amen.

I bind all the enemies' arms and ammunition against me, in Jesus' name – Amen.

The worse things happen in the battle field, but nothing whatsoever, absolutely nothing, will happen to me, in Jesus' name – Amen.

O Lord, I ask that all these confessions that I have made become operational and be a covering and a defence for me, in my spirit, in my soul and in my body. All these confessions shall go forth as a destruction to the devil and all my enemies, in Jesus' name – Amen.

As I enter into warfare, I send the word of God to damage, destroy and uproot the devil and all his followers, in the name of Jesus Christ – Amen.

Praise worship

1. Thank the Lord, because He alone is the unstoppable missile.

2. Father, make all my proposals to find favour in the sight of my divine helpers, in the name of Jesus.

3. All the demonic obstacles, that have been established in the hearts of my divine helpers against my prosperity, be destroyed, in the name of Jesus.

4. I bind and put to flight, all the spirits of fear, anxiety and discouragement, in the name of Jesus.

5. O Lord, let divine wisdom fall upon all who are supporting me in these matters.

6. I break the backbone of any spirit of conspiracy and treachery, in the name of Jesus.

7. O Lord, hammer my matter into the minds of those who will assist me, so that they do not suffer from demonic loss of memory.

8. I paralyse the handiwork of household enemies and envious agents in this matter, in the name of Jesus.

9. All evil competitors, stumble and fall, in the name of Jesus.

10. O Lord, let all my adversaries make mistakes that will advance my cause, in the name of Jesus.

11. O Lord, let all the adversaries of my breakthroughs be put to shame, in the name of Jesus.

12. I claim the power to overcome and to excel among all other competitors, in the name of Jesus.

13. O Lord, let every decision by any panel be favourable unto me, in the name of Jesus.

14. Every negative word and pronouncement against my success, be completely nullified, in Jesus' name.

15. All competitors with me in this issue will find my defeat unattainable, in the name of Jesus.

16. I claim supernatural wisdom to answer all questions in a way that will advance my cause, in the name of Jesus.

17. I confess my sins of exhibiting occasional doubts.

18. I bind every spirit manipulating my beneficiaries against me, in the name of Jesus.

19. I remove my name from the book of those who see goodness without tasting it, in the name of Jesus.

20. You the cloud, blocking the sunlight of my glory and breakthrough, disperse, in the name of Jesus.

21. O Lord, let wonderful changes begin to be my lot from this week.

22. I reject every spirit of the tail in all areas of my life, in the name of Jesus.

23. Oh Lord, bring me into favour with all those who will decide on my advancement.

24. Oh Lord, cause a divine substitution to happen if this is what will move me ahead.

25. I reject the spirit of the tail and I claim the spirit of the head, in the name of Jesus.

26. All evil records, planted by the devil in anyone's mind against my advancement, shatter to pieces, in the name of Jesus.

27. Oh Lord, transfer, remove or change all human agents that are bent on stopping my advancement.

28. Oh Lord, smoothen my path to the top by Your hand of fire.

29. I receive the anointing to excel above my contemporaries, in the name of Jesus.

30. O Lord, catapult me into greatness as You did for Daniel in the land of Babylon.

31. O Lord, help me to identify and deal with any weakness in me that can hinder my progress.

32. I bind every strongman, delegated to hinder my progress, in the name of Jesus.

33. Oh Lord, despatch Your angels to roll away every stumbling block to my promotion, advancement and elevation.

34. O Lord, let power change hands in my place of work to the hands of the Holy Spirit.

35. Fire of God, consume any rock, tying me down to the same spot, in the name of Jesus.

36. All demonic chains, preventing my advancement, break, in the name of Jesus.

37. All human agents, delaying / denying my advancement, I bind the evil spirits controlling your minds in this respect, in the name of Jesus.

38. Holy Spirit, direct the decisions of any panel in my favour, in the name of Jesus.

39. I refuse to fail, at the edge of my miracle, in the name of Jesus.

40. O Lord, release Your angels to fight my battle.

41. O Lord, let warrior angels be released to fight my battles in the heavenlies, in the name of Jesus.

42. I bind every deception and manipulation, targeted at my life, in the name of Jesus.

43. O Lord, let the rain of . . . (pick from the following) fall upon my life in abundance.

- love - power - sound mind   - knowledge   - understanding

- revelation   - wisdom   - freedom   - deliverance

- boldness   - zealousness   - purity   - holiness

- excellence   - praise   - joy   - peace

- longsuffering   - gentleness   - goodness   - faith

- word of wisdom   - word of knowledge   - healing

- working of miracles   - prophecy

- discerning of spirits   - divers kinds of tongues

- interpretation of tongues   - grace   - mercy

- life   - health   - healing   - restoration

- well-being   - counsel   - might   - strength

44. Thank You Lord for setting the machinery for my advancement in motion.

LET MY CHILDREN GO

This prayer programme is specially designed for parents who are concerned and eager to see their children get married successfully. It is a comprehensive prayer programme for those who want to intercede for their children, loved ones or neighbours who want to get married.

This programme has worked for many and will definitely produce wonderful results in the lives of those whom you intercede for.

Confessions: Josh. 24:15; Ps: 8:4-8 Isa. 54:13,17; 49:2; Matt. 7:7; Philippians 2:9; Colossians 2:13; Rev. 12:12; Luke 1:37.

PRAISE WORSHIP

PRAYER POINTS

1. Thank God because He alone is the perfect matchmaker.

2. Thank the Lord because this year is your year of dumbfounding miracles.

3. Lord, release the man/woman You have pre-ordained as my daughter's/son's husband/wife.

4. O Lord, cause it to happen that the divine match will come forth soon.

5. O Lord, let it be a person who loves You wholeheartedly.

6. O Lord, establish their home, in accordance with Ephesians 5:20-28.

7. Father, let all satanic banners, keeping them from meeting be dissolved, in the name of Jesus.

8. O Lord, send forth Your warring angels to battle on their behalf.

9. O Lord, I believe You have created my daughter/son for a special man/woman of God; bring it to pass, in Jesus' name.

10. I stand in the gap and call him/her out of obscurity into his/her life, in the name of Jesus.

11. I reject the provision of counterfeit by the enemy, in the name of Jesus.

12. I cut off the flow of any inherited marital problem into the life of my children, in the name of Jesus.

13. O Lord, let patience reign in the life of ... *(mention the name of the person)* until the right person comes, in Jesus' name.

14. Father, in the name of Jesus, just as Abraham sent his servant to find his son, Isaac, a wife, send the Holy Spirit to bring my daughter/son, a husband/wife.

15. O Lord, make known to _ _ _ the secrets needed for his marital breakthrough.

16. Help _ _ _ Lord, to discover his real self.

17. Every imagination of the enemy, against the marital life of _ _ _ be rendered impotent, in the name of Jesus.

18. Let _ _ _ refuse to co-operate with any anti-marriage spell and curse, in the name of Jesus.

19. I cancel every bewitchment, fashioned against the settling down of _ _ _ in marriage, in the name of Jesus.

20. Every force, magnetizing the wrong people to _ _ _ be paralysed, in the name of Jesus.

21. I break every covenant of marital failure and late marriage for _ _ _ in the name of Jesus.

22. I cancel every spiritual wedding, conducted consciously or unconsciously on behalf of _ _ _ in Jesus' name.

23. I remove the hand of household wickedness from the marital life of _ _ _, in the name of Jesus.

24. Every incantation, incision, hex and other spiritually harmful activities, working against the marriage of _ _ _ ,be completely neutralized, in the name of Jesus.

25. All forces of evil manipulation, delaying or hindering the marriage

of _ _ _ be completely paralysed, in the name of Jesus.

26. Let all evil anti-marriage covenants in the life of _ _ _ break, in the name of Jesus.

27. O Lord, restore _ _ _ to the perfect way in which You created him if he has been altered.

28. Father, let Your fire destroy every satanic weapon, fashioned against the marriage of _ _ _, in the name of Jesus.

29. I forsake any personal sin that has given ground to the enemy on the marital issue of _ _ _, in the name of Jesus.

30. I reclaim all the ground I have lost to the enemy, concerning the marital life of _ _ _ , in the name of Jesus.

31. Blood of Jesus, speak against every power working against the marriage of _ _ _ .

32. I apply the Blood of Jesus to remove all consequences of evil operations and oppression, in the life of _ _ _, in Jesus' name.

33. I break the binding effect of anything evil, ever put upon _ _ _ from any source, in the name of Jesus.

34. I remove the right of the enemy to afflict the plan of _ _ _ to get married, in the name of Jesus.

35. I break every bondage of inherited marital confusion, in the life of _ _ _, in the name of Jesus.

36. I bind and plunder the goods of every strongman, attached to the marriage of _ _ _, in the name of Jesus.

37. Angels of the living God, roll away the stone blocking the marital

breakthroughs of _ _ _, in Jesus' name.

38. O God arise and let all the enemies of the marital breakthroughs of _ _ _ scatter, in the name of Jesus.

39. Fire of God, melt away the stones hindering the marital blessings of _ _ _, in the mighty name of Jesus.

40. You evil cloud, blocking the sunlight of the marital breakthroughs of _ _ _ disperse, in Jesus' name.

41. All evil spirits, masquerading to trouble the marital life of _ _ _, be bound, in the name of Jesus.

42. O Lord, let wonderful changes be the lot of _ _ _ this year.

43. O Lord, turn away all who would jilt, disappoint or fail _ _ _, in the name of Jesus.

44. Any witchcraft, practised under any water against the life of _ _ _, receive immediate judgment of fire, in the name of Jesus.

45. Every evil altar, under any water where certain evils are done against _ _ _, roast, in the name of Jesus.

46. Every priest, ministering at any evil altar, against _ _ _ inside any water, fall down and die, in the name of Jesus.

47. Any power, under any river or sea, remote-controlling the life of _ _ _, be destroyed by fire and I shake him/her loose from your hold, in the name of Jesus.

48. Any evil monitoring mirror, ever used against _ _ _ under any water, crash to irredeemable pieces, in the name of Jesus.

49. Every marine witchcraft that has introduced spirit husband/wife

or child into the dreams of _ _ _ roast by fire, in Jesus' name.

50. Every agent of marine witchcraft, posing as _ _ 's husband/wife or child, in his/her dreams, roast by fire, in Jesus' name.

51. Every agent of marine witchcraft, physically attached to the marriage of _ _ _ to frustrate it, fall down and perish now, in the name of Jesus.

52. Every agent of marine witchcraft, assigned to attack the finances of _ _ _ through dream, fall down and perish, in the name of Jesus.

53. I pull down every stronghold of bewitchment, enchantment, jinx and divination, fashioned against _ _ _ by marine witches, in Jesus' name.

54. Thunderbolts of God, locate and destroy every marine witchcraft coven where deliberations and decisions were ever fashioned against _ _ _, in the name of Jesus.

55. Any water spirit from my village or the place of my birth, practising witchcraft against _ _ _ , be amputated by the word of God, in Jesus' name.

56. Every spiritual weapon of wickedness, fashioned against _ _ _ under any river or sea, be roasted by the fire of God, in the name of Jesus.

57. Any power of marine witchcraft, holding any blessing of _ _ _ in bondage, receive the fire of God and release it, in Jesus' name.

58. I loose the mind and soul of _ _ _ ,from the bondage of marine witches, in the name of Jesus.

59. Any marine witchcraft chain, binding the hands and feet of _ _ _ from prospering, break and shatter to pieces, in Jesus' name.

60. Every arrow, shot into the life of _ _ _ from under any water through witchcraft, come out and go back to your sender, in the name of Jesus.

61. Any evil material, transferred into the body of _ _ _ through contact with any marine witchcraft agent, roast by fire, in the name of Jesus.

62. Every sexual pollution of marine spirit husband/wife in the body of _ _ _, be flushed out, by the blood of Jesus.

63. Any evil name, given to _ _ _ under any water, I reject and cancel it with the blood of Jesus.

64. Every image, constructed under any water to manipulate _ _ _, be roasted by fire, in the name of Jesus.

65. Any evil, done against _ _ _ so far, through marine witchcraft, oppression and manipulation, be reversed by the blood of Jesus.

66. Spirit husband/spirit wife, release _ _ _ by fire, in Jesus' name.

67. Every spirit wife/ husband, die, in the name of Jesus.

68. Everything you spirit husband/wife has deposited in the life of _ _ _, come out by fire, in Jesus' name.

69. Every power, that is working against the marriage of _ _ _, fall down and die, in the name of Jesus.

70. I divorce and renounce the marriage of _ _ _ with any spirit husband or wife, in the name of Jesus.

71. I break all covenants entered into with the spirit husband or wife, in the name of Jesus.

72. Thou thunder fire of God, burn to ashes, the wedding gown, ring, photographs and all other materials, used for the marriage, in Jesus' name.

73. I send the fire of God to burn the marriage certificate to ashes, in the name of Jesus.

74. I break every blood and soul-tie covenant with the spirit husband or wife, in the name of Jesus.

75. I send the thunder fire of God to burn to ashes the children born to the marriage, in Jesus' name.

76. I withdraw the blood, sperm or any other part of the body of _ _ _, deposited on the altar of the spirit husband or spirit wife, in the name of Jesus.

77. You spirit husband or spirit wife, tormenting the life and earthly marriage of _ _ _, I bind you with hot chains and fetters of God, and cast you out of his/her life into the deep pit and I command you not to ever come into his/her life again, in the name of Jesus.

78. Every property of - - - in your possession in the spirit world, including the dowry and whatsoever was used for the marriage and covenants, be returned, in the name of Jesus.

79. I drain _ _ _, of all evil materials deposited in his/her body, as a result of his sexual relationship, in the name of Jesus.

80. O Lord, send Your Holy Ghost fire into the root of _ _ _, and burn out all unclean things deposited in it by the spirit husband

or spirit wife, in Jesus' name.

81. I break the head of the snake deposited into the body of _ _ _
    by the spirit husband or spirit wife to do him harm and command
    it to come out, in the name of Jesus.

82. Every evil material, deposited in the life of _ _ _, to prevent him
    from having children on earth, be purged out by the blood of
    Jesus.

83. O Lord, repair and restore every damage done to any part of the
    body and earthly marriage of _ _ _, by the spirit husband or
    spirit wife, in the name of Jesus.

84. I reject and cancel every curse, evil pronouncement, spell, jinx,
    enchantment and incantation, placed upon _ _ _ by the spirit
    husband or wife, in the name of Jesus.

85. O Lord, let _ _ _ take back and possess all his earthly belongings
    in the custody of the spirit husband or wife, in Jesus' name.

86. You spirit husband or wife, turn your back on _ _ _ forever, in
    Jesus' name.

87. I renounce and reject the name given to _ _ _ by the spirit
    husband or wife, in the name of Jesus.

88. I hereby declare and confess that the Lord Jesus Christ is the
    Husband of _ _ _ for eternity, in Jesus' name.

89. I soak _ _ _ in the blood of Jesus and cancel the evil mark placed
    on him, in Jesus' name.

90. I set _ _ _ free from the stronghold, domineering power and
    bondage of the spirit husband or spirit wife, in Jesus' name.

91. I paralyse the remote control power and work, used to destabilise the earthly marriage of _ _ _ and to hinder her from bearing children for her earthly husband, in the name of Jesus.

92. I announce to the heavens that _ _ is married forever to Jesus.

93. Every trademark of evil marriage, be shaken out of the life of _ _ _, in Jesus' name.

94. Every evil writing, engraved by iron pen, be wiped off by the blood of Jesus.

95. I bring the blood of Jesus upon the spirit that does not want to let _ _ _ go, in the name of Jesus.

96. I bring the blood of Jesus on every evidence that can be tendered by wicked spirits against _ _ _.

97. I file a counter-report in the heavens against every evil marriage, in the name of Jesus.

98. I refuse to supply any evidence, that the enemy may use against _ _ _, in the name of Jesus.

99. Satanic exhibitions, be destroyed by the blood of Jesus.

100. I declare to you spirit wife / spirit husband that there is no vacancy for you in the life of _ _ _, in the name of Jesus.

101. O Lord, make _ _ _ a vehicle of deliverance.

102. O Lord, water _ _ _ from the waters of God.

103. O Lord, let the unrelenting siege of the enemy be dismantled.

104. O Lord, defend Your interest in the life of _ _ _.

105. Everything written against _ _ _ in the cycle of the moon, be blotted out, in the name of Jesus.

106. Everything programmed into the sun, moon and stars against _ _ _, be dismantled, in Jesus' name.

107. Every evil thing, programmed into the genes of _ _ _, be blotted out by the blood of Jesus.

108. O Lord, shake out seasons of failure and frustrations from the life of _ _ _

109. I overthrow every wicked law, working against the life of _ _ _, in Jesus' name.

110. I ordain a new time, season and profitable law for _ _ _, in the name of Jesus.

111. I speak destruction unto the palaces of the queen of the coast and of the rivers, in Jesus' name.

112. I speak destruction unto the headquarters of the spirit of Egypt and blow up their altars, in the name of Jesus.

113. I speak destruction unto the altars speaking against the purpose of God for the life of _ _ _, in the name of Jesus.

114. I declare _ _ _ a virgin for the Lord, in the name of Jesus.

115. Every evil veil upon the life of _ _ _ be torn open, in Jesus' name.

116. Every wall between _ _ _ and the visitation of God, break, in Jesus' name.

117. You counsel of God, prosper in the life of _ _ _, in Jesus' name.

118. I destroy the power of any demonic seed in the life of _ _ _

from the womb, in the name of Jesus.

119. I speak unto the umbilical gate of _ _ _ to overthrow all negative parental spirits, in the name of Jesus.

120. I break the yoke of the spirits, having access to the reproductive gates of _ _ _, in the name of Jesus.

121. O Lord, let Your time of refreshing come upon _ _ _.

122. I bring fire from the altar of the Lord, upon every evil marriage, in the name of Jesus.

123. I redeem _ _ _from every sex trap by the blood of Jesus, in Jesus' name.

124. I erase the engraving of the name of _ _ _ on any evil marriage record, in the name of Jesus.

125. I confess that Jesus is the original spouse of _ _ _, and is jealous over him.

126. O Lord, bring to the remembrance of _ _ _, every spiritual trap and contract.

127. Blood of Jesus, purge _ _ _, of every contaminated material, in the name of Jesus.

128. O Lord, contend with those who are contending with the marital life of _ _ _

129. O God arise and scatter every enemy of the marriage of _ _ _

130. Begin to thank God, for your deliverance.

DEALING WITH THE EVIL POWERS OF YOUR FATHER'S HOUSE

The evil power of your father's house is one problem you must face squarely. If you want to fulfil your destiny, rise above your root and achieve what your ancestors did not achieve, you must deal with all the attacks that are sponsored by powers of your father's house. You cannot attain the highest level attainable in life, unless you deal with these powers.

You can cut yourself off from every evil link by making use of these prayer points. You can exceed the limits set by the powers of your father's house by binding them with chains and fetters of iron. This is your season of total freedom and unprecedented breakthroughs. With this prayer programme, you will shine like a star in your lineage.

Confessions: Philip. 2:9-11: Wherefore God also hath highly exalted him, and given him a name which is above every name: [10]That at the name of Jesus every knee should bow, of *things* in heaven, and *things* in earth, and *things* under the earth; [11]And *that* every tongue should confess that Jesus Christ *is* Lord, to the glory of God the Father. Psalm 56:9: When I cry *unto thee,* then shall mine enemies turn back: this I know; for God *is* for me.

1. I repent of all ancestral idol worship, in the name of Jesus.

2. Every idol of my father's house, loose your hold over my life, in the name of Jesus.

3. Every strongman of my father's house, die, in the name of Jesus.

4. I silence the evil cry of the evil powers of my father's house, fashioned against me, in the name of Jesus.

5. All consequences of the worship of evil powers of my father's house upon my life, I wipe you off, by the blood of Jesus.

6. Holy Ghost fire, burn down all spiritual shrines of my father's house, in the name of Jesus.

7. Oppressive agenda of the evil powers of my father's house, die, in the name of Jesus.

8. Any blood, speaking against my generational line, be silenced by the blood of Jesus.

9. Every evil power of my father's house, speaking against my destiny, scatter, in the name of Jesus.

10. I break all ancestral covenants with the evil powers of my father's house, in the name of Jesus.

11. Every bitter water, flowing in my family from the evil powers of my father's house, dry up, in the name of Jesus.

12. Any rope, tying my family line to any evil power of my father's house, break, in the name of Jesus.

13. Every landlord spirit, troubling my destiny, be paralysed, in the name of Jesus.

14. Every outflow of satanic family name, die, in the name of Jesus.

15. I recover every benefit, stolen by the evil powers of my father's house, in the name of Jesus.

16. Where is the God of Elijah, arise, disgrace every evil power of my father's house, in the name of Jesus.

17. Every satanic priest, ministering in my family line, be retrenched, in the name of Jesus.

18. Arrows of affliction, originating from idolatry, loose your hold, in the name of Jesus.

19. Every influence of the evil powers of my father's house on my life, die, in the name of Jesus.

20. Every network of the evil powers of my father's house in my place of birth, scatter, in the name of Jesus.

21. Every satanic dedication that speaks against me, be dismantled by the power in the blood of Jesus.

22. I vomit every food with idolatrous influence that I have eaten, in the name of Jesus.

23. Every unconscious evil, internal altar, roast, in the name of Jesus.

24. You stone of hindrance, constructed by the evil powers of my father's house, be rolled away, in the name of Jesus.

25. The voice of foundational powers of my father's house will never speak again, in the name of Jesus.

26. Every strongman, assigned by the evil powers of my father's house against my life, die, in the name of Jesus.

27. Every satanic promissory note, issued on my behalf by my ancestors, catch fire, in the name of Jesus.

28. Garments of opposition, designed by the evil powers of my father's house, roast, in the name of Jesus.

29. Every satanic cloud, upon my life, scatter, in the name of Jesus.

30. My glory, buried by the evil powers of my father's house, come alive by fire, in the name of Jesus.

31. Thou power of strange gods, legislating against my destiny, scatter, in the name of Jesus.

32. Evil powers of my father's house in my place of birth, I break your chain, in the name of Jesus.

33. I fire back every arrow of my family idols, in the name of Jesus.

34. Every evil power from my father's house, die, in Jesus' name.

35. Every evil power from my mother's house, die, in Jesus' name.

36. O God arise and let all stubborn problems die, in Jesus' name.

37. Where is the Lord God of Elijah? Arise and manifest Your power, in the name of Jesus.

38. The voice of my enemy will not prevail over my destiny, in the name of Jesus.

39. Every terror of the night, scatter, in the name of Jesus.

40. Every witchcraft challenge of my destiny, die, in Jesus' name.

41. Every seed of the enemy in my destiny, die, in the name of Jesus.

42. Every dream of demotion, die, in the name of Jesus.

43. Power of God, uproot wicked plantations from my life, in the name of Jesus.

44. Every destiny vulture, vomit my breakthroughs, in Jesus' name.

45. Every evil power that pursued my parents and is now pursuing me, release me, in the name of Jesus.

46. I fire back every witchcraft arrow, fired into my life as a baby, in the name of Jesus.

47. Fire of God, thunder of God, pursue my pursuers, in Jesus' name.

48. Holy Ghost fire, purge my blood of satanic injection, in the name of Jesus.

49. Every evil power of my father's house that will not let me go, die, in the name of Jesus.

50. Every power, designed to spoil my life, scatter, in Jesus' name.

51. Every herbal power, working against my destiny, die, in the name of Jesus.

52. I kill every sickness in my life, in the name of Jesus.

53. Every power of the idols of my father's house, die, in the name of Jesus.

54. Every evil power, pursuing me from my father's house, die, in the name of Jesus.

55. Every evil power, pursuing me from my mother's house, die, in the name of Jesus.

56. Every witchcraft tree, binding my placenta, die, in Jesus' name.

57. Where is the Lord God of Elijah? Arise and fight for me, in the name of Jesus.

58. Every destiny-demoting dream, scatter, in the name of Jesus.

59. Every foundational bondage, break, in the name of Jesus.

60. Every dream, sponsored by witchcraft, die, in the name of Jesus.

61. Every witchcraft vulture, vomit my destiny, in the name of Jesus.

62. Thou power of repeated oppression from the evil powers of my father's house, die, in the name of Jesus.

63. O Lord, let Your power reverse every evil decree issued against me by the evil powers of my father's house, in the name of Jesus.

64. Every handwriting of the evil powers of my father's house contrary to my peace, be wiped off, in the name of Jesus.

65. Every stranger from the evil powers of my father's house in my body, come out and die, in the name of Jesus.

66. Fire of God, burn off every inherited oppression from the evil powers of my father's house, in the name of Jesus.

67. Every serpent of the evil powers of my father's house behind my case, die, in the name of Jesus.

68. Environmental oppression of the evil powers of my father's house, scatter by fire, in the name of Jesus.

69. Every tongue of the evil powers of my father's house, cursing my life, be silenced, in the name of Jesus.

70. My benefits, jump out of the captivity of the evil powers of my father's house and locate me, in the name of Jesus.

71. Every attack against my destiny from the womb, by the evil powers of my father's house, scatter, in the name of Jesus.

72. O voice of God, speak terror into the camp of the evil powers of my father's house, in the name of Jesus.

73. Every cycle of oppression and affliction of the evil powers of my father's house, break, in the name of Jesus.

74. My glory arise and shine above the imaginations of the evil powers of my father's house, in the name of Jesus.

75. Owners of evil load of oppression, carry your load, in Jesus' name.

DEALING WITH THE EVIL POWERS OF YOUR FATHER'S HOUSE 2

The evil power of your father's house is one problem you must face squarely. If you want to fulfil your destiny, rise above your root and achieve what your ancestors have never achieved, you must tackle all the attacks that are sponsored by powers of your father's house. You cannot attain the highest level attainable in life, unless you deal with these powers.

You can cut yourself off from every evil link by making use of these prayer points. You can exceed the limits set by the powers of your father's house by binding them with chains and fetters of iron. This is your season of total freedom and unprecedented breakthroughs. With this prayer programme, you will shine like a star in your lineage.

Confessions

Philip. 2:9-11: Wherefore God also hath highly exalted him,

and given him a name which is above every name: [10]That at the name of Jesus every knee should bow, of *things* in heaven, and *things* in earth, and *things* under the earth; [11]And *that* every tongue should confess that Jesus Christ *is* Lord, to the glory of God the Father.

Psalm 56:9: When I cry *unto thee,* then shall mine enemies turn back: this I know; for God *is* for me.

1. I repent of all ancestral idol worship, in the name of Jesus.

2. Every idol of my father's house, loose your hold over my life, in the name of Jesus.

3. Every strongman of my father's house, die, in the name of Jesus.

4. I silence the evil cry of the evil powers of my father's house, fashioned against me, in the name of Jesus.

5. All consequences of the worship of evil powers of my father's house upon my life, I wipe you off by the blood of Jesus.

6. Holy Ghost fire, burn down all spiritual shrines of my father's house, in the name of Jesus.

7. Oppressive agenda of the evil powers of my father's house, die, in the name of Jesus.

8. Any blood, speaking against my generational line, be silenced by the blood of Jesus.

9. Every evil power of my father's house, speaking against my destiny, scatter, in the name of Jesus.

10. I break all ancestral covenants with the evil powers of my father's house, in the name of Jesus.

11. Every bitter water, flowing in my family from the evil powers of my father's house, dry up, in the name of Jesus.

12. Any rope, tying my family line to any evil power of my father's house, break, in the name of Jesus.

13. Every landlord spirit troubling my destiny, be paralysed, in Jesus' name.

14. Every outflow of satanic family name, die, in the name of Jesus.

15. I recover every benefit, stolen by the evil powers of my father's house, in the name of Jesus.

16. Where is the Lord God of Elijah? Arise, disgrace every evil power of my father's house, in the name of Jesus.

17. Every satanic priest ministering in my family line, be retrenched, in the name of Jesus.

18. Arrows of affliction originating from idolatry, loose your hold, in the name of Jesus.

19. Every influence of the evil powers of my father's house on my life, die, in the name of Jesus.

20. Every network of the evil powers of my father's house in my place of birth, scatter, in the name of Jesus.

21. Every satanic dedication that speaks against me, be dismantled by the power in the blood of Jesus.

22. I vomit every food with idolatrous influence that I have eaten, in the name of Jesus.

23. Every unconscious evil, internal altar, roast, in the name of Jesus.

24. You stone of hindrance, constructed by the evil powers of my father's house, be rolled away, in the name of Jesus.

25. The voice of foundational powers of my father's house will never speak again, in the name of Jesus.

26. Every strongman assigned by the evil powers of my father's house against my life, die, in the name of Jesus.

27. Every satanic promissory note, issued on my behalf by my ancestors, catch fire, in the name of Jesus.

28. Garments of opposition, designed by the evil powers of my father's house, roast, in the name of Jesus.

29. Every satanic cloud upon my life, scatter, in the name of Jesus.

30. My glory, buried by the evil powers of my father's house, come alive by fire, in the name of Jesus.

31. Thou power of strange gods legislating against my destiny, scatter, in the name of Jesus.

32. Evil powers of my father's house in my place of birth, I break your chain, in the name of Jesus.

33. I fire back every arrow of my family idols, in the name of Jesus.

34. Every doorway and ladder to satanic invasion in my life, be abolished forever, by the Blood of Jesus.

35. I loose myself from curses, hexes, spells, bewitchments and evil domination directed at me, through dreams, in the name of Jesus.

36. You ungodly powers, release me by fire, in the name of Jesus.

37. All past satanic defeats in the dream, be converted to victory, in the name of Jesus.

38. All tests in the dream, be converted to testimonies, in Jesus' name.

39. All trials in the dream, be converted to triumphs, in Jesus' name.

40. All failures in the dream, be converted to success, in Jesus' name.

41. All scars in the dream, be converted to stars, in Jesus' name.

42. All bondage in the dream, be converted to freedom, in Jesus' name.

43. All losses in the dream, be converted to gains, in Jesus' name.

44. All oppositions in the dream, be converted to victory, in Jesus' name.

45. All weaknesses in the dream, be converted to strength, in Jesus' name.

46. All negative situations in the dream, be converted to positive situations, in Jesus' name.

47. I release myself from every infirmity, introduced into my life through dreams, in the name of Jesus.

48. All attempts by the enemy to deceive me through dreams, fail woefully, in the name of Jesus.

49. I reject evil spiritual husband, wife, children, marriage, engagement, trade, pursuit, ornament, money, friend, relative, etc., in the name of Jesus.

50. Lord Jesus, wash my spiritual eyes, ears and mouth, with Your blood.

51. The God who answereth by fire; answer by fire whenever any spiritual attacker comes against me.

52. Lord Jesus, replace all satanic dreams with heavenly visions and divinely-inspired dreams.

53. Wonderful Lord, I reverse any defeat that I have ever suffered in the dream, in the name of Jesus.

54. Any dream that I have dreamt that is good and from God, I receive it; and those that are satanic, I reject them, in the name of Jesus.

55. Every night dream attacks and their consequences, be nullified, in Jesus' name.

56. I claim freedom from satanic and restless dreams, in Jesus' name.

57. I claim freedom from importing anxiety and shameful thoughts, into my dream, in Jesus' name.

58. I stand against every dream of defeat and its effect, in the name of Jesus.

59. All satanic designs of oppression against me in dreams and visions, be frustrated, in the name of Jesus.

60. Every demonic influence, targeted at destroying my vision, dream and ministry, receive total disappointment, in the name of Jesus.

61. Every witchcraft hand, planting evil seeds in my life through dream attacks, wither and burn to ashes, in Jesus' name.

62. By the blood of Jesus, I rebuke every frightening dream, in the name of Jesus.

63. O Lord, let the evil vision and dream about my life evaporate in the camp of the enemy, in the name of Jesus.

64. Every curse of demotion in the dream, in my life, be nullified by the blood of Jesus.

65. Every curse of confused and unprogressive dreams, in my life, be nullified by the blood of Jesus.

66. Every curse of harassment in the dreams by familiar faces, be nullified by the blood of Jesus.

67. I send the bullets of any gun shot in the dream back to sender, in the name of Jesus.

68. I paralyse all the night caterers and I forbid their food in my dreams, in the name of Jesus.

69. All pursuers in my dreams, begin to pursue yourselves, in Jesus' name.

70. All the contaminations in my life, through dreams, be cleansed by the blood of Jesus.

71. I cancel every dream of backwardness, in the name of Jesus.

72. Every dream of demotion to junior school, be dismantled. I shall go from glory to glory, in the name of Jesus.

73. By the power in the blood of Jesus, I cancel the maturity dates of all evil dreams on my life.

74. You God of promotion, promote me beyond my wildest dreams, in the name of Jesus.

75. Every sickness, planted into my life in the dream, get out now and go back to your sender, in the name of Jesus.

76. O Lord, let life be squeezed out of my dream attackers, in Jesus' name.

77. By the power in the blood of Jesus, all my buried good dreams and visions, come alive.

78. By the power in the blood of Jesus, all my polluted good dreams and visions, receive divine solution.

79. By the power in the blood of Jesus, all dream and vision killers, that are working against the manifestation of my good dreams and visions, be paralysed.

80. By the power in the blood of Jesus, every good dream and vision, that has been stolen away, be restored with fresh fire.

81. By the power in the blood of Jesus, every good dream and vision, that has been transferred, be restored with fresh fire.

82. By the power in the blood of Jesus, every good dream and vision, that has been poisoned, be neutralised.

83. By the power in the blood of Jesus, every good dream and vision, that has been amputated, receive divine strength.

84. All the contaminations in my life, through dreams, be cleansed by the blood of Jesus.

85. Any anti-progress arrow, fired into my life through dreams, be nullified, in the name of Jesus.

86. I resist the threat of death in my dreams by fire, in Jesus' name.

87. Every evil dream, that other people have had about me, I cancel it in the astral world, in the name of Jesus.

88. Every image of satan in my dream, I curse you, catch fire now, in the name of Jesus.

89. Every dream of demotion, backfire, in Jesus' name.

90. Every arrow of death in the dream, come out and go back to your sender, in the name of Jesus.

91. Every sponsored dream of poverty, by household wickedness, vanish, in the name of Jesus.

92. I dash every poverty dream to the ground, in the name of Jesus.

93. I cancel the manipulation of every satanic dream, in the name of Jesus.

94. You powers of the night, polluting my night dreams, be paralysed, in the name of Jesus.

95. Every anti-prosperity dream, die, in the mighty name of Jesus.

96. All satanic designs of oppression against me in dreams and visions, be frustrated, in Jesus' name.

97. I paralyse the spirits who bring bad dreams to me, in the name of Jesus.

98. I cancel and wipe off all evil dreams, in the name of Jesus.

99. Blood of Jesus, erase all evil dreams in my life, in the name of Jesus.

100. My dreams, my joys and my breakthroughs, that have been buried in the dark world, come alive and locate me now, in Jesus' name.

101. Every dream serpent, go back to your sender, in Jesus' name.

102. Every power, planting affliction into my life in the dream, be buried alive, in the name of Jesus.

103. Any evil programme, positioned into my life from my dream, be dismantled now, in the name of Jesus.

104. I fire back every arrow of my family idols, in the name of Jesus.

105. Every evil power from my father's house, die, in the name of Jesus.

106. Every evil power from my mother's house, die, in the name of Jesus.

107. O God arise and let stubborn problems die, in the name of Jesus.

108. Every cycle of hardship, break, in the name of Jesus.

109. Where is the Lord God of Elijah? Arise and manifest Your power, in the name of Jesus.

110. I decree that the voice of my enemy will not prevail over my destiny, in the name of Jesus.

111. Every terror of the night, scatter, in the name of Jesus.

112. Every witchcraft challenge of my destiny, die, in Jesus' name.

113. Every seed of the enemy in my destiny, die, in the name of Jesus.

114. Every dream of demotion, die, in the name of Jesus.

115. Power of God, uproot wicked plantations from my life, in Jesus' name.

116. Every destiny vulture, vomit my breakthroughs, in Jesus' name.

117. Every evil power, that pursued my parents and is now pursuing me, release me, in the name of Jesus.

118. I fire back every witchcraft arrow, fired into my life as a baby, in the name of Jesus.

119. Fire of God, thunder of God, pursue my pursuers, in the name of Jesus.

120. Holy Ghost fire, purge my blood of satanic injection, in the name of Jesus.

121. Every evil power of my father's house, that will not let me go, die, in the name of Jesus.

122. Every power, designed to spoil my life, scatter, in the name of Jesus.

123. Every herbal power, working against my destiny, die, in the name of Jesus.

124. I kill every sickness in my life, in the name of Jesus.

125. Every power of the idols of my father's house, die, in the name of Jesus.

126. Every evil power, pursuing me from my father's house, die, in the name of Jesus.

127. Every evil power, pursuing me from my mother's house, die, in the name of Jesus.

128. Every witchcraft tree, sitting on my placenta, die, in the name of Jesus.

129. Where is the Lord God of Elijah. Arise and fight for me, in the name of Jesus.

130. Every destiny-demoting dream, scatter, in the name of Jesus.

131. Every foundational bondage, break, in the name of Jesus.

132. Every dream, sponsored by witchcraft, die, in the name of Jesus.

133. Every witchcraft vulture, vomit my destiny, in the name of Jesus.

DEALING WITH THE STRONGMAN

Who is a strongman?

☞ The controller over a group of evil spirits

☞ The ruling spirit over a group of evil spirits.

☞ The power source and the dominating influence in a particular situation

☞ The principal demon or leading demon

☞ He is the dominant demon

☞ He is the head demon

☞ The prison warden of the devil

☞ The main root or the power energizing an

activity

☞ Commanding general of evil army

☞ Spiritual Sergent major calling evil commands

These prayers are needed when you notice the following

1. Little or no progress in spite of hard efforts

2. Chain problems

3. Prayer resistance

4. Unpardonable errors

5. Demons overcoming the person with ease

6. Nothing going smoothly

7. Planting much but reaping little

8. The whole of life becomes a struggle

9. Profitless hardwork

10. Problems remain the same after deliverance ministrations

11. Labour so much but achieve nothing

12. Devourers working against you

13. Acidic poverty

14. Prayers become ordinary noise

Praise worship

Scriptures

Jeremiah 7:18: The children gather wood, and the fathers kindle the fire, and the women knead *their* dough, to make cakes to the queen of heaven, and to pour out drink offerings unto other gods, that they may provoke me to anger.

Jeremiah 44:17-19: But we will certainly do whatsoever thing goeth forth out of our own mouth, to burn incense unto the queen of heaven, and to pour out drink offerings unto her, as we have done, we, and our fathers, our kings, and our princes, in the cities of Judah, and in the streets of Jerusalem: for *then* had we plenty of victuals, and were well, and saw no evil. [18]But since we left off to burn incense to the queen of heaven, and to pour out drink offerings unto her, we have wanted all *things,* and have been consumed by the sword and by the famine. [19]And when we burned incense to the queen of heaven, and poured out drink offerings unto her, did we make her cakes to worship her, and pour out drink offerings unto her, without our men?

Jeremiah 44:25: Thus saith the LORD of hosts, the God of Israel, saying; Ye and your wives have both spoken with your mouths, and fulfilled with your hand, saying, We will surely perform our vows that we have vowed, to burn incense to the queen of heaven, and to pour out drink offerings unto her: ye will surely accomplish your vows, and surely perform your vows.

Isaiah 49:24-25: Shall the prey be taken from the mighty, or the lawful captive delivered? [25]But thus saith the LORD, Even the captives of the mighty shall be taken away, and the prey of the terrible shall be delivered: for I will contend with him that contendeth with thee, and I will save thy children.

Psalm 124:7: Our soul is escaped as a bird out of the snare of the fowlers: the snare is broken, and we are escaped.

Psalm 56:9: When I cry *unto thee,* then shall mine enemies turn back: this I know; for God *is* for me.

Psalm 91:13: Thou shalt tread upon the lion and adder: the young lion and the dragon shalt thou trample under feet.

Psalm 18:37-40: I have pursued mine enemies, and overtaken them: neither did I turn again till they were consumed. [38]I have wounded them that they were not able to rise: they are fallen under my feet. [39]For thou hast girded me with strength unto the battle: thou hast subdued under me those that rose up against me. [40]Thou hast also given me the necks of mine enemies; that I might destroy them that hate me.

Psalm 35:4-6: Let them be confounded and put to shame that seek after my soul: let them be turned back and brought to confusion that devise my hurt. [5]Let them be as chaff before the wind: and let the angel of the LORD chase *them*. [6]Let their way be dark and slippery: and let the angel of the LORD persecute them.

Psalm 11:6-7: Upon the wicked he shall rain snares, fire and brimstone, and an horrible tempest: *this shall be* the portion of their cup. [7]For the righteous LORD loveth righteousness; his countenance doth behold the upright.

Psalm 129:4: The LORD *is* righteous: he hath cut asunder the cords of the wicked.

Psalm 6:8-10: Depart from me, all ye workers of iniquity; for the LORD hath heard the voice of my weeping. [9]The LORD hath heard my supplication; the LORD will receive my prayer. [10]Let all mine enemies be ashamed and sore vexed: let them return *and* be ashamed suddenly.

Psalm 140:9-10: *As for* the head of those that compass

me about, let the mischief of their own lips cover them.
[10]Let burning coals fall upon them: let them be cast into
the fire; into deep pits, that they rise not up again.

Psalm 58:6-7: Break their teeth, O God, in their mouth:
break out the great teeth of the young lions, O LORD. [7]Let
them melt away as waters *which* run continually: *when* he
bendeth *his bow to shoot* his arrows, let them be as cut in
pieces.

Psalm 118:7: The LORD taketh my part with them that help
me: therefore shall I see *my desire* upon them that hate
me.

Psalm 118:12: They compassed me about like bees; they
are quenched as the fire of thorns: for in the name of the
LORD I will destroy them.

Psalm 31:17-18: Let me not be ashamed, O LORD; for I
have called upon thee: let the wicked be ashamed, *and* let
them be silent in the grave. [18]Let the lying lips be put to
silence; which speak grievous things proudly and
contemptuously against the righteous.

Psalm 92:9-11: For, lo, thine enemies, O LORD, for, lo,
thine enemies shall perish; all the workers of iniquity shall
be scattered. [10]But my horn shalt thou exalt like *the horn
of* an unicorn: I shall be anointed with fresh oil. [11]Mine eye

also shall see *my desire* on mine enemies, *and* mine ears shall hear *my desire* of the wicked that rise up against me.

Matthew 4:10: Then saith Jesus unto him, Get thee hence, Satan: for it is written, Thou shalt worship the Lord thy God, and him only shalt thou serve.

Matthew 28:18: And Jesus came and spake unto them, saying, All power is given unto me in heaven and in earth.

Luke 10:19: Behold, I give unto you power to tread on serpents and scorpions, and over all the power of the enemy: and nothing shall by any means hurt you.

Luke 11:21-22: When a strong man armed keepeth his palace, his goods are in peace: [22]But when a stronger than he shall come upon him, and overcome him, he taketh from him all his armour wherein he trusted, and divideth his spoils.

John 12:31: Now is the judgment of this world: now shall the prince of this world be cast out.

John 16:11: Of judgment, because the prince of this world is judged.

Romans 16:20: And the God of peace shall bruise Satan under your feet shortly. The grace of our Lord Jesus Christ *be* with you. Amen.

2 Cor. 10:3-5: For though we walk in the flesh, we do not

war after the flesh: [4](For the weapons of our warfare *are* not carnal, but mighty through God to the pulling down of strong holds;) [5]Casting down imaginations, and every high thing that exalteth itself against the knowledge of God, and bringing into captivity every thought to the obedience of Christ;

Col. 2:15: *And* having spoiled principalities and powers, he made a shew of them openly, triumphing over them in it.

Hebrews 2:14-15: Forasmuch then as the children are partakers of flesh and blood, he also himself likewise took part of the same; that through death he might destroy him that had the power of death, that is, the devil; [15]And deliver them who through fear of death were all their lifetime subject to bondage.

James 4:7: Submit yourselves therefore to God. Resist the devil, and he will flee from you.

1 John 3:8: He that committeth sin is of the devil; for the devil sinneth from the beginning. For this purpose the Son of God was manifested, that he might destroy the works of the devil.

1 John 4:4: Ye are of God, little children, and have overcome them: because greater is he that is in you, than he that is in the world.

Rev. 12:11: And they overcame him by the blood of the Lamb, and by the word of their testimony; and they loved not their lives unto the death.

Rev. 20:10: And the devil that deceived them was cast into the lake of fire and brimstone, where the beast and the false prophet *are,* and shall be tormented day and night for ever and ever.

Matthew 25:41: Then shall he say also unto them on the left hand, Depart from me, ye cursed, into everlasting fire, prepared for the devil and his angels:

1. I consume the shrine of the strongman in my family with the fire of God, in the name of Jesus.

2. Let stones of fire pursue and dominate all the strongmen in my life, in the name of Jesus.

3. I smash the head of the strongman on the wall of fire, in Jesus' name.

4. I cause open disgrace to all strongmen in my family, in Jesus' name.

5. The strongman from my father's side; the strongman from my mother's side, begin to destroy yourselves in the name of Jesus.

6. I bind and I render to nothing all the strongmen that are currently troubling my life, in the name of Jesus.

7. You strongman of body destruction, loose your hold over my body, fall down and die, in the name of Jesus.

8. Every demon, strongman and associated spirits of financial collapse, receive the hailstones of fire and be roasted beyond remedy, in Jesus' name.

9. Let the finger of God unseat my household strongman, in the name of Jesus.

10. I bind you the strongman in my life and I clear my goods from your possession, in the name of Jesus.

11. You strongman of mind destruction, be bound, in Jesus' name.

12. You strongman of financial destruction, be bound, in Jesus' name.

13. Every strongman of bad luck, attached to my life, fall down and die, in Jesus' name.

14. I bind every strongman, militating against my home, in the name of Jesus.

15. I bind and paralyse every strongman of death and hell, in the name of Jesus.

16. You evil strongman, attached to my destiny, be bound, in Jesus' name.

17. Every strongman of my father's house, die, in the name of Jesus.

18. Every strongman, assigned by the evil powers of my father's house against my life, die, in the name of Jesus.

19. Every strongman, assigned to weaken my faith, catch fire, in the name of Jesus.

20. I bind and I render to nought, all the strongmen that are currently troubling my life, in the name of Jesus.

21. Let the backbone of the stubborn pursuer and strongman break, in the name of Jesus.

22. I bind every strongman, having my goods in his possessions, in the name of Jesus.

23. I clear my goods from the warehouse of the strongman, in the name of Jesus.

24. I withdraw the staff of the office of the strongman delegated against me, in the name of Jesus.

25. I bind every strongman, delegated to hinder my progress, in the name of Jesus.

26. I bind the strongman behind my spiritual blindness and deafness, and paralyse his operations in my life, in the name of Jesus.

27. Let the stubborn strongman delegated against me fall down to the ground and become impotent, in Jesus' name.

28. I bind the strongman over myself, in the name of Jesus.

29. I bind the strongman over my family, in the name of Jesus.

30. I bind the strongman over my blessings, in the name of Jesus.

31. I bind the strongman over my business, in the name of Jesus.

32. I command the armour of the strongman to be roasted completely, in the name of Jesus.

33. I release myself from the hold of any religious spiritual strongman, in the name of Jesus

34. I release myself from the hold of any evil strongman, in the name of Jesus.

35. I bind and plunder the goods of every strongman, attached to my marriage, in the name of Jesus.

36. I release my money from the house of the strongman, in the name of Jesus.

37. Let the backbone of the strongman in charge of each problem be broken, in the name of Jesus.

38. Any satanic strongman, keeping my blessings as his goods fall down and die, I recover my goods now.

39. Every jinx upon my _ _ _, be broken, in the name of Jesus.

40. Every spell upon my _ _ _, be broken, in the name of Jesus.

41. Let the rod of the wrath of the Lord come upon every enemy of my _ _ _, in the name of Jesus.

42. Let the angels of God invade them and lead them into darkness, in the name of Jesus.

43. Let the hand of the Lord turn against them day by day, in the name of Jesus.

44. Let their flesh and skin become old, and let their bones be broken, in the name of Jesus.

45. Let them be compassed with gall and travail, in the name of Jesus.

46. Let Your angels hedge them about and block their paths, in the name of Jesus.

47. O Lord, make their chains heavy.

48. When they cry, shut out their cries, in the name of Jesus.

49. O Lord, make their paths crooked.

50. O Lord, make their ways to be strewn with sharp stones.

51. Let the power of their own wickedness fall upon them, in the name of Jesus.

52. O Lord, turn them aside and cut them into pieces.

53. O Lord, make their ways desolate.

54. O Lord, fill them with bitterness and let them be drunken with wormwood.

55. O Lord, break their teeth with gravel stones.

56. O Lord, cover them with ashes.

57. O Lord, remove their souls far from peace and let them forget prosperity.

58. I crush under my feet, all the evil powers trying to imprison me, in the name of Jesus.

59. Let their mouth be put in the dust, in the name of Jesus.

60. Let there be civil war in the camp of the enemies of my _ _ _, in the name of Jesus.

61. Le the power of God pull down the stronghold of the enemies of my _ _ _, in the name of Jesus.

62. O Lord, persecute them and destroy them in anger, in the name of Jesus.

63. Let every blockage in my way of _ _ _ clear off by fire, in the name of Jesus.

64. Every demonic claim of the earth over my life, be dismantled, in the name of Jesus.

65. I refuse to be chained to my place of birth, in Jesus' name.

66. Any power pressing the sand against me, fall down and die, in the name of Jesus.

67. I receive my breakthroughs, in the name of Jesus.

68. I release my money from the house of the strongman, in the name of Jesus.

69. Let the blood of Jesus and the fire of the Holy Ghost cleanse every organ in my body, in the name of Jesus.

70. I break and loose myself from every inherited evil covenant of the earth, in the name of Jesus.

71. I break and loose myself from every inherited evil curse of the earth, in the name of Jesus.

72. I break and loose myself from every form of demonic bewitchment of the earth, in the name of Jesus.

73. I release myself from every evil domination and control from the earth, in the name of Jesus.

74. Let the blood of Jesus be transfused into my blood vessel.

75. I release panic upon my full time enemies, in the name of Jesus.

76. Let stubborn confusion come upon the headquarters of my enemies, in the name of Jesus.

77. I loose confusion upon the plans of my enemies, in the name of Jesus.

78. Every stronghold of darkness, receive acidic confusion, in the name of Jesus.

79. I loose panic and frustration on satanic orders issued against me, in the name of Jesus.

80. Every evil plan against my life, receive confusion, in the name of Jesus.

81. All curses and demons programmed against me, I neutralise you through the blood of Jesus.

82. Every warfare prepared against my peace, I command panic upon you, in the name of Jesus.

83. Every warfare prepared against my peace, I command havoc upon you, in the name of Jesus.

84. Every warfare prepared against my peace, I command chaos upon you, in the name of Jesus.

85. Every warfare prepared against my peace, I command pandemonium upon you, in the name of Jesus.

86. Every warfare prepared against my peace, I command disaster upon you, in the name of Jesus.

87. Every warfare prepared against my peace, I command confusion upon you, in the name of Jesus.

88. Every warfare prepared against my peace, I command spiritual acid upon you, in the name of Jesus.

89. Every warfare prepared against my peace, I command destruction upon you, in the name of Jesus.

90. Every warfare prepared against my peace, I command hornets of the Lord upon you, in Jesus' name.

91. Every warfare prepared against my peace, I command brimstone and hailstone upon you, in the name of Jesus.

92. I frustrate every satanic verdict issued against me, in Jesus' name.

93. Let the finger, vengeance, terror, anger, fear, wrath, hatred and burning judgment of God be released against my full time enemies, in the name of Jesus.

94. Every power, preventing the perfect will of God from being done in my life, receive failure and defeat, in the name of Jesus.

95. Let the warring angels and Spirit of God arise and scatter every evil gathering sponsored against me, in the name of Jesus.

96. I disobey any satanic order, programmed by inheritance into my life, in the name of Jesus.

97. I bind and cast out every power causing internal warfare, in the name of Jesus.

98. Every demonic doorkeeper, locking out good things from me, be paralysed by fire, in the name of Jesus.

99. I command every evil power fighting against me to fight against and destroy one another, in Jesus' name.

100. Every breakthrough hindering, delaying, preventing, destroying and breaking demons, receive confusion, in the name of Jesus.

101. Let divine power and control attack the spirits of violence and torture, in the name of Jesus.

102. Let the spirit of witchcraft attack familiar spirits fashioned against me, in the name of Jesus.

103. Let there be a civil war in the kingdom of darkness, in the name of Jesus.

104. Lord, loose judgment and destruction upon all stubborn, disobedient and reluctant spirits that fail to follow my commands promptly.

RECEIVE YOUR DELIVERANCE

The devil is a technical game player who ensures that batons are passed from one hand to another to make problems persistent. His intention and plan are to make the end of a problem the beginning of another. By so doing, he uses some of the weapons of repeated problems to weary his victims. Thank God for spiritual warfare. There is a type of prayer to pray when problems are repeated, time and again. These prayer points will prevent the repetition of problems that are sponsored by the devil.

These prayer points will enable you to deal with repeated problems. They will break the covenants strengthening the problems and destroy the spirits behind them. You must delete your name from the list of candidates for repeated problems.

CONFESSIONS - Galatians 3:13-14 : Christ hath redeemed us from the curse of the law, being made a curse for us: for it is written, Cursed is every one that hangeth on a tree: That the blessing of Abraham might come on the Gentiles through Jesus Christ; that we might receive the promise of the Spirit through faith.

2 Tim. 4:18: And the Lord shall deliver me from every evil work, and will preserve me unto his heavenly kingdom: to whom be glory for ever and ever. Amen.

Col. 1:13: Who hath delivered us from the power of darkness, and hath translated us into the kingdom of his dear Son:

Col. 2:15: And having spoiled principalities and powers, he made a shew of them openly, triumphing over them in it.

Praise worship

1. Thank God for His mighty power to save to the uttermost, for His power to deliver from any form of bondage.

2. Confess your sins and those of your ancestors, especially those sins linked to evil powers and idolatry.

3. I cover myself with the blood of Jesus.

4. O Lord, send Your axe of fire to the foundation of my life and destroy every evil plantation therein.

5. Let the blood of Jesus flush out of my system every inherited satanic deposit, in the name of Jesus.

6. I release myself from the grip of any problem transferred into my life from the womb, in the name of Jesus.

7. I break and loose myself from every inherited evil covenant, in the name of Jesus.

8. I break and loose myself from every inherited evil curse, in Jesus' name.

9. I command all foundational strongmen attached to my life to be paralysed, in the name of Jesus.

10. I cancel the consequences of any evil local name attached to my person, in the name of Jesus.

11. I break and loose myself from every form of demonic bewitchment, in the name of Jesus.

12. Let the blood of Jesus be transfused into my blood vessel.

13. Lord Jesus, walk back into every second of my life; deliver me where I need deliverance, heal me where I need healing and transform me where I need transformation.

14. Let the blood of Jesus remove any unprogressive label from every aspect of my life.

15. O Lord, renew a right spirit within me.

16. O Lord, ignite my calling with Your fire.

17. O Lord, establish me a holy person unto You.

18. O Lord, let the anointing to excel in my spiritual and physical life fall on me.

19. O Lord, let the anointing of the Holy Spirit break every yoke of backwardness in my life.

20. Holy Ghost fire, ignite me to the glory of God.

21. I take back all the grounds given to satan by my ancestors, in the name of Jesus.

22. Let everything that has been transferred into my life by demonic laying on of hands loose its hold right now, in the name of Jesus.

23. Let fire fall on every spirit of death and hell, fashioned against my life, in the name of Jesus.

24. Let the spiritual bat and spiritual lizard, that have been introduced into my head receive the fire of God, in the name of Jesus.

25. Father Lord, reveal to me any hidden covenant that the devil might have arranged against me, in the name of Jesus.

26. Every tree that the Father did not plant in my life, be uprooted, in the name of Jesus.

27. Let every hidden evil covenant break, in Jesus' name.

28. I apply the blood of Jesus to break all consequences of parental sins.

29. O Lord, turn all the evil directed at me to good.

30. O God, make everything the enemy has said is impossible in my life possible, in the name of Jesus.

31. I release myself from any inherited bondage, in Jesus' name.

32. Let the blood of Jesus flush out of my system every inherited satanic deposit, in the name of Jesus.

33. Let the blood of Jesus and the fire of the Holy Ghost cleanse every organ in my body, in the name of Jesus.

34. I break and loose myself from every collective curse, in Jesus' name.

35. I command all foundational strongmen, attached to my life to be paralysed, in the name of Jesus.

36. I cancel the consequences of any evil local name, attached to my person, in the name of Jesus.

37. Pray aggressively against the following roots of collective captivity. Pray as follows: Every effect of . . . (*pick from the under listed one by one*) upon my life, come out with all your roots, in the name of Jesus.

   - Evil physical design   - Evil dedication

   - Parental curses   - Demonic marriage

   - Envious rivalry   - Demonic sacrifice

   - Demonic incisions   - Inherited infirmity

- Dream pollution   - Evil laying on of hands

- Demonic initiations   - Wrong exposure to sex

- Demonic blood transfusion- Exposure to evil diviners

- Demonic alteration of destiny

- Fellowship with local idols - Fellowship with family idols

- Fellowship with demonic consultants

- Unscriptural manner of conception

- Destructive effect of polygamy

38. I refuse to drink from the fountain of sorrow, in Jesus' name.

39. Ask God to remove any curse He has placed on your life as a result of disobedience.

40. Let all curses issued against me be converted to blessings, in the name of Jesus.

41. You will now place blessings on yourself by saying, "There shall be no more poverty, sickness, etc in my life, in Jesus' name."

42. I vomit every satanic poison that I have swallowed, in Jesus' name.

43. I cancel every demonic dedication, in the name of Jesus. Be repeating, "I cancel you, in the name of Jesus."

44. (Place your two hands on your head.) I break every evil authority over my life, in the name of Jesus. Be repeating, "I break you, in the name of Jesus."

45. Mention the underlisted with authority and say, "Break, in the name of Jesus." Repeat, seven hot times.

   - Every evil authority of family shrine or idol

   - Every evil authority of witchcraft and family spirits

   - Every evil authority of remote control powers

   - Every evil authority of the strong man

46. Every owner of evil loads, carry your load, in the name of Jesus. (If it is sickness or bad luck, let them carry it.)

47. Every doorway and ladder to satanic invasion in my life be abolished forever by the Blood of Jesus.

48. I loose myself from curses, hexes, spells, bewitchments and evil domination, directed against me through dreams in Jesus' name.

49. I command you ungodly powers, release me in the name of Jesus.

50. Let all past satanic defeats in the dream be converted to victory in the name of Jesus.

51. Let all tests in the dream be converted to testimonies, in Jesus' name.

52. Let all trials in the dream be converted to triumphs, in Jesus' name.

53. Let all failures in the dream be converted to success, in Jesus' name.

54. Let all scars in the dream be converted to stars, in Jesus' name.

55. Let all bondage in the dream be converted to freedom, in Jesus' name.

56. Let all losses in the dream be converted to gains, in Jesus' name.

57. Let all oppositions in the dream be converted to victory, in Jesus' name.

58. Let all weaknesses in the dream be converted to strength, in Jesus' name.

59. Let all negative in the dream be converted to positive, in Jesus' name.

60. I release myself from every infirmity, introduced into my life through dreams in the name of Jesus.

PRAYERS TO RE-FIRE AND NOT RETIRE

Conception is the work of God. Every expectant mother or couple will do well to carry out this all-important prayer programme.

When you pray for the miracle of supernatural conception, you are placing your trust in the unfailing power of God, while you are waging war against every power that has decreed that your conception will be an aborted dream. This prayer programme will make conception possible, as well as safeguard your pregnancy. It is a spiritual insurance for the fruit of the womb. You must take the prayer points by faith, while making sure that spiritual aggression is added to it to make God's plan for becoming a joyful mother a glorious reality. Whether you are in an environment where medical facilities are poor or you are being attended to in an environment where there are state-of-the art medical facilities, you need this prayer programme. Use these prayer points and your testimony will gladden your heart.

CONFESSIONS: John 5:21: For as the Father raiseth up the dead, and quickeneth them; even so the Son quickeneth whom he will.

John 6:63: It is the spirit that quickeneth; the flesh profiteth nothing: the words that I speak unto you, they are spirit, and they are life.

Romans 4:17: (As it is written, I have made thee a father of many nations,) before him whom he believed, even God, who quickeneth the dead, and calleth those things which be not as though they were.

John 11:25: Jesus said unto her, I am the resurrection, and the life: he that believeth in me, though he were dead, yet shall he live:

John 1:1-5: In the beginning was the Word, and the Word was with God, and the Word was God. The same was in the beginning with God. All things were made by him; and without him was not any thing made that was made. In him was life; and the life was the light of men. And the light shineth in darkness; and the darkness comprehended it not.

Genesis 1:1-3: In the beginning God created the heaven and the earth. And the earth was without form, and void;

> and darkness was upon the face of the deep. And the Spirit of God moved upon the face of the waters. And God said, Let there be light: and there was light.

Praise Worship

1. Thou faith-weakening powers, loose your hold, in the name of Jesus.

2. I refuse to become weak in the days of adversity, in the name of Jesus.

3. Thou powers assigned to weaken my faith, die, in the name of Jesus.

4. I reject and resist anything that would weaken my faith, in Jesus' name.

5. Let my faith be barricaded by the fire of God, in the name of Jesus.

6. Every strongman assigned to weaken my faith, catch fire, in Jesus' name.

7. Every anti-miracle power, clear away, in the name of Jesus.

8. I reject every opinion that weakens my faith or discourages, in the name of Jesus.

9. I reject every man's negative opinion concerning my child-bearing, in the name of Jesus.

10. Increasing age will not weaken my faith, in the name of Jesus.

11. I shall believe the report of the Lord, in the name of Jesus.

12. Impatience will not demote my faith, in the name of Jesus.

13. I reject every spirit of frustration, in the name of Jesus.

14. Medical reports will not weaken my faith, in the name of Jesus.

15. I reject every negative medical report, in the name of Jesus.

16. I reject every report of _ _ _ (pick from the underlisted), in the name of Jesus.

- abnormal ovaries   - absence of ovaries   - hormonal imbalance

- absence of ovulation   - bilateral blockage of fallopian tubes

- abnormal womb (uterus)

- surgical removal of the womb

- congenital absence of the womb

- previous occurrence of a miscarriage

- tumour such as uterine fibroid

  - low sperm count (oligospermia)

- absence of sperm (azoospermia)

- surgical removal or congenital absence of testis

- undescended testis or abnormal testis

17. O God arise and overrule every negative report by Your divine supernatural verdict, in the name of Jesus.

18. I cancel every spiritual or physical verdict contrary to the promises of God for my life, in the name of Jesus.

19. O God, arise and transform my sperm to the ones that will supernaturally achieve a successful conception, in the name of Jesus.

20. O God, arise and transform my sperm count to a supernatural sperm count that will divinely achieve a successful conception, in Jesus' name.

21. O God, arise and replace every abnormal sperm with a normal sperm, in the name of Jesus.

22. O God, arise and replace every non-motile sperm with a motile sperm, in the name of Jesus.

23. O God, arise and replace every sluggish sperm with an active supernaturally energised sperm, in the name of Jesus.

24. O God, arise and replace every dead sperm with a living sperm, in the name of Jesus.

25. Every strongman assigned to give me low sperm count be dismantled, in the name of Jesus.

26. Every power that is responsible for low sperm count, die, in the name of Jesus.

27. I command my semen stolen by the powers of darkness to be restored to me seven-fold, in the name of Jesus.

28. I refuse to consider the deadness of the womb of my wife, in the name of Jesus.

29. I reject every deadness of the womb of my wife, in the name of Jesus.

30. I hereby command the womb of my wife to be converted from a functionally dead womb to a functionally reproductive womb, in the name of Jesus.

31. I refuse to consider the negative medical report of infertile womb, in the name of Jesus.

32. I reject and cancel every negative medical report of infertile womb, in the name of Jesus.

33. O Lord, let the negative medical report of infertile womb be converted to God's own supernatural report of fertile womb, in the name of Jesus.

34. I command my hormones to be balanced, in the name of Jesus.

35. I refuse to consider the negative medical report of lack of ovulation, in the name of Jesus.

36. I bind the spirit of lack of ovulation, in the name of Jesus.

37. I command my ovaries to be ovulating normally, in the name of Jesus.

38. I command my normal ovulation to be restored, in the name of Jesus.

39. I command my ovaries to respond supernaturally to hormones that control ovulation, in the name of Jesus.

40. O Lord, let every surgically or congenitally missing ovary be restored by Your creative power, in the name of Jesus.

41. I bind the spirit of blockage of fallopian tubes, in Jesus' name.

42. I command the fire of God to burn to ashes everything that is blocking my fallopian tubes, in the name of Jesus.

43. I command my fallopian tubes to be loosed and free from every pelvic adhesions, in the name of Jesus.

44. I command the lumen (passages) of my fallopian tubes to be bilaterally patent and opened, in the name of Jesus.

45. O Lord, let every surgically or congenitally missing fallopian tube be restored by Your creative power, in the name of Jesus.

46. I reject and cancel every negative medical report of abnormality of my womb, in the name of Jesus.

47. I command every abnormality of my womb to be divinely and supernaturally corrected, in the name of Jesus.

48. I command every evil growth in my womb such as uterine fibroid to die, in the name of Jesus.

49. I reject and cancel every negative medical report of the congenital or surgical absence of the uterus, in the name of Jesus.

50. O Lord, let every congenitally or surgically missing uterus be restored to me supernaturally and divinely, in the name of Jesus.

51. Holy Spirit, create a conducive environment in my womb that would favour conception, in the name of Jesus.

52. Holy Spirit, create a conducive environment in my womb that would favour the growth of my fetus to maturity, in Jesus' name.

53. Every agenda of the power of darkness for my womb, die, in the name of Jesus.

54. I break every witchcraft curse and spell on my womb, in Jesus' name.

55. I break every ancestral curse on my womb, in the name of Jesus.

56. I soak my womb in the blood of Jesus.

57. I command the demon that has been assigned to give me a barren womb to loose its hold on me, in the name of Jesus.

58. O Lord, let my womb be spiritually and physically compatible with the semen of my spouse, in the name of Jesus.

59. Any component of my womb stolen by the powers of darkness to be restored to me now by fire, in the name of Jesus.

60. I retrieve my blood hormones, ovaries, fallopian tubes, uterus and vagina from the coven of darkness, in the name of Jesus.

61. I reverse the effects of the ageing process on my reproductive structures, in the name of Jesus.

62. O Lord, as I grow older in age, let me become more fertile supernaturally, in the name of Jesus.

63. Let every ovarian failure be converted to ovarian success, in the name of Jesus.

64. Thou resurrection power of our Lord Jesus Christ, fall upon every deadness in my ovulation, in the name of Jesus.

65. Thou resurrection power of our Lord Jesus Christ, fall upon every deadness in my ovaries, in the name of Jesus.

66. You evil spirit guards at the doors of my fallopian tubes, I relieve you of your post, in the name of Jesus.

67. Let every legal ground the enemy is claiming for closure of the doors of my fallopian tubes be withdrawn by fire, in Jesus' name.

68. Let every clinical report of blocked fallopian tubes be cancelled over my life, in the name of Jesus.

69. Let every blood supply to fibroids in my uterus be cut off, in the name of Jesus.

70. Let the liquid fire of God flow into my uterus and melt away every fibroid, in the name of Jesus.

71. Let the liquid fire of God flow into my uterus and dissolve every adhesion, in the name of Jesus.

72. Let every negative effect of ageing on my uterus be nullified, in the name of Jesus.

73.	Holy Ghost fire, purge my womb from every satanic deposit, in the name of Jesus.
74.	Let all the doors of my womb become an expressway to conception, in the name of Jesus.
75.	Every power chanting anti-conception incantations into the heavenlies against me, die, in the name of Jesus.
76.	Let every barrenness programmed into my star be deprogrammed, in the name of Jesus.
77.	Age shall not limit my conception, in the name of Jesus.
78.	Every power accelerating my age towards premature menopause, loose your hold upon my life and die, in the name of Jesus.
79.	Every negative power battling to control the doors of my womb, be paralysed, in the name of Jesus.
80.	Thou power of God that connected Zechariah and Elizabeth to their angel of breakthrough, connect me now to my angel of breakthrough, in the name of Jesus.
81.	By the power that directed angel Gabriel to Zechariah, let the angel of my miracle baby locate me now, in the name of Jesus.
82.	I command the strongman that has been assigned to give me miscarriage womb to fall down and die, in the name of Jesus.
83.	I reject miscarriages and abortion, in the name of Jesus.
84.	I reject bleeding in pregnancy, in the name of Jesus.

85.	I reject threaten-abortion, in the name of Jesus.
86.	I reject inevitable abortion and complete abortion, in Jesus' name.
87.	I reject complicated pregnancy, in the name of Jesus.
88.	I reject maternal and child death, in the name of Jesus.
89.	I reject every abnormal baby, in the name of Jesus.
90.	I reject every miscarriageable baby, in the name of Jesus.
91.	O Lord, let my baby be beautiful and normal, in Jesus' name.
92.	I reject every baby that is the product of the devil's workmanship, in the name of Jesus.
93.	I reject every abnormal chromosome, in the name of Jesus.
94.	I reject all babies that are prone to chromosomal abnormalities, in the name of Jesus.
95.	O Lord, grant unto me, babies that are resistant to every form of infection, in the name of Jesus.
96.	O Lord, let every abnormal structure in my womb be converted to normal structure, in the name of Jesus.
97.	I command the fire of God from heaven to burn every tumour in my womb to ashes, in the name of Jesus.
98.	O Lord, I repent of every personal damage done to my cervix in the past through a traumatic D & C, in the name of Jesus.

99. I command anything in my womb that can cause ectopic pregnancy to die, in the name of Jesus.

100. I command the strongman that has been assigned to siphon or drain away my progesterone and other hormones, to fall down and die, in the name of Jesus.

101. I command the demon behind corpus luteum insufficiency to loose its hold on me now, in the name of Jesus.

102. O Lord, remove every anxiety over old age from me, in the name of Jesus.

103. I receive divine mandate to prayerfully enforce my right of conception, in the name of Jesus.

104. Let every satanic road block mounted against the transport of my egg and spouse's sperm in my fallopian tube be dismantled by fire, in the name of Jesus.

105. Let every satanic wall of partition between my egg and spouse's sperm be broken down by fire, in the name of Jesus.

106. Let my fallopian tubes be freed from every adhesions, in the name of Jesus.

107. I withdraw my fallopian tubes from every evil altar, in the name of Jesus.

108. Let every inherited obstruction in my fallopian tubes, die, in the name of Jesus.

109. Let every evil seed of barrenness in my foundation, die, in the name of Jesus.

110. Let every infection in my fallopian tubes, die, in the name of Jesus.

111. Let every microorganism causing infection in my womb be roasted, in the name of Jesus.

112. Thou power of God that transformed the destiny of Hannah, fall upon me now and give me my own Samuel, in the name of Jesus.

113. Thou power of the Holy Spirit, overshadow my life now and connect me to my own baby, in the name of Jesus.

114. Holy Spirit, overhaul my womb by your fire to produce a divine conception, in the name of Jesus.

115. Let every child formed in my womb be preserved by the fire of God and the Blood of Jesus, in the name of Jesus.

116. Healing winds of God, blow upon all the organs of my body, in the name of Jesus.

117. O God arise and withdraw my organs from every satanic blood bank, in the name of Jesus.

118. Fire of God, boil infirmities out of my blood, in the name of Jesus.

119. Thou creative power of God, work upon my life, in the name of Jesus.

120. Glory of God, overshadow my body, soul and spirit, in the name of Jesus.

121. Create new organs to replace sick or dead ones, in Jesus' name.

122. O God supply organ spare parts to my body, in the name of Jesus.

123. Heavenly surgeon, visit me now, in the name of Jesus.

124. Power of God, pull down every stronghold of stubborn infirmities, in the name of Jesus.

125. Fire of God, purge my organ for newness, in the name of Jesus.

126. Let my youth be renewed as Eagle, in the name of Jesus.

127. Every handwriting of darkness targeted against my health, be wiped off, in the name of Jesus.

128. My organs receive creative miracles, in the name of Jesus.

129. Spirit of God, move upon every organ in my body, in the name of Jesus.

130. Creative power of God, work for me now, in the name of Jesus.

131. I bind every spirit of death operating in my . . ., in the mighty name of Jesus.

132. Let Your resurrection power come upon my . . ., in the mighty name of Jesus.

133. I command every dead bone in my . . . to come alive, in Jesus' name.

134. You evil hand laid on my . . ., receive the thunder and the fire of God and be roasted, in the name of Jesus.

135. I command every evil monitoring gadget fashioned against my . . . to be destroyed, in the name of Jesus.

136. I breathe in the life of God and I reject every spirit of death and hell, in the name of Jesus.

137. I recover every miracle that I have lost through unbelief, in the name of Jesus.

138. Father, let Your creative power operate afresh in . . . area of my life, in the name of Jesus.

139. Father, let the fire of the Holy Ghost enter into my blood stream and cleanse my system, in the name of Jesus.

140. I release my . . . from the cage of every household wickedness, in the name of Jesus.

141. Let every information about my . . . be erased from every satanic memory, in the name of Jesus.

142. I command every evil plantation in my life: Come out with all your roots, in the name of Jesus! (Lay your hands on your stomach and keep repeating the emphasized area.)

143. Evil strangers in my body, come all the way out of your hiding places, in the name of Jesus.

144. I cough out and vomit any food eaten from the table of the devil, in the name of Jesus. (Cough them out and vomit them in faith. Prime the expulsion.)

144. I cough out and vomit any food eaten from the table of the devil, in the name of Jesus. (Cough them out and vomit them in faith. Prime the expulsion.)
145. Let all negative materials circulating in my blood stream be evacuated, in the name of Jesus.
146. I drink the blood of Jesus. (Physically swallow and drink it in faith. Keep doing this for some time.)
147. Lay one hand on your head and the other on your stomach or navel and begin to pray like this: Holy Ghost fire, burn from the top of my head to the sole of my feet. Begin to mention every organ of your body; your kidney, liver, intestine, blood, etc. You must not rush at this level, because the fire will actually come and you may start feeling the heat.
148. I cut myself off from every spirit of . . . (mention the name of your place of birth), in the name of Jesus.
149. I cut myself off from every tribal spirit and curses, in the name of Jesus.
150. I cut myself off from every territorial spirit and curses, in Jesus' name.
151. Holy Ghost fire, purge my life.
152. I claim my complete deliverance, in the name of Jesus, from the spirit of . . . (mention those things you do not desire in your life).
153. I break the hold of any evil power over my life, in Jesus' name.
154. I move from bondage into liberty, in the name of Jesus.
155. Thank God for answers to your prayer points.

PRAYERS FOR RAPID SPIRITUAL GROWTH

Confession: Gal. 2:20: I am crucified with Christ: nevertheless I live; yet not I, but Christ liveth in me: and the life which I now live in the flesh I live by the faith of the Son of God, who loved me, and gave himself for me.

Praise Worship

1. Let my wounded parts receive healing, in the name of Jesus.

2. Let my worried parts encounter the power in the blood of Jesus, in the name of Jesus.

3. I refuse to be divided against myself, in the name of Jesus.

4. O Lord, pour Your healing oil into my troubled soul, in the name of Jesus.

5. O Lord, hold me in Your arms of healing, in the name of Jesus.

6. Let every weariness of the mind melt away, in Jesus' name.

7. O Lord, heal my bruised heart, in the name of Jesus.

8. Any coldness towards the Lord in my heart, let the fire of the Holy Ghost melt it away, in the name of Jesus.

9. Every power, holding me down from touching the helm of the garment of the Lord, break away, in the name of Jesus.

10. O Lord, cleanse me and sweeten the springs of my being, in the name of Jesus.

11. Let the freedom and light of the Lord flow into my mind, in the name of Jesus.

12. O Lord, let Your grace and love, be my true rest, in Jesus' name.

13. In the dark places of human life, let the light of the Lord shine on me, in the name of Jesus.

14. Every wrestling match with self pity in my life, die, in the name of Jesus.

15. Every power that is threatening to swallow me up, loose your hold, in the name of Jesus.

16. O Lord, take me in Your arms and heal me, in the name of Jesus.

17. Let the power in the blood of Jesus dissolve my pride, in the name of Jesus.

18. My Jacob, arise and wrestle into your breakthroughs, in the name of Jesus.

19. In the wound of my soul, Holy Spirit, pour Your healing oil, in the name of Jesus.

20. O Lord, anoint my wounds with the oil of healing, in Jesus' name.

21. Every cry of frustration, be silenced, in the name of Jesus.

22. Every anti-harvest power of my father's house, be dismantled, in the name of Jesus.

23. O Lord, remake me to enable me fulfil my destiny, in Jesus' name.

24. Thou power of self-imprisonment, die, in the name of Jesus.

25. Power of God, draw my scattered blessings together, in the name of Jesus.

26. O God arise and sharpen my senses that I may truly see what I am looking at, in the name of Jesus.

27. Let the water of my circumstances be turned into wine by the power of the Lord, in the name of Jesus.

28. O Lord, pick me up and re-arrange my life for breakthroughs, in the name of Jesus.

29. O Lord, stay at the centre of my life, in the name of Jesus.

30. Every fountain of bitterness, dry up, in the name of Jesus.

31. Let the cock crow in my heart whenever I am about to go astray, in the name of Jesus.

32. Cobwebs of poverty, be melted away by the fire of God, in the name of Jesus.

33. O Lord, fill me with Your love and peace, in the name of Jesus.

34. Every power, weighing me down, be dismantled, in Jesus' name.

35. Every ancestral power, tying my hands, be uprooted, in the name of Jesus.

36. O Lord, give me the power to abandon my idols, in Jesus' name.

37. Holy Ghost fire, illuminate my darkness, in the name of Jesus.

38. Thou Great Physician, heal me and make me whole, in the name of Jesus.

39. Let the oil of the anointing of the Lord penetrate every cell in my body, in the name of Jesus.

40. O God of wholeness, manifest Your power in my life, in the name of Jesus.

41. Hold me, o Lord, and do not let me fall, in the name of Jesus.

42. Whenever I want to hurt others, o Lord, deflect my action, in the name of Jesus.

43. O Lord, let my desire to be true to You prevail over everything else, in the name of Jesus.

44. I receive deliverance from the bondage of unnecessary words, in the name of Jesus.

45. O Lord, teach me when to be silent, in the name of Jesus.

46. Holy Spirit, let all my words be well used, in the name of Jesus.

47. O Lord, defend Your interest in my life, in the name of Jesus.

48. By Your mountain-moving power, o Lord, stay beside me to defend me, in the name of Jesus.

49. By the power that divided the Red Sea, o Lord, stay before me to lead me, in the name of Jesus.

50. By the power that changed the lot of Jabez, o Lord, stay above me to bless me, in the name of Jesus.

51. O Lord, make me open to Your wisdom, in the name of Jesus.

52. O Lord, make me receptive to Your will, in the name of Jesus.

53. My life will not be ruled by fear of what anyone can do to me, in the name of Jesus.

54. I shall not die inwardly, in the name of Jesus.

55. I release myself from every bondage of fear, in Jesus' name.

56. O Lord, remember me as You remembered the dying man next to You at the cross, in the name of Jesus.

57. My Father, transform me in the fire of Your love, in Jesus' name.

58. Thou power of God, clear away my inner rubbish, in Jesus' name.

59. O Lord, use my life to bless many people, in the name of Jesus.

60. O Lord, make my life a garden in which You can work in this world, in the name of Jesus.

61. O Lord, fill me with the spirit of healing and peace, in the name of Jesus.

62. O Lord, set my whole heart with Holy Ghost fire, in the name of Jesus.

63. O Lord, let me be a channel of blessings to others, in the name of Jesus.

64. O God, let me be employed by You, in the name of Jesus.

65. O Lord, let me be exalted by You, in the name of Jesus.

66. O Lord, let me be set aside for You, in the name of Jesus.

67. Let the Spirit of God dwell richly in me, in the name of Jesus.

68. O Lord, use me to affect my generation positively, in Jesus' name.

69. O Lord, make me part of the mystery of Your presence in the world, in the name of Jesus.

70. Let every part of my life be overshadowed by You, O Lord, in the name of Jesus.

71. Ignite my cold love with Your fire, O Lord, in the name of Jesus.

72. Let holy fervency come upon me, in the name of Jesus.

73. Empower me, O Lord, to be selfless in all my spiritual activities, in the name of Jesus.

74. Let the bonds of evil and death be broken, in the name of Jesus.

75. Let the light of the Lord flood the darkness in my life, in the name of Jesus.

76. O Lord, let me be Your delight in this planet, in Jesus' name.

77. O Lord, simplify my life and take possession of me, in Jesus' name.

78. O Lord, forgive me for relying on my own strength, in the name of Jesus.

79. Father, empower me to climb to my mountain of fulfilment, in the name of Jesus.

80. O Lord, let Your splendour shine forth in my life, in Jesus' name.

81. O God, grant me journey mercies, till my journey's end, in Jesus' name.

82. Lord, let Your light radiate through me, in the name of Jesus.

83. O Lord, help me to empty myself before You, in the name of Jesus.

84. O Lord, teach me to be quiet in Your presence, in Jesus' name.

85. My Father, give unto me untold riches, in the name of Jesus.

86. I thank You Lord for the unimaginable gift of the gospel.

87. O Lord, keep me thankful all my days, in the name of Jesus.

88. No matter what is going on, I shall not loose sight of hope, in the name of Jesus.

89. Thank You Lord for all the insults You have borne for me, in the name of Jesus.

90. O Lord, empower me to know You deeper, in the name of Jesus.

91. Hold me, O Lord, in the palm of Your hands, in Jesus' name.

92. Hide me, O Lord, in the hollow of Your hands, in Jesus' name.

93. O Lord, let me be wholly available to You on this earth, in the name of Jesus.

94. O Lord, give me a generous heart and open hands, in Jesus' name.

95. Blood of Jesus, heal every damage done to my body, soul and spirit, in the name of Jesus.

96. O Lord, pour into my heart the gentle balm of Your Spirit, in the name of Jesus.

97. O light of God, surround me always, in the name of Jesus.

98. O presence of God, envelope my life, in the name of Jesus.

99. O God, be the light in my darkness, in the name of Jesus.

100. O God, be my refuge and strength in times of fear, in the name of Jesus.

101. O Lord, help me to be a good listener, in the name of Jesus.

102. O Lord, give me the ability to learn from my mistakes, in the name of Jesus.

103. O Lord, give me love in my thinking, in the name of Jesus.

104. O Lord, give me love in my speaking, in the name of Jesus.

105. I receive deliverance from the effect of every physical or verbal abuse, in the name of Jesus.

106. O God, by Your power, make me wise, in the name of Jesus.

107. Lord, give me wisdom and integrity to be Your true servant, in the name of Jesus.

108. I shall not live for nothing, in the name of Jesus.

109. Let every chain of spiritual laziness break from my hands, in the name of Jesus.

110. O God, arise and break open every prison which holds me captive, in the name of Jesus.

111. Let my life celebrate Your beauty, O Lord, in Jesus' name.

112. Every satanic smoke in my nostrils, clear away, in Jesus' name.

113. Every satanic dust in my mouth, be cleansed by the blood of Jesus.

114. Empower me, O Lord, to work for the deliverance of others, in the name of Jesus.

115. O God arise and heal every wound of the past in my life, in Jesus' name.

116. O Lord, purge me in every area of my life where I am corrupt, in the name of Jesus.

117. Direct me, O Lord, whenever I am threatened by error, in the name of Jesus.

118. Strengthen and build up my faith, O Lord, in Jesus' name.

119. By Your mercy which is like a refining fire, O Lord, touch my being, in the name of Jesus.

120. O Lord, make me sensitive in listening to others, in the name of Jesus.

121. O Lord, keep me from being judgmental, in the name of Jesus.

122. Let me grow into deeper knowledge of You, O Lord, in the name of Jesus.

123. Let my life, O Lord, send Your light into the world, in Jesus' name.

124. Let all my inspiration and joy be drawn from You, O Lord, in the name of Jesus.

125. O Lord, I hold out my life to You, fill my vessel, in Jesus' name.

126. Let my life reflect Your life in me, in the name of Jesus.

127. Help me, O Lord, to redeem my past mistakes, in Jesus' name.

128. I arise by the mighty strength of God and suppress my suppressors, in the name of Jesus.

129. Let the hand and wisdom of God guide me, in Jesus' name.

130. I arise by the death and resurrection of the Lord Jesus Christ and possess my possessions.

131. I arise by the power of the Holy Ghost and claim 24 hour breakthroughs, in the name of Jesus.

132. Lord, let me dream Your dreams, in the name of Jesus.

133. O Lord, let my life reflect Your love, in the name of Jesus.

134. O Lord, hide me under the shadow of Your wings, in the name of Jesus.

135. Refresh my weariness, O Lord, in the name of Jesus.

136. Visit my home Lord, and drive far from it all the snares of the enemy, in the name of Jesus.

137. O God, break through my deafness and possess me, in the name of Jesus.

138. O Lord, breathe Your fragrance on me and give me favour, in the name of Jesus.

139. Let the eagle in me come alive and fly, in the name of Jesus.

140. Holy Spirit, let the power of prayer rise without effort in my heart always, in the name of Jesus.

141. My Father, make my soul Your bride, in the name of Jesus.

142. O Lord, teach me to seek You, in the name of Jesus.

143. My spirit man, hate those sins that separate You from God, in the name of Jesus.

144. Show me Your glory, O Lord, and promote my life, in the name of Jesus.

145. O Lord, open my eyes to Your presence and my lips to Your praises, in the name of Jesus.

146. O God, let me be exalted for You, in the name of Jesus.

147. O Lord, lead me, guide me, hold me in Your wonderful way, in the name of Jesus.

148. My Father, I abandon myself into Your hands, do what You will with me, in the name of Jesus.

149. O Lord, let my thoughts and words flow from You, in the name of Jesus.

150. O Lord, remove from my life all that blocks my way to You, in the name of Jesus.

151. O Lord, plant into my life all that would make me speed towards You My Father, in the name of Jesus.

152. O Lord, let me begin to shine as You shine, in Jesus' name.

153. I refuse to live a useless life in the name of Jesus.

154. O Lord, increase my vision of glory in the name of Jesus.

155. O Lord, increase my love for You in the name of Jesus.

156. O Lord, make me an instrument of deliverance, in Jesus' name.

157. I say no to all that keep me from following the Lord in the name of Jesus.

158. I say yes to all that brings me closer to the Lord in Jesus' name.

159. Make me, O Lord, like a tree planted by the waterside in the name of Jesus.

160. O Lord, let Your love shine through my eyes, in Jesus' name.

161. O Lord, let the Holy Spirit inspire my words, in Jesus' name.

162. My Father, cause Your wisdom to fill my heart, in Jesus' name.

163. Let me be changed, O Lord, unto Your likeness from glory to glory in the name of Jesus.

164. Transform my talents into means of bringing joy to others, O Lord in the name of Jesus.

165. I shall not bury my talents, I shall use them to make the Lord better known to the people of the world, in the name of Jesus.

166. O Lord, whatever the world may say, let me only pay attention to what You are saying to me, in the name of Jesus.

167. O God, deliver me from every internal slavery, in Jesus' name.

168. Let me confess Your name, O Lord, to the end, in Jesus' name.

169. I cause all the traps and dark powers of this world to bow before me, in the name of Jesus.

170. O Lord, let every moment of my life be Your moment, in the name of Jesus.

171. Let Your kingdom, O Lord, grow mightily in me, in Jesus' name.

172. O Lord, make me part of the mystery of Your presence in the world, in the name of Jesus.

173. O Lord, help me to see my real needs which are concealed from me, in the name of Jesus.

174. Lord, by Your blood, cleanse and sweeten the springs of my being, in the name of Jesus.

175. Let Your freedom and light flow into my mind, O Lord, in Jesus' name.

176. Encircle me, O Lord, with the wall of fire, in Jesus' name.

177. Encircle me, O Lord, with the wall of Your blood, in Jesus' name.

178. Encircle me, O Lord, with the wall of Your angel, in Jesus' name.

179. Encircle me, O Lord, with the wall of Your feather, in the name of Jesus.

180. Water me, O Lord, from Your fountain of blessings, in Jesus' name.

181. O Lord, make me Your reflection, in the name of Jesus.

182. Deliver me, O Lord, from the distraction of trying to impress others, in the name of Jesus.

183. Teach me, O Lord, to learn from criticism, in Jesus' name.

184. O Lord, pick me up firmly on the narrow way that leads to freedom, in the name of Jesus.

185. Take away from me, O Lord, all over-confidence and boasting, in the name of Jesus.

186. Take away from me, O Lord, all vain thoughts and desires to excuse myself from sin, in the name of Jesus.

187. Christ who overcame in the wilderness, fight for me, in the name of Jesus.

188. Christ who cleansed the temple, clear the temple of my heart, in the name of Jesus.

189. Christ of Gethsemane, intercede for me, in the name of Jesus.

190. Christ of calvary, fill me with Your victory, in Jesus' name.

191. Christ of the empty tomb, release me from every bondage, in the name of Jesus.

192. Panic will not drown the still small voice of the Holy Spirit in my life, in the name of Jesus.

193. O Lord, fill me with the spirit of intelligence and wisdom, in the name of Jesus.

194. Holy Ghost, instruct my speech and touch my lips, in the name of Jesus.

195. O Lord, make me keen to understand Your word, in the name of Jesus.

196. Make me quick, O Lord, to learn and remember Your words, in the name of Jesus.

197. O Lord, give me power to accurately name what is evil, in the name of Jesus.

198. O Lord, let me never stray from You, in the name of Jesus.

199. Let the darkness of ignorance be scattered, in Jesus' name.

200. O Lord, increase and multiply Your mercy upon me, in the name of Jesus.

201. O Lord, create in me a hunger for Your word, in Jesus' name.

202. I shall not utter empty prayers which have no fire, in the name of Jesus.

203. Lord, give me a grateful heart, in the name of Jesus.

204. Any power that wants to divide me against myself, scatter, in the name of Jesus.

205. Revive, redeem and restore me, O Lord, in the name of Jesus.

206. Thou enemy of my salvation, die, in the name of Jesus.

207. O Lord, make me a good example for my generation, in Jesus' name.

208. I shall not mortgage my salvation on the altar of Delilah, in the name of Jesus.

209. Every power hindering my holy walk with the Lord, scatter and die, in the name of Jesus.

210. Begin to thank God for answers to your prayers in this section.

INIQUITY SHALL NOT DWELL IN MY TENT

PRAYERS FOR SPIRITUAL GROWTH

Confession: Isa. 40:28-30: Hast thou not known? hast thou not heard, that the everlasting God, the LORD, the Creator of the ends of the earth, fainteth not, neither is weary? there is no searching of his understanding. He giveth power to the faint; and to them that have no might he increaseth strength. Even the youths shall faint and be weary, and the young men shall utterly fall:

Praise Worship

1. Thank the Lord for the power of the Holy Spirit.

2. Confession of sins and repentance.

3. Father Lord, let the Holy Spirit fill me afresh, in Jesus' name.

4. Father Lord, let every unbroken area in my life be broken, in the name of Jesus.

5. Father Lord, incubate me with the fire of the Holy Spirit, in Jesus' name.

6. Let every anti-power bondage break in my life, in Jesus' name.

7. Let all strangers flee from my spirit and let the Holy Spirit take control, in the name of Jesus.

8. O Lord, catapult my spiritual life to the mountain top.

9. Father Lord, let heavens open and let the glory of God fall upon me, in the name of Jesus.

10. Father Lord, let signs and wonders be my lot, in Jesus' name.

11. I decree the joy of the oppressors upon my life to be turned into sorrow, in the name of Jesus.

12. Let all multiple strongmen operating against me be paralyzed, in the name of Jesus.

13. O Lord, open my eyes and ears to receive wondrous things from You.

14. O Lord, grant me victory over temptations and satanic devices.

15. O Lord, ignite my spiritual life so that I will stop fishing in unprofitable waters.

16. O Lord, release Your tongue of fire upon my life and burn away all spiritual filthiness present within me.

17. Father Lord, make me to hunger and thirst for righteousness, in the name of Jesus.

18. O Lord, help me to be ready to do Your work without expecting any recognition from others.

19. O Lord, give me victory over emphasizing the weaknesses and sins of other people while ignoring my own.

20. Marks of sin in my life, go. Marks of purity, come upon my life, in the name of Jesus.

21. Holy Ghost fire, incubate my spirit man, in the name of Jesus.

22. Every anti-repentant spirit in my life, I bind you and cast you out now, in the name of Jesus.

23. I receive fresh fire to move forward in my spiritual life, in the name of Jesus.

24. Let my steps be withdrawn from every wickedness, in the name of Jesus.

25. Let my seat be the seat of purity, in the name of Jesus.

26. Every iniquity, flee from me, in the name of Jesus.

27. Power to live a godly life, come upon me now, in Jesus' name.

28. I soak myself in the blood of Jesus and in the word of God, in the name of Jesus.

29. Every inner strife against holiness in my life, die, in Jesus' name.

30. Vagabond spiritual life, I reject you, in the name of Jesus.

31. Thou tongue of fire from heaven, purify my destiny, in the name of Jesus.

32. O Lord, give me depth and root in my faith.

33. O Lord, heal every area of backsliding in my spiritual life.

34. O Lord, help me to be willing to serve others rather than wanting to exercise authority.

35. O Lord, open my understanding concerning the scriptures.

36. O Lord, help me to live each day recognizing that the day will come when You will judge secret lives and innermost thoughts.

37. O Lord, let me be willing to be the clay in Your hands, ready to be moulded as You desire.

38. O Lord, wake me up from any form of spiritual sleep and help me to put on the armour of light.

39. O Lord, give me victory over all carnality and help me to be at the centre of Your will.

40. I stand against anything in my life that will cause others to stumble, in the name of Jesus.

41. O Lord, help me to put away childish things and put on maturity.

42. O Lord, empower me to stand firm against all the schemes and techniques of the devil.

43. O Lord, give me a big appetite for the pure milk and solid food in the word.

44. O Lord, empower me to stay away from anything or anybody who might take God's place in my heart.

45. Holy Spirit, do not leave my house desolate, in Jesus' name.

46. O Lord, I want You to break me, I want the self in me to die.

47. O Lord, whatever would make You to replace me, remove it from my life now.

48. O Lord, give me the power to walk in the spirit.

49. O Lord, let holiness be my food.

50. O Lord, reveal to me, anything that is hindering my spiritual growth.

51. O Lord, help me to put on the garment of righteousness.

52. O Lord, help me to crucify my flesh.

53. O Lord, help me to hate sin with perfect hatred.

54. O Lord, save me from myself.

55. O Lord, let me be lost in You.

56. O Lord, crucify . . . (put your own name).

57. Holy Spirit, possess me completely, in the name of Jesus.

58. O Lord, divorce me from every sin of self.

59. O Lord, break me and mould me according to Your will.

60. Father Lord, let me experience Your kingdom in every department of my life, in the name of Jesus.

61. My flesh, I command you to die to sin, in Jesus' name.

62. Every enemy of brokenness in my life, depart, in Jesus' name.

63. I paralyse all my Delilah, in the name of Jesus.

64. O Lord, break me down to the depth of my spirit.

65. My shaven Samson, receive your hair, in the name of Jesus.

66. O God who quickeneth the dead, give life to every dead area of my life today, in the name of Jesus.

67. Holy Spirit, take my hands off my own life and possess me Yourself, in the name of Jesus.

68. Every evil inherited character in my life, be demolished, in the name of Jesus.

69. Father Lord, let Your will be done in my life.

70. Every nest that builders of evil nests have built for me, be roasted, in the name of Jesus.

71. O Lord, break me in my unbroken areas.

72. O Lord, I welcome brokenness in every department of my life.

73. O Lord, break me!

74. O Lord, make me a living sacrifice.

75. I refuse to be caged by the enemy, in the name of Jesus.

76. O God, stretch me and renew my strength, in the name of Jesus.

77. O Lord, renew a right spirit within me.

78. O Lord, renew my mind in Your word.

79. O Lord, let Your renewing power renew my life like the eagle's.

80. Let my youth be renewed like the eagle's, in the name of Jesus.

81. Let every impurity in my life be flushed out by the blood of Jesus, in the name of Jesus.

82. O Lord, create within me hunger and thirst after purity and holiness.

83. O Lord, cleanse all the soiled parts of my life.

84. O Lord, refresh every dry area of my life.

85. O Lord, heal every wounded part of my life.

86. O Lord, bend every evil rigidity in my life.

87. O Lord, re-align every satanic straying in my life.

88. O Lord, let the fire of the Holy Spirit warm every satanic freeze in my life.

89. O Lord, give me a life that kills death.

90. O Lord, kindle in me the fire of charity.

91. O Lord, glue me together where I am opposed to myself.

92. O Lord, enrich me with Your gifts.

93. O Lord, quicken me and increase my desire for the things of heaven.

94. By Your rulership, O Lord, let the lust of the flesh in my life die.

95. Lord Jesus, increase daily in my life.

96. Lord Jesus, maintain Your gifts in my life.

97. O Lord, refine and purge my life by Your fire.

98. Holy Spirit, inflame and fire my heart, in the name of Jesus.

99. Lord Jesus, lay Your hands upon me and quench every rebellion in me.

100. Holy Ghost fire, begin to burn away every self-centredness in me, in the name of Jesus.

101. Father Lord, breathe Your life-giving breath into my soul, in the name of Jesus.

102. O Lord, make me ready to go wherever You send me.

103. Lord Jesus, never let me shut You out.

104. Lord Jesus, never let me try to limit You to my capacity.

105. Lord Jesus, work freely in me and through me.

106. O Lord, purify the channels of my life.

107. Let Your heat, O Lord, consume my will, in the name of Jesus.

108. Let the flame of the Holy Spirit, blaze upon the altar of my heart, in the name of Jesus.

109. Lord Jesus, come like blood into my veins.

110. O Lord, order my spirit and fashion my life in Your will.

111. O Lord, let Your fire burn all that is not holy in my life.

112. O Lord, let Your fire generate power in my life.

113. Lord Jesus, impart to me thoughts higher than my own thoughts.

114. Holy Spirit, come as dew and refresh me, in Jesus' name.

115. Holy Spirit, guide me in the way of liberty, in Jesus' name.

116. Holy Spirit, blow upon me such that sin would no more find place in me, in the name of Jesus.

117. Holy Spirit, where my love is cold, warm me up, in Jesus' name.

118. O Lord, give me the power to embarrass my enemies.

119. Every spiritual coffin I have constructed for myself, be destroyed by the fire of God, in the name of Jesus.

120. O Lord Jesus, choose me for miracles every day of my life.

121. O Lord, speak Your word of power into my situation.

122. O Lord, deliver me from the mouth of the lion.

123. O Lord, forgive me for bringing problems into my life.

124. O Lord, empower me to dwell in Noah's Ark.

125. O Lord, empower me to prosper.

126. O Lord, remove from my life anything that will make me to miss the rapture.

127. Let the blood of Jesus and the fire of the Holy Ghost purge out of my life, every sin that will take me to hell fire, in Jesus' name.

128. O Lord, empower me to dwell in safety.

129. I vomit every food of sin in my life, in the name of Jesus.

130. O Lord, speak life and fire into my life today.

131. I swallow the pill of aggressive resistance against sin and unrighteousness, in the name of Jesus.

132. Jesus, pray for me so that I will not be winnowed like the chaff of wheat by the devil.

133. O Lord, bring help for me from above and disgrace my oppressors.

134. I move from minimum to maximum for the glory of God, in Jesus' name.

135. I paralyse every satanic opposition to my progress, in Jesus' name.

136. All my dragons shall be disgraced, in the name of Jesus.

137. I destroy the works of the destroyer upon my life, in Jesus' name.

138. Every wicked tree growing in my foundation, be uprooted now, in the name of Jesus.

139. I break every egg that the serpent has laid in any department of my life, in the name of Jesus.

140. Every serpentine and scorpion power, militating against my life, be disgraced, in the name of Jesus.

141. O Lord, let all the serpents and scorpions assigned against me begin to fight themselves, in the name of Jesus.

142. Every serpent, sent to destroy me, return to your sender, in the name of Jesus.

143. Every dumb and deaf spirit, loosen your hold upon my life now, in the name of Jesus.

144. My spiritual strength, sapped by the serpent, receive the touch of God and be restored, in the name of Jesus.

145. You serpent, loose your grip upon my spiritual strength, in the name of Jesus.

146. Every pollution done to my spiritual life and health by the serpent, be cleansed by the blood of Jesus, in Jesus' name.

147. Every serpentine manipulation of my health, be frustrated and be rendered impotent, in the name of Jesus.

148. All you serpents, I command you to vomit my prosperity, health, marriage, finances and spiritual strength that you have swallowed, in the mighty name of Jesus.

149. I climb the hills of God by the power of the Holy Spirit, in Jesus' name.

150. Let the power of the Holy Ghost energize my body, soul and spirit, in the name of Jesus.

151. I refuse to be a Judas, in the name of Jesus.

152. Every power, working against my journey to heaven, I destroy you, in the name of Jesus.

153. I move from spiritual insignificance to spiritual significance, in the name of Jesus.

154. Every enemy of holiness programmed into my life, die, in the name of Jesus.

155. Every blockage on my way of righteousness, be eliminated by fire, in the name of Jesus.

156. Every handwriting of iniquity upon my destiny, be wiped off by the blood of Jesus.

157. Every power, planning spiritual disgrace for me, be dismantled, in the name of Jesus.

158. I arise above destructive habits by the power in the blood of Jesus.

159. Every spiritual oppressor, working against my spiritual breakthroughs, I destroy your power, in the name of Jesus.

160. I arise above every evil family root by the power in the blood of Jesus.

161. Holy Ghost fire, destroy every internal iniquity, in Jesus' name.

162. I shall not bury my own glory, in the name of Jesus.

163. Every power sitting on my spiritual talent, be unseated by the power in the blood of Jesus.

164. Let the fruit of the Spirit manifest afresh in my life, in the name of Jesus.

165. Anointing that breaks the yoke, break every yoke of iniquity in my life, in the name of Jesus.

166. Every curse of backsliding, be broken, in the name of Jesus.

167. I declare that I am saved by God; no evil power shall cut me down, in the name of Jesus.

168. O Lord, give me power to be faithful to You, in Jesus' name.

169. I receive the anointing to remain steady, committed and consistent in my spiritual life, in the name of Jesus.

170. I shall not deviate into spiritual error, in the name of Jesus.

171. O Lord, give me the heart of a servant so that I can experience Your blessings everyday, in the name of Jesus.

172. I receive power to rise up with wings as eagles, in Jesus' name.

173. The enemy will not waste my salvation, in the name of Jesus.

174. The devil will not swallow my salvation, in the name of Jesus.

175. Power for effective development in my spiritual life, come upon me now, in the name of Jesus.

176. I declare war against spiritual ignorance in my life, in the name of Jesus.

177. I bind and cast out every unteachable spirit in my life, in the name of Jesus.

178. I receive the anointing for success in my spiritual life, in the name of Jesus.

179. I shall not be an enemy of integrity, in the name of Jesus.

180. I shall not disgrace the salvation of God upon my life, in the name of Jesus.

181. I shall work in holiness everyday, in the name of Jesus.

182. I bind the spirit of sexual immorality, in the name of Jesus.

183. I receive the culture of loyalty in my spiritual life, in the name of Jesus.

184. I shall not become an old king that is resistant to advice, in the name of Jesus.

185. I shall not live a wasteful and extravagant spiritual life, in the name of Jesus.

186. I shall not serve my wonderful Saviour for filthy financial gain, in the name of Jesus.

187. My wife/husband shall not destroy my salvation, in Jesus' name.

188. Every Judas in my salvation, fall into your own trap, in the name of Jesus.

189. My marriage will not destroy my salvation, in Jesus' name.

190. I claim progress and excellence for my spiritual life, in the name of Jesus.

191. Multitude will go to heaven because of my salvation, in the name of Jesus.

192. I kill every attack on my salvation; I shall prevail, in the name of Jesus.

193. I shall not engage in rebellion, in the name of Jesus.

194. Every power of my father's house, working against my salvation, die, in the name of Jesus.

195. Anointing for excellence, fall upon me, in the name of Jesus.

196. On issues about my salvation, I will not surrender to the enemy, in the name of Jesus.

197. I shall not die before my time, in the name of Jesus.

198. I shall not capture the prosperity of Naaman, in Jesus' name.

199. Let God arise and let every enemy of my salvation scatter, in the name of Jesus.

200. I receive fresh fire and fresh anointing, in the name of Jesus.

201. Holy fire of revival, fall upon my life, in the name of Jesus.

202. Spirit of rebellion, depart from my life, in the name of Jesus.

203. Spirit of stubbornness, depart from my life, in Jesus' name.

204. O Lord, let me have pure hands and a pure heart, in the name of Jesus.

205. O Lord, let the words of my mouth and the meditation of my heart be acceptable in Your sight always, in Jesus' name.

206. I reject every agenda of the enemy to make me walk in the paths of sinners, in the name of Jesus.

207. Spirit of the living God, fall afresh upon me, in Jesus' name.

208. Spirit of the living God, mould my life to become what God wants me to be, in the name of Jesus.

209. Every blessing I received in this section will remain permanent in my life, in the name of Jesus.

210. Thank God for what He has done for you in this section.

POWER AGAINST EVIL SPIRITUAL MARRIAGES

The supernatural world is as real as the physical. What takes place in the spiritual realm affects us physically in our day to day lives.

The subject of the evil spiritual marriage has been grossly mis-understood by many people. While some hold erroneous views, others demonstrate partial knowledge of this all-important subject. The problem of evil marriage goes beyond dilettantish purposes.

Evil marriage is a deep subject. It affects many people. From our spiritual research and statistical findings, we have gathered that seven out of ten ladies who profess to be born again are involved, consciously or unconsciously, with evil spiritual marriage. In the same vein, seven out of every ten Christian men are, consciously or unconsciously, affected by evil spiritual marriages.

There are some terrible powers known as spirit spouses.

> More than any other power, these spirits have destroyed marriages.

> Many women suffer from astral sex regularly. Astral sex is the ability to project one's spirit man into the victim's body and have intercourse with it. This practice is very common amongst satanists. They leave their physical bodies in a dormant state while they project their spirits into the body of whoever they want to have sex with.

Pray these prayers when you notice any of the following:

1. Marital distress

2. Sexual relationships in dreams

3. Hatred of marriage

4. Being jilted

5. Unpardonable sexual error

6. Wrong decisions

7. Neglect and abandonment by the opposite sex

8. Demonic dream assistance

9. Swimming or seeing a river in the dream

10. Missing one's menstrual period in the dream

11. Pregnancy in the dream

12. Breast-feeding a baby in the dream

13. Backing a baby in the dream

14. Having a family in the dream

15. Shopping with a man / woman in the dream

16. Seeing a man sleeping by one's side in the dream

17. Hatred by earthly spouse

18. Serious gynaecological problems

19. Having a miscarriage after sexual dreams

20. Dream marriages

Praise worship

Confession

1. Spirit husband/spirit wife, release me by fire, in the name of Jesus.

2. Every spirit husband/wife, I divorce you by the blood of Jesus.

1. Every spirit wife/every spirit husband, die, in the name of Jesus.

2. Everything you have deposited in my life, come out by fire, in the name of Jesus.

3. Every power that is working against my marriage, fall down and die, in the name of Jesus.

4. I divorce and renounce my marriage with the spirit husband or wife, in the name of Jesus.

5. I break all covenants entered into with the spirit husband or wife, in the name of Jesus.

6. I command the thunder fire of God to burn to ashes the wedding gown, ring, photographs and all other materials used for the marriage, in Jesus' name.

7. I send the fire of God to burn to ashes the marriage certificate, in the name of Jesus.

8. I break every blood and soul-tie covenants with the spirit husband or wife, in the name of Jesus.

9. I send thunder fire of God to burn to ashes the children born to the marriage, in Jesus' name.

10. I withdraw my blood, sperm or any other part of my body deposited on the altar of the spirit husband or wife, in the name of Jesus.

11. You spirit husband or wife tormenting my life and earthly marriage I bind you with hot chains and fetters of God and cast you out of my life into the deep pit, and I command you not to ever come into my life again, in the name of Jesus.

12. I return to you, every property of yours in my possession in the spirit world, including the dowry and whatsoever was used for the marriage and covenants, in the name of Jesus.

13. I drain myself of all evil materials deposited in my body as a result of our sexual relation, in Jesus' name

14. Lord, send Holy Ghost fire into my root and burn out all unclean things deposited in it by the spirit husband or wife, in the name of Jesus.

15. I break the head of the snake, deposited into my body by the spirit husband or wife to do me harm, and command it to come out, in the name of Jesus.

16. I purge out, with the blood of Jesus, every evil material deposited in my womb to prevent me from having children on earth.

17. Lord, repair and restore every damage done to any part of my body and my earthly marriage by the spirit husband or wife, in the name of Jesus.

18. I reject and cancel every curse, evil pronouncement, spell, jinx, enchantment and incantation placed upon me by the spirit husband or wife, in the name of Jesus.

19. I take back and possess all my earthly belongings in the custody of the spirit husband or wife, in Jesus' name.

20. I command the spirit husband or wife to turn his or her back on me forever, in Jesus' name.

21. I renounce and reject the name given to me by the spirit husband or wife, in the name of Jesus.

22. I hereby declare and confess that the Lord Jesus Christ is my Husband for eternity, in Jesus' name.

23. I soak myself in the blood of Jesus and cancel the evil mark or writings placed on me, in Jesus' name.

24. I set myself free from the stronghold, domineering power and bondage of the spirit husband or wife, in the name of Jesus.

25. I paralyse the remote control power and work used to destabilise my earthly marriage and to hinder me from bearing children for my earthly husband or wife, in the name of Jesus.

26. I announce to the heavens that I am forever married to Jesus.

27. Every trademark of evil marriage, be shaken out of my life, in the name of Jesus.

28. Every evil writing, engraved by iron pen, be wiped off by the blood of Jesus.

29. I bring the blood of Jesus upon the spirit that does not want to go, in the name of Jesus.

30. I bring the blood of Jesus on every evidence that can be tendered by wicked spirits against me.

31. I file a counter-report in the heavens against every evil marriage, in the name of Jesus.

32. I refuse to supply any evidence that the enemy may use against me, in the name of Jesus.

33. Let satanic exhibitions be destroyed by the blood of Jesus.

34. I declare to you spirit wife / husband that there is no vacancy for you in my life, in the name of Jesus.

35. O Lord, make me a vehicle of deliverance.

36. I come by faith to mount Zion. Lord, command deliverance upon my life now.

37. Lord, water me from the waters of God.

38. Let the careful siege of the enemy be dismantled, in the name of Jesus.

39. O Lord, defend Your interest in my life.

40. Everything, written against me in the cycle of the moon, be blotted out, in Jesus' name.

41. Everything, programmed into the sun, moon and stars against me, be dismantled, in Jesus' name.

42. Every evil thing programmed into my genes, be blotted out by the blood of Jesus.

43. O Lord, shake out seasons of failure and frustrations from my life.

44. I overthrow every wicked law, working against my life, in the name of Jesus.

45. I ordain a new time, season and profitable law, in Jesus' name.

46. I speak destruction unto the palaces of the queen of the coast and of the rivers, in Jesus' name.

47. I speak destruction unto the headquarters of the spirit of Egypt and blow up their altars, in the name of Jesus.

48. I speak destruction unto the altars, speaking against the purpose of God for my life, in Jesus' name.

49. I declare myself a virgin for the Lord, in Jesus' name

50. Let every evil veil upon my life be torn open, in Jesus' name.

51. Every wall between me and the visitation of God, be broken, in the name of Jesus.

52. Let the counsel of God prosper in my life, in the name of Jesus.

53. I destroy the power of any demonic seed in my life from the womb, in the name of Jesus.

54. I speak unto my umbilical gate to overthrow all negative parental spirits, in the name of Jesus.

55. I break the yoke of the spirits, having access to my reproductive gates, in the name of Jesus.

56. O Lord, let Your time of refreshing come upon me.

57. I bring fire from the altar of the Lord upon every evil marriage, in the name of Jesus.

58. I redeem myself by the blood of Jesus from every sex trap, in the name of Jesus.

59. I erase the engraving of my name on any evil marriage record, in the name of Jesus.

60. I reject and renounce every evil spiritual marriage, in the name of Jesus.

61. I confess that Jesus is my original spouse and is jealous over me.

62. I issue a bill of divorcement to every spirit wife / husband, in the name of Jesus.

63. I bind every spirit wife / husband with everlasting chains, in the name of Jesus.

64. Let heavenly testimony overcome every evil testimony of hell, in the name of Jesus.

65. O Lord, bring to my remembrance every spiritual trap and contract.

66. Let the blood of Jesus purge me of every contaminating material, in the name of Jesus.

67. Let the spirit husband/wife fall down and die, in Jesus' name.

68. Let all your children attached to me fall down and die, in the name of Jesus.

69. I burn your certificates and destroy your rings, in the name of Jesus.

70. I execute judgement against water spirits and I declare that you are reserved for everlasting chains in darkness, in the name of Jesus.

71. O Lord, contend with those who are contending with me.

72. Every trademark of water spirit, be shaken out of my life, in the name of Jesus.

DISMANTLING CANCER

CONFESSIONS: Proverbs 4:20-22: My son, attend to my words; incline thine ear unto my saying. 21Let them not depart from thine eyes; keep them in the midst of thine heart. 22For they are life unto those that find them, and health to all their flesh.

2 Tim. 1:7: For God hath not given us the spirit of fear; but of power, and of a sound mind.

2 Tim. 3:3: But the Lord is faithful, who shall stablish you, and keep you from evil.

Matthew 15:13: But he answered and said, Every plant, which my heavenly Father hath not planted, shall be rooted up.

Mark 11:23: For verily I say unto you, That whosoever shall say unto this mountain, Be thou removed, and be thou cast into the sea; and shall not doubt in his heart, but shall believe that those things he saith shall come to pass; he shall have whatsoever he saith.

Mark 11:24: Therefore I say unto you, What things soever ye desire, when ye pray, believe that ye receive them, and ye shall *have them.*

Jeremiah 30:15-17: Why criest thou for thine affliction? Thy sorrow is incurable for the multitude of thine iniquity: because thy sins were increased, I have done these thing unto thee. 16Therefore all they that devour thee shall be devoured; and all thine adversaries, every one of them, shall go into captivity; and they that spoil thee shall be a spoil, and all that prey upon thee will i give for a prey. 17For i will restore health unto thee, and i will heal thee of thy wounds, saith the LORD; because they called thee an Outcast, saying, This is Zion, whom no man seeketh after.

PRAISE WORSHIP

1. All the activities of silent killers in my body, die, in the name of Jesus.

2. You the symptom of cancer in any area of my body, die, in the name of Jesus.

3. Every evil growth in my body, I curse you to die, in Jesus' name.

4. I fire back every arrow of cancer, in the name of Jesus.

5. Every abnormal production and uncontrollable behaviour of cells in my body, stop, in the name of Jesus.

6. I bind every spirit of death and hell, in the name of Jesus.

7. Every negative consequence of abnormal production of cells in my body, die, in the name of Jesus.

8. I shall not die but live to declare the works of God, in Jesus' name.

9. You mass of extra tissue/tumour that has become malignant in my breast, be melted by the fire of God, in the name of Jesus.

10. Every demon of cancer, I bind you and cast you out, in Jesus' name.

11. Every break away cancer cell from malignant tumour that has entered my bloodstream (Lymphatic system), be flushed away by the blood of Jesus.

12. Every vampire spirit, release my life, in the name of Jesus.

13. You the malignant tumour, go back to your own kind by fire, in the name of Jesus.

14. O Great Physician, deliver me now.

15. Every spread of cancer (metastasis) in my body, stop and I command normalcy to my body system, in the name of Jesus.

16. Lay your hands on the affected parts and pray like this:

    - Evil growth, dry up and die, in the name of Jesus.

    - Satanic instructions to my body, be dismantled, in Jesus' name.

    - Every poison in my body, come out through the mouth and through the nose, in the name of Jesus.

    - Every spirit behind this cancer, come out with all your roots, in the name of Jesus.

    - Every cancer anchor in my body, be dismantled, in Jesus' name

- Every cancer anchor in my body, be dismantled, in the name of Jesus.

- Every vehicle of cancer, crash, in the name of Jesus.

- Power of cancer, die, in the name of Jesus.

- Holy Ghost fire, burn away every cancer, in the name of Jesus.

- Caldron of witchcraft cooking my flesh, die, in the name of Jesus.

- Let the fire of God kill bewitched cells in my body, in the name of Jesus.

- Blood of Jesus, move upon every area of my life.

- I dismantle every hand of witchcraft, in the name of Jesus.

17. The power of cancer, die, in the name of Jesus.

18. Every threat to my life, my God shall threaten you to death, in the name of Jesus.

19. Holy Ghost, break the yoke of cancer in my life, in Jesus' name.

20. Every devastating attack on my beauty through the attack on my breast, die, in the name of Jesus.

21. Every power behind unprofitable growth, die, in the name of Jesus.

22. Every cancer initiation beginning from the duct in my breast, die, in the name of Jesus.

23. The spirit of cancer, loose your hold and die, in the name of Jesus.

24. You cancer of any kind, I am not your candidate, therefore, leave me alone, in the name of Jesus.

25. Cancer of_ _ _, I command you to dry up and die, in the name of Jesus.

26. Every power jingling the bell of untimely death on my life, you, your bell and pronouncements, die, in the name of Jesus.

27. I curse every cancerous cell to die, in the name of Jesus.

28. Every disease of Egypt, I am not your candidate, in Jesus' name

29. You demon of unprofitable growth and cell multiplication, I bind you and cast you out, in the name of Jesus.

30. Every re-occurrence of breast cancer in my life, die, in the name of Jesus.

31. Father Lord, let Your power move away every mountain of infirmity in my life, in the name of Jesus.

32. Every sign of inflammatory of breast cancer, die, in the name of Jesus.

33. I receive deliverance from every inherited spirit, in the name of Jesus.

34. Every unusual change in size, shape or colour of my breast, die, in the name of Jesus.

35. Holy Ghost arise and kill every satanic agent in my life, in the name of Jesus.

36. Every satanic discharge from my nipple, dry up to source, in the name of Jesus.

37. By the power that divided the Red Sea, let every evil growth dry up, in the name of Jesus.

38. Every solid lump or thickening in any area of my body, be melted away by fire, in the name of Jesus.

39. Every circulating serpent in my body, come out by fire, in the name of Jesus.

40. Any stage breast cancer has reached in my life, today, I terminate your advancement and I command a reversal now, in the name of Jesus.

41. I decree you will not spread to any other part of my body, in the name of Jesus.

42. Let my body reject every handwriting of darkness, in Jesus' name.

43. There shall be no reinforcement or regrouping of any cancer attack against me anymore, in the name of Jesus.

44. Let the arrow of darkness release my blood and my organs, in the name of Jesus.

45. Satan, hear me and hear me very well, I am not a death carrier but I am a life carrier, in the name of Jesus.

46. I speak destruction unto every cancerous cell, in the name of Jesus.

47. Blood of Jesus, mop up all the poison of cancer, in the name of Jesus.

48. Every arrow of cancer, come out now, in the name of Jesus.

49. Every power battling my health, receive the fire of God, in the name of Jesus.

50. By the power in the striped of Jesus, I kill every power of cancer, in the name of Jesus.

51. The power of pain, be dissolved by fire, in the name of Jesus.

52. O God arise and let every enemy of my sound health scatter, in the name of Jesus.

53. O cancer, hear the power of the Lord, I command you to dry up, in the name of Jesus.

54. Poison and insects programmed into my body, come out now, in the name of Jesus.

55. I cancel by fire the evil instructions given to my body, in Jesus' name.

56. I received deliverance from the grip of destructive spirit, in the name of Jesus.

57. Holy Ghost fire and blood of Jesus, destroy every contrary handwriting of infirmity.

58. Begin to thank God for your healing.

POWER AGAINST INTROJECTS

Prayers when one is under astral projection attacks. When one has been infiltrated by astral projection into his body.

Confessions Psalm 18:44-45: As soon as they hear of me, they shall obey me: the strangers shall submit themselves unto me. The strangers shall fade away, and be afraid out of their close places.

Luke 10:19: Behold, I give unto you power to tread on serpents and scorpions, and over all the power of the enemy: and nothing shall by any means hurt you.

Deut. 7:15: And the Lord will take away from thee all sickness, and will put none of the evil diseases of Egypt, which thou knowest, upon thee; but will lay them upon all them that hate thee.

Praise Worship

Prayer Points

1. Holy Ghost fire, incubate my life, in the name of Jesus.

2. I charge my body with the fire of the Holy Ghost, in the name of Jesus.

3. Every agenda of astral attack for my life, die, in the name of Jesus.

4. I pull out the messenger of satan from my body, in the name of Jesus.

5. Every astral projection into my _ _ _ _ (head, chest, stomach, womb), I bind you and I cast you out, in the name of Jesus.

6. My head, reject the landing space of darkness, in the name of Jesus.

7. Every introject power, die, in the name of Jesus.

8. Let my body be too hot for any introject, in the name of Jesus.

9. Power of astral sex, upon my life, die, in the name of Jesus.

10. I reject every satanic authority laying claim upon my life, in the name of Jesus.

11. I break every curse of the victim syndrome, in the name of Jesus.

12. Ladders of darkness, permitting evil infiltration into my life, scatter, in the name of Jesus.

13. Yokes of darkness, harassing my health, scatter, in Jesus' name.

14. Programme of the enemy for my body, I disapprove you now, in the name of Jesus.

15. Introject spirits, come out of my life, in the name of Jesus.

16. Every power assigned to possess me, die, in the name of Jesus.

17. Spirits of death and hell, ordained against my life, loose your hold, in the name of Jesus.

18. I cancel every spell, enchantment and divination assigned against me, in the name of Jesus.

19. Dark strangers, release my life, in the name of Jesus.

20. Every unwelcome visitor in the habitation of my life, get out now, in the name of Jesus.

21. Every astral projection into my body, scatter by fire, in the name of Jesus.

22. Every astral altar assigned against my body, soul and spirit, catch fire, in the name of Jesus.

23. Blood of Jesus, sanitise my body, soul and spirit.

PRAYERS TO HEAL DIABETES

CONFESSIONS

Psalm 103:3: Who forgiveth all thine iniquities; who healeth all thy diseases;

Psalm 107:20: He sent his word, and healed them, and delivered them from their destructions.

Psalm 138:1-8: I will praise thee with my whole heart: before the gods will I sing praise unto thee. 2I will worship toward thy holy temple, and praise thy name for thy lovingkindness and for thy truth: for thou hast magnified thy word above all thy name. 3In the day when I cried thou answeredst me, and strengthenedst me with strength in my soul. 4All the kings of the earth shall praise thee, O Lord, when they hear the words of thy mouth. 5Yea, they shall sing in the ways of the Lord: for great is the glory of the Lord. 6Though the Lord be high, yet hath he respect unto the lowly: but the proud he knoweth afar off.

7Though I walk in the midst of trouble, thou wilt revive me: thou shalt stretch forth thine hand against the wrath of mine enemies, and thy right hand shall save me. 8The Lord will perfect that which concerneth me: thy mercy, O Lord, endureth for ever: forsake not the works of thine own hands.

Proverbs 12:18: There is that speaketh like the piercings of a sword: but the tongue of the wise is health.

Jeremiah 17:14: Heal me, O Lord, and I shall be healed; save me, and I shall be saved: for thou art my praise.

Jeremiah 33:6: Behold, I will bring it health and cure, and I will cure them, and will reveal unto them the abundance of peace and truth.

1 Peter 3:12: For the eyes of the Lord are over the righteous, and his ears are open unto their prayers: but the face of the Lord is against them that do evil.

James 5:16: Confess your faults one to another, and pray one for another, that ye may be healed. The effectual fervent prayer of a righteous man availeth much.

3 John 1:2: Beloved, I wish above all things that thou mayest prosper and be in health, even as thy soul prospereth.

Praise worship

1. Every power planning to kill, steal and destroy my body, release me by fire, in the name of Jesus.

2. Every spirit of tiredness, release me, in Jesus' name.

3. Every spirit of diabetes, come out with all your roots, in Jesus' name

4. Every bondage of diabetic spirits, come out with all your roots, in the name of Jesus.

5. Any evil power running through my body, loose your hold, in the name of Jesus.

6. Every evil power touching my brain, release me, in Jesus' name.

7. Every tentacle spirit moving about in my body, come out by fire, in the name of Jesus.

8. Every spirit of migraine and headache, come out by fire, in the name of Jesus.

9. Every dark spirit working against the kingdom of God in my life, come out by fire, in Jesus' name.

10. Every power working on my eyes and reducing my vision, be eliminated completely, in the name of Jesus.

11. Every demon of insulin deficiency, depart by fire, in Jesus' name.

12. Every spirit of diabetes, release my liver, in the name of Jesus.

13. Every evil power planning to amputate my leg, I bury you alive, in the name of Jesus.

14. Every spirit of diabetes, release my bladder, in Jesus' name.

15. Every spirit of excessive urination, release me, in Jesus' name.

16. Every spirit of diabetes, release my skin and ears, in the name of Jesus.

17. Every spirit of itching, depart, in the name of Jesus.

18. Every spirit of diabetes, release my lungs, in the name of Jesus.

19. Every spirit of diabetes, release my reproductive areas, in the name of Jesus.

20. I release myself from every spirit of drowsiness, tiredness and impaired vision, I bind you and cast you out, in Jesus' name.

21. Every spirit of infirmity generating tiredness, loose your hold, in Jesus' name.

22. Every spirit of excessive thirst and hunger, I bind you and cast you out, in the name of Jesus.

23. I bind every spirit of loss of weight, in Jesus' name.

24. I bind every spirit of rashes, in the name of Jesus.

25. I bind every spirit of slow healing of cuts and bruises, in the name of Jesus.

26. I bind every spirit of bed-wetting, in the name of Jesus.

27. I bind every spirit of enlargement of the liver, in Jesus' name.

28. I bind every spirit of kidney disease, in the name of Jesus.

29. I bind every spirit of gangrene, in Jesus' name.

30. I bind every spirit of hardening of the arteries, in Jesus' name.

31. I bind every spirit of confusion, in Jesus' name.

32. I bind every spirit of convulsion, in Jesus' name.

33. I bind every spirit of loss of consciousness, in Jesus' name.

34. The spirit of the fear of death, depart from my life, in the name of Jesus.

35. The evil doorkeeper of insulin, loose your hold, in Jesus' name

36. Every power destroying insulin in my body, I bind you and cast you out, in Jesus' name.

37. Every power hindering the co-ordination between my brain and my mouth, I bind you and cast you out, in Jesus' name.

38. Every spirit of torment, release me, in Jesus' name.

39. Every power attacking my blood sugar, loose your hold, in the name of Jesus.

40. I break every curse of eating and drinking blood from ten generations backward on both sides of my family lines, in the name of Jesus.

41. Every door opened to diabetic spirits, be closed by the blood of Jesus.

42. Every inherited blood disease, loose your hold, in Jesus' name.

43. All bloodline curses, be broken, in Jesus' name.

44. Every curse of breaking the skin of my body unrighteously, be broken, in Jesus' name.

45. I bind every demon in my pancreas and I cast them out, in the name of Jesus.

46. Any power affecting my vision, I bind you, in the name of Jesus.

47. Every satanic arrow in my blood vessel, come out by fire, in the name of Jesus.

48. Every demon of stroke, come out with all your roots, in the name of Jesus.

49. Every spirit of confusion, loose your hold, in Jesus' name

50. Anything inhibiting my ability to read and meditate on the word of God, be uprooted, in the name of Jesus.

51. I bind and cast out every spirit of _ _ _

    - convulsion

    - abdominal problems

    - fear - guilt

    - hopelessness

    - impotence - palsy

    - candor   - swelling

    - stress   - worry

- anxiety   - deafness

- high blood pressure

- animal

- nerve destruction

- kidney destruction

come out of my pancreas, in the name of Jesus.

52. I bind and cast out familiar spirits travelling through family bloodlines to cause diabetes and other sickness, in Jesus' name.

53. I cast out _ _ _ (pick from the under listed), in Jesus' name.

    - demons in abdomen

    - acute pain

    - amputation

    - animal spirits

    - bed wetting

    - anger

    - beta cell destroyer

    - demons in bladder

- the fear of death
- accelerated hardening of the arteries
- anxiety
- beef insulin   - blackwell
- blood diseases
- blood resricting
- demons in blood vessels
- bondage   - bowel disease
- brain migraine
- cancer of the pancreas
- cataracts
- circulation problems
- confusion
- convulsions
- diverse diseases
- drowsiness - cold feet
- breathing problems
- depression - destroyer
- diabetes melitus
- dim vision   - dropsy

- demons in DNA
- dumb   - dumb and deaf
- enlargement of the liver
- evil diseases of Egypt
- excessive hunger
- excessive thirst
- eye damage   - fear
- feet damage
- gain of weight
- gene damage   - guilt
- demons in glucose
- headache
- heart damage
- demons in heart
- infections
- insulin destroyer
- demons in intestines
- excessive foot odor
- excessive itching
- excessive urination
- genetic demons

- hardening of the arteries	- slow healing of cuts
- hearing backwards	- type I diabetes
- heart attacks - mourning	- weight loss
- incurable disease	- inability to digest
- loss of consciousness	- type II diabetes
- nerve damage	- witchdoctor
- rashes - stink	- water in the heart
- slow healing of bruises	- water in the kidneys
- leaking blood vessels	- water in the brain
- lunatic - mind control	- water in the ear
- rotten legs	- water in the inner ear
- narrow blood vessels	- water in the liver
- pregnancy problems	

BREAKING THE YOKE OF SATANIC DELAY

This prayer section should be done with fasting when you notice the following

☞ **Unexplainable delay when you are expecting a breakthrough**

☞ **When you begin to have dream of blockages and delays**

☞ **When you have already received promises and for a long time, they are not coming to pass**

☞ **When you are tired of stagnancy**

☞ **When you are convinced that the delay is not from God, but attacks from the enemy**

Praise worship

Scripture Reading - 1 Samuel 1 & 2

Confessions - Psalm 27:14

1. Every arrow of evil delay, fired into my star, die, in the name of Jesus.

2. Every arrow of backwardness, fired into my star, die, in Jesus' name.

3. Chains of stagnation, break, in the name of Jesus.

4. Delay tactics, organised against my joy, scatter, in the name of Jesus.

5. Every delay, programmed to tie me down, die, in the name of Jesus.

6. Every arrow of disappointment, die, in the name of Jesus.

7. Thou power of hard-life, die, in the name of Jesus.

8. Every arrow of shame, targeted at my life, backfire, in the name of Jesus.

9. Every power ordained to make me rise and fall, die, in the name of Jesus.

10. Every power of my father's house, delaying my breakthroughs, die, in the name of Jesus.

11. Curses and covenants of satanic delay, die, in the name of Jesus.

12. Deep pit, swallowing my virtues, vomit them by fire, in the name of Jesus.

13. Chain of delay, holding my star, break, in the name of Jesus.

14. Cloud of darkness around my breakthroughs, scatter, in the name of Jesus.

15. I pull down every stronghold of satanic delay, in the name of Jesus.

16. Every strongman assigned against my progress, die, in the name of Jesus.

17. Satanic decree over my picture, die, in the name of Jesus.

18. Every evil power draining my virtues, die, in the name of Jesus.

19. Failure and calamity shall not be my identity, in the name of Jesus.

20. Power of stagnation, dry up, in the name of Jesus.

21. Every padlock holding down my progress, catch fire, in the name of Jesus.

22. Book of generational failure, bearing my name, catch fire, in the name of Jesus.

23. Every satanic court, summoned to deliberate on my progress, scatter, in the name of Jesus.

24. My wasted years, be restored by fire, in the name of Jesus.

25. Every child of darkness, covering my future, catch fire, in the name of Jesus.

26. Wind of the spirit, carry me to my destination, in the name of Jesus.

27. I decree failure is not my portion, in the name of Jesus.

28. Household strongman, assigned against my destiny, die, in the name of Jesus.

29. Every anti-favour oil on my head, dry up, in the name of Jesus.

30.	Blessings from unexpected quarters, locate me by fire, in the name of Jesus.
31.	Covenant of hard labour of my father's house, die, in the name of Jesus.
32.	Holy Ghost fire, convert my delay to speed by fire, in the name of Jesus.
33.	Glory of the later house, catch up with my star, in the name of Jesus.